Charlottesville Day School
200 Four Seasons Drive
Charlottesville, Virginia 22901
(434) 817-2371

Skills for Preschool Teachers

Seventh Edition

JANICE J. BEATY

Elmira College, Emerita

PEARSON

Merrill
Prentice Hall

Upper Saddle River, New Jersey
Columbus, Ohio

Library of Congress Cataloging-in-Publication Data

Beaty, Janice J.
   Skills for preschool teachers / Janice J. Beaty.—7th ed.
      p. cm.
   Includes bibliographical references and index.
   ISBN 0-13-048609-4 (pbk.)
      1. Child development. 2. Education, Preschool. 3. Preschool teachers—Training of. I.
Title.

LB1115 .B325 2004   2002030939
372.21—dc21

Vice President and Publisher: Jeffery W. Johnston
Executive Editor: Kevin M. Davis
Associate Editor: Christina M. Tawney
Editorial Assistant: Autumn Crisp
Production Editor: Sheryl Glicker Langner
Design Coordinator: Diane C. Lorenzo
Cover Designer: Jeff Vanik
Cover photo: Getty One
Production Manager: Laura Messerly
Director of Marketing: Ann Castel Davis
Marketing Manager: Amy June
Marketing Coordinator: Tyra Poole

This book was set in Zapf Humanist by Carlisle Communications, Ltd. It was printed and bound by R. R. Donnelley & Sons Company. The cover was printed by Phoenix Color Corp.

Photo Credits: All photos courtesy of Janice J. Beaty

Copyright © 2004, 2000, 1996, 1992, 1988, 1984, 1979 by Pearson Education, Inc., Upper Saddle River, New Jersey 07458. Pearson Prentice Hall. All rights reserved. Printed in the United States of America. This publication is protected by Copyright and permission should be obtained from the publisher prior to any prohibited reproduction, storage in a retrieval system, or transmission in any form or by any means, electronic, mechanical, photocopying, recording, or likewise. For information regarding permission(s), write to: Rights and Permissions Department.

Pearson Prentice Hall™ is a trademark of Pearson Education, Inc.
Pearson® is a registered trademark of Pearson plc
Prentice Hall® is a registered trademark of Pearson Education, Inc.
Merrill® is a registered trademark of Pearson Education, Inc.

Pearson Education Ltd.
Pearson Education Singapore Pte. Ltd.
Pearson Education Canada, Ltd.
Pearson Education—Japan

Pearson Education Australia Pty. Limited
Pearson Education North Asia Ltd.
Pearson Educación de Mexico, S.A. de C. V.
Pearson Education Malaysia Pte. Ltd.

10 9 8 7 6 5 4 3 2 1
ISBN: 0-13-048609-4

*To Head Start teachers and teacher assistants
across the nation
for making a lasting contribution
to the lives of young children
and their families*

About the Author

Janice J. Beaty, professor emerita, Elmira College, Elmira, New York, is a full-time writer of early childhood college textbooks and a consultant and trainer in early childhood education from her new home in Gulf Breeze, Florida. Some of her textbooks include: *Observing Development of the Young Child* (5th Ed.), *Prosocial Guidance for the Preschool Child,* and, most recent, *Early Literacy in Preschool and Kindergarten* with Dr. Linda Pratt. Dr. Beaty is also involved in an early literacy mentoring program with Foster Grandparents in schools and Head Start centers in central Missouri.

Preface

This text presents and discusses basic classroom skills for preschool teachers. It is designed for use by college students preparing to be teachers in preschool, center-based child care, Head Start, and prekindergarten. It is also useful for in-service teachers, assistant teachers, and volunteers who are updating their skills or preparing for the national CDA (Child Development Associate) credential.

The skills for working with 3- to 5-year-old children in a classroom setting are presented in 13 chapters. Each chapter is a self-contained learning module with objectives, text, learning activities, end-of-chapter questions, an evaluation sheet, and lists of references, supplementary readings, and videotapes. Some chapters contain lists of children's computer programs, music distributors, and book toy distributors. Students may progress through each chapter at their own pace using the Self-Taught Module Approach. College instructors or trainers can use the text as assigned reading in courses and workshops, or for student teaching. Checklists and forms placed throughout chapters may be photocopied and used again and again.

To gain the greatest value from this program, the student should be in an early childhood classroom setting to apply the ideas with young children. Many college and university programs place students in a nursery school or lab school setting for several mornings a week so that they may accomplish the prescribed learning activities with young children.

College and university programs that use this text as a resource for a practicum or internship often expect students to complete three or four modules in one semester. To determine which module chapters a student should work on, some programs carry out an initial assessment of the students as they work in an early childhood classroom. The instructor uses the Teacher Skills Checklist (see Introduction) as an observation tool in an initial assessment of the students' skills. Students are also asked to complete a self-evaluation using the Teacher Skills Checklist as described in the Introduction. The instructor and each student then have a conference, during which they compare checklist results and determine on which of the thirteen skill areas the student needs to concentrate, thus providing an individualized training program based on student strengths and needs.

Observation tools in the text that focus on the strengths and needs of young children include the Large Motor Checklist, Small Motor Checklist, Creative Movement Checklist, Cognitive Concepts Checklist, Children's Curiosity Checklist, Self-Concept Checklist, Social Skills Checklist, and Child Involvement Checklist. The physical environment and materials of the early childhood classroom are assessed with observation tools such as the Classroom Safety Checklist, Classroom Cleanliness Checklist, Learning Center Checklist, Learning Center Location Checklist, and Book Selection Checklist. In addition to the Teacher Skills Checklist, the text also includes a Teacher Listening and Speaking Checklist.

The 13 chapters of the text are arranged in the same order as the skills in the Teacher Skills Checklist and the 13 CDA functional areas. Each chapter provides theoretical background on the particular skill topic, as well as ideas for practical application in working with young children and their families in an early childhood classroom.

New Features in the Seventh Edition

This seventh edition of *Skills for Preschool Teachers* has been revised to include new material in each chapter, with special emphasis on creating a calm and happy atmosphere in the classroom conducive to learning. New material describes teacher behavior in emergency situations to dissipate children's fears, support mental and emotional health of children, and help them cope with traumatic events. Brain research on stress is described as the basis for providing a high-activity, low-stress environment.

A new Creative Movement Checklist helps teachers find ways to involve children in this important area, supported by the latest brain research on movement and music. A new Cognitive Concepts Checklist helps teachers focus on the basic concepts necessary for children's learning. A continued discussion of children's natural emergence into reading and writing includes new picture books and computer programs to support the hands-on activities offered. Using picture song books to encourage chanting, acting out verses, and even creating a sandbox theater with cutout characters is described. A discussion of cultural influences on a child's self-concept helps teachers recognize how family values may affect child behavior in the classroom. An expanded discussion of how children learn to make friends gives teachers suggestions for creating a "kindness class," for developing "listening partners," and for helping children with special needs to find friends. A discussion of the child as a spiritual being reinforces these ideas, encouraging children's appropriate behavior and development of self-control. Family classroom meetings are described as an important means of family involvement in the program.

In the chapter on "program management" (Chapter 12) a discussion of managing time contrasts American practices with those of Reggio Emilia programs in Italy. Other new ideas and knowledge in the field of early childhood education are described in the chapter on "promoting professionalism" (Chapter 13) along with the latest information on the National Association for the Education of Young Children's "Code of Ethical Conduct" and the training necessary to make it meaningful to classroom staff. Finally, a new section, Appendix A: Becoming a CDA: Child Development Associate, describes this process in greater detail.

As in previous editions of *Skills for Preschool Teachers*, this seventh edition features how to use the latest children's picture books, including 40 new ones added to the 200 children's books also described.

Use as a Companion Text

This seventh edition of *Skills for Preschool Teachers* is designed to be used as a companion volume with the author's text *Observing Development of the Young Child* (Merrill/Prentice Hall, 2002). While *Skills* is intended as a teacher development textbook, the companion volume *Observing* is a child development book that focuses on six major areas of development: emotional, social, motor, cognitive, language, and creative.

Like this text, *Observing Development of the Young Child* is based on an observational checklist, the Child Skills Checklist, with each major area of the checklist represented by a chapter in the book: self-identity, emotional development, social play, prosocial behavior, large motor development, small motor development, cognitive development, spoken language, prewriting and prereading skills, art skills, and imagination. The observational items on the checklist represent subheadings in each chapter, just as they do in this text.

Observing Development of the Young Child presents ideas and activities to promote child development in each of the child skill areas. Planning for individual children based on checklist results helps student interns as well as teachers to provide developmentally appropriate activities for their children.

Students and instructors are encouraged to obtain a copy of *Observing Development of the Young Child* to be used in conjunction with this seventh edition of *Skills for Preschool Teachers*.

ACKNOWLEDGMENTS

My special thanks goes once again to Bonny Helm for her critical reading of the text and her numerous ideas and suggestions, especially for the CDA competency statements in Appendix A. Thanks also to the Human Development Corporation in Columbia, Missouri, and Noah's Ark Preschool in Taos, New Mexico, for allowing me to photograph children in their early childhood classes. Your children are so photogenic! To Ann Davis, my former editor at Merrill, goes my continued gratitude for her suggestions and support. Finally, I appreciate the helpfulness of the several professionals in the field who reviewed the proposal for the seventh edition of this text: Frank Miller, Pittsburgh State University; Barbara F. Boyd, Radford University; and J. Christine Catalani, San Antonio College.

Janice J. Beaty

Discover the Companion Website
Accompanying This Book

The Prentice Hall Companion Website: A Virtual Learning Environment

Technology is a constantly growing and changing aspect of our field that is creating a need for content and resources. To address this emerging need, Prentice Hall has developed an online learning environment for students and professors alike—Companion Websites—to support our textbooks.

In creating a Companion Website, our goal is to build on and enhance what the textbook already offers. For this reason, the content for each user-friendly website is organized by topic and provides the professor and student with a variety of meaningful resources. Common features of a Companion Website include:

For the Professor—

Every Companion Website integrates **Syllabus Manager™**, an online syllabus creation and management utility.

- **Syllabus Manager™** provides you, the instructor, with an easy, step-by-step process to create and revise syllabi, with direct links into Companion Website and other online content without having to learn HTML.
- Students may logon to your syllabus during any study session. All they need to know is the web address for the Companion Website and the password you've assigned to your syllabus.
- After you have created a syllabus using **Syllabus Manager™**, students may enter the syllabus for their course section from any point in the Companion Website.
- Clicking on a date, the student is shown the list of activities for the assignment. The activities for each assignment are linked directly to actual content, saving time for students.
- Adding assignments consists of clicking on the desired due date, then filling in the details of the assignment—name of the assignment, instructions, and whether or not it is a one-time or repeating assignment.
- In addition, links to other activities can be created easily. If the activity is online, a URL can be entered in the space provided, and it will be linked automatically in the final syllabus.

- Your completed syllabus is hosted on our servers, allowing convenient updates from any computer on the Internet. Changes you make to your syllabus are immediately available to your students at their next logon.

For the Student—

- **Introduction**—General information about the topic and how it will be covered in the website.
- **Web Links**—A variety of websites related to topic areas.
- **Timely Articles**—Links to online articles that enable you to become more aware of important issues in early childhood.
- **Learn by Doing**—Put concepts into action, participate in activities, examine strategies, and more.
- **Visit a School**—Visit a school's website to see concepts, theories, and strategies in action.
- **For Teachers/Practitioners**—Access information you will need to know as an educator, including information on materials, activities, and lessons.
- **Current Policies and Standards**—Find out the latest early childhood policies from the government and various organizations, and view state, federal, and curriculum standards.
- **Resources and Organizations**—Discover tools to help you plan your classroom or center and organizations to provide current information and standards for each topic.
- **Electronic Bluebook**—Paperless method of completing homework or essays assigned by a professor. Finished work can be sent to the professor via email.
- **Message Board**—Virtual bulletin board to post and respond to questions and comments from a national audience.

To take advantage of these and other resources, please visit the *Skills for Preschool Teachers,* Seventh Edition, Companion Website at

www.prenhall.com/beaty

Brief Contents

Contents

4 Advancing Physical Skills   102

5 Advancing Cognitive Skills   130

6 Advancing Communication Skills   160

7 Advancing Creative Skills   192

8 Building a Positive Self-Concept   218

9 Promoting Social Skills   242

12 Providing Program Management   316

13 Promoting Professionalism   352

Appendix A   Becoming a CDA: Child Development Associate   379

Index   387

Introduction

 THE SELF-TAUGHT MODULE APPROACH

This text introduces the Self-Taught Module Training Program, a unique approach to training teachers, student teachers, and teaching assistants in early childhood classroom skills. It is based on the premise that people learn more effectively when they become deeply involved in their own instruction. Although this text can be used in a traditional college course, students and instructors also have the option of using the text as follows. The Self-Taught Module Approach allows students to do the following tasks:

1. Help determine their own needs.
2. Participate in selecting a trainer.
3. Assist in setting up a training prescription.
4. Work at their own pace in an early childhood setting.
5. Help determine when they have accomplished the objectives and finished the training.
6. Contribute to their own evaluation of skills gained from the training.

The approach is the same as for children in the preschool setting. They also strive to become independent and self-directed in their learning. Thus, it is appropriate that their teachers develop classroom skills to assist them in achieving that end through their own self-taught training.

The Self-Taught Module Approach is also based on the premise that training in classroom skills should be individualized to be effective. This program contains 13 module chapters that can be prescribed separately or in any combination or sequence to meet the individual's training needs. Each chapter in the program is self-contained and can be used independently to upgrade particular skills during in-service training. For college students in preservice training, the entire text can be used to provide the basic skills necessary for successful preschool teaching.

The skills derive from the original six competency goals developed by the federal Administration for Children, Youth, and Families and refined by the Council for Early Childhood Professional Recognition, sponsored by the National Association for the Education of Young Children for the Child Development Associate (CDA) training program. These goals represent basic competencies for persons with primary responsibility for groups of young children 3 to 5 years of age. From these competency goals, 13 key words known as Functional Areas have been extracted to serve as the focus for teacher training. Each of these Functional Areas serves as the basis for one of the 13 chapters of this textbook. Each of these 13 CDA Functional Areas also appears as a heading for the items appearing on the Teacher Skills Checklist. *Skills for Preschool Teachers* has thus integrated the CDA competencies into a college-based teacher preparation program, as well as an in-service training program for teachers, assistants, student teachers, and volunteers in the classroom. (See Appendix A, "Becoming a CDA: Child Development Associate.")

CDA Goals, Functional Areas, and Book Chapters

1. Establishing and maintaining a safe, healthy learning environment

SAFE	Chapter 1 Maintaining a Safe Classroom
HEALTHY	Chapter 2 Maintaining a Healthy Classroom
LEARNING ENVIRONMENT	Chapter 3 Establishing a Learning Environment

2. Advancing physical and intellectual competence

PHYSICAL	Chapter 4 Advancing Physical Skills
COGNITIVE	Chapter 5 Advancing Cognitive Skills
COMMUNICATION	Chapter 6 Advancing Communication Skills
CREATIVE	Chapter 7 Advancing Creative Skills

3. Supporting social and emotional development and providing guidance

SELF	Chapter 8 Building a Positive Self-Concept
SOCIAL	Chapter 9 Promoting Social Skills
GUIDANCE	Chapter 10 Providing Guidance

4. Establishing positive and productive relationships with families

FAMILIES	Chapter 11 Promoting Family Involvement

5. Ensuring a well-run, purposeful program responsive to participant needs

PROGRAM MANAGEMENT	Chapter 12 Providing Program Management

6. Maintaining a commitment to professionalism

PROFESSIONALISM	Chapter 13 Promoting Professionalism

True learning occurs when students have opportunities to make practical applications of theoretical ideas. Therefore, the classroom skills acquired through the Self-Taught Module Approach should be performed in actual preschool settings. If already serving as a teacher, assistant, or volunteer in a Head Start program, child-care center, nursery school, Montessori program, or prekindergarten program, the student may use the children's classroom as the location for completing the prescribed module chapters. If enrolled in a college or university early childhood program, the student will need to volunteer at least three mornings a week in a nearby preschool classroom.

Students will also need a trainer to assist with their progression through the training program. The trainer will help with each student's initial assessment, review answers to question sheets, observe students in the early childhood classroom, and meet regularly with the student to provide support and assistance as the learning activities are completed. The trainer, in other words, serves as a support and resource person who responds to the student's work and activities. The primary responsibility for progress through the Self-Taught Module Training Program belongs to the student. Students will be involved in activities such as the following:

1. initial assessment of student's present skills in an early childhood classroom based on observations by the trainer using the Teacher Skills Checklist
2. self-assessment of current skills by the student using the Teacher Skills Checklist
3. an assessment conference with the trainer to discuss and compare the results of the two checklists
4. development of a training prescription consisting of particular module chapters based on the results of the assessment conference
5. step-by-step, self-directed progression through each of the assigned chapters
6. observation by the trainer in the preschool classroom as the student carries out chapter activities
7. regular meetings with the trainer to discuss assigned chapter activities

The intent of the Self-Taught Module Training Program is to assist the student in acquiring classroom skills through a wide variety of learning techniques. Reading from the text, writing answers to questions, responding orally to a trainer's questions, doing supplementary reading, viewing videotapes, performing focused observations of children, making file cards of classroom activities, creating special games and activities to meet children's needs, working directly with children and classroom team members in an early childhood classroom, demonstrating evidence of competence through classroom performance—all of these learning activities are a part of each chapter.

This seventh edition of *Skills for Preschool Teachers* presents a comprehensive program for training primary caregivers in early childhood programs. It will also help those already employed in programs to assess their areas of need and strengthen their skills. It will help those preparing to work in such programs to develop entry-level skills in a classroom setting.

Initial Assessment

Students in the Self-Taught Module Training Program begin with an initial assessment to help them determine what classroom skills they possess and what skills they will need to strengthen through training. The initial assessment is a threefold process involving both the student and the trainer or instructor. It consists of the following:

1. a classroom observation of the student by the trainer or college instructor using the Teacher Skills Checklist
2. a self-evaluation by the student using the Teacher Skills Checklist
3. a conference between the student and the trainer or instructor to compare checklist results and develop a personalized training prescription

In a self-taught program, the student always initiates any activity. Therefore, it is up to you, the student, to begin the process.

Selecting the Trainer

You will need to arrange for a trainer to make the initial assessment of you in an early childhood classroom. If you are a college student, your early childhood instructor or supervising teacher may automatically become your trainer. In other instances, someone in the early childhood program where you work or volunteer may serve as the trainer.

If you are employed in an early childhood program, it is possible for a master teacher, education coordinator, or director to be your trainer. Or your program may wish to contract for the services of an outside trainer through a local college, university, or Head Start office. It is important that the trainer be someone you have confidence in, who has had experience in an early childhood classroom, and who can evaluate your classroom skills objectively and help and support you throughout your training program.

Teacher Skills Checklist

This checklist was developed and field tested by the author for use as an initial assessment instrument and training tool by college students and CDA trainees and candidates. It is based on the previously mentioned Competency Goals and Functional Areas developed by the Council for Early Childhood Professional Recognition.

Each item of the checklist stands for one Functional Area and contains three representative indicators that demonstrate competence in the particular skill area. Each chapter of the text then discusses one of these Functional Areas, with the indicators serving as specific objectives for the chapter and as subheadings within the chapter. Thus the Teacher Skills Checklist serves not only as an initial assessment tool but also as an outline for this text. It is important for the student to refer to the particular sections of the text to clarify or interpret the various checklist items.

Assessment by the Trainer

Again, it is up to you, the student, to arrange for an initial assessment by the trainer. The assessment should take place as soon as you are comfortably involved with the children and their activities. Then you can invite your trainer to make the observation.

The trainer will place a check mark next to each item on the Teacher Skills Checklist that she/he observes you performing and then will indicate the "evidence" for each check mark.

Self-Assessment

Next, you should go through the same process yourself, checking off the items on the Teacher Skills Checklist that you have performed. Be honest. Check only those items you have actually performed, and then record the evidence. A self-assessment is often a difficult type of evaluation. But you need to do it carefully and accurately for your training plan to be effective. If you are not sure about an item, put down an "N."

Your responses on the checklist are just as important as the trainer's responses in determining your training prescription. After each item, you should also write down the evidence on which you base your check mark. For example, for the item "Promotes toy and material safety within each curriculum area," you might record that you "survey the room using the Classroom Safety Checklist each morning."

Assessment Conference

When both you and the trainer have finished filling out your Teacher Skills Checklists, arrange a meeting to discuss the results. At this time, you should go over your two checklists together, discussing the items that were checked as well as those that were not checked. If one checklist has a blank for a particular item while the other has a check mark for the same item, this may be an area of confusion you will want to clarify. If both checklists contain a blank for the same item, this may serve as a focus for the training to come.

Training Prescription

The training itself should be designed around the strengths of the student as indicated by the check marks on the checklist. As you and your trainer go over the checklist together, jot down these areas of strength on the Training Prescription form. Then indicate the training needs as indicated by blanks on the checklist. To determine what learning activities should be prescribed, you and your trainer can choose the chapters that address the particular needs indicated and follow the learning activities listed at the end of each chapter.

Teacher Skills Checklist

Name _____   Observer _____

Program _____   Dates _____

Directions
Put a "✓" for items you see the student perform regularly.
Put an "N" for items where there is no opportunity to observe.
Leave all other items blank.

Item	**Evidence**	**Date**

1. SAFE

_____ Promotes toy and material
safety within each learning center.   _____

_____ Plans and implements necessary
emergency procedures.   _____

_____ Provides a safe classroom atmosphere
through teacher behavior.   _____

2. HEALTHY

_____ Encourages children to follow
common health and nutrition practices.   _____

_____ Recognizes unusual behavior or
symptoms of children who may be
ill and provides for the children.   _____

_____ Supports the mental and emotional
health of every child.   _____

3. LEARNING ENVIRONMENT

_____ Sets up stimulating learning centers
in appropriate spaces.   _____

_____ Provides appropriate materials for
children's self-directed play and
learning.   _____

_____ Promotes a high-activity, low-stress
environment where children can play
and learn happily together.   _____

4. PHYSICAL

_____ Assesses children's large motor skills and provides appropriate equipment and activities.

_____ Assesses children's small motor skills and provides appropriate materials and activities.

_____ Provides opportunities for children to engage in creative movement.

5. COGNITIVE

_____ Helps children develop curiosity about their world through sensory exploration.

_____ Helps children develop basic concepts about their world by classifying, comparing, and counting objects in it.

_____ Helps children apply basic concepts about the natural world through hands-on experiences.

6. COMMUNICATION

_____ Talks with individual children to encourage listening and speaking.

_____ Uses books and stories to motivate listening, speaking, and emergent reading.

_____ Provides materials and activities to support emergent writing.

7. CREATIVE

_____ Gives children time, opportunity, and freedom to do pretending and fantasy role play.

_____ Provides a variety of art materials and activities for children to explore on their own.

_____ Encourages children to create and have fun with music.

8. SELF

_____ Accepts self and every child as worthy and uses nonverbal cues to let children know they are accepted.

_____ Accepts diversity in children and helps children to accept one another.

_____ Helps every child experience success in the classroom.

(continued)

(continued)

9. SOCIAL

_____ Helps children learn to work and play cooperatively through sharing and turn-taking.

_____

_____ Helps children learn to enter ongoing play without disruptions.

_____

_____ Helps children learn to make friends.

_____

10. GUIDANCE

_____ Uses positive prevention measures to help eliminate inappropriate behavior in the classroom.

_____

_____ Uses positive intervention measures to help children control their inappropriate behavior.

_____

_____ Uses positive reinforcement techniques to help children learn appropriate behavior.

_____

11. FAMILIES

_____ Involves parents in participating in children's program.

_____

_____ Recognizes and supports families of different make up.

_____

_____ Builds teacher-family relationships through family classroom meetings.

_____

12. PROGRAM MANAGEMENT

_____ Uses a team approach to plan a flexible curriculum.

_____

_____ Plans and implements an emergent curriculum to assure a quality program.

_____

_____ Evaluates curriculum outcomes through child observations and team conferences.

_____

13. PROFESSIONALISM

_____ Makes a commitment to the early childhood profession.

_____

_____ Behaves ethically toward children and their families.

_____

_____ Takes every opportunity to improve professional growth.

_____

Permission is granted by the publisher to reproduce this checklist for evaluation and record keeping.

Training Prescription

Student _____ Date _____

Trainer _____ Classroom _____

Strengths

1. _____

2. _____

3. _____

Training Needs

1. _____

2. _____

3. _____

Learning Activities

1. _____

2. _____

3. _____

Permission is granted by the publisher to reproduce this prescription for evaluation and record keeping.

Maintaining a Safe Classroom

▢ ### GENERAL OBJECTIVE

To be able to set up and maintain a safe classroom environment and reduce and prevent injuries

☑ ### SPECIFIC OBJECTIVES

____ Promotes toy and materials safety within each learning center

____ Plans and implements necessary emergency procedures

____ Provides a safe classroom atmosphere through teacher behavior

S afety is a basic concern for all teachers of preschool children. Before you can offer developmental activities for children who come to center-based programs, you must first guarantee them a safe environment. Their parents assume this to be the case. As a child-caregiver, you make the same assumption. However, you have the responsibility to see that your classroom is actually safe. You or a staff member assigned to the task must inspect each learning center in the room every day before the children's arrival and again while children are busily playing with the equipment to be sure the safety hazards sometimes found in particular centers are not present in yours.

In addition, you must check the condition of the bathroom, the exits, the stairs, and the outdoor play area daily to be sure they are clean, clear, and safe. Although a maintenance person may have the responsibility for cleaning and repairing the building and grounds, it is also up to you as the leader of a group of young children to see that the environment is truly safe.

Making your classroom safe can prevent injuries if you are aware of the potential dangers of sharp objects, hazardous materials, electrical equipment, climbing apparatus, and water spills. Children need to learn how to keep themselves safe in the classroom, on the playground, and on the streets by following the common safety practices you present to them. You also need to learn how to help children feel safe and remain safe when unsafe conditions are present.

Safety Checklist

A safety checklist is one of the most effective methods for establishing and maintaining a safe environment. It will help you to set up the classroom initially with safety in mind and will assist you in checking daily on the condition of the classroom. The Classroom Safety Checklist in Table 1–1 serves this purpose.

Table 1–1 Classroom Safety Checklist

Art Center

_____ Scissors use supervised

_____ Water spills cleaned up

_____ Hazardous materials ellminated (sprays, solvents, glazes, permanent markers)

Block-Building Center

_____ Building space adequate

_____ Blocks free from splinters

_____ Construction height within limits

_____ Toy accessories free of sharp edges, broken parts

Book Center

_____ Floor area covered

_____ Heating vents, pipes covered

_____ Rocking chairs away from children on floor

Computer Center

_____ Electric cords, plugs out of children's reach

_____ Located away from water

_____ Children seated with computer on low table or stand

Cooking Center

_____ Cooking appliances in compliance with local safety codes

_____ Electric appliances, microwave ovens controlled by adult

_____ Sharp implement use supervised by adult

_____ Number of children in area limited

Dramatic Play Center

_____ Clothes hooks away from eye level

_____ Plastic dishes, cutlery unbroken

_____ Play jewelry, earrings, beads unbroken

_____ Dolls, toys with no small removable parts (e.g., buttons)

Large-Motor Center

_____ Climbing, sliding equipment cushioned

_____ Wheeled vehicle use controlled

_____ Safety rules established and enforced by adult

Manipulative/Math Center

_____ Tiny beads, counters eliminated

_____ Sharp or pointed objects eliminated

_____ Objects with splinters, peeling paint, broken parts discarded

Music Center

_____ Cords on record players, radios, tape recorders out of reach
_____ Equipment using small batteries eliminated

Sand/Water/Sensory Center

_____ Sand or water spills cleaned up
_____ Broken, rusty, or sharp-edged toys removed
_____ Glass implements eliminated
_____ Safety goggles used at sand table

Science/Discovery Center

_____ Aquarium and incubator wires out of reach
_____ Houseplants nonpoisonous

Woodworking Center

_____ Adult-size tools supervised
_____ Safety goggles used
_____ Safety rules established and enforced by adult
_____ Number of children limited

General Room Conditions

_____ Floor covering smooth, unbroken, and untorn
_____ Traffic patterns between areas clear
_____ Heaters, pipes, vents covered and sectioned off
_____ Electrical cords, wires, plugs out of children's reach
_____ Electrical outlets covered
_____ Smoke detectors in appropriate locations
_____ Fire extinguishers accessible
_____ Peeling paint removed, refinished
_____ Broken furniture, toys removed, repaired
_____ Sharp corners of room dividers padded
_____ Emergency procedures, phone numbers clearly posted

Bathroom

_____ Sinks, toilets child-size
_____ Stands, stools sturdy
_____ Slippery floors cleaned up
_____ Cleaning and disinfecting materials locked up
_____ First-aid kit out of children's reach; accessible to adults

Stairs/Exits

_____ Exits clearly labeled
_____ Stair steps smooth, unbroken, of nonskid material
_____ Carpeting, mats smooth, untorn, not slippery
_____ Stair railings reachable by children
_____ Two exits in every classroom
_____ Stairs well-lighted

(continued)

Table 1–1   *continued*

Outdoor Playground

_____	Playground enclosed with fence
_____	Debris, broken glass removed
_____	Cushioning under climbers, slides
_____	Large equipment anchored in ground
_____	Swings of safe material (belts, tires)
_____	Young–child-size equipment used
_____	Railings around high platforms, on steps
_____	Sharp edges, missing or loose parts, splinters on equipment corrected
_____	Adequate supervision when in use

Permission is granted by the publisher to reproduce this checklist for evaluation and record keeping.

PROMOTES TOY AND MATERIALS SAFETY WITHIN EACH LEARNING CENTER

Art Center

The art center should be located near a source of water so brushes and hands can be cleaned easily and water for painting is not so easily spilled. The center may consist of one or more easels for painting, one or more tables for flat painting and crafts, and shelves at children's level for youngsters to select and return art materials on their own. Teachers' art supplies are better stored in cabinets inaccessible to children.

Sharp scissors are less dangerous for young children to use than dull ones, which may slip and cut a child. Small sharp scissors can help young children develop manipulative skills safely. An adult should keep a watchful eye on children when scissors are out, however, and have children put the scissors away in scissors holders on nearby shelves when not in use.

Replace art materials that are hazardous with nontoxic materials. Use water-based nontoxic paints and glues. Even rubber cement is toxic if inhaled. Instead, use white glue. When the class is using modeling sand, be sure children wear safety goggles to prevent them from wiping their eyes with sandy fingers. When using glitter, have children apply it from a shaker and keep hands away from it. If glitter gets on fingers be sure children wipe or wash it off because glitter can be dangerous to eyes, which children tend to rub. All art materials for young children should be nontoxic, nonflammable, and water-based. (Taylor, 2002) Do not use tiny craft and collage beads, buttons, and gems that the youngest children may put in mouths, noses, or ears.

You will want to establish block-building rules with the children at the outset.

Block-Building Center

Blocks should be stored lengthwise on shelves for easy selection and return. Be sure the block shelves are steady, against the wall if necessary, so that someone bumping against them will not tip them over on children playing in the center. The principal safety feature of block-building areas is the height of constructions. Some teachers permit children to build with wooden unit blocks or large hollow blocks only as high as a child's own height. Others allow children to climb on chairs to build towers as high as they can reach. The danger is that the tall building may fall on another child or that the climbing child may fall and be injured. You must decide whether this situation poses a problem with your children. If this is a safety priority with you, you will want to establish block-building rules with the children at the outset.

Since preliterate children are not able to read written rules, why not post illustrated rules for them to follow? You can draw an outline of a block building next to the outline of a child to show the allowable height and another that shows a building that is too tall. Below each picture write a simple rule such as "Just Right" or "Too Tall." Most children will soon figure out what the words say as well as what the illustrations mean.

Book Center

Your library or reading corner should be a comfortable place for children to stretch out on the floor or curl up on a soft couch to read. Make sure the floor is covered with a rug to keep it warm enough in cold weather, and locate the reading corner in an area that is free from drafts. If you use pillows on the floor, make sure that heating vents are not covered accidentally. If you have a rocking chair, help children learn to control it. Children tend to get carried away with child-size rockers and may tip over or rock on someone's fingers.

Computer Center

The computer center is new in many preschool programs. Young children can teach themselves to use these powerful interactive learning tools if teachers set up the area for their convenience and safety. Children should sit and not stand when using this valuable piece of equipment. Two children at a time can be seated in child-size chairs in front of one computer with the monitor screen on a table at their eye level, not on a shelf high above them. Electric cords should be plugged into a wall outlet behind the machine and out of the children's reach. Do not use long extension cords that people might trip over. Instead, plug computers into "surge bar" outlets (available at hardware or computer-supply stores). Keep water and sticky fingers away from the computer keyboard. Children should wash their hands before using the computer. When the computer is not in use, cover the keyboard or move it out of reach to prevent children from playing with keys or inserting tiny objects.

Cooking Center

Most states have licensing and insurance regulations governing safety in child-care centers. You also need to learn the local safety regulations governing hot food preparation in schools and child-care centers. Some schools do not allow electric appliances, microwave ovens, hot plates, or blenders in the classroom. Some require only special kitchen areas for hot cooking, while food preparation without heating can be carried out within the classroom. Whatever the case, an adult should always be in the area during food preparation. Electrical equipment can be plugged into counter-top outlets that are otherwise covered when not in use. Young children can learn to use knives and scrapers safely, but an adult should supervise.

Dramatic Play Center

The dramatic play center can be sectioned off for children's pretend play with child-size cupboards, refrigerator, stove, and sink. Toy safety is a particular concern in the dramatic play area. Check dolls for small parts that a child could twist off and swallow accidentally. Remove dolls with buttons, glass eyes, and beads that are sewn or wired on. Be sure that earrings are large and that strings of beads are unbroken. Tiny objects sometimes find their way into young children's noses or ears. Also remove toys with springs, wires, or sharp parts.

If you use plastic dishes, knives, or spoons, make sure they are not broken. Cutting knives, of course, should not be used for play. Be sure hooks for hanging dress-up clothes are not at children's eye level.

Large Motor Center

Indoor climbing equipment should be cushioned with pads or other materials thick enough to prevent injuries in case a child falls. Establish safety rules for climbers at the outset. If you have wheeled riding vehicles, establish safety rules with traffic signs and safety games. This is how young children learn safety rules—through games and fun activities.

Choose equipment appropriate for young children for indoor play. Teeter-totters are too difficult for most preschoolers to use without injury. Lofts should be no higher than 4 or 5 feet off the ground. A sturdy railing around the top is important. If the railing contains slats, they should be spaced close enough that children's heads cannot be entrapped. How do children get up onto the loft? Fye and Mumpower (2001) suggest: "A loft with a removable ladder makes it possible for an adult to control access to the area. Lofts should be monitored at all times and the number of children playing in them limited" (p. 22).

Children with physical impairments should be involved in all activity areas of the classroom, including the large-motor center. Find ways to give them safe access to large motor experiences. Children in wheelchairs can throw and catch soft balls or inflated balls. True *inclusion* means that all children are included in all classroom activities. Use your ingenuity to accommodate everyone. For example, in a catch-and-toss game, have everyone sit in chairs just as a wheelchair-bound child does.

Manipulative/Math Center

If you have 3-year-olds or younger children in your program, be sure the stringing beads and counters are large. Three-year-olds often put small objects into their mouths, noses, and ears. Use large counting and sorting items whenever possible, and keep them stored in clear plastic containers on nearby shelves. Check games and toys for broken parts and discard anything with splinters, wires, or peeling paint.

Music Center

Cords on record players, tape recorders, and electronic keyboards should be out of children's reach. Children should not be allowed to plug in or unplug the equipment. Better to use battery-operated players when possible. However, avoid equipment with small mercury-type batteries that could be swallowed accidentally. If children use headsets for listening to records or tapes, be sure to control the volume on the player in a permanent manner so that children's hearing is not damaged if the volume is too loud.

Sand/Water/Sensory Table

When playing at the sand table, children should wear safety goggles to keep sand out of their eyes. Spilled water and sand around tables are slippery and should be cleaned up. Spilled rice from a sand table is especially slippery. Keep a child-size mop, broom, and dust pan in the area so that children can help with cleanup. They will not only take pride in themselves and their classroom by performing this adult-type task but also learn safety practices useful in other settings. To prevent spills in the first place, keep ingredients at low levels in the play tables. Children can have just as much fun and learn just as much with a few inches of water as they do with a filled water table—and they will stay drier.

Be sure toys and implements for sand and water play are not broken, rusty, or sharp-edged. Glass containers such as baby-food jars or glass eyedroppers should not be used. Replace them with plastic cups, containers, bottles, funnels, droppers, and basters.

Science/Discovery Center

Display children's collections of seeds or beans under clear plastic wrap instead of leaving them open for handling. As mentioned previously, some young children put such items in their mouths, and certain seeds or beans may be poisonous.

Certain houseplants are highly poisonous if ingested and thus pose a hazard to young children who may be tempted to eat a leaf or berry. If you have plants in your classroom, keep them out of reach. Rather than warning children against eating such leaves or berries, it is better to remove the temptation. If you stress "no eating," certain young children who had no notion of eating a plant part will try it just because you mentioned not doing it! Figure 1–1 lists the more common poisonous plants.

Woodworking Center

In woodworking, as in playing with sand, children should wear safety goggles, and most love the experience. Use small-size adult hammers, saws, pliers, and screwdrivers. Most children's toy sets are not made for use with real wood and nails. Children can learn the safe use of real tools by having a staff member or a parent demonstrate how. An experienced child can also show a beginner. Limiting the number of children in the area will also reduce safety hazards.

Woodworking generates much interest for both boys and girls. Roofing nails and ceiling tiles are easier for beginners to use successfully. To cut down on noise, put rug squares under the pounding materials.

Figure 1–1   Common Poisonous
Plants

Poisonous Indoor Plants	
Philodendron	
Mistletoe berries	
Dieffenbachia	
Poinsettia leaves	
Amaryllis	
Poisonous Outdoor Plants	
Holly	Yew
Mustard	Lily-of-the-valley
Hydrangea	Mushroom
Buttercup	Bittersweet berries
Azalea	Black locust tree
Castor bean	Rhubarb leaves
Rhododendron	Cherry tree
Datura	Oleander

General Room Conditions

Check the heating system in your room. Exposed pipes should not be allowed unless they are thoroughly protected with asbestos-free insulation. Radiators and space heaters should be sectioned off to prevent children's direct contact. Portable electric or kerosene heaters are generally prohibited by fire codes or insurance regulations. Be sure that safety equipment such as smoke detectors and fire extinguishers are in working order and that staff member know what to do and how to use them in the event of a fire.

Electric cords and wires should not be accessible to children. Avoid using extension cords whenever possible. Place aquariums, incubators, and other classroom electrical equipment near outlets that are inaccessible to little hands. Exposed outlets should be covered with safety plugs.

Check your walls, furniture, and cupboards for peeling paint. Children love to pick off the pieces and put them in their mouths. Be sure the surfaces are sanded and refinished with lead-free paint. Remove broken toys and furniture and have them repaired. Don't wait until someone gets hurt. Check wooden equipment and room dividers for splintery surfaces and have them refinished. What about the corners of the room dividers? Will children be hurt if they stumble against the edges? You may need to tape padding onto edges that are sharp.

Be sure your rugs and carpeting lie flat. Wrinkles in carpets cause tripping. Area rugs should have nonskid backing. Use carpets where children will be sitting and playing on the floor. Loop pile carpeting is especially good because it retains its appearance and is easily accessible for wheelchairs. In eating and art areas where spills are likely, washable floor coverings are more practical (Fye & Mumpower, 2001).

Check the physical environment of your classroom to see if you need to modify it for children with special needs. You may need shelves or water containers at special heights for such children.

Bathroom

Slippery floors may be the most common cause of injuries. Make it a practice to check bathroom floors from time to time during the day, and clean them whenever there are spills. Sinks and toilets should be cleaned and disinfected and floors mopped daily. If the sink is not child-size, use a sturdy nonskid stool for children to reach it. Water temperature should not exceed 110 degrees. Mark the faucets with hot and cold symbols in red and blue.

Always store bathroom cleaning and disinfecting materials in cabinets out of the reach of children, and be sure that cabinets containing caustic or poisonous materials are locked. If first-aid kits or materials are stored in the bathroom, keep them out of reach of children, but accessible to adults.

Stairs/Exits

What about stairs leading into or out of the building? Can children reach the railings? Are steps sturdy and unbroken? If covered with carpet, is the carpeting smooth and in good condition? As a teacher of young children, you are accountable for all aspects of children's safety in the building. Although others may be responsible for repairs and replacements, it is up to you to ensure safety by reporting problems and making sure they are corrected. Cutout footprints mounted as a trail can guide children to exits.

Outdoor Playground

Select outdoor play equipment with care, making sure it is developmentally appropriate for preschool children in size, usage, and location. Belt or tire swings are preferable to swings with hard seats, since the latter cause many injuries. The U.S. Consumer Product Safety Commission (1997) recommends a minimum 8-foot safety zone around each play unit, such as swings or slides, as well as a resilient safety surface under and around each unit. A cushioning of sand, wood chips, bark, or special mats may be used, but grass, dirt, concrete or blacktop are not acceptable.

Use child-size equipment with railings and platforms on the slides. Swings should not be attached to climbing structures as in backyard sets. Climbing, sliding, and swinging equipment should be securely anchored in the ground with concrete. Eliminate dangerous equipment such as merry-go-rounds and teeter-totters. The teeter-totter is a dangerous piece of playground equipment for preschoolers. A young child can be thrown off even a small teeter-totter when the child at the lower end jumps off unexpectedly. The safe use of a teeter-totter is too complex a concept for

A cushioning of wood chips or bark under climbing equipment makes a resilient safety surface.

most 3 and 4-year-olds to learn; most teachers prefer not to have them. Merry-go-rounds are also too difficult for most preschool children to use safely. Children can be thrown to the ground while getting on and off merry-go-rounds that are moving, and trying to stay on when they are spinning fast is beyond the capabilities of most preschoolers. Even supervising adults have difficulty preventing spills when merry-go-rounds are going.

Is the equipment on your playground in safe condition? Check to make sure there are no loose parts, sharp edges, or slivers. There also should be no spaces or protrusions where children's heads or body parts can become trapped or their clothing entangled. Safety product guidelines are available from the U.S. Consumer Product Safety Commission by calling 1-800-638-2772.

You as teacher, teaching assistant, or student teacher are an especially important safety feature on the playground. You must accompany children whenever they go outside, preceding them to the playground and making sure conditions are safe for them to follow. Should there be a strange animal or person on the grounds, you will then be able to address the situation, sending the children back inside if necessary.

While the children play you should be an alert observer, not spending time visiting with another adult, but watching for possible dangerous situations among children on the climbing, swinging, or sliding equipment.

Finally, the playground should be properly fenced off from roads, driveways, or parking lots. Each time you use the playground, you should make sure to check it first for broken glass or other dangerous debris. Your children deserve a fun-to-use, hazard-free playground.

Books to Read

Children can help to keep themselves safe if you include them in talking about safety precautions on the playground. Read a picture book about children on the playground such as *So What?* (Cohen, 1982). A book in the familiar "Jim" series, this story shows Jim and his friends hanging upside down on the jungle gym. Although the story focuses on the concepts of "easy" and "hard," playground safety can easily be included when you talk about the story. In the animal story *Chicken Chickens* (Gorbachev, 2001) Mother Hen takes her two little chickens to the playground, but they are afraid to try the various pieces of play equipment until Beaver helps them down the slide on his tail. Ask your children what they would do in each case.

PLANS AND IMPLEMENTS NECESSARY EMERGENCY PROCEDURES

As you plan for the safety needs of the children in your care, be sure to consider unexpected emergencies that may arise. These may include illnesses or injuries where prompt emergency action is necessary; weather emergencies where prompt indoor precautions must be taken; and fires, floods, explosions, or earthquakes where emergency exiting is required. It is particularly important to have the children practice emergency exiting in fire drills.

Emergency Illnesses or Injuries

Know your children well. Do any of them have chronic illnesses such as asthma or diabetes? Heart problems? Breathing problems? Seizure disorders? Allergic reactions? Bleeding problems? A health record for each child should be on hand in the classroom for quick reference. Plans for children with emergency health needs should be made at the beginning of the year with the advice of parents and the program health professional. Be sure to have emergency access to someone who speaks the language of every non-English-speaking child in the program. Be alert to symptoms and learn to recognize signs that may signal an emergency. Know the location of the nearest emergency room and how long it takes to get there. Have transportation available at all times.

Figure 1–2 Emergency Management Conditions

Source: From *Caring for Our Children, National Health and Safety Performance Standards: Guidelines for Out-of-Home Child Care Programs* (p. 23) by the American Academy of Pediatrics and the American Public Health Association, 1992. Reprinted with permission.

- Bleeding
- Burns
- Poisoning
- Choking
- Injuries including insect, animal, and human bites
- Shock
- Convulsions or nonconvulsive seizures
- Sprains, fractures
- Dental emergencies
- Head injuries
- Allergic reactions
- Eye injuries
- Loss of consciousness
- Electric shock
- Drowning

Preparing for Accidents

Post near your telephone emergency numbers for police, sheriff, fire department, doctor, ambulance, hospital, and poison control center. All adults in the classroom should be familiar with the location of these numbers. Also, post near telephones simple directions for handling emergencies, written in two languages if your program is bilingual. A list of children's home telephone numbers, parents' cell phone numbers, and the names and numbers of persons to contact if no one is home should be available near your telephone, as well.

All staff involved in direct care of children should be certified in pediatric first aid that includes rescue breathing and first aid for choking as developed by one of the following organizations: the American Red Cross, American Heart Association, or National Safety Council. Such a course should include emergency management of the conditions listed in Figure 1–2.

Make plans with the staff about each person's duties during an emergency. Practice together to see how you best can respond as a team. Your program also should devote a staff meeting to emergency procedures and first aid. Keep two well-stocked first-aid kits available at all times, one for the classroom and one to take on field trips. Make sure each staff member knows how to use it. Figure 1–3 lists the contents of a first-aid kit as approved by the American Academy of Pediatrics and the American Public Health Association (1992).

In addition, be sure to have on hand near the telephone or first-aid kit an easy-to-use, easy-to-read first-aid emergency handbook. Two excellent spiral-bound handbooks with illustrated, step-by-step first-aid procedures for common medical and health emergencies are *A to Z Health and Safety in the Child Care Setting* (Stoll, 2000) and *Childhood Emergencies: What to Do* (Marin Child Care Council, 2000), also in Spanish.

Book to Read

Children can also become aware of situations requiring first aid by hearing stories about helping someone who has been injured or by playing doctor or nurse in the dramatic play area. You can read them a story such as *Maybe a Band-Aid Will Help* (Hines, 1984), about a little girl who tries to help her "injured" doll.

Figure 1–3   Contents of First-Aid Kit

From *Caring for Our Children, National Health and Safety Performance Standards: Guidelines for Out-of-Home Child Care Programs* (p. 162) by the American Academy of Pediatrics and the American Public Health Association, 1992. Reprinted with permission.

- Disposable nonporous gloves
- Sealed packages of alcohol wipes or antiseptic
- Scissors
- Tweezers
- Thermometer
- Bandage tape
- Sterile gauze pads
- Flexible roller gauze
- Triangular bandages
- Safety pins
- Eye dressing
- Pen/pencil and notepad
- Syrup of ipecac
- Cold pack
- Standard first-aid text
- Coins for use in pay phone
- Insect sting preparation
- Poison control center telephone number
- Water
- Small plastic or metal splints
- Soap

If an injury should occur, make a note of what happened and when, the child's reaction, and your response. Pass such information on to parents and emergency personnel on your center's accident report form, and keep a copy for your own program.

Weather Emergencies

Violent weather can cause emergencies in which teachers and child-care workers must help protect children. When warnings for tornadoes, hurricanes, typhoons, thunderstorms, flash floods, tidal waves, windstorms, or dust storms are issued or sirens are sounded, emergency procedures must be followed immediately. Different rules are necessary for different types of storms. Learn the rules that apply to your area, and practice them with the children under your care until they can respond quickly and without panic.

Books to Read

An ordinary thunderstorm does not require emergency procedures but may frighten the children, nevertheless. You could read them a story such as *Thunder Cake* (Polacco, 1990) and then help them prepare together a real thunder cake. The story describes a little Caucasian girl's visit to her grandmother's farm during a fierce thunderstorm and how her grandmother helps her overcome her fear by gathering ingredients and making a thunder cake. It is a counting tale, as well, for grandmother instructs: "When you see the lightning, start counting . . . real slow. When you hear the thunder, stop counting. That number is how many miles away the storm is."

Use the recipe at the end of the story or have your own recipe and ingredients ready for your emergency. If the electricity goes off, involve the children in a cool cooking activity such as "banana-sicles" (call them "thunder-sicles"). Peel a banana (or an apple); cut it crosswise into two pieces; insert a Popsicle stick in each half; spread peanut butter on the fruit; then crumble graham crackers and roll fruit in crumbs. Be sure to have the children count the seconds between the lightning flash and the thunder to see how many miles away the storm is.

Storm in the Night (Stolz, 1988) tells the story of young African-American Thomas, his grandfather, and his cat Ringo on the night a thunderstorm puts out the lights before it is time to go to bed. They watch the storm from inside and then out on the porch, listening to the sounds in the night. Have your children listen for and de-scribe the sounds they hear, just as Thomas does.

Emergency Exiting

Certain situations demand rules and order. Emergency exiting from the building is one of them. Fire drills, earthquake drills, chemical spills, bombs, civil disturbances, or other street emergencies call for buildings to be cleared as quickly as possible. Children should practice this procedure repeatedly so that everyone understands how to do it without panic. Do not wait for a fire inspector to make this happen. It is your responsibility to yourself, the children, and their families to see that emergency evac-uations are accomplished with ease.

Children with physical disabilities may need special help. Be sure your center is in compliance with ramps, railings, and handholds in place. Classroom staff mem-bers should be assigned to children with special needs to help them move quickly but safely out of the building. Emergency exit signs and directions should be posted in several languages if your program is multilingual. Designate a safe spot outside the building where children should always go to whenever there is emergency exiting.

Books to Read

Before emergency drills take place, talk with your children and read them stories in preparation. *A Chair for My Mother* (Williams, 1982) tells the tale of a little inner-city girl who saves money to replace her mother's big easy chair, which is ruined when a fire destroys their apartment. Although this is a long story for preschoolers you can "read the pictures" and talk to the children about what happens. Talk with the chil-dren about how to exit from a burning building.

A favorite new fire safety story, *Stop Drop and Roll* (Cuyler, 2001) features wor-rywart Jessica who is learning about fire safety in school. Jessica worries about every-thing: smoke alarms, sprinklers, fire drills, escape plans, and especially about what a person should do if her clothes catch on fire. The teacher, Mr. Martin, teaches the chil-dren to say "Stop, drop, and roll," to put out clothing fire. But these words only twist Jessica's tongue into a big knot until the day she sees the flaming candles on Tom's birthday cake. She yells "Stop, drop, and roll!" and Tom drops to the floor. Of course it is a false alarm, but Jessica realizes that she really remembers what to say and do in a real emergency. Can your children practice this procedure?

PROVIDES A SAFE ATMOSPHERE THROUGH TEACHER BEHAVIOR

Teacher's Behavior

The key to helping children respond quickly and sensibly to safety emergencies is the teacher's behavior. Teachers and other classroom staff must keep their own poise, remaining calm, unstressed, and in control. No matter how uneasy you may feel, it must not show in your face, your voice, or your actions. Concentrate instead on the children and how you can help them come through the situation without becoming panicked or hysterical yourself. Here are some suggestions of what you can do:

Dissipate Fear

In today's world unexpected things happen. Teachers and staff members should be as prepared as they can be for all kinds of disasters: common and uncommon, expected and unexpected, minor and serious. One factor common to all these situations is fear. Fear is a crippling emotion that can cause panic and chaos among those experiencing it. If you recognize this fact, you can help dissipate fear among the children through your own behavior as mentioned earler. You can also talk with the children about the fears they may have, and how to handle such fears. Fears such as the fear their mother or father will not come for them; fear of the dark; fear of loud noises; and fear of animals are some of the fears they or you might mention.

Like us, young children are spiritual beings. They need to be treated as such and encouraged to develop their spiritual sides. Early childhood educators from Montessori on have been aware of this fact, but too many of today's teachers have not responded to it (Wolf, 1989). Professor of child study David Elkind believes that:

> Individuals who, in their everyday lives, exemplify the highest of human qualities such as love, forgiveness, and generosity might also be said to be spiritual. It is spirituality in the broad, nondenominational sense that I believe can be fostered by educational practice. (1992, p. 12)

When teachers show children unconditional love, they help to dissipate children's fears during times of crisis and confusion. The six examples of teacher behavior during emergency situations in Figure 1–4 are demonstrations of love toward children. This love in turn fosters reciprocal feelings of love and security within the children, helping to dissipate fear.

When teachers show children unconditional love they help to dissipate children's fears during times of crisis and confusion.

1. Be quiet: help children to become quiet; become quiet yourself; whisper.
2. Use body language: smile; nod; make eye-contact with each child.
3. Come close: touch children; hug them; hold their hands; put arm around them.
4. Use verbal cues: use calming words; use compliments.
5. Laugh quietly together: whisper a silly word or verse; make a silly face.
6. Hold hands: everyone hold hands close together in a circle (standing or seated).

Figure 1–4   Teacher Behavior in Emergency Situations

Books to Read

Ann Tompert's book (1988) *Will You Come Back for Me?* tells the story of 4-year-old Suki, an Asian-American girl who has to go to a child-care center while her mother works. Her mother takes her for a preliminary visit to meet the teacher and see how the other children play, but Suki is afraid to join in. At home Suki expresses her fears, so her mother makes a big red paper heart with her name on it. She tears it in two to show Suki she will leave part of her heart with Suki when she goes to work, but puts it back together to show Suki how she will always come back for her at 3 o'clock. Do any of your children have such fears? What can help them overcome such fears?

Naomi Judd's book (1999) *Love Can Build a Bridge* illustrates the power of love between children of different races as they help one another in crisis situations such as falling and getting hurt, being in the hospital, having a bike wreck, and being afraid of a fireworks explosion.

Fear of the dark is very common among young children. A book that may help to dissipate such a fear is Jill Tomlinson's (2001) *The Owl Who Was Afraid of the Dark* about the little barn owl, Plop, who doesn't want to be a night bird because he is afraid of the dark. His parents have him visit various night-loving people to find out why they like the dark because of watching fireworks, sitting around a campfire, waiting for Santa Claus, looking at stars through a telescope, and discovering the beauty of the dark. Have your children discuss how they feel about each of these situations.

Supervising Classroom Areas

Early childhood programs are fortunate to have more than one staff member present at all times. A teacher, an assistant, and sometimes a third staff member, student teacher, or Foster Grandparent volunteer can contribute to children's safety by supervising activities and areas where precautions are necessary. Plan during staff meetings what the role of each staff member will be. Include volunteers in your plans and give them a role where appropriate. Help them to model calm and unruffled behavior during times of crisis and accidents, and how to handle emergencies.

Overall responsibility for safety belongs to the teacher, who can survey the entire classroom as other staff members work with children in particular learning centers. Be sure that room dividers are not so high that they prevent you from seeing all the children. If your program uses more than one room at a time, be sure a staff member remains in each room.

Learning centers that need safety supervision include large motor, computer, woodworking, and cooking. The bathroom, the playground, and the stairs are other safety supervision areas. It is necessary to keep an eye on the children in all of these areas but not stand over them, unless you are demonstrating the use of a tool. The more unobtrusive that staff members can be in their supervision, the more freely children will explore activities or learning centers independently.

Anticipating Unsafe Behavior

Unsafe child behavior can take many forms. It may consist of running in the classroom or halls, pushing other children, climbing too high, playing too rough, or using materials in unsafe ways. You may be able to eliminate much unsafe behavior by anticipating it ahead of time. Arrange the physical environment so that children do not have room for uncontrolled running. Have children walk with partners in the halls or on city streets. Carefully supervise potentially unsafe situations.

Children love to play with water. If they squirt it on the floor in the classroom or in the bathroom, they have created a slippery condition for others. You need to stop them firmly, not harshly, and redirect them by involving them in helping you to clean up the water. Make the task interesting, not a punishment.

Redirecting Unsafe Behavior

Telling a child to stop climbing so high or to stop building such a tall block building will not resolve the safety problem. Commands like these only encourage young children to climb higher and build taller. A sensitive teacher knows that one of the best ways to deal with such situations often requires redirecting unwanted behavior, not by referring to it, but by calling the child's attention to something else.

For instance, go to the child personally (don't shout across a room) and ask the child to show you how he or she can climb horizontally or swing hand over hand, or to show you how a very wide building would look. Giving a child another challenge will often redirect potentially unsafe behavior into something more constructive.

Modeling Safe Behavior

You and the staff members are the models of safe behavior for your children. When they see you taking precautions with saws, hammers, knives, or electrical equipment, they will imitate you. Your behavior is much more effective than your trying to tell or "teach" children the proper rules. As you practice normal adult safety behavior, you should describe it verbally to the children. "See how I cut the pumpkin? I move the knife away from me so that I don't get cut. Now you try it." You also should not practice any unsafe behavior such as consuming hot liquids or setting a hot cup of coffee down in the classroom area.

You and your staff, including volunteers, should discuss safety practices so that all of you agree on the limits you will set for children in the classroom. This agreement will thus help you to enforce the limits consistently. Young children do not necessarily understand rules by being told. Most often they learn by doing, by being involved in the situation. For instance, you can demonstrate at the workbench how to hold the saw and make it work, or you can have a parent come in and demonstrate. Then let each child try it. When a child has learned to use the saw, let him or her show the next child how to use it. If one child can show another child how to perform the task, then that child has really learned it.

Involving Children in Safety Rules

Let the children be involved in helping to decide on the safety rules for each classroom area. All of you should agree on the rules. How many children should be allowed in the woodworking area at one time? How high can a block building be built and still

*How high can a block building
be built and still be safe?*

be safe? Should a child be allowed to stand on a chair to make the building higher than he or she can reach from the floor? The children need to know the answers to these questions. If they help make the rules, they will be more willing to follow them.

Do not overburden the children with rules. Make simple ones that everyone understands and that you can easily enforce. Children should be concerned with the safety basics such as not hurting themselves or others. We adults are sometimes overly concerned about rules and regulations. If there are too many rules, young children simply will not respond. Keep rules simple, basic, and few in number.

Teaching Car Safety Through Dramatic Play

Most states have enacted legislation governing car safety for young children. The laws state that children younger than 4 must sit in state-approved car seats when riding in private cars. As a teacher, you can encourage children to follow this practice through classroom play activities. Bring in a car seat and let them practice using it themselves or with dolls during dramatic play. Or fasten a seat belt to a chair and let children pretend to be riding in a car.

Talk to the children about bus safety. If any of the children are transported to the center by bus, have the bus driver come in at the beginning of the year to talk about bus safety. How should they sit in a moving vehicle? What should their behavior be like?

Book to Read

Read the book *The Wheels on the Bus* (Kovalski, 1987) or sing the song by the same name and discuss what the children think about the safety of the people on that particular bus.

Teaching Traffic Safety with Signs and Games

Children can learn about safety signs and signals when they go on field trips. Follow-up activities in the classroom can help reinforce these learnings. Through games, songs, and stories, they can learn that red means "stop" and green means "go." Make a traffic light from a half-gallon milk carton. Cover it with dark contact paper and cut three holes in a vertical row through one side. Cover each hole with red, yellow, or green cellophane or tissue paper. Make three small holes on the opposite side of the box, large enough to shine a pen flashlight through. Let the children play a "Red Light-Green Light" game by marching around in a circle while someone shines the flashlight through the hole to signal "stop," "wait," or "go."

You can also make or purchase wood or cardboard stop signs and other traffic signals for the children to use in block play. Follow up this activity with a visit by a police officer or school crossing guard to demonstrate street-crossing safety. Although safety videos are available for children, young preschoolers do not learn concepts as well from videos as they do from active involvement with learning. Sitting still and listening to a teacher or a video is not as effective a learning strategy as the more interactive activities mentioned.

Using Multicultural Books as Follow-Up Safety Reinforcers

Once a concept is clear to children, books can serve as a good follow-up when they are read to individuals and small groups. Trying to teach a safety concept to a large group of children by reading a book is much less effective because children need to be close enough to see the illustrations. They need to be able to respond individually to the teacher's questions, such as "Can you find the traffic light in the picture?" "What color is it?" and "Does it tell the driver to stop or go?"

Two excellent books for reinforcing traffic safety concepts are the recently reissued picture book *Red Light Green Light* (McDonald, 1944) and the wordless picture book *Truck* (Crews, 1980). Let the children make up their own story as they watch Crew's 18-wheeler following traffic signs through the city and onto the highway. Be sure to have a selection of toy cars and trucks in the block area after reading these books. As you watch and listen to the children's dramatic play you will soon learn whether the children really understand these safety concepts.

Not So Fast Songololo (Daly, 1985) is a simple story about a South African boy who helps his granny go shopping in the crowded city. In addition to the traffic lights they encounter, this book uses descriptive words and sensitive illustrations to show people from another culture involved in safety problems similar to those of American children. Multicultural education is best integrated into every classroom activity by including stories like this in which children can pretend to be book characters from another culture. What would your children do if, like Songololo, they went shopping with their grannies?

Or what do they have to say about the way African American Lizzie walks to work through the city with her mother in *Red Light Green Light, Mama and Me* (Best, 1995)? Have they ever had a ride on a subway? These books can easily stimulate the building of block roads if you put out little cars, trucks, road signs, and multiethnic figures of people in your block center. Ask the builders to tell the others what safety rules the block people and cars need to follow.

Children such as the vivacious Chinese Canadian girl in the book *Where Is Gah-Ning?* (Munsch, 1994) sometimes forget all about safety rules when they are in a hurry to get someplace. Gah-Ning takes off down the road to go shopping, first on her bicycle and then on roller blades, while her distraught father chases after her in his car. What would your children have done?

Preparing for Field Trips

Field trips require special preparations. Teachers need to familiarize themselves with the field trip site to prepare the children. Are there special safety hazards that need to be addressed? On a visit to a farm, for example, how close should children get to the animals? What about riding on a tractor? On a visit to a fire station, will the children be allowed to climb onto a fire truck?

In addition, children may need to learn how to walk in pairs, how to cross busy thoroughfares, and how to wait for the teacher before they go forward. The adults as well as the children need to understand such procedures ahead of time.

If children are transported in cars, buses, or subways, they and the drivers or parent helpers must be aware of safe and unsafe child behavior in a vehicle. One of the adults should also be certified in pediatric first aid and should take along a first-aid kit.

To anticipate the safety problems inherent in any field trip, you should make a preliminary visit to the site, if possible using the same mode of transportation the children will use. Then you can make notes about safety situations for preparing the staff and the children. Talk to the people at the site in case they have safety rules or advice you will need to know ahead of time. As you look at the field trip site, try to anticipate the kinds of exploring your active children will attempt to do. Would any of these things be dangerous? What about children becoming separated from the group or going off by themselves? One of your staff members can be assigned to check on this problem.

Books to Read

You may want to practice field trip behavior ahead of time with your children in the classroom. Reading a book such as *Don't Worry, I'll Find You* (Hines, 1986) to small groups helps children to understand what to do if they get separated. Have children role-play such a situation with a doll from the dramatic play center. In *Laney's Lost Momma* (Hamm, 1991) African-American Laney loses her mother in a large department store, but finds her when she remembers Momma's advice about what to do if you get lost. What would your children do in this situation?

Preparing Children for Personal Safety

The personal safety of the children in your care includes protecting them from harm or victimization by predatory adults. Sexual abuse of children by adults is one of the primary dangers involved. Although this is a very real threat to certain young children, many professionals believe that the child-care community has overreacted to the threat in ways that are potentially harmful to children.

Through films, diagrams, games, and exhortations, teachers have alerted young children to "stranger-danger" in centers. In addition, teachers have made children think it is their responsibility to protect themselves from such adults. However, we delude ourselves if we believe that 3-, 4-, and 5-year-old children can successfully ward off the advances of abusive adults. In addition, if children have been taught what to do, but then find they can't prevent the abuse, their own guilt feelings may add to the psychological damage, and they may come to believe that the abuse is their own fault.

As a result of this kind of overreaction to the situation on our part, we find many children in child-care centers who are afraid of the other adults in the building, who run from friendly college students, who will not let health professionals examine them, or who may even show fear when a parent undresses them for bed or a bath. In addition, some child-care professionals themselves worry that entering the bathroom area with the children in their care or helping children clean themselves after accidents may cause children to overreact and report to their parents that they were touched. Male child-care workers are especially vulnerable to such charges, and as a result, many of the much-needed male role models for young children have been driven out of the child-care profession.

We need to step back and think about the effects of instilling this kind of fear in young children. This kind of fear not only inhibits learning but also makes children all the more vulnerable to victimization. We also need to realize that most child sexual abuse occurs in the home and that 85 percent of such abuse is perpetrated by someone the child knows (Hull, 1986).

What, then, should be our role in protecting the children in our charge? We should use our common sense in helping children learn not to go with strangers or accept rides from people they do not know. However, scare tactics and the constant bombardment of children with "stranger-danger" films and lessons are out of place.

We as teachers are the ones who really need to be educated in this matter. We should look carefully at the message we want to get across to children. It should not be that there is danger in every stranger. It should not be one of "good touches" and "bad touches." How is a preschooler to distinguish between the two? With such messages, we may be producing a generation of paranoid children who will keep their distance from one another as adults. Do we want to live in a society where caring, touching, and loving are perceived as threatening acts? Instead, we should encourage children to do the following:

1. Children should talk to a trusted adult when they feel uncomfortable.
2. They should go only with a trusted adult on the street or in a car.
3. They should ask a trusted adult when they are unsure of what to do.

The child-care staff and parents need to be involved in sensitive discussions of this issue and how it is to be handled in the center and at home. You may want to invite psychologists or health professionals to contribute their expertise. A positive approach, in which children learn to feel good about themselves and the people around them, should be your goal for the children's personal safety.

You and your staff also should take special precautions in not allowing a child to leave the center with any person other than the designated parent or caregiver. If someone you do not know demands to take the child home, do not comply. Call the parent or social worker for advice on what to do. Otherwise, keep the child in your care until the proper adult caregiver responds.

SUMMARY

Information from this chapter should help you set up and maintain a safe classroom environment and to reduce and prevent injuries. You should be able to assess the curriculum areas in the room for possible safety hazards such as electrical cords, exposed heating pipes or vents, slippery floors, rugs that do not lie flat and could cause tripping, and rough edges and sharp corners on room dividers. You should understand how to promote safety in each area with illustrated signs, simple basic rules, supervision where necessary, anticipation and redirection of unsafe child behavior, and role-playing and demonstration of safe behavior.

Through games, stories, dramatic play, and other developmentally appropriate activities, children can learn the safety rules and precautions they must practice on stairs and exits, in the bathroom, on field trips, and in cars. You yourself should be aware of the importance of planning for children's emergency illnesses and injuries and of being prepared to give first aid if an accident occurs. You should also be aware of procedures to follow during weather emergencies or emergency exiting of the building during drills or real situations. Remaining calm yourself and helping to dissipate children's fears through positive, loving behaviors will help children remain calm in times of crisis. As a role model for safe behavior in the classroom, you will be taking the first step to assure children and their families that your program is making a serious commitment to each child's safety and well-being.

LEARNING ACTIVITIES

1. Read Chapter 1, Maintaining a Safe Classroom, and write out answers to Question Sheet 1.
2. Meet with your trainer or instructor and discuss answers to Question Sheet 1.
3. View one of the videotapes suggested, write out plans, and discuss with your trainer how you can apply information from this video.

4. Read one or more of the references cited or suggested readings in this chapter. Begin a card file with 10 file cards that describe in detail ideas from your reading for promoting safety in your classroom. Include the reference source on the back of each card.

5. Assess the safety of your classroom by using the Classroom Safety Checklist in Table 1–1. What changes can you suggest?

6. Have one of your staff members hold a fire drill or emergency exiting drill. Observe and record what happens. Report on the results and make recommendations for improvement.

7. Help a small group of children learn a particular safety concept using ideas and techniques from this chapter. Record the results.

8. List the contents of your classroom first-aid kit and describe a use for each item.

9. For some or all of the children, arrange and conduct a field trip during which you make appropriate use of safety measures. Write a report of the results and make suggestions for improvement.

10. Complete the Chapter 1 Evaluation Sheet and return it to your trainer or college supervisor.

QUESTION SHEET 1

1. Who is responsible for providing and maintaining a safe classroom environment, and what does that responsibility entail?

2. With what safety factors should classroom caregivers be concerned? How does your classroom fare in this regard?

3. What are some of the dangerous materials a classroom might contain? Does your classroom have any of these?

4. What dangers to young children are posed by their entering and exiting a building? How can such dangers be overcome?

5. How can you, as a teacher, model specific safety practices for the children under your care? Be specific.

6. How do children best learn safety rules? Give specific examples.

7. What are the safety aspects of field trips with which you should be concerned?

8. How would you handle an emergency such as a child's falling and being injured?

9. How can you help children maintain their personal safety without frightening them?

10. What unsafe child behavior might occur in your classroom, and how could you correct it?

11. What should be your main safety concerns when equipping your playground?

12. What is the most dangerous aspect of climbers? How can you minimize this danger?

13. What are the most dangerous aspects of slides and swings? How can you minimize these dangers?

14. What activities in the classroom and on the playground should be supervised for safety reasons? How should this be done?

15. If you could change the physical arrangement of the classroom and the outside playground to improve children's safety, what would you do and why?

REFERENCES

American Academy of Pediatrics and American Public Health Association. (1992). *Caring for our children, national health and safety performance standards: Guidelines for out-of-home child care programs.* St. Paul, MN: Redleaf Press.

Elkind, D. (1992). Spirituality in education. *Holistic Education Review. 21.*

Hull, K. (1986). *Safe passages: A guide for teaching children personal safety.* Dawn Sign Press.

Fye, M. A. S., & Mumpower, J. P. (2001). Lost in space? Designing learning areas for today. *Dimensions of Early Childhood, 29*(2), 16–22.

Marin Child Care Council. (2000). *Childhood emergencies: What to do.* St. Paul, MN: Redleaf Press.

Stoll, B. H. (2000). *A to Z health and safety in the child care setting.* St. Paul, MN: Redleaf Press.

Taylor, B. J. (2002). *Early childhood program management: People and procedures* (4th ed.). Upper Saddle River, NJ: Merrill/Prentice Hall.

Wolf, A. D. (Ed.). (1989). *Peaceful children, peaceful world: The challenge of Maria Montessori.* Hollidaysburg, PA: Parent Child Press.

U.S. Consumer Product Safety Commission. (1997). *Handbook for public playground safety.* Washington, DC: U.S. Government Printing Office.

SUGGESTED READINGS

Cook, R. E., Tessier, A., & Klein, M. D. (2000). *Adapting early childhood curricula for children in inclusive settings* (5th ed.). Upper Saddle River, NJ: Merrill/Prentice Hall.

Copeland, M. L. (1996). Code Blue! Establishing a child care emergency plan. *Child Care Information Exchange, 107,* 17–22.

Hudson, S. D., Thompson, D., & Mack, M. G. (2000). Safe playgrounds: Increased challenges, reduced risks. *Dimensions of Early Childhood, 29*(1), 18–23.

Jordan, N. H. (1993). Sexual abuse prevention programs in early childhood education: A caveat. *Young Children, 48*(6), 76–79.

National Association for the Education of Young Children. (2001). Helping young children in frightening times. *Young Children, 56*(6), 6–7.

Shallcross, M. A. (1999). Family child care homes need health and safety training and emergency rescue system. *Young Children, 54*(5), 70–73.

Taylor, S. I., & Morris, V. G. (1996). Outdoor play in early childhood settings: Is it safe and healthy for children? *Early Childhood Education Journal, 23*(3), 153–158.

Taylor, S. I., Morris, V. G., & Cordeau-Young, C. (1997). Field trips in early childhood settings: Expanding the walls of the classroom. *Early Childhood Education Journal, 25*(2), 141–146.

CHILDREN'S BOOKS

Best, C. (1995). *Red light green light, Mamma and me.* New York: Orchard.

Cohen, M. (1982). *So what?* New York: Dell.

Crews, D. (1980). *Truck.* New York: Greenwillow.

Cuyler, M. (2001). *Stop drop and roll.* New York: Simon & Schuster.

Daly, N. (1985). *Not so fast Songololo.* New York: Viking Penguin.

Gorbachev, V. (2001). *Chicken chickens.* New York: North-South Books.

Hamm, D. J. (1991). *Laney's lost momma.* Morton Grove, IL: Whitman.

Hines, A. G. (1986). *Don't worry, I'll find you.* New York: Dutton.

Hines, A. G. (1984). *Maybe a Band-Aid will help.* New York: Dutton.

Judd, N. (1999). *Love can build a bridge.* New York: HarperCollins.

Kovalski, M. (1987). *The wheels on the bus.* Boston: Little Brown.

McDonald, G. (1944). *Red light green light.* Garden City, NY: Doubleday.

Munsch, R. (1994). *Where is Gah-Ning?* Toronto: Annick.

Polacco, P. (1990). *Thunder cake.* New York: Philomel.

Stolz, M. (1988). *Storm in the night.* New York: Harper.

Tomlinson, J. (2001). *The owl who was afraid of the dark.* Cambridge, MA: Candlewick Press.

Tompert, A. (1988). *Will you come back for me?* Morton Grove, IL: Albert Whitman.

Williams, V. B. (1982). *A chair for my mother.* New York: Greenwillow.

VIDEOTAPES

American Academy of Pediatrics (Producer). *Part 4: Setting up for healthy and safe care.* Washington, DC: National Association for the Education of Young Children. (Part of set #820)

Massachusetts Dept. of Public Health. (Producer). *Family child care health and safety video and checklist.* St. Paul, MN: Redleaf Press.

National Association for the Education of Young Children. *Make a difference: Report child abuse and neglect.* Washington, DC: NAEYC #890.

Video Active Productions. (Producer). *Safe active play: A guide to play area hazards.* Washington, DC: National Association for the Education of Young Children.

CHAPTER 1 EVALUATION SHEET
MAINTAINING A SAFE CLASSROOM

1. Student _____

2. Trainer _____

3. Center where training occurred _____

4. Beginning date _____ Ending date _____

5. Describe what student did to accomplish General Objective.

   _____

   _____

6. Describe what student did to accomplish Specific Objectives.

   Objective 1 _____

   _____

   Objective 2 _____

   _____

   Objective 3 _____

   _____

7. Evaluation of student's Learning Activities

   _____

Signature of Trainer: Signature of Student:

_____   _____

Comments:

   _____

   _____

   _____

Perrmission is granted by the publisher to reproduce this page for evaluation and record keeping.

Maintaining a Healthy Classroom

GENERAL OBJECTIVE

To be able to set up and maintain a healthy classroom that promotes good child health and nutrition and is free from factors contributing to illness

SPECIFIC OBJECTIVES

____ Encourages children to follow common health and nutrition practices

____ Recognizes unusual behavior or symptoms of children who may be ill and provides for the children

____ Supports the mental and emotional health of every child

HEALTH practices, like those of safety, are best taught to young children through behavior modeling on the part of classroom adults, as well as through lighthearted games, stories, and activities involving the children. Nutrition facts, for example, become meaningful for young children, not by learning the basic food groups, but through fun classroom experiences with real food. Children learn to wash their hands before meals, not because they know it kills germs, but because they see the teacher doing it.

ENCOURAGES CHILDREN TO FOLLOW COMMON HEALTH AND NUTRITION PRACTICES

Exercising

In the eyes of many adults, young children are always on the go. Why should the preschool provide more exercising activities than children already engage in naturally, you may wonder? Children's energy is deceiving. It may be evident to everyone, but the opportunities to express it are vanishing in most children's everyday life. No longer can youngsters run and play freely when streets are unsafe. Young children who formerly walked with their parents to school in the morning more often ride or are bussed nowadays. And instead of playing vigorous sidewalk games, most children spend more time watching television after school. It has become a sedentary society for children as well as adults.

Preschool programs are thus called upon to help fill this important need—that is, the need to help children develop healthy bodies through exercise. Every preschool must provide large motor equipment for both the classroom and the outside playground, and this equipment must be made available to all on a daily basis. You should also plan time daily for strenuous running and movement in a gymnasium or outdoor playground. If neither is available, instead take the children for a follow-the-leader run around the building.

For programs that do not have an indoor or outdoor space large enough for running, have children run in place to a chant. Start out slowly and increase the speed with every verse.

Step, step, step,
Make your feet trep, trep,
Make your legs hep, hep,
As you keep in step.

Trot, trot, trot,
Makes your toes dot, dot,
Make your heels hot, hot,
As you trot, trot, trot.

Faster, faster, faster,
Make your feet go faster, faster,
Make your legs go even faster,
And you won't have a disaster.
STOP!

Children enjoy such body action chants and want them repeated over and over. But you need to control the action and take a "breather" from time to time. As noted by Werner, Timms, and Almond (1996): "Young children have small bodies and lack muscular endurance. They tire easily and quickly, yet they also recover quickly. Activities should be designed with this in mind. Exercise should be in short bouts with time-outs for rest and recovery. Then, it's off again for more activity" (p. 50).

If you want to keep children interested in such daily movement exercises, ask them to help make up some of their own running chants. They love to be included in planning activities, and they love variety in their activities even more. "Everybody get ready to run in place like Alex's gerbil! Can you do it holding hands? Let's see how fast you can go."

Allow children who cannot stand and run to sit and make movements with their feet or hands, to play catch with a beanbag, or provide some other activity that encourages them to move. For example, have wheelchair-bound children touch their toes, knees, shoulders, and heads to a different chant while seated. Everyone can enjoy this kind of body action chanting if they are all seated. Make up your own chants with the children's help, and you may be surprised at the creative rhyming words they invent.

Resting

Healthy young children seem to be perpetual motion machines, never stopping to take a breath. Yet they do need to practice a balance of active and quiet activities. The classroom staff should make sure a rest time is also part of the daily program.

This does not mean the teacher should make the children put their heads down on the table for 15 minutes every day at 10 A.M. whether or not they need a rest. Rest time should come as a natural follow-up to exertion, rather than as a formal period at a certain time of day. If there has been no strenuous activity during the morning, a group rest time is unnecessary. If you schedule one anyway, you will probably spend most of the time trying to keep the children quiet. On the other hand, when children are truly tired, they welcome a quiet period.

Children with physical disabilities or health impairments may tire more quickly than do others. You and your staff should recognize the situation, provide a quiet place for such children, and make sure they stop to rest when they need it.

Some programs have a quiet period just before lunch, when the children put mats on the floor and pursue quiet activities by themselves. Playing soft music is conducive to calming children down and encouraging quiet activities. Solitary activity is a refreshing change of pace if children have been with a large and active group all morning or have just come in from the playground.

If yours is an all-day program, you should provide a formal nap period in the afternoon. Use cots or mats wherever you have spare space. If you are using the regular classroom space, section off an area for children who no longer take afternoon naps. Dim the lights in the room, but after the nappers have fallen asleep, you can whisper to the nonsleepers that they may go to this special area and play quietly. Individual mats marked with the children's names help make this a quiet time for nonsleepers as well.

Books to Read

Astronauts Are Sleeping (Standiford, 1996) shows three astronauts floating lazily through space as a child asks what could they be dreaming about? What do they see in their dreams? In *Hush! A Thai Lullaby* (Ho, 1996) a Thai mother hushes all the animals so that Baby can sleep. A mosquito, lizard, cat, mouse, frog, pig, monkey, water buffalo, and elephant all become so quiet everyone can rest—everyone but Baby, who stays awake the whole time. But the lyrical rhythms may soothe your listeners into falling asleep. *Olivia* (Falconer, 2000) is a little girl pig who is always on the go. She wears out everyone around her, and finally even herself, when her mother reads her to sleep.

Washing

Hand-washing can do more to prevent the spread of infectious diseases than almost any other health practice. Children must learn to wash their hands upon arrival, before meals, after using the bathroom, and after handling pets. Do you serve as their model? They will do it because you ask them to and because it is an interesting sort

Hand washing can do more to prevent the spread of infectious diseases than almost any other health practice.

of task, but you should model the same behavior. They should see you washing your hands, too. Demonstrate with liquid soap how to wash the front and back of the hands, between the fingers, and under the fingernails. Then rinse, dry your hands with a paper towel, wipe off the faucet, and dispose of the towel in the trash container.

Be sure you wash your own hands when you arrive, before preparing food, before eating, after helping a child use the toilet, and especially after wiping a child's nose. All of the classroom staff should do the same to prevent the spread of germs.

Discuss with the children how germs cause diseases and then have the youngsters practice their own hand-washing skills to get rid of pretend germs that you will put on their hands. Sprinkle cinnamon on their hands and let each one try to wash it off. Did they get rid of every "germ"?

It is essential to have a sink in the classroom as well as in the bathroom. If you do not, set up a hand-washing stand with plastic basins for washing and rinsing, and devise a method for disposing of the water after use.

You can promote the practice of cleanliness through washing in other ways. For example, have the children bathe the dolls in the dramatic play area once a week. If the classroom does not have a toy sink in the area, bring in a plastic tub. Both boys and girls can have an enjoyable time with water. Let them wash the dolls' clothes as well. This activity presents another good opportunity to talk about cleanliness and how it keeps us healthy and free from disease.

Children especially love to play with water, so approach these activities with a sense of pleasure rather than drudgery. Hand-washing may be a daily routine, but it can be fun if you and the children make it so. Have each child take turns bathing one of the plastic dinosaurs in a small basin, for instance. (Don't forget to change the water every time.) Then read them the hilarious book *The Beast in the Bathtub* (Stevens, 1985), a story about little Lewis, who doesn't want to bathe because there's a big green beast in his bathtub. Put out a green monster toy in the water table after this one.

Nutrition

Children learn very quickly what foods we consider important, not by what we say, but by observing the kinds of food we serve in the classroom. Do you serve cookies and milk for a snack? Do you serve cake, cupcakes, or candy for birthdays? Sugar found in such foods has been linked to the formation of dental cavities and to obesity. If you want children to become acquainted instead with delicious fruits and interesting vegetables, plan some exciting food activities with these foods as well. Talk to parents about sending in something besides cake or cupcakes for birthdays or about coming in to help the children prepare their own treats.

How about a "Banana Surprise" or a "Smoothie" or a "Hairy Harry" for a birthday celebration? The children can have the fun of making their own party refreshments as well as eating them. "Banana Surprise" uses bananas, graham cracker crumbs, and peanut butter and gives children practice with the small-motor skills of peeling the banana, spreading it with peanut butter, and rolling it in cracker crumbs. If you substitute raisins for the cracker crumbs, you will be making "Ants on a Log."

"Smoothies" are a blend of orange and lemon juice, mashed bananas, honey, and milk. Children also enjoy making "Hairy Harrys" out of apple slices spread with peanut butter and topped with alfalfa sprouts and raisins. To make their own peanut butter, have them grind up peanuts.

In addition to parties, let the children also make their own daily snacks, such as stuffed celery. In addition to scrubbing and cutting the celery, they can make fillings from cream cheese or peanut butter. Other nutritious snacks include low-fat yogurt or cottage cheese that can be spread on crackers or used as a dip for carrots, celery, broccoli, or strawberries (Rothlein, 1989).

Pretend Soup and Other Real Recipes (Katzen & Henderson, 1994) is a fine child-oriented cookbook with illustrated recipes for "bagel faces" and 18 other child-tested treats. Print and draw simple illustrated recipes on newsprint for the children to follow, and you add the dimension of "emergent literacy" prereading experiences to the activity (see Chapter 6).

Do the children in your care eat breakfast? It is important for young children to start the day with a nutritious meal. If they skip breakfast, they may become cranky and inattentive. Research shows that children who eat breakfast are more alert and may even learn more during late morning hours. Consider providing breakfast for your children. Fruit or juice, milk, and cereal can be varied with nontraditional breakfast foods such as melted cheese on toast or a peanut butter sandwich on whole-grain bread (Rothlein, 1989). Don't forget to serve as a model by eating breakfast with the children.

Once children have had some experiences with healthful foods, teachers can introduce other fun nutrition activities. Food puppets can visit the class to talk about their favorite foods. How about a "junk-food puppet" who thinks everyone should eat nothing but candy bars, potato chips, and soda? How will your children respond?

Books to Read

This is the time for reading the book *Gregory, the Terrible Eater* (Sharmat, 1980), the hilarious story of a little goat who craves human food but must learn to eat "correctly" by being served one piece of goat food at a time (e.g., "spaghetti and a shoelace in tomato sauce"). Can your children make up nutritious menus for their own pets? For themselves?

Do any of your children have younger siblings who have trouble eating the food on the table? They will enjoy hearing *Eat Up, Gemma* (Hayes, 1988), a humorous family story about Baby Gemma, who will not eat anything she is given, only impossible items like the decorations on a lady's hat. Her African-American family is ready to give up, until Gemma's brother has the brilliant idea of arranging grapes and bananas on a plate to look like the lady's hat that Gemma tried to eat. Can your children arrange the fruit you provide in tempting combinations for their own snack?

Plan a cooking activity every week. If you have the equipment to cook hot foods (e.g., a stove, a microwave oven, a hot plate, or a hot pot), you may want to start with vegetable soup. As a lead-in, read the comical book *To Market, To Market* (Miranda, 1997), with its eye-popping animals that the lady brings home from the market one by one, creating chaos in the kitchen, until the animals end up doing the shopping and bringing home the proper vegetables.

Picture books are excellent nutrition lesson lead-ins to introduce the activity, as well as follow-ups later to help children reconstruct in their minds what they did compared with what the book characters did. In *Warthogs in the Kitchen, A Sloppy Counting Book* (Edwards, 1998), children will chuckle over the antics of warthogs in aprons making a mess in the kitchen as they bake pickle cupcakes. Be sure to compare the two cupcake recipes at the end: One is for humans; and the other, which begins with "1. Wash hooves," is for warthogs.

It's Grandma's birthday in *Bunny Cakes* (Wells, 1997), and little bunny Max wants to make her an earthworm birthday cake. But his sister Ruby insists on a real angel surprise cake, for which Max is sent to the store time after time to buy each ingredient he manages to damage. He tries to add his own ingredient, "red-hot marshmallow squirters," and finally Grandma is so thrilled with the results she doesn't know which cake to eat first. Making a list, scribble writing, finding items at the store, counting, measuring, stirring, and baking take on real meaning when children have the kind of hands-on experiences that Max had.

Family Involvement in Food Activities

In *Everybody Cooks Rice* (Dooley, 1991), the youngsters can enjoy a multiethnic food experience as Lewis's sister goes around the neighborhood looking for Lewis and finding instead all of her neighbors cooking different rice dishes. She samples black-eyed peas and rice from Barbados, turmeric rice with pigeon peas from Puerto Rico, fish sauce for rice from Vietnam, basmati rice from India, rice with tofu and vegetables from China, rice and beans from Haiti, and finally back home, rice with green peas from her great-grandmother's Italian recipe. The recipes for these dishes appear at the end of the story. Invite parents from different cultures to help you and the children cook a different rice dish every month.

In *Dumpling Soup* (Rattigan, 1993), a multicultural extended family in Hawaii celebrates the New Year by going to Grandma's house to cook and eat dumpling soup. Marisa, the Asian-American narrator of the story, gets to help make dumplings for the first time as her Korean, Japanese, Chinese, Hawaiian, and Caucasian relatives gather. The children may want to celebrate the New Year with their own nutritious dumplings, made with the help of parents or neighbors. If you celebrate holidays with cooking or eating activities, be sure to make them multiethnic like this.

A favorite activity for children and families alike is a potluck meal, with each family bringing its own special dish. Two wonderful alphabet potluck books are available to spice up the event: *Potluck* (Shelby, 1991), in which a different child brings each alphabetical item (from Acton with asparagus soup to Zeke and Zelda with zucchini casserole), and *Alligator Arrived with Apples, A Potluck Alphabet Feast* (Dragonwagon, 1987), a thanksgiving feast by 26 alphabetical animals.

Be sure to include plastic foods for children to pretend with in the dramatic play center, as a follow-up to the real food and nutrition activities they have experienced. School-supply catalogs now provide plastic foods from many cultures: Italian pizzas, Chinese dumplings and egg rolls, Mexican tacos and tortillas, Japanese sushi, Chinese dim sum, and Middle Eastern kabobs, as well as plastic breads from around the world.

Medical Tests and Examinations

Although a classroom teacher is not usually responsible for setting up medical tests and examinations for children, you can clearly support the health specialist who does. You and the specialist need to work together to plan and carry out classroom activities to acquaint children with these examinations to make them less threatening.

Before an eye test, for instance, let the children practice holding a card over one eye and responding to letters on an eye chart. Later they can give a similar "test" of their own to the dolls in the dramatic play center. Before an ear test, have the health specialist demonstrate or talk to the children about what will occur. The nurse in one Head Start program pasted together a three-dimensional model of an ear inside a shoe box. Through a hole in one end of the box, the children could shine a pen flashlight to see the inner parts of the "ear," just as the doctor does. Be honest with children about what will happen. If their fingers will be pricked to draw blood, arrange for a demonstration with a nurse. Invite a dental hygienist to demonstrate a dental checkup.

Before taking your class on a field trip to a clinic, read them *Robby Visits the Doctor* (Davidson, 1992). Afterward display doctor or dental props for children to play with in the dramatic play center. Listen to what they are saying to determine how much they have learned about health checkups. According to Texas Child Care (1994):

> After offering these experiences as a foundation, set up a pretend medical office or hospital in the dramatic play center. If children have had frightening experiences, role-playing will help them work through their fears and hurts. If they've never been to the dentist or eye doctor, dramatic play will help them prepare for the first visit and feel secure. (pp. 22–26)

It is important for young children to act out their feelings about doctors, nurses, having shots, and going to the hospital. Thus, medical role-playing in the dramatic play area of the classroom serves a therapeutic as well as an educational role for the youngsters. Some children can pretend to be the doctor or nurse giving shots to other children or dolls, and others can pretend to be the patients who roll up their sleeves for shots. This is scary business for youngsters. Working out their fears of doctors and shots in this nonthreatening manner helps children to prepare for the real thing.

Books to Read

As a follow-up to this medical role-playing, you can read the book *No Measles, No Mumps for Me* (Showers, 1980), a story about a little boy who is immunized against childhood diseases. In simple terms and illustrations, the story explains what happens inside the body after an immunization shot. Ask the children what happens if they get chicken pox. Some of the children know already. Read the simple but funny *Itchy, Itchy, Chicken Pox* (Maccarone, 1992) for everyone to find out.

Other Health Practices

Again, you are the model for the children to follow. Be sure your own health practices are exemplary. If you want children to eat some of every food on their plates, then you should set the example. If you smoke, do it in a private place away from the children. If you want children to stop biting their fingernails, be sure you don't bite yours.

Be sure that children have separate combs and hair brushes. Do not use the same comb or brush for more than one child. Precaution also needs to be taken whenever anyone is exposed to blood or body fluids containing blood discharged from injuries. Use disposable gloves when cleaning up bloody areas and then use an antiseptic on the area.

Brushing teeth after meals is an important habit for your children to learn. Each child needs his or her own individual brush, marked with a name or symbol that the child can recognize. Also, put the child's mark on the place where children store their

Each child needs his own individual toothbrush and tube of toothpaste.

brushes. You might use an inverted egg carton, or a parent could make a wooden toothbrush holder.

Using only one tube of toothpaste increases the possibility of passing germs from one child to the next. Have small marked individual tubes for each child. Some centers turn small paper cups upside down and place a blob of toothpaste on each cup bottom. The child then swipes the paste off the bottom of the cup and onto his or her toothbrush. After brushing, the child can rinse with the cup and then throw it away. However you prefer to do it, make sure children brush hygienically after each meal.

Keeping the Classroom Clean

The classroom must be clean and sanitary. Even when a janitorial staff does the cleaning, it is your responsibility to make sure they have done it properly and that it remains in good condition throughout the day. Floors, tabletops, and food serving areas should be kept clean. Food should be stored properly and garbage disposed of promptly. Keep your classroom clean and sanitized to prevent the spread of diseases.

To disinfect toys and surfaces the children have touched, wash or wipe them with a solution of ¼ cup of bleach to 1 gallon of water, prepared fresh each day. Whenever children have been exposed to a communicable disease, such as chicken pox, be sure

Figure 2–1   Classroom Cleanliness Checklist

Permission is granted by the publisher to reproduce this checklist for evaulation and record keeping.

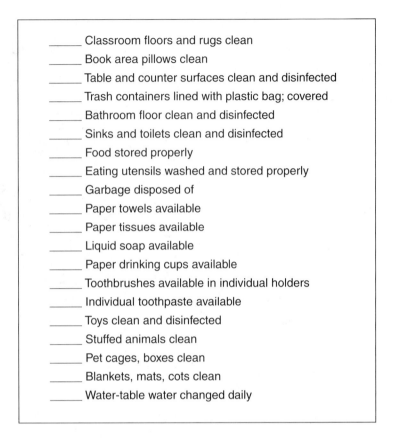

_____ Classroom floors and rugs clean

_____ Book area pillows clean

_____ Table and counter surfaces clean and disinfected

_____ Trash containers lined with plastic bag; covered

_____ Bathroom floor clean and disinfected

_____ Sinks and toilets clean and disinfected

_____ Food stored properly

_____ Eating utensils washed and stored properly

_____ Garbage disposed of

_____ Paper towels available

_____ Paper tissues available

_____ Liquid soap available

_____ Paper drinking cups available

_____ Toothbrushes available in individual holders

_____ Individual toothpaste available

_____ Toys clean and disinfected

_____ Stuffed animals clean

_____ Pet cages, boxes clean

_____ Blankets, mats, cots clean

_____ Water-table water changed daily

to notify parents. Use the Classroom Cleanliness Checklist each day to make sure your center is clean and sanitary (see Figure 2–1).

Light, heat, and ventilation should be kept at healthful levels. Children and their parents need to be informed about the type of clothing children should wear at the center. If an extra sweater is necessary, you should be ready to provide it if the family does not. Keep a supply of clean extra clothing items on hand in case children have spills or accidents or lose items such as mittens. Be sure to launder the clothing after use.

Your outside playground should also be kept clean and free of debris. If you have a sandbox, keep it covered so that animals cannot get in it. If you have tire swings or climbers, have holes punched in them so that water does not collect and provide a breeding place for germ-carrying mosquitoes.

Your classroom also needs a basic supply of tissues, paper towels, paper cups, and liquid soap. If you use sheets or blankets for napping, these must be individually labeled and washed periodically. To prevent the spread of germs, be sure children use only their own labeled sheets and blankets for naps. Also make sure eating utensils are washed at temperatures hot enough to kill bacteria, and then stored properly.

RECOGNIZES UNUSUAL BEHAVIOR OR SYMPTOMS OF CHILDREN WHO MAY BE ILL, AND PROVIDES FOR THE CHILDREN

Sick days for the children in your program are inevitable, and you need to be prepared. Can you recognize when children are ill? Does your center have the space and staff to provide for them? If not, have you arranged with parents for alternate caregivers?

Policies about caring for sick children must be discussed with the staff and communicated to the parents so that everyone is familiar with the procedures. First, you must make sure that all of the children are immunized against diphtheria-tetanus-whooping cough, measles-mumps-rubella, polio, hepatitis, and influenza type B.

You must also check on children when they arrive each day. Any of the following symptoms may indicate the child is ill and needs attention:

unusual paleness	unusual tiredness	fever, chills
skin rash	abdominal pain	sore throat
red, watery eyes	nausea, vomiting	earache
swollen neck glands	diarrhea	bruise marks
stomachache	headache	burns

How sick is too sick? Child-caregivers need to know general information about the seriousness of children's illnesses. For instance, children with a runny nose, slight cough, slight headache, or slight stomachache may remain in the classroom if this is your policy. But children with a fever, vomiting, an earache, a congested cough, a severe headache, or a sore throat should be sent home or to the alternate caregiver. Until the child leaves, the child needs to be isolated from the others, with someone on hand to offer help and comfort. These arrangements should be set up ahead of time by the program and the family.

You should also be familiar with children's health needs. Are any of the children on medication? Do any of them have asthma or allergies? What about physical limitations? Some children become fatigued more easily than others do. Whether or not you are responsible for keeping the children's health records, you should familiarize yourself with them, talk with parents, and be prepared to respond to individual needs.

Acquired Immune Deficiency Syndrome (AIDS)

AIDS is a life-threatening, communicable viral disease that attacks the human immune system, leaving it unable to fight off infection. An increasing number of children are born with AIDS to mothers who have the disease. However, you may not know whether a child in your classroom has AIDS or is HIV (human immunodeficiency virus) positive. The child may not be aware that he or she has the disease. Because of the potential for discrimination against such youngsters, many states do not require parents to report this information to schools or child-care programs.

AIDS is not passed to others by skin contact, saliva, biting, hugging, kissing, or sharing the bathroom or water fountain. The greater concern in an early childhood program is that a child who is HIV positive may pick up a disease from the other children and be unable to fight it off. Children with AIDS may have fragile physical health (Deiner, 1993). Discuss with parents how best you can help their child, as you would with any child with a health impairment.

Book to Read

Come Sit by Me (Merrifield, 1990) tells the sensitive story about Karen who loves to play with the other children in her preschool, especially when they play doctor and rescue Erica from a burning house, make wet paper casts for her broken legs, and give Jonathan medicine for his fever. But she is worried because the new boy, Nicolas, isn't her friend yet. Nicolas, who is out sick a lot, finally begins to play with Karen, but not with some of the other children. They won't play with him because he has AIDS. Then the other children won't play with Karen because she plays with Nicolas. Finally her parents call for a parent meeting to talk about AIDS. Afterward, when Nicolas comes in the next day, all the children call to him to come sit by them.

Allergies and Asthma

Allergies are sensitivities to substances that most people find harmless. They are the most common health impairment of young children and account for one-third of all chronic health conditions of preschool children. Plant pollen, dust, and animal dander may give allergic children the coldlike symptoms of red and puffy eyes, dark circles under eyes, frequent runny nose, sneezing (four or five times in a row), a dry hacking cough, mouth breathing, frequent nosebleeds, skin irritations, or rashes. If children exhibit such symptoms, especially related to weather or the allergy season, contact the families to learn whether the children have known allergies or should be tested for them (Deiner, 1993).

You may need to have the classroom scrubbed and vacuumed frequently, and not merely dusted. Air conditioner and heating system filters should be cleaned or replaced often. The classroom animal pets may need to be exchanged for pets without fur or feathers.

Common foods are another source of potential allergies. Ninety percent of food allergies are caused by eating legumes (peas, beans, and nuts, especially peanuts), chocolate, citrus fruits (especially oranges), cereal and grain products, fish, shellfish, milk, eggs, cola drinks, berries, tomatoes, cinnamon, and food colorings (Deiner, 1993). If a child exhibits an allergic reaction after eating, contact the parents or the health specialist.

Insect bites pose serious problems for certain allergic children and can even be fatal. Swelling or hotness around the face and neck followed by difficulty in breathing must be responded to immediately. Field trips to sites where wild plants grow and bees or mosquitoes live can cause problems for allergic children. Be sure to find out what reaction such a child is likely to have, what you should do, and what the side effects of any medication may be (Deiner, 1993). Children sometimes pick up fuzzy caterpillars like the woolly bear. These caterpillars frequently cause skin reactions such as itching or rashes. Wash the affected areas thoroughly.

Asthma affects about 2 percent of the population and often develops in early childhood, and afflicts twice as many boys as girls. Asthma is caused by an obstruction of the small bronchial tubes and results in shortness of breath, coughing, wheezing, and choking. Allergies are the most common cause, although excitement or exertion can also trigger an attack. Asthma attacks come more frequently in the early morning and may occur without warning, thus frightening the child and others around him or her. Teachers should know ahead of time how to help the child use the prescribed medication or inhaler, and how to sit (not lie down) during an attack (Deiner, 1993).

Dramatic play can help children who have allergies or asthma work out their fears, just as it does for children who are afraid of doctors and shots. Some classrooms set up their dramatic play areas as an emergency room with pretend examining tables, X-ray machines, and a breathing apparatus. Children wear personalized face masks "so we don't catch germs from each other," says one pretend player (Goldberg, 1994). Teachers invite nurses or clinicians to talk to the children. A visiting nurse declared: "Children in this age group need this kind of play. It helps them cope with things that worry them. Injuries, accidents, violence, and bad people are big worries for children" (Goldberg, 1994, p. 35).

Attention-Deficit Hyperactivity Disorder (ADHD)

Although not an illness, ADHD is the current term for a disability that 3 percent to 5 percent of children may exhibit. Children with ADHD are excessively overactive, inattentive, unable to concentrate on a task long enough to complete it, and impulsive in their responses to events and people. Again, the disorder is more prevalent in boys than in girls (Landau & McAninch, 1993).

Children with this attention deficit find it difficult in preschool to stay still, to share or take turns, to wait for anything, or to cooperate with others. They may exhibit excessive body movements and vocalizations, and some may fight or be extremely disruptive. Sugar consumption is not the cause of this disability, as was once thought, nor is a particular child-rearing practice (Landau & McAninch, 1993).

Because excessive activity, impulsive responding, and inability to pay attention are also normal behaviors among many preschool children, teachers and parents need professional help in diagnosing this disorder. For some children, a highly structured environment itself causes them to react in a hyperactive manner. Other children are naturally hyperactive, especially during the preschool years. As noted by Berk (1993):

> Most children who are diagnosed by competent mental health professionals as having attention-deficit hyperactivity disorder do; but as early childhood educators, we must always ensure that our classrooms are developmentally appropriate and that children are not being inappropriately labeled because our classroom is inappropriate. (p. 49)

Your best response to hyperactive children is to show them you accept them as they are.

Your best response to hyperactive children is to show them you accept them as they are, to redirect their inappropriate behavior into constructive channels, and to praise them for even the smallest success. They are often rejected by peers and thus may have a low self-esteem. These are often bright children who deserve compliments rather than criticism. Praise for their efforts and a loosely structured environment with many activities they can freely choose from works best. Giving them choices helps them develop the self-control necessary for being successful in activities and getting along with others.

Work daily with parents to discuss how their child is behaving at home and what is working best in the classroom. For certain children with attention-deficit disorder, a large center-based program may be overwhelming. They may do better in a smaller family child-care setting.

Child Abuse

Abused children are children whose parents or caregivers have mistreated, neglected, or intentionally injured them. As a teacher or child-care worker, it is your responsibility to report suspected cases of child abuse. This type of mistreatment of children includes physical, emotional, verbal, and sexual abuse, as well as physical and emotional neglect. Physical abuse is usually easiest to recognize because of its visible signs, but it is possible for you to identify other forms of abuse as well.

Physically abused children may display repeated or unexplained injuries, burns, bruises, welts, or missing patches of hair. They may complain of harsh treatment or be unusually fearful of adults, including parents. Sometimes they may appear to be malnourished or dehydrated. They may also be withdrawn or sometimes disruptive. Physically neglected children are often unclean and may have bad odors or wear shoes and clothing of the wrong size. They may have untreated illnesses or injuries. They may be chronically hungry or tired and may spend much time alone.

Emotionally abused or neglected children are more difficult to identify, but they are generally unhappy and seldom smile. Sometimes they, too, are withdrawn or disruptive. Often they react without emotion to unpleasant statements or situations. They may appear apathetic and seldom participate in classroom activities.

Sexually abused children may have underclothing that is torn or stained. They may complain of pain or itching in the genital area or may have difficulty urinating. They may also be withdrawn or have trouble getting along with others.

Such children need help of two kinds. First, you must accept them as worthy human beings in your classroom and let them know it. They will need to experience success and be praised for it. At the same time, the abuse must be stopped.

The law requires that child-caregivers report cases of child abuse. Most states have toll-free hot lines available 24 hours a day. The telephoned report must be followed by a written report within 24 hours. The state then contacts the local Department of Social Services, which sends caseworkers to investigate and take action with the family involved.

If you suspect that a child is a victim of abuse or neglect, you should contact your center director, principal, or health specialist to evaluate the situation. You should also be aware of the policy your center or school has adopted for reporting child abuse. If you are not, ask to have an in-service program to outline policies for dealing with abuse and neglect.

Ear Infections

Ear infections are the second most frequent illness among young children; only the common cold occurs more often. It is important for teachers and child caregivers to recognize this illness because children with ear infections have fluid in their middle ear that may cause mild to moderate hearing loss for weeks and sometimes months. When such a hearing loss is experienced over long periods of time, children can have difficulty in learning language or paying attention (Watt, Roberts, & Zeisel, 1993).

Teachers can help reduce the incidence of ear infections by trying to prevent the spread of colds in the classroom, since colds often lead to ear infections. Help children with colds to cover their noses and mouths when they cough and sneeze, and be sure that you, they, and everyone practices frequent and careful hand washing after using tissues. Also clean and disinfect any toys, faucets, or equipment handled by the children. If any children exhibit a hearing loss, contact the family and suggest that they have the child's hearing tested. Ear infections are generally treated with antibiotics, but in persistent infections, the child's ears may also be drained with tubes.

Your classroom environment can also facilitate children's hearing if you make speaking easier to hear. Rugs on floors, curtains at windows, hangings on walls, and acoustical tiles on ceilings help absorb background noise. Have children use headsets when they are listening to music rather than adding music to the background noise in the room. Work with children in small activity groups rather than the entire class. Sit or stand close to children when speaking and make eye contact with them so they can see your lips moving. Children with other types of hearing impairment will also benefit from an environment where speaking is easier to hear.

Physical and Mental Disabilities

Increasing numbers of preschool children with physical and mental disabilities are being included, or mainstreamed into regular preschool programs. Young children in braces and wheelchairs, children with cerebral palsy, and children with mild mental retardation can make significant developmental gains in such inclusive programs. Research has shown that "Children with disabilities display more advanced play in inclusive settings with nondisabled children than they do in self-contained classrooms" (Diamond, Hestenes, & O'Connor, 1994, p. 69).

Children without disabilities gain, as well. They become more accepting of human differences, more comfortable with children who have disabilities, and more helpful to others in general.

What about the health needs of such children? As a teacher in a program that includes children with disabilities, you should be aware of the special health needs of these individuals, such as medication or a special diet. They may become fatigued more easily than other children and need fewer strenuous activities or more rest. The program health specialist together with the children's parents can help you determine whether other accommodations are required.

PL 99-457, which governs special needs children in preschool, requires that the teacher, health and special needs professionals, and parents develop an Individualized Family Service Plan (IFSP) to promote the development of children with disabilities. It is important to maintain close contact with parents of these children so that they can let you know their expectations and concerns. Can such children move freely, easily, and safely in the classroom? You may have to rearrange furniture, widen walkways, or make activity areas more accessible. What about special toys, equipment, and activities? Books such as *The Practical Guide to Assessing Infants and Preschoolers with Special Needs* (Bondurant-Utz, 2002); *Adapting Early Childhood Curricula for Children in Inclusive Settings* (Cook, Tessier, & Klein, 2000); *Resources for Teaching Children with Diverse Abilities* (Deiner, 1993); and *Creating Inclusive Classrooms* (Salend, 2001) can help you plan your curriculum to include every child's needs.

Do your children accept children with disabilities as a matter of fact? If you treat all of your children with the same care and concern, the youngsters themselves should model this behavior with one another. You may also want to include picture books in your library area featuring children with disabilities as main characters whether or not your classroom contains such children.

Books to Read

Susan Laughs (Willis, 2000) is a simple illustrated story of a little red-haired Caucasian girl who laughs, sings, dances, and swings on each page until you discover on the last page that Susan also sits in a wheelchair. *Darlene* (Greenfield, 1980) shows a little African-American girl in a wheelchair playing with her cousin and uncle while waiting for her mother to return. *I Have a Sister—My Sister Is Deaf* (Peterson, 1977) is the story about an Asian girl who tells about the accomplishments of her very special deaf sister. *A Button in Her Ear* (Litchfield, 1976) is Angela Perkins's own story about how she came to wear a hearing aid. In *Harry and Willy and Carrothead* (Caseley, 1991), Harry, who was born without a hand, has a prosthesis, but he plays ball as well as Willy. In *The Balancing Girl* (Rabe, 1981), Margaret uses leg braces, crutches, and a wheelchair but proves to be the best balancer in first grade.

SUPPORTS THE MENTAL AND EMOTIONAL HEALTH OF EVERY CHILD

Brain Research and Mental Health

Health for young children is more than developing and maintaining physically healthy bodies. It also involves promoting and maintaining mental and emotional health. Research findings on how the brain works show that high levels of stress can inhibit learning and functioning. Children assimilate large amounts of information about what's going on around them through their senses. These sensory stimuli are relayed to the brain through the chemical and electrical firing of the nerve cells' *dendrites.* The information is then transmitted to various parts of the brain that control appropriate responses. If the information is threatening, children may freeze up and be unable to function normally. (Rushton, 2001)

Teachers can help to relieve such stress when they maintain their own calm and control and help children feel good about themselves in the classroom environment. When a child feels safe and secure the brain releases *endorphins,* hormones that can help a child to relax. What goes on in young children's families, communities, and classrooms has an effect on their mental and emotional health. When stressful occurrences take place, young children are definitely affected. The preschool teaching staff needs to recognize such occurrences to help children cope.

The breakup of families is one of the reasons many young children are under stress today. Other reasons include hospitalization of the child or a family member, moving, a parent's loss of a job, abuse of alcohol or drugs by a family member, the absence of a family member, the death of a family member, or a new baby or adopted child. Your contact with families should alert you to any causes of stress within the family, and you should discuss with the family how your program can help their child during such times. Your two-way communication with families can also alert them when you observe children displaying symptoms of stress. These symptoms include uncharacteristic thumb sucking, wetting, whining, moping around, unusual aggressiveness, tiredness, not eating, or not sleeping at nap time.

Moving

Reading books dealing with a stressful situation and then talking about the stories can be therapeutic for children. In our mobile society, many children suffer their first stressful situation when they move from their families' surroundings to a new and unknown place. No matter how adults prepare them for the move, it is still traumatic for most children. Reading books about moving to individual children when they are about to move may help them if they can identify with the books' main characters.

In *The Leaving Morning* (Johnson, 1992) an apartment-dwelling African-American brother and sister spend time telling their neighbors and cousins good-bye on the leaving morning. This sensitively illustrated story is told in lavish double-page pictures with just a few bittersweet words. In *Maggie Doesn't Want to Move* (O'Donnell, 1987), Maggie's brother uses the excuse that Maggie, his baby sister, doesn't want to move to express his own concern. In *Gila Monsters Meet You at the Airport* (Sharmat, 1980), a New York City boy does not want to move out West with his family because of all the strange things he has heard about the West.

Adoption

Adoption is often difficult for children to understand, but it does not have to be traumatic for them if it is handled sensitively. Picture books that you can read to individual children who let you know they have been adopted include *Tell Me a Real Adoption Story* (Lifton, 1993), about the conversation between a little girl and her mother concerning adoption stories. Some are made-up stories, but she wants to hear the real one about how she came to live with her family. *Through Moon and Stars and Night Sky* (Turner, 1990) tells the story of an Asian boy who is adopted into an American family. But this story starts in Southeast Asia and brings a young boy to America, where he identifies with his family from photos they have sent him. Simplest of all the stories is *The Day We Met You* (Koehler, 1990), told by the excited parents who finally get the word that their baby is ready. They hurry to prepare for it and finally get to see and love their new child.

New Baby

Having a new baby in the house is sometimes a stressful occasion for the preschooler who has previously been the center of attention. You can help individual children in your classroom deal with their feelings of jealousy if parents or the child lets you know about a new baby. Two little books deal with a brother's jealousy before the baby is born, *When the New Baby Comes I'm Moving Out* (Alexander, 1979), and afterward, *Nobody Asked Me If I Wanted a Baby Sister* (Alexander, 1971). An Ezra Jack Keats classic, *Peter's Chair* (1967), tells the story of African-American Peter who decides to run away when he sees that his old crib and high chair are being painted pink for his new little sister. Little girls finally coming to love their new siblings is the theme of *My Little Brother* (Gliori, 1992) and *I Love My Baby Sister (Most of the Time)*, (Edelman, 1984). Both boys and girls can enjoy all of these stories about new siblings, and especially their own new roles in the family.

A hilarious Robert Munsch farcical story *Alligator Baby* (1997) has Kristen's mother waking up and yelling that she is having a baby. The father tries to zoom her to the hospital but gets lost and ends up in the zoo. When they come home with the new baby wrapped in a blanket, Kristen notices that he doesn't have a people tail, or a people claw, or a people face. When her mother says, "Don't be jealous," out pops an alligator baby! So back they go and back they return with another wrong baby, a seal baby. Once again they try, only to bring home a gorilla baby. It's up to Kristen to ride her bike to the zoo and finally rescue her new baby brother. Be sure to talk with the child listener afterward about whether this story could be true or not. Then have a good laugh together.

Death of a Family Member

Overcoming grief and anguish caused by the death of a loved one cannot be accomplished by reading a book to a child. But sometime afterward it may help to share with the child another child's experience from a picture book. The sensitively written and illustrated book *You Hold Me and I'll Hold You* (Carson, 1992) is a first-person story told from the point of view of a vivacious little girl who has experienced the loss of her mother through divorce, of a pet hamster who dies, and of an aunt whose funeral she attends. What makes it finally bearable, she decides while in the arms of her father, is if "you hold me and I'll hold you."

Your most helpful response to mental and emotional stress of any kind in children is your acceptance of them in bad times as well as good, and your display of that acceptance with smiles, hugs, concerned inquiries, and redirection of them into activities that will take their minds away from the stressful situation for a while, but will also show them that no matter what, you cherish them just as they are.

Community

Many communities in the United States are no longer the safe places they used to be. Most young children learn about violence in schools, bombings, and terrorism by hearing family members talk about them, but especially by watching the scenes—often violent images—on television. While we are ourselves are often horrified, grieving, afraid, and angry, we sometimes believe that young children don't understand what is happening and thus will not be affected by violence in communities. This is not the case. As noted by the National Association for the Education of Young Children:

Show children by your actions and reactions that they are safe in the classroom and things are all right here.

Sometimes we think that young children don't understand anyway, that they won't notice our sadness or fear, or that it is better to protect children from any mention of such terrible events. But we should remember that even very young children notice a great deal and they can quickly tune into any sorrow or anxiety that surrounds them. (2001, p. 6)

What can you as a teacher or staff member of an early childhood program do to help children cope with such traumatic events? The National Association for the Education of Young Children gives several suggestions:

1. Give reassurance and physical comfort.
2. Provide structure and stability.
3. Let children know that feeling upset is okay.
4. Help children to talk if they are ready.
5. Turn off the television.
6. Provide activities that help children release tension and cope with feelings. (2001, pp. 6–7)

Classroom

Show children by your own actions and reactions that they are safe in the classroom and things are all right here. Follow your normal classroom schedule and routines so that children have the stability they are used to. If they seem to be upset by events they have seen or heard about, let them know it is normal to feel upset. If they want to talk about it, help them to express their feelings. It is better to do this in small groups or one-to-one. Young children tend to get lost in large groups and feel too unsure of themselves to speak out. Obviously you do not have a television in the classroom, but you can talk with children's parents and suggest that they turn off the television when children are around. Children are definitely affected by what they see and hear, and there is no need for them to watch violent scenes being replayed. Put out therapeutic play materials such as character dolls, play dough, water play, finger paints, and sand. Put out appropriate props in the dramatic play center where children may want to pretend to be doctors or nurses, firefighters or rescue workers.

SUMMARY

You should be able to set up and maintain a classroom that promotes good health and nutrition and is free from factors contributing to illness. You will be providing daily opportunities for your children to exercise both indoors and outdoors whether or not a large space is available. The balance of active and quiet activities you set up will include rest periods as a natural follow-up to exertion, although you will accommodate individual needs for children who no longer nap during the day. Washing hands and brushing teeth will be an important part of the program, with care taken to prevent transfer of germs during toothbrushing. Nutritional needs for the children under your care will be met through snacks and meals. In addition, they will learn good food habits through their own fun experiences with nutritional foods.

You will use the Classroom Cleanliness Checklist in Figure 2–1 as a reminder of specific areas that need special attention or cleaning.

Your children will be prepared to take medical tests and examinations through preliminary classroom activities set up by you or a health specialist. You will be able to recognize symptoms of illness in children and know how to deal with them. You will also be familiar with the characteristics of abused children and with the ways that you and your program must respond. Children with health impairments such as AIDS, allergies, asthma, attention-deficit disorder, and physical and mental disabilities also can be accommodated in the classroom through your careful planning with parents and health specialists.

The mental and emotional health of every child in times of family stress such as divorce, moving, a new baby, or the death of a family member, as well as traumatic happenings in the community will be responded to in the classroom with sensitivity, reassurance, and activities to help children release tension and cope with feelings.

LEARNING ACTIVITIES

1. Read Chapter 2, Maintaining a Healthy Classroom, and write out answers to Question Sheet 2.

2. Meet with your trainer or instructor and discuss answers to Question Sheet 2.

3. View one of the videotapes listed and write out and discuss with your trainer how you can apply information from this video.

4. Read one or more of the references cited or suggested readings. Make 10 file cards with specific ideas for promoting health and nutrition in your classroom. Include the reference source on each card.

5. Use the Classroom Cleanliness Checklist in Figure 2–1 for a week, making any corrections

necessary to keep the room clean and sanitary. Discuss results with your trainer.

6. Make a card for each child in your class on which you can record information about general health, energy level, napping habits, eating habits, any special health concerns, and, where necessary, suggestions for health improvement.

7. Use ideas from this chapter to help a small group of children learn a particular health or nutrition practice.

8. Celebrate a child's birthday with one of the nutritious food ideas described in this chapter.

9. Choose one of the illnesses or impairments discussed in this chapter and learn all you can about it: how to prevent it, how to help a child in the classroom who has acquired it, and what agencies in the community can be called on for help.

10. Complete the Chapter 2 Evaluation Sheet and return it to your trainer or college supervisor.

QUESTION SHEET 2

1. How are good health practices best taught to young children?

2. How should you provide for large-muscle exercise?

3. When should children have rest time in the classroom? What can you do to encourage your own children to rest or nap?

4. How can children best be encouraged to keep clean?

5. How can children learn what foods are the best for them?

6. What kinds of foods besides cookies and cake can you provide for a birthday celebration? Why?

7. How can you prepare children for an eye examination?

8. What can you do to keep the classroom and playground clean and sanitary? Make a list and explain the items on it.

9. How can you recognize whether a child is ill, and what should you do about it?

10. What should you do about a child in the program who has AIDS?

11. How can you help prevent children with allergies from having an allergic reaction?

12. How can you help a hyperactive child to gain the most from the program?

13. How can you recognize child abuse, and what should you do about it?

14. How can you recognize whether a child has an ear infection that may cause hearing impairment, and what can you do to help?

15. How can you promote the mental and physical well-being of children in your classroom in times of violence or terrorism?

REFERENCES

Berk, L. E. (Ed.). (1993). Young children with attention deficits. *Young Children, 48*(4), 49–58.

Bondurant-Utz , J. A. (2002). *The practical guide to assessing infants and preschoolers with special needs.* Upper Saddle River, NJ: Merrill/Prentice Hall.

Cook, R. E., Tessier, A., & Klein, M. D. (2000). *Adapting early childhood curricula for children in inclusive settings.* Upper Saddle River, NJ: Merrill/Prentice Hall.

Deiner, P. L. (1993). *Resources for teaching children with diverse abilities* (2nd ed.). Fort Worth, TX: Harcourt.

Diamond, K. E., Hestenes, L. L., & O'Connor, C. E. (1994). Integrating young children with disabilities in preschool: Problems and promise. *Young Children, 49*(2), 68–75.

Goldberg, E. (1994). Including children with chronic health conditions: Nebulizers in the classroom. *Young Children, 49*(2), 34–37.

Katzen, M., & Henderson, A. (1994). *Pretend soup and other real recipes, A cookbook for preschoolers and up.* Berkeley, CA: Tricycle Press.

Landau, S., & McAninch, C. (1993). Young children with attention deficits. *Young Children, 48*(4) 49–58.

National Association for the Education of Young Children. (2001). Helping young children in frightening times. *Young Children, 56*(6), 6–7.

Rothlein, L. (1989). Nutrition tips revisited: On a daily basis, do we implement what we know? *Young Children, 44*(6), 30–36.

Rushton, S. P. (2001). Applying brain research to create developmentally appropriate learning environments. *Young Children, 56*(5), 76–82.

Salend, S. J. (2001). *Creating Inclusive Classrooms.* Upper Saddle River, NJ: Merrill/Prentice Hall.

Texas Child Care. (1994). The doctor is in: Medical offices for dramatic play. *Texas Child Care Quarterly, 18*(3), 22–27.

Watt, M. R., Roberts, J. E., & Zeisel, S. A. (1993). Ear infections in young children: The role of the early childhood educator. *Young Children, 49*(1), 65–72.

Werner, P., Timms, S., & Almond, L. (1996). Health-stops: Practical ideas for health-related exercise in preschool and primary classrooms. *Young Children, 51*(6), 48–55.

SUGGESTED READINGS

Austin, J. S. (2000). When a child discloses sexual abuse: Immediate and appropriate teacher responses. *Childhood Education, 77*(1), 2–5.

Black, S. M. (1999). HIV/AIDS in early childhood centers: The ethical dilemma of confidentiality vs. disclosure. *Young Children, 54*(2), 39–45.

Bromer, B. L. (1999). Who's in the house corner? Including young children with disabilities in pretend play. *Dimensions of Early Childhood, 27*(2), 17–23.

Dahl, K. (1998). Why cooking in the classroom? *Young Children, 53*(1), 81–83.

Desrochers, J. (1999). Vision problems: How teachers can help. *Young Children, 54*(2), 36–38.

Dooling, M. V., & Ulione, M. S. (2000). Health consultation in child care: A partnership that works. *Young Children, 55*(2), 23–27.

Endres, J. B., & Rockwell, R. S. (1994). *Food, nutrition, and the young child* (4th ed.). Upper Saddle River, NJ: Merrill/Prentice Hall.

Fuhr, J. E., with Barclay, K. H. (1998). The importance of appropriate nutrition and nutrition education. *Young Children, 53*(1), 74–80.

Greenberg, J. (2001). "She is so my real mom!" Helping children understand adoption as one form of family diversity. *Young Children, 56*(2), 90–93.

Jordon, N. H. (1993). Sexual abuse prevention programs in early childhood education: A caveat. *Young Children, 48*(6), 76–79.

Marotz, L., Cross, M., & Rush, J. (1997). *Health, safety and nutrition for the young child.* Albany, NY: Delmar.

Miller, R. (1996). *The developmentally appropriate inclusive classroom in early childhood education.* Albany, NY: Delmar.

Moukaddem, V. (1990). Preventing infectious diseases in your child care setting. *Young Children, 45*(2), 28–29.

Rose, D. F., & Smith, B. J. (1993). Preschool mainstreaming: Attitude barriers and strategies for addressing them. *Young Children, 48*(4), 59–66.

Vacca, J. J. (2001). Dealing with the aftermath: Helping young children with post traumatic stress disorder (PTSD). *Dimensions of Early Childhood, 29*(2), 18–24.

Wardle, F. (1990). Bunny ears and cupcakes for all: Are parties developmentally appropriate? *Child Care Information Exchange, 74*, 39–41.

Zeiger, M. D., & Munoz-Furlong, A. (1992). *Off to school with food allergies: A guide for parents and teachers.* Fairfax, VA: The Food Allergy Network.

CHILDREN'S BOOKS

Alexander, M. (1971). *Nobody asked me if I wanted a baby sister.* New York: Dial.

Alexander, M. (1979). *When the new baby comes I'm moving out.* New York: Dial.

Carson, J. (1992). *You hold me and I'll hold you.* New York: Orchard.

Caseley, J. (1991). *Harry and Willy and Carrothead.* New York: Greenwillow.

Davidson, M. (1992). *Robby Visits the Doctor*. New York: Random.

Dooley, N. (1991). *Everybody cooks rice*. Minneapolis, MN: Carolrhoda.

Dragonwagon, C. (1987). *Alligator arrived with apples, A potluck alphabet feast*. New York: Macmillan.

Edelman, E. (1984). *I love my baby sister (most of the time)*. New York: Puffin.

Edwards, P. D. (1998). *Warthogs in the kitchen, A sloppy counting book*. New York: Hyperion.

Falconer, I. (2000). *Olivia*. New York: Atheneum.

Gliori, D. (1992). *My little brother*. Cambridge, MA: Candlewick.

Greenfield, E. (1980). *Darlene*. New York: Methuen.

Hayes, S. (1988). *Eat up, Gemma*. New York: Mulberry.

Ho, M. (1996). *Hush! A Thai Lullaby*. New York: Orchard.

Johnson, A. (1992). *The leaving morning*. New York: Orchard.

Keats, E. J. (1967). *Peter's chair*. New York: Penguin.

Koehler, P. (1990). *The day we met you*. New York: Bradbury.

Lifton, B. J. (1993). *Tell me a real adoption story*. New York: Knopf.

Litchfield, A. B. (1976). *A button in her ear*. Morton Grove, IL: Whitman.

Maccarone, G. (1992). *Itchy, itchy, chicken pox*. New York: Scholastic.

Merrifield, M. (1990). *Come sit by me*. Toronto, Ontario, Canada: Women's Press.

Miranda, A. (1997). *To market, to market*. San Diego: Harcourt.

Munsch, R. (1997). *Alligator baby*. New York: Scholastic.

O'Donnell, E. L. (1987). *Maggie doesn't want to move*. New York: Macmillan.

Peterson, J. W. (1977). *I have a sister—my sister is deaf*. New York: Harper.

Rabe, B. (1981). *The balancing girl*. New York: E. P. Dutton.

Rattigan, J. K. (1993). *Dumpling soup*. Boston: Little Brown.

Sharmat, M. (1980). *Gregory the terrible eater*. New York: Scholastic.

Sharmat, M. (1980). *Gila monsters meet you at the airport*. New York: Macmillan.

Shelby, A. (1991). *Potluck*. New York: Orchard.

Showers, P. (1980). *No measles, no mumps for me*. New York: Crowell.

Standiford, N. (1996). *Astronauts are sleeping*. New York: Knopf.

Stevens, K. (1985). *The beast in the bathtub*. New York: Harper.

Turner, A. (1990). *Through moon and stars and night sky*. New York: HarperCollins.

Wells, R. (1997). *Bunny cakes*. New York: Dial.

Willis, J. (2000). *Susan laughs*. New York: Holt.

VIDEOTAPES

American Academy of Pediatrics & National Association for the Education of Young Children. (Producers). *Caring for our children, national health and safety performance standards. Part 6: Illness in child care*. (Six-part video series). Washington, DC: National Association for the Education of Young Children. (#820)

Kendrick, A. S., Gravell, J., & Massachusetts Dept. of Public Health. (Producer). *Family child care health & safety video and checklist*. St. Paul, MN: Redleaf Press.

National Association for the Education of Young Children. *Food for thought: Nutrition and Children*. Washington, DC: Author. (#892 English; #892S Spanish)

National Association for the Education of Young Children. *Make a difference: Report child abuse and neglect*. Washington, DC: Author. (#890 English; #890S Spanish)

Project MAINSTREAM. (Producer). *Mainstreaming in child care settings*. Child Development Media, Inc., 5632 Van Nuys Blvd., Suite 286, Van Nuys, CA 91401.

Video Active Productions (Producer). *Child care and children with special needs*. Washington, DC: National Association for the Education of Young Children. (#818)

CHAPTER 2 EVALUATION SHEET
MAINTAINING A HEALTHY CLASSROOM

1.   Student _____

2.   Trainer _____

3.   Center where training occurred _____

4.   Beginning date _____ Ending date _____

5.   Describe what student did to accomplish General Objective.
     _____
     _____

6.   Describe what student did to accomplish Specific Objectives.

     Objective 1 _____

     _____

     Objective 2 _____

     _____

     Objective 3 _____

     _____

7.   Evaluation of student's Learning Activities
     _____

Signature of Trainer: Signature of Student:

_____   _____

Comments:
     _____
     _____
     _____

Permission is granted by the publisher to reproduce this page for evaluation and record keeping.

Establishing a
Learning Environment

GENERAL OBJECTIVE

To be able to set up and arrange an early childhood classroom with stimulating activities that motivate children to become involved

SPECIFIC OBJECTIVES

_____ Sets up stimulating learning centers in appropriate spaces

_____ Provides appropriate materials for children's self-directed play and learning

_____ Provides a high-activity, low-stress environment where children can learn happily together

The **learning environment** in early childhood classrooms is based partially on the physical arrangement of equipment and materials. This arrangement is one way of conveying to children what kinds of activities are available for them and what they can and cannot do with the materials.

Wide-open spaces may encourage them to run and shout. Small, closed-in spaces indicate quiet and limited access for only a few children at a time. Carpeted areas tempt children to sit on the floor, while pillows near bookshelves invite them to relax and look at a book. Water tables filled to the brim are asking to be spilled. Several inches of water in the bottom gives children the freedom to move it around without spilling. Tall shelves stuffed with art materials say, "This is not for you to touch," to many children. To the adventurous ones they say, "See if you can reach us!" One puzzle on the table with four chairs bids four children to sit down, but it also invites a squabble. Thus, how you arrange your classroom helps decide what will take place in it.

What do you want to happen? The primary goals of many early childhood programs are to promote children's positive self-images, their self-direction, and their joy of learning. If these are your goals, you will want to arrange your classroom in a way that will help children feel good about themselves as people, motivate them to become involved in the activities, and help them to become self-directed in their learning. The classroom can do this if you keep the children in mind when you arrange the learning centers.

SETS UP STIMULATING LEARNING CENTERS IN APPROPRIATE SPACES

Learning Centers as Brain Stimulators

Learning centers are the areas in your classroom devoted to particular curriculum activities such as block-building, art, literacy, dramatic play, math, science, music, and large motor activities. It is these centers, in fact, and not a written plan, that primarily determine the curriculum of early childhood programs. Why have learning centers? When set up appropriately, learning centers help children to choose and focus on particular activities, giving them the freedom to pursue these activities on their own. When children are actively involved in their own learning, they tend to find such hands-on experiences meaningful and relevant in their own lives. As Rushton (2001) notes:

> Research on the brain discloses that neurons change during such experiences. As a child experiences an event for the first time, for example, new dendrites form on nerve cells. The belief is that the greater number of dendrites and connections of dendrites to each other, the greater the speed of recall and memory. The classroom environment determines, to some degree, the functioning ability of children's brains. (p. 79)

Determining Learning Centers

The number and kinds of learning centers in your classroom depend on your program goals, space available, and number of children. Although state and federal regulations may vary, an early childhood program serving children 3 to 5 years of age should plan on having 40 to 60 square feet of space per child. Where there is a high density of children and little room for necessary activities there is often a marked increase of negative and idle behavior (Taylor, 2002, p. 367).

Many programs follow a rule of thumb that counts four to six children to a large learning center. Thus, if you serve 18 to 20 children, you will need at least five large sectioned-off centers, more if possible. Smaller centers that include a maximum of two to four children can be permanent fixtures or alternated with one another. Ideally, you should be able to include the learning centers shown in Figure 3–1.

Room Layout

To determine where in the room you should place each learning center, first look at the room layout as a whole and locate the permanent features:

doors (entrance, exit, and bathroom doors)

openings (halls or between rooms)

sink

windows

Large	Small
Block-building	Music
Books/listening	Writing
Dramatic play	Science/Discovery
Manipulative/math	Computer
Arts and crafts	Water/sand
Large motor	Woodworking
	Cooking

Figure 3–1   Learning Centers

closet

walls

The space leading to doors and openings must be reserved for people to pass in and out. You may need to section off nearby learning centers so that walkers will not interfere with the children's activities. Close to the entrance door locate the youngsters' cubby area, where outside clothing is hung and personal items stored. In some centers, cubbies are outside the classroom; but if your cubbies are inside, be sure they are near the entrance so that children need not walk across the room for coats or sweaters.

Location of the sink helps determine where to place wet activities. For example, the art center should be as close as possible to the sink because children will be getting and returning water, rinsing brushes, and washing hands. A water table can be farther away because the teachers will fill it. Although cooking also uses water, it is often a temporary activity that can be set up on a counter near the sink whenever necessary.

Windows also help determine where to place learning centers. A bay window with a window seat, for instance, makes the ideal location for the book or library area. The science area can be set up in front of a regular window to provide sun for plant-growing experiments. Windows are also essential as a source of natural lighting: daylight. Its importance in a classroom is pointed out by Caples, an award-winning school-facilities architect:

> We strongly believe that daylight is a necessity in each classroom, especially for full-day programs. Not only does sunlight destroy mold and bacteria and provide a needed source of vitamin D, it also contributes to a sense of optimism and offers connection with the natural world. (1996, p. 16)

What use do you make of a classroom closet? Is it for the usual storage area or teachers' coats? Why not convert the closet to a learning center extension? A closet with its door removed makes a unique extra room for the dramatic play area. Children need to be in sight at all times, so be sure to remove the closet door. A classroom closet can also become an extension of the large motor area if you outfit it as a jumping room with inflated floor cushions and wall bars, handholds, or a rope climber.

Separating Activities

In addition to taking advantage of permanent classroom features such as doors, windows, and closets, teachers need to separate the various learning centers from one another so that children can clearly see what activities are available and can make independent choices without confusion. A book center, science center, and manipulative center all in a row along one side of the room may be understandable to teachers but bewildering for children unless each area is clearly sectioned off.

Most classrooms use shelves, cubbies, or dividers to separate the learning centers from one another. Use your ingenuity to section off your own areas. Instead of placing bookshelves against the wall, for instance, use them as dividers between the book area and another learning center. Use block shelves the same way. The play stove, sink, and refrigerator can serve as dividers in a dramatic play area, rather than standing against a classroom wall. As Caples notes:

> The furniture used to create the dividers should be selected for "merchandizing appeal," allowing children to see and select items, whether they be blocks arranged by shape, books with their covers facing out, or musical instruments on pegboards. (1996, p. 15)

Dividers should not be so high that they conceal children from one another or the teacher. The room itself should be open and cheerful, with spaces used effectively. In lieu of room dividers, place large furniture to section off areas. For example, use easy chairs or couches with colored corrugated cardboard fastened to their backs as dividers for particular areas.

Some classrooms install a loft to give it interesting extra spaces not only for large motor climbing activities but also for learning center extensions on top and underneath. Music activities with players and headsets, for example, work especially well under a loft. The entire loft, both above and below, can also be part of a dramatic play area.

Use room walls as the backs of learning centers, with dividers forming the sides. Mount photos, posters, pictures, and hangings appropriate to the area on the walls, as well. Pictures of buildings, bridges, and towers at children's eye level serve as great motivators for building in the block area, for example. After a field trip, mount photos from the trip or cut out appropriate pictures from magazines.

Be careful not to enclose each area so completely that it is cut off from the other learning centers. Young children like to see what is happening in other centers and need to be able to move easily from one to another. A completely enclosed area with only a small opening also causes group-entry problems. The children inside may decide that the center is their private space and try to prevent others from entering. You need to anticipate potential behavior problems like this as you organize the centers.

Before you begin rearranging the classroom, step back and watch how the children use it as it is now. Do they all crowd together in one area? Do they mill around in the center of the room without much direction? Do they have to walk through the

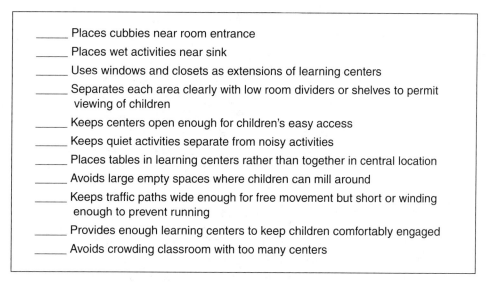

_____ Places cubbies near room entrance

_____ Places wet activities near sink

_____ Uses windows and closets as extensions of learning centers

_____ Separates each area clearly with low room dividers or shelves to permit
           viewing of children

_____ Keeps centers open enough for children's easy access

_____ Keeps quiet activities separate from noisy activities

_____ Places tables in learning centers rather than together in central location

_____ Avoids large empty spaces where children can mill around

_____ Keeps traffic paths wide enough for free movement but short or winding
           enough to prevent running

_____ Provides enough learning centers to keep children comfortably engaged

_____ Avoids crowding classroom with too many centers

Figure 3–2   Learning Center Location Checklist

Permission is granted by the publisher to reproduce this checklist for evaluation and record keeping.

block center to get to the bathroom? Are certain centers more popular than others? What seems to make the difference?

To rearrange learning centers so that children can choose them freely and use them with ease, spend time to determine how the room works in its present arrangement. Use Figure 3–2 to assess your current room arrangement.

Floor Planning

Next make a simple floor plan of the present arrangement and record directly on it as you observe children during the free-choice period for 15 minutes on three different days. Use symbols such as *x*'s and *o*'s for girls and boys. Record directly on the plan where individual children are located for the 15 minutes of your observation. Use arrows to show how children move from one center to another. This exercise will help you to step back and objectively evaluate the children's use of the classroom. Discuss your findings with members of your team. If movement, work, and play are not orderly or not even taking place in certain centers, you may want to make some changes.

What will the changes be? The answer depends on how much empty space you have. Large areas of empty space encourage children to run around wildly or aimlessly. Would your program be better served if you sectioned off some of that space into learning centers? You may think you need the space for circle time, creative movement, or other whole-group activities. Instead, consider using the block area for large-group activities when the blocks are on the shelves. Whole-group activities do not require exclusive space when little is available or when such space will reduce the number of necessary learning centers.

Even though some teachers place all tables together in the center of the room, try to determine if this is necessary in your classroom. Wouldn't the room be more interesting if the large central space were sectioned off and the tables moved into appropriate learning centers? The size and shape of the room help to determine this arrangement, as well as the children's use of the space.

Is there an activity area that few children use? Why does this happen? Some classroom book centers consist only of a bookshelf against the wall with one chair nearby. Few children may use this area because it is not sectioned off for privacy, because it is too close to a noisy area, or because it is just not inviting. Pull the bookshelf away from the wall and use it as a divider. Bring in some bright pillows, stuffed animals, or puppets that go with the books. Put a fluffy area rug on the floor. Be sure that your books are in good condition and appropriate for the age and interest of the youngsters. Mount colorful book posters on the walls of the area at the children's eye level. When a learning center like this becomes attractive, it will soon fill up with youngsters.

How do the children get from one area to another? Can they move freely? They should not have to squeeze between tables and room dividers or step over someone's block structure. On the other hand, you need to avoid one long traffic lane that encourages running from one end of the room to the other. Simply arrange a shelf or divider to redirect the traffic and prevent uncontrolled movement. See the sample floor plan in Figure 3–3.

Self-Regulating Methods

Do your observations indicate problems with too many children in any one area? Children can regulate their own numbers if you make it interesting for them. For example, you can mount pictures of four fish on the wall by the water table, six construction workers in the block center, or four books in the book center, with a hook under each picture. Then children who want to play in the particular area can hang their name tags on chosen hooks. When the hooks are full, newcomers must either trade a place or play elsewhere.

Wearing colored tags is another method for helping children choose a learning center. The tags can be kept on a Velcro board in front of the room for the children to choose from, or color-coded Velcro signs can be mounted in each learning center. Other classrooms use necklaces hanging in each learning center for youngsters to wear when they are playing in the center of their choice.

Giving children choices like this is especially important if we want them to gain confidence in their own abilities. When teachers direct children into certain centers, tell them how many can play there, or tell them what materials they must use, they make the youngsters more dependent on them and less sure of their own newly developing abilities. As noted by Shepherd and Eaton (1997):

> Children are likely to become more self-directed rather than teacher-directed if they can make choices and decisions about materials to use. . . . When children are given real choices, they are more likely to remain at an experience or a task for an extended period of time. (1997, p. 45)

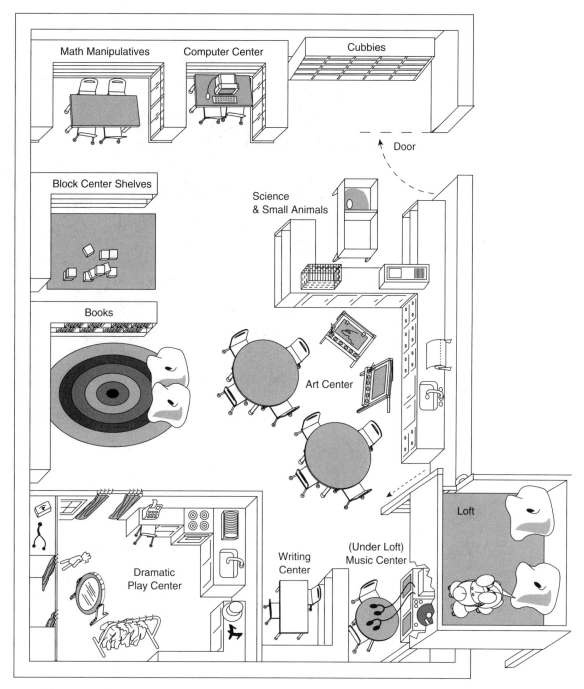

Figure 3–3 Floor Plan

Children can regulate their own numbers by hanging their name tags on a hook in the learning center of their choice.

We need to remember that the classroom belongs to the children, too, and should be arranged for them to use on their own as much as possible.

Follow-Up Planning

When you have decided how to rearrange the room, try it out on paper first. Make another floor plan that you discuss with your team and the children. Don't forget that it is their room as well as yours. You may want to change only one area at a time to see how the children respond. Many youngsters prefer the stability of keeping things the same; thus a total rearrangement can be disorienting for them.

After you have rearranged the room, check to see if movement, work, and play are more orderly than before. If other changes are necessary, repeat the space assessment process to determine what else needs to be done. A final floor plan on paper can show what the new arrangement will look like before you begin moving furniture. Let everyone join in. If children are included in making room arrangements, they are more likely to accept them.

PROVIDES APPROPRIATE MATERIALS FOR CHILDREN'S SELF-DIRECTED PLAY AND LEARNING

Play as Learning

Children 3 to 5 years old spend a great deal of time playing. We understand about their playing with toys; that's what toys are for. But then we notice that they also seem to play with materials that are not toys; for example, pens, paintbrushes, flashlights, computer keyboards. Such materials, in fact, become toys for these youngsters, and they often play with them in ways that were never meant to be. Don't they know any better?

The fact is that they do know better. This is exactly what they should be doing, for play is the natural process by which young children learn. Because adults do not use play in the same manner, we often mistake children's play for recreation or inconsequential activity. "Play time is over," we say to them. "Let's put the blocks away now and learn about numbers." Because play has little to do with learning for most adults, we tend to feel the same about play for children—that it has little to do with their learning. We are wrong.

Preschool children do not learn numbers by sitting down, being quiet, and listening to the teacher. They do not really learn how to use the computer by following adult directions. Instead, they accomplish most of their learning by the hands-on method of playing with materials and equipment to find out how they work. Every object becomes a toy that they manipulate playfully until they learn what it does. We call this the *self-discovery method* of learning, and it is very effective. The wise preschool teacher sets up her entire classroom so that children can spend the majority of their time teaching themselves through play. Maxim (1989) points out the importance of play:

> Play is a need of every child. . . . And when we observe children at play, we often see enjoyment and delight. Because of this fun aspect, adults sometimes think of play as a form of amusement or fun only; not as something to be taken seriously. However, play is an important childhood activity that helps children master all developmental needs. (p. 261)

Equipping Learning Centers

The preschool teaching staff must equip each of the learning centers with appropriate materials that children can choose and use in a self-directed manner. The Learning Center Checklist in Figure 3–4 assists teachers in seeing at a glance the necessary ingredients and arrangement they must consider.

Use the checklist as a guide to setting up a new classroom or as an assessment tool to evaluate your current arrangement. Then you must consider how to arrange the materials so that children can use them for self-directed learning. Following this checklist are suggestions on how to set up each of the 13 learning centers so that children can use them most effectively.

Observer_____Classroom_____Date_____

1. Provide classroom centers for:
_____ Block building
_____ Book activities
_____ Dramatic play
_____ Manipulative/math activities
_____ Arts and crafts
_____ Large motor activities
_____ Music
_____ Science
_____ Writing
_____ Computer activities
_____ Sand/water play
_____ Woodworking
_____ Cooking

2. Organize BLOCK-BUILDING CENTER to contain:
_____ Blocks lengthwise on shelves
_____ Enough blocks for building large structures
_____ Small figures, trucks, and other accessories
_____ Shelves marked with symbols of blocks and accessories

3. Organize BOOK CENTER to contain:
_____ Books on shelves at children's height, with covers visible
_____ Books in good condition
_____ Multiethnic books
_____ Puppets and other book extension objects
_____ Pillows, cushions, and comfortable chairs

4. Organize DRAMATIC PLAY CENTER to contain:
_____ Appropriate equipment, furniture, and accessories
_____ Men's and women's dress-up clothes and prop boxes
_____ Clothes arranged for easy selection and return
_____ Full-length mirror
_____ Dolls of different skin colors
_____ Language props such as two telephones

5. Organize MANIPULATIVE/MATH CENTER to contain:
_____ Tables, floor space, and nearby materials on shelves
_____ Puzzles, table blocks, and sorting and matching games and puzzles
_____ Shape, color, counting, and number games
_____ Cash registers, abacus, number beads, and rods
_____ Necessary parts and pieces not missing from games and puzzles

Figure 3–4   Learning Center Checklist

Permission is granted by the publisher to reproduce this checklist for evaluation and record keeping.

6. Organize ART CENTER to contain:

_____ Easels and tables set up for daily use
_____ Paper, paints, brushes, crayons, scissors, and collage materials on nearby shelves
_____ Clay, play dough, yarn, fabrics, and stamping materials for use throughout the year

7. Include in classroom LARGE MOTOR CENTER:

_____ Climbing equipment (bars, ladder, climber, loft)
_____ Balancing equipment (balance beam, blocks)
_____ Jumping equipment (inflated mat, trampoline)
_____ Children's basketball net and ball
_____ Lifting materials (large hollow blocks)
_____ Wooden riding vehicles

8. Include in MUSIC CENTER:

_____ Sound- and rhythm-producing materials
_____ Tape recorders, tapes, CD players, and headsets (or record players)
_____ Electronic keyboard
_____ Strumming instruments
_____ Percussion instruments (drums, xylophones)

9. Include in SCIENCE/DISCOVERY CENTER:

_____ Magnifying glasses, balance scale, magnets
_____ Animal, fish, or insect pets
_____ Plants and seed-growing experiments
_____ Children's collections
_____ Books about science activities in progress

10. Include in WRITING CENTER:

_____ Desk to write on and to store writing supplies
_____ Pens, pencils, markers, chalk, and chalkboard
_____ Paper, pads, notebooks, file cards, and envelopes
_____ Ruler, stapler, scissors, hole punch, and paper clips
_____ Rubber stamps and pad, peel-off stickers, and stamps
_____ Typewriter and/or computer

11. Include in COMPUTER CENTER:

_____ Computer on low table with two chairs
_____ Printer and paper
_____ Several appropriate software programs
_____ Games, puzzles, and materials to extend each program

12. Include in SAND/WATER PLAY CENTER:

_____ Squeeze bottles, basters, and eggbeaters
_____ Children's water play aprons and safety goggles
_____ Small trucks, figures, shovels, sifters, and sand toys
_____ Clean-up tools for children's use

(continued)

---

13. Provide in WOODWORKING CENTER:
_____ Usable pounding and sawing tools and safety goggles
_____ Marked tool storage shelves or pegboard
_____ Woodworking table or stump; vise
_____ Wood scraps, ceiling tiles, and nails

14. Include in COOKING CENTER:
_____ Knives, spoons, beaters, scrapers, and food mill
_____ Bowls, pans, measuring cups, and mixing spoons
_____ Microwave or toaster oven, blender, electric fry pan, crockpot, or hot plate
_____ Illustrated recipe charts

15. Provide general room area with:
_____ Cubby, shelf, or box for each child's possessions
_____ Private area or private space for each child
_____ Pictures, photos, and displays at child's eye level

Figure 3–4   *continued*

Block-Building Center

---

2. Organize BLOCK-BUILDING CENTER to contain:
_____ Blocks lengthwise on shelves
_____ Enough blocks to build large structures
_____ Small figures, trucks, and other accessories
_____ Shelves marked with symbols of blocks and accessories

Wooden unit blocks have played an important role in early childhood programs since their introduction during the early years of the century by American early childhood educator Carolyn Pratt. Her units, half units, double units, quadruples, arches, and ramps stimulate children's imaginations and creativity in building structures of all sizes and shapes. The blocks help develop children's perceptual skills, such as eye-hand coordination as they match sizes or balance one block on another in building towers and bridges. Block building also promotes counting and categorizing skills as children learn to sort shapes and sizes during pickup. Concepts gained on field trips can be reinforced when children use them to reconstruct, for example, the fire station or farm they have just visited.

Many prepackaged nursery school sets of unit blocks contain too few blocks for children to construct even a small number of moderate-size buildings at one time. Try out a set and see what your children do with it. If you note that they don't have

If you want children to return toys to their places, mount cutouts of them on the shelves where they belong.

enough blocks for several children to build large buildings, then order more. You can't have enough unit blocks, most teachers agree.

Store blocks lengthwise on low shelves so that children can see their sizes and shapes and decide easily what they need for building. A cutout or outline of the block at the back of the shelf enables children to return the blocks to the proper shelves during pickup and helps them learn to match the block with its outline. Careful arrangements like this allow children to become independent and self-directed in their play.

It is also important to store building accessories in the same area with the unit blocks so that children will know they are available and can use them with the blocks. Small figures of people and animals, especially dinosaurs, are popular if you want to encourage dramatic play in the block area. Sometimes children prefer to play only with blocks, but often they want to pretend that people and animals are doing things in the block structures. Although small vehicles are appropriate accessories, large wooden riding vehicles belong in the large motor area, not in the block area, where they can knock down the carefully constructed buildings. If you want children to return the toys to their places, don't forget to mount cutouts of accessories on the shelves where they belong.

If you are following a particular curriculum theme throughout the classroom you will need to hang an appropriate "book-on-string" on the wall in this center along with supporting props and accessories. For a class exploring an "astronaut and space ship" theme, one teacher clipped the book *Zoom! Zoom! Zoom! I'm Off to the Moon* (Yaccarino, 1997) to a string that was fastened to the wall, along with several little plastic space vehicles and space people. The children enjoyed hearing this simple story over and over, and then building their own "space port."

Book Center

> **3. Organize BOOK CENTER to contain:**
>
> _____ Books on shelves at children's height, with covers visible
>
> _____ Books in good condition
>
> _____ Multiethnic books
>
> _____ Puppets and other book extension objects
>
> _____ Pillows, cushions, and comfortable chairs

Early childhood specialists tell parents that reading to their preschool children is one of the most important things they can do to improve their children's literacy development. Preschool programs must go even further. You should not only read to the children but also provide opportunities for children to use books on their own. To succeed in school and develop essential verbal skills, young children need to find their way to books as early as possible. A picture book should be available in every learning center to support a particular curriculum theme as noted under "Block-Building Center." These can be hung from plastic "kitchen clips" fastened to wall in the centers and changed frequently.

The book center itself should be one of the most comfortable and inviting areas in your classroom. A soft throw rug, bright puffy pillows, and a beanbag or upholstered child-size chair may be the items you choose. Children enjoy participating in furnishing the book corner. Bring in square rug samples and have the youngsters help carpet the floor with them.

Because the book center needs to be quiet, it should be separated from noisy areas by room dividers or placed next to other quiet activities such as writing or manipulatives. Display books in the most inviting way possible. The covers should always be facing out so that children are attracted to particular books by their covers and can make easy choices. If book covers are torn or missing, repair them or replace the books. Torn books are not inviting to children. Torn books imply that teachers are not concerned about keeping books in good condition and, therefore, that books are not important. Or children may decide that it must be all right to tear a book, since someone already has.

If you have a large book collection, consider displaying only part of it and changing the books from time to time. Putting out too many books at once tends to confuse young children. Be sure the books are displayed at children's eye level. Bookshelves made for older children should be scaled down to your children's height. Making the book area as easy to use as possible promotes children's self-directed learning.

Where do the books come from? A bookmobile? A library? A catalog? A resource room? Private donations? No matter what their source, you should be the one to choose the books for your classroom. Preschool children do not yet know how to select the best books. With the large number of children's books currently being published, you must become familiar not only with the best books but also with selection techniques; thus, you will be able to choose picture books that meet your curriculum needs as well as your children's interests (see Book Selection Checklist, chapter 6).

Some books should feature multiethnic characters. Whether or not you have African American, Hispanic, Native American, or Asian American children in your classroom, you should have books that portray the multiethnicity of American life. Excellent picture books are available today showing children of almost every race or culture (see Beaty & Pratt, 2003).

Children enjoy extending their experiences with favorite books if you also stock the book area with character dolls, puppets, and stuffed animals to go with the books. Children's book departments and school supply companies such as Constructive Playthings (1-800-448-4115) and Lakeshore Learning Materials (1-800-421-5354) offer both multiethnic dolls and puppets that can serve as book characters. Call for catalogs. Cooking supply stores also stock hotpad gloves in the shapes of animals, which make excellent hand puppets; or you and the children can make your own hand puppets from mittens, small paper bags, and socks. A book center should also contain a cassette recorder with headphones and book tapes to accompany some of the books on the shelves. (For more information on children's books, see Chapter 6.)

Dramatic Play Center

---

4. Organize DRAMATIC PLAY CENTER to contain:

_____ Appropriate equipment, furniture, and accessories

_____ Men's and women's dress-up clothes and prop boxes

_____ Clothes arranged for easy selection and return

_____ Full-length mirror

_____ Dolls of different skin colors

_____ Language props such as two telephones

Young children live in a world of pretending. To adults who often view fantasy with misgivings, this may seem unhealthy, but it is quite the contrary. Through pretending, young children are not trying to escape from reality; they are, in fact, trying to understand it. They are doing their best to deal with people and circumstances that sometimes confuse them. Dramatic play helps to bring some sense, order, and control into their world.

To assist them in their pretending, we provide a classroom learning center that encourages imaginative play. Some programs call it the "housekeeping center," "home center," or "dress-up area." Others prefer to call it the "family life area." This center often contains child-size kitchen furnishings such as a stove, refrigerator, sink, cupboards, and table. Some programs set up a store with shelves of empty food packages. Some have a bedroom with a mirror, dresser, and doll beds, or a restaurant with tables and chairs.

All these arrangements are familiar to children and encourage them to dress up and play a variety of roles without teacher involvement. These roles include that of mother, father, uncle, aunt, grandmother, grandfather, sister, brother, baby, storekeeper, and waitress. Playing these roles helps children experience life from another point of view. It helps them to understand these roles and, in many instances, helps them to work out fears and frustrations in their own lives. Fears of going to the doctor and getting a shot, for example, can be directly faced in such pretending. Self-directed dramatic play experiences like this help a child gain a healthy and positive self-concept.

You need to provide both men's and women's clothing, hats, shoes, belts, wallets, and purses. Teenagers' clothes are just as appropriate and fit the children even better than adult sizes. Don't forget filmy scarves for princesses, a wand, a walking stick, and hats of every variety. Hang the clothes on separate hooks or hangers for the children's easy selection and return. Cramming clothing into a box or drawer makes it difficult for youngsters to see what is available.

Prop boxes, however, are the exception. Each box should contain the clothes and props needed for a special role, for instance, a firefighter. Such a prop box might contain a firefighter's hat, boots, and raincoat. After each field trip, fill a cardboard prop box with appropriate items to help children recreate the trip. Mark the boxes with illustrated signs and place them on shelves in the dramatic play area.

Children learn much about themselves through dramatic play. They quickly learn how other children respond to them in the frank give-and-take of peer play. They should also be able to look at themselves in the full-length mirror that is part of every good dramatic play area. Then children can see what they look like dressed up as someone else. Such pretend roles give children an entirely different perspective of themselves and others.

Have a large selection of baby dolls in this area. They should be of different skin colors, whether or not your children are, to introduce children as early as possible to the fascinating variety of people in America. Attitudes that last a lifetime develop in the early years. Also include at least two toy telephones (or several cell phones) to encourage children's language development as they play out their pretend roles.

Keep the area neat if you want youngsters to use it. When play is finished, children can help pick up and clean up by putting clothes back on the dolls, props in the boxes, dress-up clothes on hooks, or a baby doll asleep in the crib, and by getting the table set for its next role-players. (For more information on dramatic play, see Chapter 9.)

Manipulative/Math Center

5. Organize MANIPULATIVE/MATH CENTER to contain:

_____ Tables, floor space, and nearby materials on shelves

_____ Puzzles, table blocks, sorting and matching games

_____ Shape, color, counting, and number games

_____ Cash registers, abacus, number beads, and rods

_____ Necessary parts and pieces not missing from games and puzzles

Manipulative skill is the ability to use one's hands and fingers with dexterity. It is important for young children to develop such skills so that they learn not only to button and zip clothes, tie shoes, and hold a pencil with ease, but also to learn to read without difficulty later on. Eye–hand coordination is important for developing the visual perception necessary to read from left to right.

Math is a manipulative skill that preschoolers can practice. Children need experiences with concrete three-dimensional materials in sorting, classifying, and counting before they can progress to more abstract work with number symbols. Many commercial manipulative materials are currently available to fill your shelves: knob puzzles, wooden puzzles, magnetic shapes, interlocking blocks, stacking toys, snapping blocks, stringing beads, threading spools, lacing shapes, stick pegboards, button boards, parquetry blocks, dominoes, counting frames, sorting trays, interlocking cubes, and more.

Nevertheless, you will want to add teacher-made games to the area. You can not only save money with homemade materials but also provide directly for the children's particular needs. Homemade picture puzzles showing each child's face, for instance, promote positive self-concepts as well as their motor skills.

These puzzles, sets, and games can be stored on shelves backed by cutout symbols for children to match when they return the items. As with books, do not put out all the manipulative materials at once, for too large a selection can be overwhelming. Check periodically to make sure the puzzle pieces and game parts are not missing. If pieces are missing, either replace them or discard the item. Some classrooms use plastic containers with an outline of a part traced on the cover to help children locate particular materials and return the pieces to the container where they belong during pickup. Opening and closing these containers give children additional practice in small motor coordination.

The manipulative center should be large enough to contain at least one table as well as floor space near the shelves of materials. Although teachers often put out puzzles on the table before children arrive, let the youngsters make their own choices too. If the materials are arranged simply and attractively on nearby shelves, children should have no trouble finding what they want. If the puzzle they select first is too difficult, they can return it and take another.

Art Center

> **6. Organize ART CENTER to contain:**
>
> _____ Easels and tables set up for daily use
>
> _____ Paper, paints, brushes, crayons, scissors, and collage materials on nearby shelves
>
> _____ Clay, play dough, yarn, fabrics, and stamping materials for use throughout the year

Most early childhood programs use art activities almost every day. Unfortunately, adults seem to control art projects more often than almost any other activity. Teachers or aides often get out the art supplies, pass out the paper, give instructions, and then remain in the area to make sure their instructions are carried out.

If we truly want children to become self-directed in their learning, we should allow them to be as independent in art as in dramatic play or block building. Freedom to explore and experiment encourages creativity. Although directions are surely appropriate in certain crafts projects, we should also give children the opportunity to try out paints and brushes of their own choosing with paper they select.

This independence is possible when child-level shelves hold the art materials near the tables or easels where they will be used, when materials are arranged for easy selection and return by the children, and when children are allowed and encouraged to participate in setting up and cleaning up art activities. When children become independent in art, they will happily choose this activity on their own during the daily free-choice period.

Teachers may want to have easels set up with paints and brushes ready for children on a daily basis. But children can also learn to choose their own paper from the shelf and put it up with the teacher's help. On days when prepared play dough will be used, children can help get it out of storage. Other times, they can help mix it.

If you have a water source in the room, the art center should be nearby. With minimum direction, children can become entirely independent in setup and cleanup when the materials are nearby. (For more information on art activities, see Chapter 7.)

Large Motor Center

> **7. Include in classroom LARGE MOTOR CENTER:**
>
> _____ Climbing equipment (bars, ladder, climber, loft)
>
> _____ Balancing equipment (balance beam, blocks)
>
> _____ Jumping equipment (inflated mat, trampoline)
>
> _____ Children's basketball net and ball
>
> _____ Lifting materials (large hollow blocks)
>
> _____ Wooden riding vehicles

If your program has a well-equipped outside playground, you may wonder why you should provide a large motor area inside. It is essential during the preschool years for children to practice large motor skills as often as possible every day, whether or not they go outside. An indoor wooden climber is perhaps the best single piece of equipment if you have room for only one piece. Molded plastic climbing and sliding equipment is popular in some programs; others use giant plastic waffle blocks with tunnels and slides that snap together. A homemade substitute can be a packing crate and a ladder or a loft with a ladder and slide. Cardboard cartons with low doors cut in both ends make fine tunnels to promote crawling skills. Commercial foam or cloth tunnels are also popular.

Ordinary chairs and tables can serve as climbing, jumping, and crawling stations in an obstacle course, when nothing else is available. Creative teachers find that almost anything is possible with masking tape and a little imagination. Children, too, enjoy making their own balance beams from unit blocks placed together in a long or winding road.

In classrooms with little or no space for a permanent large motor area, you can use a corner to fasten climbing bars or a climbing rope with a mat cushion underneath; or you could consider converting a closet into a large motor jumping room as described earlier in this chapter. Free-standing or mounted basketball rims can also be used in an out-of-the-way corner, with foam balls that will not bounce into other areas. Ask the children what other climbing and jumping activities they want to try in the room.

Use your own judgment about wooden riding vehicles. If you include them in the classroom, be sure there is space enough for children to ride them without running into things. They can help you mark out roads and make traffic signals if necessary. (For more information on motor activities, see Chapter 4.)

Music Center

```
   8.  Include in MUSIC CENTER:
_____   Sound- and rhythm-producing materials
_____   Tape recorders, tapes, CD players, and headsets
          (or record players)
_____   Electronic keyboard
_____   Strumming instruments
_____   Percussion instruments (drums, xylophones)
```

Music is important in the early childhood classroom. Young children are at a stage in their growth and development when they want to express themselves freely in all sorts of ways. Music is one of those ways. It is up to you to provide an atmosphere where music is as much a natural part of the day as conversation. Chanting, singing, moving to rhythm, listening to tapes or records, and playing instruments should be a part of every day's activities for both children and adults.

Store rhythm instruments separately on shelves or attached to pegboards in the music area so that children can see what is available and make independent choices. Mount a tracing of each instrument on its shelf or board space to give children yet another opportunity to match shapes and return materials to their proper places. Every classroom music center needs a tape recorder or record player with headsets for children's private listening. Records and tapes, however, should not be the extent of your classroom music. Children also need opportunities to make their own music, for example, singing, humming, whistling, or playing a drum or keyboard. (For more information on music, see Chapter 7.)

Science/Discovery Center

---

9. Include in SCIENCE/DISCOVERY CENTER:

_____ Magnifying glasses, balance scale, magnets

_____ Animal, fish, or insect pets

_____ Plants and seed-growing experiments

_____ Children's collections

_____ Books about science activities in progress

In some programs, science activities are relegated to a side cupboard or window ledge. But teachers and assistants who realize that such an area can be the most exciting spot in the classroom often reserve much more space: a cozy corner with a table for the daily "science object," shelves for children's collections, and space for the tools of science. The tools of science include a stand-up magnifying glass and several small magnifying glasses, a giant magnet, an assortment of small magnets, tweezers, prisms, a tape measure or windup ruler, a balance scale, a fish net, and several see-through plastic jars.

Is there space in your classroom for a terrarium full of ferns, moss, and wintergreen gathered on a trip to the woods? You might also include an aquarium for goldfish or tropical fish, with a book nearby for identifying them. An ant farm, insect habitat, or butterfly bower can display the latest occupants. A cage on the counter may have a gerbil or guinea pig in residence. Shelves closest to the window can contain bean sprouts in paper cups.

An exciting activity of some kind happens daily in such a classroom. It may be an egg carton full of a bean-seed mixture that encourages children to sort and classify or to weigh the items with the balance scale. A chart to record how many inches each child's beans have grown invites all kinds of measuring with the windup ruler. A sealed box in the middle of the table with a sign, "Guess what's inside! Tell your guess to the tape recorder," has the curious ones trying to find out what the sign says, shaking the box vigorously, and cautiously recording their guesses. Another sign, "Bring something green tomorrow," sets off a babble of ideas.

Children in such a classroom expect to be challenged to find out something independently. They know they must use their five senses plus the available science tools to discover "how much" or "what kind" or "how many." What's more, these youngsters can learn to do it on their own because of the careful arrangement of the materials and the stimulating manner in which science objects are displayed.

Make space in your classroom for an aquarium with tropical fish or a terrarium with ferns and moss.

Writing Center

> **10. Include in WRITING CENTER:**
> _____ Desk to write on and to store writing supplies
> _____ Pens, pencils, markers, chalk, and chalkboard
> _____ Paper, pads, notebooks, file cards, and envelopes
> _____ Ruler, stapler, scissors, hole punch, and paper clips
> _____ Rubber stamps and pad, peel-off stickers, and stamps
> _____ Typewriter and/or computer

The news about preschool children and writing is good indeed. Child development specialists and teachers around the world are discovering a growing number of young children who have taught themselves to write (and even to read) naturally. Some preschool youngsters have always had this ability to advance from scribbles into writing on their own, but it was seldom recognized and therefore not encouraged. Instead, children had to wait until elementary school where writing would be taught formally. Now we know better. Today both preschools and kindergartens are setting up a writing area for children to experience this natural emergence into writing through play with writing implements just as they play with painting implements.

Early childhood teachers can facilitate this natural process by encouraging children to experiment with writing, but not teaching them formally how to make letters or words. As noted by Mills and Clyde (1991):

> Because children naturally interact with print in functional and meaningful ways, children can read and write in their own ways before entering school and continue to learn through authentic reading and writing lessons. (p. 58)

Because writing is more often done at a desk, it makes sense to set up a classroom writing area around a desk. A child's home desk with drawers is ideal, or you can develop a little "office area" with a small file cabinet and shelves to store the materials. A table can serve for scribbling space or as a typewriter stand. Ask a parent or a business to donate an old manual typewriter for your children's use. Children's toy typewriters do not work as well. The classroom computer can be located here if you choose not to set up a separate computer area. Keep the computer on a separate table, however, with two chairs for two children to use at the same time.

Children relish the opportunity to try out all kinds of writing implements. Stock the area with pencils and pens of all sizes and shapes. Some children prefer gripping the thick primary pencils, but a few like to use regular adult pencils. The all-time favorites seem to be felt-tip markers of every color. They make marks easier than pens or pencils, with young children's stubby fingers. Be sure your markers and ballpoint pens are water-soluble.

The types of writing, printing, and stamping materials you supply will influence the kinds of scribbles, mock writing, and print the children produce. Put out only a few kinds of writing implements, paper, and tablets at first to get them started. Then from time to time add other materials, such as blank postcards, greeting cards, stationery, and envelopes.

Children especially enjoy receiving and sending letters even when their writing is still in the scribble stage. Be sure to include mailboxes in the writing area to motivate letter writing. Shoe boxes decorated by the children and labeled with their names and pictures make good mailboxes when stacked together on a shelf in the writing center. Add a bulletin board for children to display their own writing products. (For more information on writing, see Chapter 6.)

Computer Center

---

11. Include in COMPUTER CENTER:

_____   Computer on low table with two chairs

_____   Printer and paper

_____   Several appropriate software programs

_____   Games, puzzles, and materials to extend each program

This is a new learning center for many preschool programs. Adults who are unfamiliar with the computer may be surprised that preschools and kindergartens are encouraged to set up such a learning center or that young children are invited to use it on their own. To an adult, a computer seems to be an expensive, complicated, high-tech piece of equipment that only older children could learn to use.

As it turns out, appropriate computer programs are no more complicated to operate for children 3 to 5 years of age than are television programs. With the proper software and a minimum of instruction, young children can teach themselves to operate the programs by themselves. Computers, in fact, are set up to teach in the same manner that young children are set up to learn: through playing around with the keys, by trial and error, and through playful self-discovery.

Software programs for preschool children in the form of simple games can involve the youngsters in learning about themselves, their families, the environment, animals, vehicles, letters, numbers, shapes, and colors. But be sure your center is set up for two children to use at once. Children can then teach one another how to operate the program. They also learn turn-taking, cooperation, and problem solving as they try to work the programs through trial and error.

Because computers are an expensive item for most preschools and kindergartens, teachers and directors should ask for help from parents or businesses in acquiring them. Often an older, less powerful model of a computer can be donated that easily accommodates the early childhood software you will be using. Choose the computer on the basis of the software programs available.

To choose the software, it is important to understand how children will use it. You should make yourself familiar with popular programs for young children through a hands-on approach. Visit a public school computer resource center or a library or museum software collection and borrow sample programs for trial use by you and the children.

The number of software programs you purchase will depend on the particular curriculum areas of the classroom in which you plan to integrate computer software, as well as the developmental levels of the programs. Some teachers start by purchasing one or two programs each for shapes, colors, opposites, numbers, letters, drawing, painting, and constructing. They introduce the programs one by one, leaving them in the area for the children to try out for a week or so at a time before introducing a new program.

Meanwhile, teachers can include concrete activities related to each program in other learning centers. For example, when an alphabet program is in use on the computer, a magnetic letters game can be put out. A mixed-up animals puzzle can be in the manipulative area when a mixed-up animals computer program is being used. In this way, computer programs are translated into three-dimensional hands-on classroom activities so necessary for young children's learning. (For more about computers, see Chapter 5.)

Sand/Water Play Center

---

12. Include in SAND/WATER PLAY CENTER:

_____ Squeeze bottles, basters, and eggbeaters

_____ Children's water play aprons and safety goggles

_____ Small trucks, figures, shovels, sifters, and sand toys

_____ Clean-up tools for children's use

Water has an irresistible appeal for youngsters. Watch them wash their hands or get a drink. The splashing and squirting that often occur are not so much misbehavior as they are a part of the playful discovery process that children use to learn about new things. Yet it is more than that. Water seems to have a mesmerizing effect on children. They revel in its smooth or bubbly feel, its gushing and gurgling sound, and the way they can squirt it, spray it, or pour it. Even children with short attention spans can play with it for hours. The hyperactive or unruly child often quiets down remarkably during water play. Its calming effect makes it an excellent quiet activity, a wonderful change of pace after a hectic morning.

The physical arrangement of the water play area, just as with the rest of your classroom, determines whether children can enjoy playing in water on their own or whether there will always be squabbling and the necessity for close adult supervision. If you have a water table, put only a few inches of water in it. Children can have fun with this much water and still keep themselves and the floor fairly dry. Have equipment for use in the water table on nearby shelves or hanging from a pegboard rack in the area. To avoid arguments, be sure to have more than one of the favorite toys. Most children especially enjoy large plastic basters and eggbeaters. A supply of empty plastic squeeze bottles of various sizes, as well as plastic pitchers, plastic bottles, plastic hoses, and eye droppers should be standard equipment. Plastic or wooden boats and figures of people are also popular.

To keep children's clothes dry, have aprons available, either hanging on hooks or folded on shelves nearby, so that the children can get the aprons by themselves. A water table can usually accommodate a maximum of four children. Place the number *4* or four stick figures of children in the center, and let the children regulate themselves.

If you don't have a water table, use four plastic dishpans on a regular classroom table. The sink in the housekeeping area also makes a good, if small, water play area for doing the dolls' dishes or laundering doll clothes. Put a squirt of liquid detergent in the water at times and let children play with bubbles. Another day, let them use food coloring and droppers to mix colors.

Water tables can easily be converted to sand tables for another activity children really enjoy. The same directions apply. Generally, 2 or 3 inches of sand are plenty. Keep sand accessories and clean-up equipment in the area. Help children understand a few simple rules—for example, that they must keep the sand in the table and that only four children are allowed in the play area at a time. Then enforce the rules with quiet, consistent firmness. If sand is spilled, children can help sweep it up.

Small containers, sifters, hoppers, scoops, shovels, small dump trucks, and figures of people are popular sand toys. Be sure to have enough for four to play without squabbles. Have the children wear safety goggles to keep sand out of their eyes.

Woodworking Center

---

13. Provide in WOODWORKING CENTER:

_____ Usable pounding and sawing tools and safety goggles

_____ Marked tool storage shelves or pegboard

_____ Woodworking table or stump; vise

_____ Wood scraps, ceiling tiles, and nails

Wood is another medium especially attractive to children. You can see this by the way they handle wooden blocks. The fact that wood can be pounded and turned into something other than itself makes it as creative a medium as paint. Both boys and girls love to pound. Thus, woodworking is an excellent channel for acceptable venting of frustration. Children can pound wood and let off steam harmlessly.

Not every early childhood program can afford a workbench. Tree stumps make an excellent substitute and are even more effective for pounding on. Just for the fun of pounding, let children nail things onto the tops of tree stumps. A box of nails of many sizes and another of pine wood scraps are enough to keep your woodworking area going for many days. Children should wear safety goggles for this activity. Putting on goggles for an activity like this makes children feel really grown-up.

Some teachers substitute ceiling tiles for wood because with this softer substance children have better control over hammers and nails. Building supply dealers will sometimes donate extra tiles. Children can also pound nails more easily through leather scraps or Styrofoam boards than through wood. Small adult tools are more effective than children's toolbox toys. They can be stored on shelves or hung from pegboards, with their outlines traced so that children can match shapes and return the tools easily.

Cooking Center

> **14. Include in COOKING CENTER:**
> _____ Knives, spoons, beaters, scrapers, and food mill
> _____ Bowls, pans, measuring cups, and mixing spoons
> _____ Microwave or toaster oven, blender, electric fry pan, crockpot, or hot plate
> _____ Illustrated recipe charts

Adults sometimes misunderstand the idea of cooking in the preschool classroom. Teaching a child to cook is not the purpose. Cooking is instead an exceptional vehicle for promoting learning experiences such as eye–hand coordination, small muscle strength, cause and effect, prereading skills, sequencing, measurement, nutrition, and sensory exploration. For example, peeling shells from hard-boiled eggs offers unparalleled practice in small motor skills. Scraping carrots, dicing potatoes, mixing batter, and turning the handle of an eggbeater strengthen hand and arm muscles.

Children's intense interest in food and food preparation provides the motivation for learning, and your ingenuity supplies the activities. There are no limits to the learning possibilities of a cooking center. Cooking is especially fascinating to children because it is a real activity, not a pretend one, and they can eat the results!

A cooking center need not be a permanent fixture. Cooking can take place in the classroom at a table set up for it, on a counter near an electrical outlet, or in the center kitchen. A microwave oven, a toaster oven, or an electric fry pan can supply the heat if your safety and insurance regulations permit hot cooking. (For more information on cooking, see Chapter 2.)

Child's Private Area

A child's private area is not a curriculum area as such, but it should be provided on a permanent basis if your goal is to promote a child's positive self-image. It is a place where a child can get away by himself or herself when the need arises. If yours is an all-day program, such a location is a necessity. Three- and 4-year-olds, especially, find large groups of children overwhelming if they must be with them any length of time.

An overstuffed chair in a comfortable corner away from noisy activities may be all that is needed. Some classrooms use a large cardboard carton with a cutout door and window for a hut or playhouse. This can serve as the private area when dramatic play is finished. A packing crate serves the same purpose. So does a card table covered with a blanket for the child to crawl under. A colorfully painted claw-footed bathtub lined with pillows makes a wonderful retreat. Some centers have a loft that can be used for a child's private space. The book area of some classrooms makes a cozy retreat as well. Bunnett and Davis (1997) explain:

> We discovered that children need more than one "cozy nest," and designed several soft and quiet places. Over the years, we have used mattresses, bean chairs, hammocks, and rag pillows, to name a few. We found that with additional quiet spaces children can do their work with fewer disruptions, feel less fatigued, and can retreat to a quiet place without negative connotations. (p. 44)

It is important that the private area be located in the classroom and not isolated in another part of the building. Children need to be by themselves, but at the same time, they like to know what others are doing. Being isolated in another room is too much like punishment.

Accommodations for Children with Special Needs

Children with hearing or vision impairments and physical or mental disabilities may need special accommodations in the classroom. Simplifying the environment may be all that is necessary. This means that learning centers are clearly designated. Areas are kept uncluttered with only the materials in use kept on open shelves. All curriculum materials have cutout illustrations marking their spaces on the shelves. Walls are painted in soothing pastel colors and kept uncluttered. Children's art and writing are displayed in one location rather than spread around the room. Noise is kept at minimum levels through the use of floor carpeting, wall curtains, and acoustical ceiling tiles. Pathways through the room are wide enough for a wheelchair.

Other accommodations can be arranged depending on the need. Talk with parents and health specialists about including children with special needs without calling attention to disabilities. (For more about children with special needs, see Chapter 2.)

Developmentally Appropriate Materials

Children of different ages have distinct preferences for the toys and materials they want to play with. Toddlers, for instance, often prefer push-toys that make sounds as they roll across the floor. Preschoolers disdain such toys but may flock to shelves containing trucks, cars, and figures of people and animals. Likewise children at different developmental levels may use the same materials in different ways. Some 3-year-olds, for instance, fill containers with building blocks and then dump them out. Others build roads, towers, and even bridges with the same blocks.

Some materials are obviously more appropriate than others for children of different ages and at various stages of development. Yet for preschool programs to satisfy all of their youngsters' widely divergent interests and needs, teachers must also understand children's development as they progress from one level to another.

Developmental Levels

Observers of young children have noted that most children begin to explore a new object in the same way. They play around with it, exploring it with their senses. With a toy telescope, for instance, they may first use it as a hammer, a horn, or a tower, or they may look through the wrong end and laugh before figuring out its real use. With a paintbrush, they may swish paint around on a paper, change hands and slap on another color of paint, change hands again and cover the paper with still another color. We call this beginning exploration of a new material *manipulation.* Young children everywhere seem to try out new objects in the same manipulating manner.

Once children have accomplished this beginning exploration and learned how to work the material, they go on to a second phase of use: *mastery.* Here they repeat the correct use of the object or material over and over. With a toy telescope, they may push it together to close it, open it, look through it, and close it again—over and over. Or they may grip a paintbrush in the right hand while they fill their paper with lines and take another sheet and fill that with lines—again and again. It is almost as though they are practicing the skill they have just learned.

Finally, many—but not all—children evolve into a third stage of exploration: *meaning.* Here children put the same object or material to some new and different use, giving it their own meaning. For example, with a telescope, they might use it in their large block "spaceship" as a control lever. With a paintbrush, they may begin painting suns and people.

These three developmental learning levels that most children work through spontaneously with no outside help can be referred to as the *3-M's: manipulation, mastery,* and *meaning.* For teachers and assistants in early childhood programs, it is important to recognize these levels as they witness children playing with materials. It helps to know, for example, that Sarah, who is filling page after page of paper with lines of scribbles, must be at the mastery level in spontaneous writing. Don't try to stop her. She is engaged in her own play-practice and will progress beyond her repetitive actions when she has mastered line-scribbling. Nor should you try to redirect Zack's efforts at the easel as he slaps paint every which way on his paper first with one hand and then the other. He is still manipulating the medium.

Over the years observers of children have determined the sequences most children follow as they interact on their own with particular objects and materials. For example, children begin manipulating unit blocks by filling containers with blocks and then dumping them out. They eventually progress to the mastery level by stacking blocks in horizontal lines (roads) or vertical lines (towers). Finally, they emerge into inventive construction of buildings and bridges, giving meaning to their work. It is fascinating for adult observers to watch this progression of levels develop in a child and to note that every child seems to follow the same progression and in almost the same manner.

Teachers, teaching assistants, student teachers, and volunteers should be aware of these developmental levels as they make their plans for individuals and the total group. By carefully observing and recording how children interact with materials, teachers can determine whether each child is in the manipulation, mastery, or meaning stage. After this determination is made, teachers can add appropriate materials to each of the learning centers to support children's own progression through their levels of exploration. For example, provide new and challenging puzzles in the manipulative center when children have made the old ones over and over. For children who are still filling and dumping table blocks rather than building with them, let them continue this beginning exploration before adding new materials but support their current efforts by giving them new containers to use. (For more information about observing children and Child Involvement Checklist, see Chapter 12.)

Changing Materials

Look around your classroom and what do you see? Some classrooms appear to be the same all year round. The same books are on the shelves of the library area; the same paint colors fill the jars at the easel; the same science project occupies the shelf by the window. These materials may have appealed to the children at first, but after continued use over long periods of time, they eventually lose their attraction. It is time for a change, but not a complete change.

Young children need new stimulation but within the comfortable learning centers they are used to. This means you should add new materials to each of the classroom centers from time to time. Put away a few items for the time being and add something new to each area at least once a month. Researchers Petrakos and Howe (1996) note:

> There is evidence to support the notion that the physical arrangement of the play setting may directly influence the types of children's play. Although the housekeeping corner is designed to encourage dramatic play, it can be limited and static in terms of the arrangement of space, equipment, and theme. (p. 66)

If yours is a center where the toy refrigerator, stove, and sink remain in the same position for an entire year, consider bringing in a large cardboard refrigerator box and letting the children invent their own setting. With your help they can cut out doors and windows and even paint their new "house," "ticket booth," or "castle."

One program enclosed its housekeeping center with walls containing acrylic windows that went up and down, a doorbell, a mailbox, and a small lamp on a dresser table inside (Bunnett & Davis, 1997). Another program brought in a steamer trunk with drawers and compartments containing fancy dress-up clothes, costume jewelry, and accessories. Children suddenly became motivated to dress up as actors and put on plays for each other.

In addition to renewing the children's interest in the program, new materials can also support youngsters' learning as you choose items based on curriculum topics you are featuring. For instance, after a picnic at a park or beach, put sand and sand toys in the former water table. In the block center, hang a book-on-a-string such as *Tar Beach* (Ringgold, 1991), about the African-American family who takes their blankets and picnic supplies to the rooftop of their New York apartment for a picnic under the stars. In the art center put out *Beach Feet* (Reiser, 1996), describing what people's feet and animals' feet look like and do at the beach. In the cooking center put out *Famous Seaweed Soup* (Martin, 1993) about a little girl who goes to the beach with her family where she makes her famous pretend seaweed soup. At the same time put pieces of black paper for the rooftops and figures of African American people for the picnickers in the block center, and watch what the children build. In the art area, cover the floor with paper and put out pans of paint for children to step in barefooted and make their own "beach feet." Put out real supplies in the cooking center and cook up some real "seaweed" soup in the crock pot for everyone.

Evaluating Room Arrangement

Your children's behavior in the classroom will tell you whether you have planned and arranged well for them. Large groups of children milling around aimlessly may mean there is too much open space or not enough learning centers. A great deal of running may mean that open areas need to be sectioned off with room dividers.

On the other hand, your room could be too cluttered, so that children, especially 3-year-olds, have difficulty making choices and settling down. Perhaps they are suffering from "sensory overload." Simplify the environment by putting away some of the materials and taking unnecessary pictures off the walls. When most of the children become involved in the areas and engrossed in the activities, you will know that your arrangement is working as it should.

During the year, you will want to rearrange the room for variety or for new challenges. It is best to change only one or two areas at once because young children are easily upset by abrupt changes. It helps to let them participate in the planning and re-arranging, since it is their room as much as yours.

 ## PROVIDES A HIGH-ACTIVITY, LOW-STRESS ENVIRONMENT WHERE CHILDREN CAN LEARN HAPPILY TOGETHER

Brain Research and Stress

The results of brain research of the past decade can help teachers of young children to understand why creating a high-activity, low-stress, brain-compatible learning environment is essential if young children are to grow and learn. As Rushton (2001) points out:

> A nonthreatening learning environment is crucial if students are to feel safe in encountering and exploring stimulating new ideas. (p. 76)

Start the day with an activity that gets the children laughing and feeling happy.

Research findings on how the brain functions show that high levels of stress can inhibit learning. When a teacher yells at a child or calls out his name across the room to stop him from doing something, the child and those around him often become afraid. This fear causes the brain to release the hormone cortisol which stops the child from thinking clearly. Lasting high stress or threat can reduce the brain's capacity for understanding and can interfere with higher-order thinking. (Rushton, 2001)

Teachers who belittle, ridicule, or criticize the children create situations that can hinder learning. Teachers who allow children to be bullied by other children or kept out of group activities also add to their stress. Classrooms that are too crowded or too empty create children's discomfort. Environments that are cold, sterile, and nonstimulating do the same.

On other hand, low-stress, high-activity environments treat all children as worthy individuals; provide a wide range of exciting activities for children to choose from; use colors, lamps, and music to create warm and comfortable settings; help all children to experience success; have a balance of quiet and active learning times, of total group, small group, and individual activities; and have teachers and staff who use humor, love, and affection to interact with children, while modeling positive interpersonal behaviors.

Using Humor

Young children love to be in classrooms where smiling teachers get down on the floor and have fun with them; where laughter rings out all day long and teachers know how to pretend just as children do to engage their attention. Are you excited to see the children come in every day? You need to show it. You need to tell children how happy you are to see them. You need to begin with one activity at the beginning of the day that gets them laughing and feeling happy. As Rushton (2001) notes:

> Emotions are biological functions of the nervous system, and they strongly influence attention and memory. Children engaged in interesting activities at the beginning of the day will have a more positive disposition toward the day's activities as a whole. (p. 77)

You might decide to have a surprise "drop-in-and-laugh" time in each of the learning centers, where you come in with a funny story to read to the small group or a fun activity to add to what they are already doing. For instance, in the block-building center where the children are building a space port for their rocket ships, you might drop in with the outlandishly funny *Here Come the Aliens!* (McNaughton, 1995), showing preposterous-looking beings floating in space against the black of night as they approach earth. They squeak, squawk, gobble, and munch. Table manners? Not this bunch. But as they get close to Earth, one of them produces a picture that scares them so much they reverse course and leave. "A picture of you kids—aged four! It's scared them off—away they roar. The aliens are going!" You'll know they found the story hilarious if they want it repeated.

Or perhaps you can drop into the dramatic play center where a small group is playing with the new baby doll, to read *Oonga Boonga* (Wishinsky, 1998), the story of baby Louis who wouldn't stop crying until her brother Daniel came home and said "oonga boonga" to her. Children love funny words like this as you will soon find out when you hear them whispering "oonga boonga" to one another and dissolving into gales of laughter.

Then one day, of course, you must read the book *Hug* (Alborough, 2000) to each of the learning center groups. It is the simple story of a small chimp who wanders through an African jungle noticing that all of the baby animals are being cuddled by their mothers except him, and he wants a hug. The only word used throughout is the word 'hug' which the little chimp says to each of the animals, but they only ignore him until finally his mother appears exclaiming "Bobo!" Then he gets his hug, and so does everyone else—including each of your listeners as you go around the group hugging each one.

SUMMARY

This chapter provides ideas for setting up and arranging an early childhood classroom so that children will become self-directed in their learning. You will need to articulate your own program's goals to decide what curriculum areas to include in your classroom. Using the Learning Center Checklist in Figure 3–4 should help you understand how each activity area can promote your program's goals for young children.

Since the physical arrangement of a preschool classroom is the structure for an open and flexible curriculum, you will want to arrange your room carefully, using aids such as the Learning Center Location Checklist in Figure 3-2. This checklist can help you learn to separate one area from another by pulling shelves away from the walls and using them as dividers to make the areas obvious to the children. Self-regulating devices such as hooks and tags or charts and necklaces can also help children become independent in using their environment.

You will begin to understand how children's play serves as their vehicle for learning and how they go through developmental levels of manipulation, mastery, and meaning as they explore the curriculum materials you provide. You will also learn to know the importance of changing the learning centers and adding new materials to support different curriculum topics. Then you will understand how stress prevents children from learning and how humor can keep them playing and learning together all day long. The chapters that follow extend the discussion of each learning center and describe how teachers can promote young children's natural growth and development in these areas.

LEARNING ACTIVITIES

1. Read Chapter 3, 'Establishing a Learning Environment,' and write out answers to Question Sheet 3.

2. Meet with your trainer or instructor and discuss answers to Question Sheet 3.

3. View one of the videotapes suggested and make 10 file cards of ideas for use in setting up a classroom. Include a reference source on each card.

4. Read one or more of the references cited or suggested readings. Add 10 cards to your file, with specific ideas for setting up the classroom. Include the reference source on each card.

5. Use the Learning Center Checklist in Figure 3–4 to assess your current room arrangement. Set up a new learning center or rearrange an old one based on the checklist results and ideas presented in this chapter.

6. Visit another early childhood classroom and make a floor plan showing the areas children were using during your visit. Record on file cards at least three new ideas for classroom arrangement gained from this visit.

7. Set up and implement a children's self-regulating method for choosing learning centers in your classroom.

8. Make outlines of the materials and equipment in each area and mount them on their particular shelves and hook boards. Observe how children use the materials afterward.

9. Bring in new games, books, pictures, or props that illustrate a field trip you have taken and add them to one or more learning centers. Observe how children use them.

10. Complete the Chapter 3 Evaluation Sheet and return it to your trainer or college supervisor.

QUESTION SHEET 3

1. In what ways does the physical arrangement of the classroom control the children's behavior?

2. What is one way your room arrangement can promote the children's positive self-images?

3. How can you determine what learning centers to establish in your room?

4. What are several different ways that you can separate one center from another?

5. Where can total group activities take place? Why in that location?

6. How can you set up the classroom for children to regulate their own numbers in the various centers?

7. When should you rearrange the room and how should you go about it?

8. What process do preschool children use to learn about things? What process is inappropriate for teachers to use with young children?

9. What are three ways you can make your book center more attractive and supportive of children's learning?

10. Why should a large motor center be included inside the classroom and what should it consist of?

11. How can a writing center support children's natural emergence of writing abilities?

12. Why would you include a computer center in an early childhood program and what should it contain?

13. What accommodations should you make for children with special needs?

14. Why should you establish a child's private area? What should it consist of?

15. How can you provide a low-stress environment where children can play and learn happily?

REFERENCES

Beaty, J. J., & Pratt, L. (2003). *Early literacy in preschool and kindergarten.* Upper Saddle River, NJ: Merrill/Prentice Hall.

Bunnett, R., & Davis, N. L. (1997). Getting to the heart of the matter. *Child Care Information Exchange, 114,* 42–44.

Caples, S. E. (1996). Some guidelines for preschool design. *Young Children, 51*(4), 14–21.

Maxim, G. W. (1989). *The very young child* (3rd ed.). Upper Saddle River, NJ: Merrill/Prentice Hall.

Mills, H., & Clyde, J. A. (1991). Children's success as readers and writers: It's the teacher's beliefs that make the difference. *Young Children, 46*(2), 58.

Petrakos, H., & Howe, N. (1996). The influence of the physical design of the dramatic play center on children's play. *Early Childhood Research Quarterly, 11,* 63–77.

Rushton, S. P. (2001). Applying brain research to create developmentally appropriate learning environments. *Young Children, 56*(5), 76–82.

Shepherd, W., & Eaton J. (1997). Creating environments that intrigue and delight children and adults. *Child Care Information Exchange, 117,* 42–47.

Taylor, B. J. (2002). *Early childhood program management.* Upper Saddle River, NJ: Merrill/Prentice Hall.

SUGGESTED READINGS

Diamond, K. E., Hestenes, L. L., & O'Connor, C. E. (1994). Integrating young children with disabilities in preschool: Problems and promise. *Young Children, 49*(2), 68–75.

Fye, M. A. S., & Mumpower, J. P. (2001). Lost in space? Design learning areas for today. *Dimensions of Early Childhood, 29*(2), 16–22.

Haugland, S. W. (2000). Early childhood classrooms in the 21st Century: Using computers to maximize learning. *Young Children, 55*(1), 12–18.

Hewitt, K. (2001). Blocks as a tool for learning: Historical and contemporary perspectives. *Young Children, 56*(1), 6–13.

Johnston, C. B. (1998). Four easels, five sand tables, and billions of blocks: Setting up an early childhood classroom. *Dimensions of Early Childhood, 26*(2), 24–27.

Prescott, E. (1997). 3 keys to flexible room arrangement. *Child Care Information Exchange, 117,* 48–50.

Readdick, C. A. (1993). Solitary pursuits: Supporting children's privacy needs in early childhood settings. *Young Children, 49*(1), 60–64.

Sloane, J. W. (2000). Make the most of learning centers. *Dimensions of Early Childhood, 28*(1), 16–20.

Tegano, D. W., Moran, J. D., Delong, A. J., Brickey, J., & Ramassini, K. K. (1996). Designing classroom spaces: Making the most of time. *Early Childhood Education Journal, 23*(3), 135–141.

Van Hoorn, J., Nourot, P., Scales, B., & Alward, K. (1999). *Play at the center of the curriculum* (2nd ed.) Upper Saddle River, NJ: Merrill/Prentice Hall.

Youcha, V., & Wood, K. (1997). Enhancing the environment for ALL children. *Child Care Information Exchange, 114,* 45–49.

CHILDREN'S BOOKS

Alborough, J. (2000). *Hug.* Cambridge, MA: Candlewick.

Martin, A. T. (1993). *Famous seaweed soup.* Morton Grove, IL: Whitman.

McNaughton, C. (1995). *Here come the aliens!* Cambridge, MA: Candlewick.

Reiser, L. (1996). *Beach feet.* New York: Greenwillow.

Ringgold, F. (1991). *Tar beach.* New York: Crown.

Wishinsky, F. (1998). *Oonga boonga.* New York: Dutton.

Yaccarino, D. (1997). *Zoom! Zoom! Zoom! I'm off to the moon.* New York: Scholastic.

VIDEOTAPES

Carter, M. (Producer). *Children at the center.* St. Paul, MN: Redleaf Press.

Creative Education (Producer). *Children at work.* St. Paul, MN: Redleaf Press.

Dodge, D. T. (Producer). *The creative curriculum for early childhood.* St. Paul, MN.: Redleaf Press.

Dodge, D. T. (Producer). *New room arrangement as a teaching strategy.* St. Paul, MN: Redleaf Press.

High/Scope. (Producer). *Setting up the learning environment.* Ypsilanti, MI: High/Scope.

National Association for the Education of Young Children. (Producer). *Places to grow: The learning environment. (The early childhood program: A place to learn and grow video series).* Washington, DC: Author.

Self-Dimensons & Creative Education (Producers). *Discipline and the physical environment.* St. Paul, MN: Redleaf Press.

CHAPTER 3 EVALUATION SHEET
ESTABLISHING A LEARNING ENVIRONMENT

1. Student _____

2. Trainer _____

3. Center where training occurred _____

4. Beginning date _____ Ending date _____

5. Describe what student did to accomplish General Objective.

_____

_____

6. Describe what student did to accomplish Specific Objectives.

Objective 1 _____

_____

Objective 2 _____

_____

Objective 3 _____

_____

7. Evaluation of student's Learning Activities

_____

Signature of Trainer: Signature of Student:

_____   _____

Comments:

_____

_____

_____

_____

_____

_____

_____

Permission is granted by the publisher to reproduce this page for evaluation and record keeping.

Advancing Physical Skills

GENERAL OBJECTIVE

To promote children's physical development by determining their needs and providing appropriate materials and activities

SPECIFIC OBJECTIVES

____ Assesses children's large motor skills and provides appropriate equipment and activities

____ Assesses children's small motor skills and provides appropriate materials and activities

____ Provides opportunities for children to engage in creative movement

The **physical** growth and development of young children during their preschool years is such an obvious occurrence that we sometimes take it for granted. Children will of course grow bigger, stronger, more agile, and more coordinated in their movements without outside help. It is part of their natural development. But at times, we are suddenly surprised by the 4-year-old who cannot run without stumbling, who has trouble holding a paintbrush, or who cannot walk up and down stairs easily.

We realize that individual differences in development account for many such lags. Some children are slower than others in developing coordination. Others may have neurological problems. But for many children it is the lack of opportunity to run, jump, climb, and throw freely. The streets may be dangerous and parks too far away. Unfortunately for many young children, television has replaced active play. As Pica (1997) points out: "Today's children are leading sedentary life-styles and incurring serious health risks from inactivity" (p. 4).

On the other hand, physical activity helps children develop strong and healthy bodies, builds bones and muscles, improves muscular strength and endurance, helps to control weight, to decrease blood pressure, and reduces the risk of heart disease, diabetes, and certain kinds of cancer (Staley & Portman, 2000). We also know through brain research that "the time to lay the foundation for motor control circuitry in the brain is between the prenatal period and age five" (Miller, 1999, p. 58). In other words, physical activity in early childhood programs is a necessity if we want children to develop normally.

Classroom workers in early childhood programs can and must help young children improve both large and small motor coordination by providing activities, materials, and equipment that will give them practice with basic movements. Just as important is the actual instruction in movement skills. As noted by Sanders and Yongue (1998):

> A combination of play and planned movement experiences, specifically designed to help children develop physical skills, are the most beneficial in assisting young children in their development. When frequent, regular, appropriate movement experiences are combined with daily indoor and outdoor play, children freely practice and develop their skills. (pp. 11–12)

ASSESSES CHILDREN'S LARGE MOTOR SKILLS AND PROVIDES APPROPRIATE EQUIPMENT AND ACTIVITIES

All children pass through the same sequence of stages in their physical growth, but some do it more quickly or evenly than others. Since individual children in a single classroom will be at many different levels of physical development, the teacher should determine at the outset each child's physical capacities to provide appropriate activities to promote this growth.

To provide relevant help for the children in your care, you need to determine which large motor skills they already possess, as well as the skills they need to strengthen. It is best to avoid a formal evaluation in which each child attempts the activities as you watch and record. This type of assessment tends to create a win-or-lose situation that makes children self-conscious and less free in their movements.

Instead, make an informal assessment while the children play in the large motor area, on the playground, or in the block-building area. Observe the children as they go up the steps and into the building. You will soon learn which children move with confidence and which have difficulty. Take a beanbag out on the playground and toss it back and forth to individuals. Put out tricycles for children to ride. You will soon have a comprehensive survey of each child's large muscle development.

The checklist in Figure 4–1 includes the large motor skills you will want your children to perform. Copy it onto a 5-by-7-inch card for each individual and check off items as they are accomplished in the natural environment of the classroom and playground. Add the date after each skill to keep a record of the children's accomplishments.

The activities you plan as a result of this assessment should not necessarily be singled out for a particular individual. There is no need to focus attention on an awkward child. All the children can benefit from practice with large body movements. But you will want to be sure to involve children who need special help in particular activities.

Walking

Uncoordinated children may still have trouble walking, and they need as much practice as you can give them. By playing walking games with small groups of children, you can make this practice fun for all. Play "Follow the Leader" with different kinds of walking: tramping, striding, tiptoeing, strolling, shuffling, marching, waddling. You

---

LARGE MOTOR CHECKLIST

Child's Name_____**Date**_____

_____ Walks up and down stairs

_____ Walks across a balance beam

_____ Balances on one foot

_____ Hops, jumps with both feet over a low object

_____ Runs, gallops, and skips without falling

_____ Climbs up and down a piece of climbing equipment

_____ Crawls, creeps, or scoots across the floor

_____ Picks up and carries a large object

_____ Throws a beanbag/ball

_____ Catches a beanbag/ball

_____ Rides wheeled equipment

Figure 4–1   Large Motor Checklist

Permission is granted by the publisher to reproduce this checklist for evaluation and record keeping.

might say aloud the kind of steps you are making as you walk, for example, "Tramp, tramp, tramp, shuffle, shuffle, shuffle," and so forth.

Books to Read

The children can also try to walk like certain animals (e.g., a duck, elephant, cat, or mouse) and let the others try to guess what they are. To get them started, read the book *Pretend You're a Cat* (Marzollo, 1990), a story about multiethnic children making motions like cats, dogs, birds, and bees. In *Funny Walks* (Hindley, 1994) people stride, amble, bumble, and scurry. Animals waddle, slink, and trot. Invite children to try their own funny walks after hearing this story.

Another walking activity involves cutting out and mounting a trail of contact paper stepping-stones on the floor and having the children step from one to another. Some teachers prefer to use stepping-stones of floor tile squares instead. Walking up and down stairs calls for coordination and balance. If you have a "rocking boat" piece of equipment, turn it over and it becomes up-and-down steps for children to practice on. Children can also make their own stairs with large hollow blocks pushed together.

For just plain silly walking read *Silly Sally* (Wood, 1992), a simple, brightly illustrated nonsense story about Silly Sally, who goes to town walking backward upside down. On her way she meets a series of animals who involve her in dancing a jig, playing leapfrog, and finally falling asleep. First read the story to the entire group at circle time. Then have the children try walking backward. Can they do it walking in a circle? Once they learn how, have them stop and perform each motion Sally makes as she walks. Older children can try out the "cake walk" after hearing *Mirandy and Brother Wind* (McKissack, 1988), a story about African American Mirandy who tricks Brother Wind into helping her compete in a fancy cake walk contest.

What about walking to music? Children enjoy walking around in a circle as you play a record, cassette tape, or CD with a catchy or bouncy rhythm. As they walk, have the children listen for the beat rather than the words on *Adventures in Rhythm* (Ella Jenkins), *Kids in Motion* (Steve & Greg), *Reggae for Kids* (Jamaican songs), or *Walk in Beauty My Children* (Native American songs), which can be obtained from educational supply houses. If you don't have the music, use a drum, tom-tom, or tambourine to beat out the rhythm as the children walk. Can the children clap as they walk to a beat? Then have them trot, tiptoe, or stamp to the beat.

Balancing

To make any kind of movement with confidence and stability, children must be able to balance themselves. They must maintain body stability while being stationary as well as during movement. To promote stationary balance, play "Follow the Leader" in the classroom. You be the leader, demonstrating how to stand on one foot while holding the other, then shift to the opposite foot. If you have large hollow blocks, have children try to stand on a horizontal block and then on top of a vertically placed block.

Another stationary balancing activity involves pretending to be animal and bird statues. Large pictures of animals placed around the room at the children's eye level will help them choose which one to mimic. They might choose to be a bird dog pointing, a heron standing on one leg in a frozen position, or a frog getting ready to hop. Let someone count out loud to find out how long they can hold their poses. Or have one child pretend to be one of the pictures and let the others guess which one. If you do not have animal pictures, photocopy them from the previously mentioned book *Pretend You're a Cat* (Marzollo, 1990).

Book to Read

Children with physical disabilities can do stationary balancing. The book *The Balancing Girl* (Rabe, 1981) shows Margaret balancing a book on her head while moving in a wheelchair. Then she balances herself on crutches. Read this book to your class, whether or not you have children with physical disabilities. Then bring in a wheelchair or crutches and have children try out their own balancing skills.

Activities to promote balance while moving involve the traditional balance beam. This can be purchased from a school equipment company or made by placing blocks in a row. Children can practice walking across the wide side of the beam and then the narrow edge. Children should walk on the balls of their feet and not their heels. Have them balance on the beam walking forward and then try sideways or backward.

For another walking balance activity, the teacher can cut out vinyl adhesive footprints and handprints and fasten them on the classroom floor in a series of "baby steps," "giant steps," "frog hops" (i.e., both hand and footprints), and "tiptoes" for the youngsters to follow during "Follow the Leader." Also include "crutch marks," "cane marks," and "wheelchair tracks" for everyone to follow while using this equipment. Don't limit this activity to children with disabilities. Everyone should try it.

Still another piece of balancing equipment is the commercially available "balance board," which is flat on top and curved underneath. Children can stand on the balance board, placing a foot at each end, and rock back and forth.

Children like to invent their own balancing challenges. "Ice skating" on wooden unit blocks or "skiing" down a block ramp they have built can give them wonderful practice.

Hopping/Jumping/Leaping

Once children have learned to balance on one foot, they can try hopping. The hopping movement is done on one leg. At first have youngsters practice hopping in place on one leg and then on the other. Then they can try moving forward with their hops. Make a hopping trail across the room just as you did for balancing. Place several single right footprint cutouts in a row on the right side of the trail; place single left footprints in a row on the other side. When children come to these, they will have to hop first on the right foot and then on the left foot, again on the balls of their feet rolling down to their heels.

Make a hopscotch game with masking tape and cutout contact paper symbols of geometric designs or colors. Children can call out the symbol when they hop on the design, or you can call out a symbol and see if children can hop to it. For a multicultural hopping experience, read *Hopscotch Around the World* (Lankford, 1992), with full-page illustrations of children from 17 countries playing their version of hopscotch—from "pele" on the island of Aruba, to "klassiki" in Russia, to "gat fei gei" in China.

Jumping is the same as hopping, only with both feet together. Children can try to jump in place, move forward, get over something, or get down from a height. Then have them try to jump over the "river" you create on the classroom floor with two strips of masking tape for the "river banks." Keep the banks close together at first, but widen them as the children improve their jumping skills. Encourage them to jump with both feet together and not to leap across with one foot. Once children develop the skill of jumping over lines, let them try jumping over a unit block with both feet together.

Children also enjoy jumping down from a height. You may want to use a mat for a landing pad. Jumping off a low chair is high enough for 3- and 4-year-olds. One teacher found that her children liked to measure and record their jumps. She planned a "jumping jack period" once a week in which each child from a small group jumped off a low wooden box; another child marked the landing spot; and together they measured the length of the jump. This was recorded on a "jumping jack chart." The children tried to better their own previous record, rather than seeing who could jump the farthest. Avoid competition in physical skills with young children, as it discourages those who have trouble accomplishing activities.

Preschool-size trampolines are also available commercially for practicing the skill of jumping in place. To prevent falls, the best equipment has a safety bar for children to hold as they jump. Inflated mats placed in a closet "jumping room" also help children improve this skill. Keep the closet door fastened open so the jumpers are visible.

Jumping is the same as hopping only with both feet together.

Books to Read

Children can also pretend to be various jumping creatures, such as rabbits, grasshoppers, frogs, or kangaroos. They can jump to music or the beat of a tambourine. Your "footprint trail" can also encourage jumping by mounting pairs of paper prints placed together with a space in between the next pair. Try reading a book about jumping to a small group of children, and have them jump at the proper time in the story. *One Two Three Jump!* (Lively, 1999) lends itself well to such an activity. *Moon Jump* (Matura, 1988) shows Cayal, who jumps so high he ends up on the moon. Put "moon" hula hoops on the floor and have children try jumping into and out of them.

No Jumping on the Bed! (Arnold, 1987) shows what happens when you jump one more time when you shouldn't. *Five Ugly Monsters* (Arnold, 1995) hilariously illustrates the counting chant of five monsters jumping on the bed and one falling off each time. Read this story with the children joining in the refrain as five of them jump on a floor mat. One child can jump off the mat each time until none is left.

Leaping is easier than jumping for most children. It is done from one foot and can carry the child farther than a jump. Children can pretend to be deer leaping through a forest or runners leaping over hurdles.

Running/Galloping/Skipping

Because most preschool children seem to do a great deal of running, we sometimes take this form of locomotion for granted. However, Sanders and Yongue (1998) point out:

> Running is a skill. Fast, zigzag, and forward are concepts that describe running. During a lesson for older preschoolers, where the emphasis is on developing skill in running, the challenge might be, "Can you run very fast in a zigzag path while moving forward?" (p. 14)

Children who can run well spend a great deal of time doing so, but uncoordinated children need special practice. When you plan running games, be sure all the children are included and encouraged to run. Games on the playground or in the gymnasium can include "Follow the Leader" relay races. Avoid traditional games such as *Duck, Duck, Goose; Red Rover, Red Rover;* or *Doggie, Doggie Where's Your Bone?* where children have to wait to be chosen, and often are the last to be picked. Avoid emphasizing competition with its winners and losers. Instead, praise the efforts of each child. If someone is declared the "winner," it may very well discourage a slower child, who will not want to participate in an activity for fear of being a sure "loser." Yet this is the child who needs this practice.

Galloping is a combination of a walk and a leap. The child takes a step with one foot, then brings the other foot behind it and leads off with the first foot again. In other words, one foot always leads. Children enjoy pretending to be horses and galloping around the room to music or tambourine beats. Skipping is a much more complex skill. Preschool programs should not be concerned with teaching children to skip. Most children do not master this skill much before age 5 or 6, nor should they be expected to.

Book to Read

Children enjoy body action chants using legs and feet. The traditional nursery school chant "Going on a Bear Hunt" is now in book form with sound-words and illustrations in *We're Going on a Bear Hunt* (Rosen, 1989). Read it to the children first in a seated group and then by standing in place and going through the motions along with the story characters—the father, the three children, a baby, and a dog. They go "swishy, swashy" through grass; "splash, splosh" through a river; "squelch, squerch" through mud; "stumble, trip" through a forest; "hoooo woooo" through a snowstorm; and "tiptoe, tiptoe, tiptoe" into the bear's cave.

Climbing can be done with legs or arms or both.

All of these marvelous leg and foot motions must be repeated rapidly in reverse sequence when the bear chases the whole lot of them back home. When they have completed this activity, your children should be as exhausted as the family in the story, who flop into bed and declare that they're never going on a bear hunt again! Your youngsters, however, will probably express their own feelings quite differently: "Let's do it again, teacher!" It is a large motor experience no one should miss.

Climbing

Climbing can be done with legs or arms or both. To ensure the safety of the children because of the height involved, you will want to purchase commercial materials from reliable firms. Any homemade climbing equipment (including lofts) needs to be tested carefully before children use it.

Wooden indoor climbers include jungle gyms, rung ladders, and the climbing house. Metal indoor climbers include nesting climbers of different heights that can stand alone or be used to support a walking board, a horizontal crossing ladder with wooden sliding boards. Indoor climbers are usually movable, rather than anchored to the ground like those on outdoor playgrounds. For safety's sake, classroom workers need to stand nearby when children are using them. Pads or mats should be placed underneath in case of falls.

Outdoor climbing equipment includes metal dome climbers, satellite climbers, jungle gyms, molded plastic climbers, rung ladders, rope ladders, link chain ladders, cargo nets, and tires, to mention a few. The equipment the children use outside should not include large-size playground pieces. Not only is large equipment dangerous for 3-, 4-, and 5-year-olds, but the skills required for use are beyond the capacity of most young children.

Commercial climbing equipment is expensive. You can substitute your own outdoor equipment through donations such as an old sanded-down rowboat (for climbing and dramatic play), tree stumps, and truck tires. Be sure the wooden equipment is splinter-free and that any paint used is lead-free. Drill holes in any tires that are used so that water will not collect and serve as a breeding place for mosquitoes. Outside climbing equipment should be anchored firmly to the ground and cushioned underneath with either sawdust, wood chips, bark, sand, or other soft materials.

Book to Read

Once again, a body action chant may serve for classrooms without climbing equipment. "Itsy Bitsy Spider," the all-time favorite nursery school fingerplay, is in picture-book form as *The Itsy Bitsy Spider* (Trapani, 1993). It can easily be converted to a whole-body action chant rather than a fingerplay. Better still, bring in a small ladder or a kitchen stepstool and have the children climb up and down, one at a time, while you hold the ladder and everyone else says the verses. The spider in this version climbs not only up the well-known waterspout but also up the kitchen wall, up the yellow pail, up the rocking chair, and finally up the maple tree, where she makes it to the top and spins her web.

Crawling/Creeping/Scooting

The crawling movement is made with the body flat out on the floor, with arms pulling and legs pushing. Children can pretend they are worms, snakes, lizards, beetles, caterpillars, or alligators. They can crawl to spooky music from tape or record player or to tambourine or drumbeats that the teacher makes. They can also pretend to be swimmers who are swimming across a river or lake (the room). You can read or tell the class a story about some creature and ask the children to move like the creature. You might play music while they are moving.

Creeping, on the other hand, is done on hands and knees, with the body raised above the floor. Some children have difficulty creeping in a cross-pattern (i.e., moving the opposite arm and leg in unison). If this is the case with any of your children, give them many opportunities to practice. Have them creep across the floor of the block-building area with a few blocks on their backs. Can they make it without losing the blocks? Put a few more blocks on the backs of any children who want to join in this unusual block pickup game. Have a child or two stationed at the block shelves to unload the creepers as they arrive. If the blocks on the floor are already close to the shelves, have the block carriers crawl around in a circle before they give up their loads.

Children can also pretend to be any one of a number of animals as they creep: dog, cat, horse, tiger, elephant, dinosaur. They can creep to music or drumbeats. They can creep through tunnels made from cardboard boxes, card tables, or two chairs tipped forward with their backs together. Commercial creeping equipment includes plastic barrels and fabric or foam tunnels. You can create an obstacle course around the room for creeping only, with the path marked by masking tape. Children can pretend to be an animal or a mountain climber as they creep through the course.

Scooting is done by sitting, kneeling, or standing on a movable piece of equipment and pushing it along with one or both feet. Children can also sit on a piece of cardboard and push themselves backward across a polished floor with their feet. Commercial scooter boards are for children to sit on and push with their feet or hands to move the caster wheels on the bottom. Skateboards are actually scooters. But young children do better by sitting and pushing rather than standing on skateboards. The scooter vehicle, which is operated by standing and steering while pushing with one foot, is beyond the skill of most 3- and many 4-year-olds. Many 5-year-olds, on the other hand, do well on scooters. Some trikes are moved by children's feet on the floor rather than by pedals. Children also like to push themselves around on large wooden vehicles. It is excellent exercise for leg muscles.

Picking Up/Carrying

Use hollow blocks or something similar for the children to pick up and carry one by one. When all the blocks have been moved in one direction, reverse the course. This exercise helps children develop arm and back strength as well as stamina. Children can also carry large pillows, plastic basins, empty cartons, chairs, mats, and large toys. A book to motivate picking up and carrying is *Bet You Can't* (Dale, 1987), a story that features an African American boy and his big sister challenging one another to pick up their toys in a basket and carry it.

Throwing/Catching

Many educators and parents believe children will develop physical skills on their own. For some children this is true, but many others need to be challenged with age-appropriate activities to help them develop even the most basic skills such as throwing and catching. (Sanders, 1992, p. 4)

A great deal of practice is necessary for young children to become skilled at the arm and hand movements of throwing and catching. Catching is the more difficult of the two. For children to experience success in your classroom, start with something large, for example, a beanbag, a foam ball, a beach ball, or a small soccer ball or basketball. Children can throw to one another, to the teacher, up in the air, or at a target such as a carton or a preschool-size basketball basket. Children can perfect their underhand throwing skills with other objects, such as rings and ring-toss targets. Beanbags can be thrown into a wastebasket or a cardboard carton with a clown's face drawn on it.

Young children usually catch with both hands and their bodies. To develop catching skills, you can throw children objects like yarn balls, Nerf balls, beach balls, and beanbags at first. Later use smaller rubber balls.

Riding Wheeled Equipment

Tricycles and Big Wheels help young children learn the skills of pedaling and steering at the same time, a coordination skill. Some centers have halls that can be used

---

LARGE MOTOR CHECKLIST

Child's Name ___Duane L._____ **Date** ___4/15_____

___✓___ Walks up and down stairs

___✓___ Walks across a balance beam

___✓___ Balances on one foot

___✓___ Hops, jumps with both feet over a low object

___✓___ Runs, gallops, and skips without falling

_____ Climbs up and down a piece of climbing equipment

_____ Picks up and carries a large object

_____ Throws a beanbag/ball

_____ Catches a beanbag/ball

___✓___ Rides wheeled equipment

Figure 4–2   Duane's Large Motor Checklist

for riding activities. Others have sidewalks outside. Keep track not only of children who accomplish pedaling a trike easily, but also those who never try it. Use the color of their clothes as a cue to involving them in trike-riding without embarrassing them (e.g., "Now is the special trike-time for all the children wearing blue shirts"). Give anyone who is having trouble a hand in getting started and making the trike go.

Making Plans for Individuals

Once your assessment of a child is complete, you should begin planning for his or her continued physical development. As previously mentioned, you should not single out a child who has a particular need, but instead plan a small-group activity that will address the particular need and include that child. Focus on a skill the child already possesses. Whenever possible, you should begin with the strengths of a child to help develop an area of need. For example, see 5-year-old Duane's Large Motor Checklist, shown in Figure 4–2, which was prepared by his teacher on a 5-by-7-inch card.

The teacher was surprised at the throwing/catching results, since Duane's running and jumping skills were better than average and he was such an active boy. He seemed to love balls and would try hard to throw and catch, but without much success. It seemed strange that his arms were not as strong or coordinated as the rest of his body. A conference with his parents revealed that Duane's right arm had been injured in a car accident, and although it had healed, he did not use it as well as he should be able to. It embarrassed him not to be able to keep up with his friends in ball games.

The teacher decided to find a physical activity that would help to strengthen Duane's arm. She discussed the problem with a physical education teacher, who suggested playing with a preschool-child-size tetherball. It worked very well because

Duane enjoyed any kind of ball game. This particular activity was so new to the whole class that no one was any better at it than anyone else. As the teacher noted on the back of Duane's card, he spent a great deal of time playing tetherball, and his arm became much stronger.

ASSESSES CHILDREN'S SMALL MOTOR SKILLS AND PROVIDES APPROPRIATE MATERIALS AND ACTIVITIES

Small motor coordination involves using the fingers with dexterity to manipulate objects. This is also known as eye–hand, visual–manual, fine-motor, or perceptual-motor coordination. It is an important skill for young children to develop as a prerequisite for learning to read and write from left to right and to use a writing tool effectively. Children who experience difficulty in these checklist areas sometimes exhibit a lack of small motor coordination. Young boys frequently show less dexterity with their fingers than do girls of the same age. As with girls and large motor skills, the lag may result from inherent genetic differences, but encouragement and practice in small motor activities nevertheless benefits both boys and girls.

Small Motor Assessment

Children's small motor abilities can be assessed using a checklist, as were large motor skills. Copy the Small Motor Checklist (see Figure 4–3) onto a card for each child. Observe and use the checklist to assess the children's small motor skills as they play

---

SMALL MOTOR CHECKLIST

Child's Name_____Date_____

_____ Inserts pegs

_____ Zips a zipper

_____ Twists a nut onto a bolt

_____ Pours a liquid without spilling

_____ Strings beads

_____ Cuts with scissors

_____ Cuts with a knife

_____ Pounds nails with a hammer

_____ Traces objects with crayon, felt-tip pen

_____ Writes with an implement

_____ Paints with a brush

Figure 4–3   Small Motor Checklist

Permission is granted by the publisher to reproduce this checklist for evaluation and record keeping.

naturally during classroom activities. Be sure to provide the necessary small motor activities for children who need help in a particular skill and for other children as well. Do not make a fuss about developmental lags certain children may exhibit. Everyone has his or her own timetable for development. Individual differences in young children are to be expected.

Inserting

Small motor activities help establish handedness in young children. Most of the children will already have exhibited a preference for either right- or left-handedness by the time they enter a preschool program. You should note which hand a child uses more frequently and help the child strengthen handedness through manipulative games. Do not try to change a left-handed child. You can best help the child by providing opportunities to become proficient with the left hand. Talk with parents about this, especially if parents are trying to change the left-handedness.

Picking up small objects with the preferred hand helps children develop and strengthen their handedness. This activity also promotes eye–hand coordination, allowing children to manipulate the object they are viewing. It further helps strengthen finger muscles that will eventually be needed for grasping a writing implement.

Teacher-made sorting games are especially helpful in this area. In addition to promoting manual skills, sorting games help children develop cognitive concepts such as sorting and matching according to size, shape, or color. Shoe boxes and plastic margarine containers are handy accessories for these games. Each shoe box can contain a separate game. Label each empty margarine container with the picture and name of the item it should contain. Then cut a hole in the top large enough to permit the item to be dropped in. Have one extra container to hold the entire assortment of items. Label the outside of the shoe box with an illustration of the items so that children can identify separate games.

The idea of the game is to sort a collection of items by picking up each one and inserting it into the proper container. Each shoe box game will contain a different collection. For example, one box can hold a collection of three different kinds of beans along with a margarine cup for each kind of bean; another, a collection of three different pasta shapes and cups. Other collections may include nuts, bolts, and screws; three different kinds of buttons; poker chips of three different colors; golf tees of three colors, all with accompanying cups.

To begin, the children should pour out the collection into the top of the shoe box for ease in sorting. Once they have finished the fun task of dropping the items through the holes in the proper container tops, they should remove the tops to see how accurate they were in their sorting. If the game has captured their interest, they can pour the items back into the top of the shoe box and sort them over and over. You will recall that repeating a task again and again means the youngsters are at the mastery level of exploratory play.

Egg cartons can also be used for sorting. Either keep the top closed and puncture holes over every egg section or let the children play with the carton open. Labels of the items can be pasted on the different sections or next to the holes. All of these games should be kept on the shelves of your manipulative area near the tables where they will be used.

Puzzles require finger skill to pick up and insert a piece into a space.

Many commercial games also promote finger dexterity: wooden puzzles with knobs on each piece, Legos, pegboards, lacing boards, stringing beads, bristle blocks, slotted wheels, Montessori cylinder blocks, and shape inlays. You can make your own pegboards by acquiring scraps of pegboard material from a lumber company and using colored golf tees as pegs. Another teacher-made board for promoting finger dexterity is the geoboard. You can make one by pounding headless nails equidistant (e.g., 1 inch apart) in rows on a 12-inch-square board. Children can then stretch colored rubber bands over the nails to make various designs.

Puzzles require the same finger skill: picking up and inserting an item into a space. The first puzzles for young children are the large wooden ones with only a few pieces to be inserted into a cutout wooden frame. Children who have never assembled a puzzle are more successful when each puzzle piece represents a whole item rather than a part of an item in the picture. Check your puzzles carefully. You will need a wide selection because of the children's range of abilities.

It is important at the beginning of the year to have puzzles that new children can complete successfully. If they have had no previous experience with puzzles, you may need to sit with them for encouragement or for actual help until they complete the puzzle. They may have no clue about how to do it. Take turns with them at first, finding a piece and inserting it yourself. Then tell them to find a piece and encourage them to try it out until they discover where it fits.

A wide range of commercial puzzles is available, but you can also make your own. Enlarged photographs of each child can be glued or laminated to thick vinyl posterboard and then cut into puzzle pieces with a modeler's knife. Store the pieces in separate manila envelopes with a picture label on the front. Do not put out the puzzles for use until pictures of everyone are available. It is too distressing for children to find that they have been left out.

Zipping

You can observe and record how children zip their own clothing, or you can make or purchase a zipper board. Cut the zipper and plenty of surrounding cloth from an old skirt or jacket. Then fasten the two sides to a board. Don't forget to sand the wood so that there are no sharp edges.

Twisting/Turning

Different small muscles are developed to accomplish the skills of twisting or turning something with the hands. You can help by giving children opportunities to use tools like eggbeaters, food mills, or can openers in their cooking activities or water play.

Start collecting small plastic bottles with screw-on tops. When you have several, wash them out and put tops and bottles in a shoe box for the children to try to put together. They must practice the additional skill of matching sizes before they can screw on the tops successfully.

You can also make or purchase a board with bolts of different sizes protruding through the surface, with a container of nuts the children can screw onto the bolts. Squeezing oranges for orange juice is another activity that promotes the twisting and turning skill—if children use a hand-operated juicer. Have children make their own orange juice for a snack.

Pouring

Children need the practice of pouring liquids. Do not deprive them of it by doing all the pouring yourself. Use small pitchers for snacks or lunches, and the children will be able to pour their own juice and milk. Even programs using pint or half-pint milk cartons should empty these into small pitchers for the children to use on their own. Be sure to have plastic bottles and pitchers in the water table, as well. You may also want children to experience pouring something other than a liquid. Let them pour rice from a pitcher to a bowl and back again. Salt and sand are other pouring possibilities.

Stringing Beads

These days stringing beads can be more than an exercise in small motor development or eye–hand coordination. It can become a surprising multicultural enterprise that can bring children closer to Native Americans, Egyptians, Africans, Italians, and people all over the world who make and string their own beads.

Book to Read

Start by reading the children *A String of Beads* (Reid, 1997), the story of a little girl and her grandma who spend the story sorting out store-bought beads, making their own, learning where different beads come from, and finally stringing them into marvelous necklaces for everyone to wear. The author states that "beads are little pieces of the world that tell us their histories in fascinating fashion" (cover flap). The book illustrations are as dazzling as the beads themselves.

Your youngest children should continue to string mainly the easy-to-handle large wooden beads on thick shoelace-type strings. Older preschoolers can sort out and identify flat store beads that Grandma calls "disks," ball beads she calls "spheres," long round beads she calls "cylinders," and long tube beads she calls "bugles."

The youngsters may want to sort and string them by size or shape or even by color. Some beads are large seeds from Amazon jungles, and others are seashells from tropical waters. Some Native Americans carve animal-shape beads called "fetishes." Bead stores and hobby shops display a wide variety these days. Your children can make their own colorful beads by dying pasta of various shapes with food coloring and then stringing them on yarn for bracelets, anklets, or ponytail holders. Or they can squeeze and twist polymer clay of different colors into long rolls that they cut and roll into beads with holes made by a toothpick.

Cutting with Scissors

There are several ways to help children who have not yet learned to cut. Show them how to hold the scissors with their favored hand. If they are left-handed, provide left-handed scissors. Then hold a narrow strip of paper stretched taut between your two hands for the child to practice cutting in two. Once the child can do so without difficulty, have another child hold the paper and let her take turns holding and cutting. On another day, show the child how to hold the paper in her own hand and cut with the other hand. Let her practice on different kinds and sizes of paper, including construction paper, typing paper, and pages from old magazines. Finally, draw a line on a sheet of paper and let the child practice cutting along a line. For fun as well as practice, have children cut up colored ribbon into small pieces for confetti.

Later have a cutting day at the emptied water table after you place paper scraps and old magazine pages in it. Tie several pairs of scissors with lengths of yarn to the table and turn interested children loose during the free choice period to "cut up a storm."

Cutting with a Knife

Young children can also learn to handle knives safely. Not only does cutting with a knife provide excellent small motor coordination practice, but it is also a highly satisfying adult-type skill for young children to accomplish. You can start with table knives and soft items. Children can learn to hold the knife in one hand with the sharp edge of the blade down, while holding a peeled, hard-boiled egg, cooked potato or carrot, or peach or pear with the other hand. They may have to make a sawing motion to get started. After they have learned to control a table knife, they can begin learning to use a sharp paring knife for the same kind of soft items cutting. Eventually they should be able to help prepare food for a snack such as raw carrots, apples, or celery.

Using a vegetable scraper is another satisfying skill for children to learn. Carrots are best to begin with, but children will eventually be able to peel potatoes successfully. These are real experiences rather than games or simulations, and children understand the value of such skills because they have seen grown-ups do them. It gives children great satisfaction to realize that they too can take part in the adult world. Their teachers can feel satisfaction, as well, knowing that cooking experiences provide an excellent opportunity for children to develop small motor control.

Other cooking tools such as shredders, graters, grinders, and melon ballers are also valuable for small motor development. Have children make their own melon ball fruit cups for snacks from different kinds of melons. (For more information on cooking, see chapters 2 and 3.)

Holding and Hammering

To pound a nail with a hammer takes well-developed eye–hand coordination even for an adult. Let children practice at the woodworking table with soft materials at first such as plasterboard or ceiling tiles and large-headed nails. They can pound pieces of tile or wood together, or they can pound objects such as Styrofoam onto a board. Small adult hammers are more effective than children's toy box tools.

Be sure to bring in several slices of tree stumps and have children pound nails into them for the fun of pounding and the practice of eye–hand coordination. Put out two cross-sections of tree stumps along with hammers and nails on a classroom table to create a favorite pounding center for both girls and boys. Nails go into tree stumps easier than into boards. Put towels under the stumps to cut down on noise. When the top of a stump is covered with nails, you can have it sliced off with a chain saw, thus getting it ready for the next pounders. Once children learn the knack of holding and hammering, they can make designs or even pound their initials on the stumps. As Leithead (1996) points out:

> Hammering nails is an excellent perceptual motor exercise, an effective way for young children to build eye–hand coordination. As soon as children are old enough to grasp a hammer, few can resist the urge to pound nails. (p. 12)

Too many teachers fail to see the need for providing a woodworking center like this, perhaps because they have little interest in hammering themselves. Instead, we need to put aside our adult considerations and plug into children's own strong interests, whenever we are fortunate enough to discover them, in order to support children in their own development.

Holding and Printing/Tracing

A writing area offers children a chance to experiment with holding all kinds of writing and marking tools: pencils, pens, crayons, chalk, and markers. They can make scribbles, mock write, print, and make signs. Be sure to have paper, pads, tablets, notebooks, file cards, and envelopes on hand. Mount alphabet letters, signs, and symbols in the area. Have geometric shapes for youngsters to trace around.

Then let them practice their scribble writing and printing of letters. Some children may want to try printing their names. Others will want to trace around various objects. This is excellent practice for strengthening finger muscles and developing control of the writing tool. (For more information on emergent writing, see Chapter 6).

Book to Read

Read to children the Jewish folktale *Joseph Had a Little Overcoat* (Taback, 1999) in which a clever man takes his old and worn overcoat and converts it first into a jacket, then a vest, then a scarf, then a necktie, then a handkerchief, and finally a button as each item gets old and worn. Pages of the book have cutouts of each of these clothing items which children can trace onto pieces of paper inserted between the pages. Then they can cut out the items and color them or use them as paper doll clothes to dress Joseph. You can make a color photocopy copy of Joseph, cut it out and laminate it for the children to play with.

Planning for Individuals

Once the small motor assessment has been completed, you and your classroom team will have a better idea of the activities you should provide. Although you will be planning for individuals, be sure not to single them out as being deficient in these skills. Because a classroom of children exhibits such a wide range of motor abilities, all the children should be accepted as they are. If one child's development seems to lag behind another's, simply involve that youngster in activities that will strengthen that particular skill. As with large motor activities, all the children can benefit from the small motor activities you provide for certain children.

Children with Disabilities

Youngsters with physical impairments should be encouraged to accomplish as many large and small motor activities as they can. Once you have assessed what they are able to do, you will be ready to make appropriate individual plans to challenge them, just as you do for all of the children.

PROVIDES OPPORTUNITIES FOR CHILDREN TO ENGAGE IN CREATIVE MOVEMENT

Movement, Music, and Brain Research

Whether or not you are a dancer yourself, it is imperative that you provide opportunities for young children to move to music, to engage in creative movement, the structured or free-flowing movement activity done to music and percussion beats. As Davies (2000) reports:

> Music synchronizes the right and left hemispheres of the brain. Researchers report that the left hemisphere analyzes the structure of music, while the right hemisphere focuses on the melody. The hemispheres work together when emotions are stimulated, attention focused, and motivation heightened. Rhythm acts as a hook for capturing attention and stimulating interest. Once a person is motivated and actively involved, learning is optimized.

Where does creative movement come in? We learn that researcher Howard Gardner (1993) recognizes multiple intelligences: verbal-linguistic, logical-mathematical, musical-rhythmic, visual-spatial, bodily kinesthetic, interpersonal, intrapersonal, and naturalistic. He theorizes that people learn through combinations of these intelligences. Furthermore, Hap Palmer (2001), well-known composer of animated teaching songs for young children, suggests that "music and movement, with its rich combination of rhythm, melody, lyric, motion, and group interactions, touches each of these areas" (p. 14).

Observe how your children move when you play particular records or tapes or beat out a rhythm on a drum or tom-tom. Do some of them let loose and run around wildly? Do some make up their own steps? Do some look to you to provide the directions on how to move? Do others pull back and refuse to join in? The Creative Movement Checklist in Figure 4–4 lists some of the movements children may engage in during a creative movement activity. Copy the checklist on file cards for individual children so you can observe where their strengths lie and what areas need strengthening.

Palmer noted when he first began teaching that young children's attention span was so short and their squirminess so ceaseless, that he decided to write songs for them combining music and movement. One was "Alphabet in Motion" from his recording *Can a Jumbo Jet Sing the Alphabet?* (1998). As the children sing or listen to the bouncy tune they must also "do your moves one by one." A, arch, B, bend, C, clap, D, droop, and so on. He explains that "as the children shift from shape to shape, they develop balance, coordination, strength, and endurance; learn the elements of movement; and gain a sense of mastery of their bodies and spatial relationships. They develop confidence and self-esteem because their ideas and creative expressions are valued" (pp. 13–14).

To help children become involved in creative movement, you can start by having them stand in one place while moving their bodies. Play records with words that tell children what to do or you can sing out a movement word to any instrumental music. Accept any movement children make, whether or not it illustrates the movement

---

CREATIVE MOVEMENT CHECKLIST

Child's Name_____**Date**_____

_____ Engages in structured movement activities led by teacher

_____ Makes body movements while standing in one place

_____ Makes creative movements while moving across the floor

_____ Participates in group movement activities

_____ Moves creatively on own or with another child

_____ Moves to imitate particular animal, person, or object

_____ Uses prop (ribbon, scarf, hoop, balloon) to do creative movement

_____ Engages in unstructured movement activities

_____ Moves freely to music or drumbeats

_____ Has favorite song(s) for doing creative movement

_____ Uses arm, hand, leg, feet, body movements to express feelings

_____ Makes up own movements

Figure 4–4   Creative Movement Checklist

Permission is granted by the publisher to reproduce this checklist for evaluation and record keeping.

word. They may not have any idea what a word like *arch* means, or how a person should make an arch movement with their bodies. If you are modeling the word *arch,* children may copy your movement, or they may not. The purpose of the activity should be enjoyment of moving to music, not the accuracy of the movements. Once children get the idea, have them move across the floor doing movements to the words they hear. Basic movement words include: walk, run, jump, hop, gallop, leap, roll, crawl, clap, bend, wiggle, swing, shake, turn, twist, tiptoe, freeze. Use one word at a time until children have learned to make the movement, before proceeding to the next word.

When children are familiar with the basic movement words, Palmer suggests adding some colorful variations such as: "bounce, bubble, crinkle, crouch, dangle, dart, fling, glide, lunge, melt, ooze, plunge, quiver, rise, scamper, scatter, wobble, and zoom" (p. 14). Children love fun words like this and should soon be making up silly motions to go with them. You and they can also make up motion words to familiar tunes and then act them out while singing. For example, to "Row, Row, Row Your Boat":

Hop, hop, hop around,
Round and round the room;
Wobbly, wobbly, wobbly, wobbly,
Stop or you'll go boom!

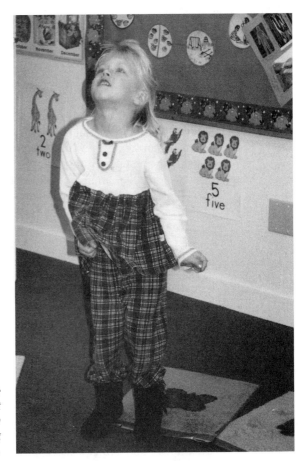

To help children become involved in creative movement you can start by having them stand in one place while moving their bodies to music.

Books to Read

Reading an appropriate book may help to get your children started making motions that illustrate words. Try reading *Cosmo Zooms* (Howard, 1999) about the little dog who wasn't very good at anything like the other dogs on his street, until he lay down on a skateboard by accident, and off he zoomed. Can your children zoom around the room like Cosmo to some cool skateboard music? Another simple book full of wonderful dance words showing colorful children rapping, tapping, gliding, and jiving to the beat is *Twist With a Burger, Jitter With a Bug* (Lowery, 1995). Be sure to play some catchy tunes when you read it because children are sure to want to get up and dance.

Imitating Animals

Once they understand the concept of moving to music, children can begin on their own with something familiar to imitate in their own way. Let them move like familiar animals. Put up pictures of dogs, cats, birds, rabbits, mice, guinea pigs, snakes, beetles, and spiders around the room at the children's eye level. Let them try to move on all fours like one of the animals. Do it to appropriate music such as Hap Palmer's *Animal Antics* or *Sally the Swinging Snake,* or from recordings such as *Animal Walks* or *Walk Like the Animals* from educational supply catalogs such as *Constructive Playthings* (phone: 1-800-448-4114). Encourage the children to watch how classroom pets move. But be sure you accept whatever movements they make as their own interpretations of animal motions.

Perhaps one or two children will want to demonstrate their own movements while the rest clap a rhythm. You may want to tap on a tambourine or drum as children move like animals. Follow the rhythm established by the children rather than making your beats faster or slower. Young children have difficulty following an outside beat at first and usually move to their own inner rhythm.

Books to Read

They may want to try certain kinds of movements without music, such as crawling like snakes or worms, leaping like cats or tigers, or waddling like ducks. Picture books such as the previously mentioned *Pretend You're a Cat* (Marzollo, 1990) can also motivate children to move like animals. Your youngsters may want to put on animal ears or a paper bag animal mask, or paint their faces to look like animals as the children do in the story. If dinosaurs have taken over your classroom, then *Saturday Night at the Dinosaur Stomp* (Shields, 1997) is the book for your children. After hearing the story, have them represent their favorite dinosaurs doing the Triassic Twist, the Brontosaurus Bump, the Raptor Rap, or the Jurassic Jump to music with a deep bass drum beat.

For children who are still uncomfortable with creative movement, read them *Giraffes Can't Dance* (Andreae, 1999), about Gerald Giraffe with his crooked knees and long skinny legs whom the other animals make fun of at the Jungle Dance because he is so awkward—until he finds he can twirl and swirl and dance to the moon music all by himself. Or as he tells the others: "We all can dance, when we find the music that we love." Have your children bring in some of their own music.

Other Motions

Awkward or shy children can often be enticed to engage in movement activities if they have an object to hide behind as they make their motions; ribbons, scarves, paper streamers, hula hoops, or balloons can be used. Then the focus is on the object, not the child. Put out movement props like these for everyone to choose from. Have them move around the room slowly at first and then faster to music or tambourine beats.

Bring in a pair of red shoes and read *Red Dancing Shoes* (Patrick, 1993), the lively story of a little African American girl whose grandmama brings her a pair of red dancing shoes. After watching her twirling and spinning her way through the story, does anyone want to try the red shoes? Put on a tape and let them dance. *My Best Shoes* (Burton, 1994) has a different girl or boy on every two pages moving with a different pair of shoes: high shoes, tap shoes, play shoes, old shoes, bright and shiny blue shoes. Have children choose a pair from your dress-up center and strut their stuff.

Some children feel free enough in the beginning to move like trees in the wind, like ocean waves, or like lightning in a thunder storm, but others need to try more structured movements before they feel free enough to let go and move creatively.

Have them try to move across the room silently, then heavily, then slowly, and then rapidly. Can they be a plane moving down the runway, an eagle soaring through the sky, or a skier going downhill? Eventually they may be able to express emotions such as happiness, sadness, anger, and surprise in their creative movements.

Sometimes the music itself creates the mood for movement. Play nature music on tape cassettes and see what happens. Some of the music cassettes available include Hap Palmer's *Quiet Places* and *Sea Gulls* from *Constructive Playthings*. Do not force children who are not ready to join the group. The activity should always be fun for individuals, not embarrassing. The children who do not participate can observe and may later try out their own movements. Hold the hand of a nonparticipant and swing it back and forth while watching the others move to music. Leave animal pictures and movement props in the music corner along with music tapes and a tambourine to encourage children to try out body movements on their own.

SUMMARY

To promote children's physical development, you should determine their needs at the outset and then provide appropriate materials and activities. The use of checklists of large and small motor skills and creative movement for informal observation of children helps the classroom worker to assess more clearly each child's motor ability. Then the teacher can make individual plans based on the child's needs by using the child's strengths as a starting place.

A child with a particular developmental need should not be singled out for special help but should be included in small-group activities designed for that child but worthwhile for others as well. Getting children involved in creative movement activities is also described, with special focus on starting with movement words. Ideas for imitating animals, using books to motivate movement, using props, moving to music, and making up their own movements help children develop physically and creatively.

LEARNING ACTIVITIES

1. Read Chapter 4, Advancing Physical Skills, and write out answers to Question Sheet 4.

2. Meet with your trainer or college instructor and discuss answers to Question Sheet 4.

3. Read one or more of the references cited or suggested readings. Then add 10 cards to your file, with specific ideas for helping children develop large and small motor skills. Include the reference source on each card.

4. Assess each child's large motor skills using the checklist in Figure 4–1.

5. On the basis of your results, construct a game, bring in materials, or conduct an activity to promote the large motor skills of children who need help as suggested in the text.

6. Assess each child's small motor skills using the checklist in Figure 4–3.

7. On the basis of your results, construct a game, bring in materials, or conduct an activity to promote the small motor skills of children who need help as suggested in the text.

8. Help a child who has not been involved in creative movement try standing in place and moving to a "movement word."

9. Read a book to the children that will lead them into a creative movement activity as described in the text.

10. Complete the Chapter 4 Evaluation Sheet and return it to your trainer or college supervisor.

QUESTION SHEET 4

1. How can you provide for children who seem awkward when they walk or have difficulty balancing?

2. What kinds of balancing activities can you provide that include both children who use a wheelchair and the rest of the class?

3. What should you do about children who have difficulty skipping?

4. What are two jumping activities children can do within the classroom?

5. What kinds of equipment can children use inside the classroom to develop climbing skills?

6. How can you help children develop the skills of throwing and catching?

7. If only one child in your classroom has difficulty throwing and catching, what should you do?

8. How can you best help a left-handed child?

9. What are the specific small motor skills necessary for young children to develop?

10. How would you help a child learn to cut with scissors?

11. How do cooking activities promote small motor development? Be specific.

12. What are some homemade materials that can promote small motor development? How?

13. Describe a beginning activity to encourage creative movement with children.

14. How might you engage a shy child in creative movement activities?

15. What should you do if children refuse to join in a movement activity?

REFERENCES

Davies, M. A. (2000). Learning . . . The beat goes on. *Childhood Education, 76*(3), 148–153.

Gardner, H. (1993). *Frames of mind: The theory of multiple intelligences.* New York: Basic.

Leithead, M. (1996). Happy hammering. . . . A hammering activity center with built-in success. *Young Children, 51*(3), 12.

Miller, S. E. (1999). Balloons, blankets, and balls: Gross-motor activities to use indoors. *Young Children, 54*(5), 58–63.

Palmer, H. (2001). The music, movement, and learning connection. *Young Children, 56*(5), 13–17.

Pica, R. (1997). Beyond physical development: Why young children need to move. *Young Children, 52*(6), 4–11.

Sanders, S. W. (1992). *Designing preschool movement programs.* Champaign, IL: Human Kinetics.

Sanders, S. W., & Yongue, B. (1998). Challenging movement experiences for young children. *Dimensions of Early Childhood, 26*(1), 9–16.

Staley, L., & Portman, P. A. (2000). Red Rover, Red Rover: It's time to move over. *Young Children, 55*(1), 67–72.

SUGGESTED READINGS

Beaty, J. J. (2002). *Observing development of the young child.* Upper Saddle River, NJ: Merrill/Prentice Hall.

Benzwie, T. (1987). *A moving experience: Dance for lovers of children and the child within.* Tucson, AZ: Zephyr Press.

Bond, K., & Deans, J. (1997). Eagles, reptiles and beyond: A co-creative journey in dance. *Childhood Education, 73*(6), 366–371.

Griffin, C., & Rinn, B. (1998). Enhancing outdoor play with an obstacle course. *Young Children, 53*(3), 18–23.

Javernick, E. (1988). Johnny's not jumping: Can we help obese children? *Young Children, 43*(2), 18–23.

Koff, S. R. (2000). Toward a definition of dance education. *Childhood Education, 77*(1), 26–31.

Pica, R. (1995). *Experiences in movement with music, activities, and theory.* Albany, NY: Delmar.

Poest, C. A., Williams, J. R., Witt, D. W., & Atwood, M. E. (1990). Challenge me to move: Large muscle development in young children. *Young Children, 45*(5), 4–10.

Roger, L. (1996). Adding movement throughout the day. *Young Children, 51*(3), 4–6.

Weikart, P. S. (1998). Facing the challenge of motor development. *Child Care Information Exchange, 121,* 60–62.

CHILDREN'S BOOKS

Andreae, G. (1999). *Giraffes can't dance.* New York: Orchard.

Arnold, T. (1987). *No jumping on the bed!* New York: Dial.

Arnold, T. (1995). *Five ugly monsters.* New York: Scholastic.

Burton, J. E. (1994). *My best shoes.* New York: Tambourine.

Dale, P. (1987). *Bet you can't.* New York: Lippincott.

Hindley, J. (1994). *Funny walks.* New York: BridgeWater Books.

Howard, A. (1999). *Cosmo zooms.* San Diego: Harcourt Brace.

Lankford, M. D. (1992). *Hopscotch around the world.* New York: Morrow.

Lively, P. (1999). *One Two Three Jump!* New York: Margaret K. McElderry Books.

Lowery, L. (1995). *Twist with a burger, jitter with a bug.* Boston: Houghton Mifflin.

Marzollo, J. (1990). *Pretend you're a cat.* New York: Dial.

Matura, M. (1988). *Moon jump.* New York: Knopf.

McKissack, P. C. (1988). *Mirandy and Brother Wind.* New York: Knopf.

Patrick, D. L. (1993). *Red dancing shoes.* New York: Tambourine.

Rabe, B. (1981). *The balancing girl.* New York: E. P. Dutton.

Reid, M. S. (1997). *A string of beads.* New York: Dutton.

Rosen, M. (1989). *We're going on a bear hunt.* New York: McElderry.

Shields, C. D. (1997). *Saturday night at the dinosaur stomp.* Cambridge, MA: Candlewick.

Taback, S. (1999). *Joseph had a little overcoat.* New York: Viking.

Trapani, I. (1993). *The itsy bitsy spider.* Boston: Whispering Coyote Press.

Wood, A. (1992). *Silly Sally.* San Diego: Harcourt Brace.

MUSIC DISTRIBUTORS

Constructive Playthings, 1227 East 119th St., Grandview, MO, 64030.

Lakeshore Learning Materials, 2695 E. Dominguez St., Carson, CA, 90749.

VIDEOTAPES

Indiana Steps Ahead. (Producer). *New games for child care settings.* Washington, DC: National Association for the Education of Young Children. (#896; in Spanish #896S).

Indiana Steps Ahead. (Producer). *Structured play: Gross motor activities for everyday.* Washington, DC: National Association for the Education of Young Children. (#883; in Spanish #883S).

National Association for the Education of Young Children. *Learning can be fun (Ella Jenkins).* Washington, DC: Author (#851).

CHAPTER 4 EVALUATION SHEET
ADVANCING PHYSICAL SKILLS

1. Student _____

2. Trainer _____

3. Center where training occurred _____

4. Beginning date _____ Ending date _____

5. Describe what student did to accomplish General Objective.

   _____

   _____

6. Describe what student did to accomplish Specific Objectives.

   Objective 1 _____

   _____

   Objective 2 _____

   _____

   Objective 3 _____

   _____

7. Evaluation of student's Learning Activities

   _____   _____

Comments:

   _____

   _____

   _____

   _____

   _____

   _____

   _____

   _____

   _____

Permission is granted by the publisher to reproduce this checklist for evaluation and record keeping.

Advancing Cognitve
Skills

GENERAL OBJECTIVE

To promote children's cognitive development by involving them in exploring their world

SPECIFIC OBJECTIVES

____ Helps children develop curiosity about their world through sensory exploration

____ Helps children develop basic concepts about their world by classifying, comparing, and counting objects in it

____ Helps children apply basic concepts about the natural world through hands-on experiences

Cognitive skills are thinking skills that grow out of children's need to know. In the past, many preschool programs downplayed this important area of child development. Somehow we believed we should not teach children to learn until they entered elementary school at age 5 or 6. The preschool, we declared, should be concerned principally with children's play.

We were right about children's play, but we were very wrong about their learning. Now we know better. Now we realize that young children learn through play. Unlike play for adults, young children's play is not only for their recreation but also for their learning: for their trying out and finding out what makes things tick. It is essential that preschool teachers understand this about children's cognitive abilities: that children develop them through their hands-on playful exploration of materials, animals, plants, fish, birds, and insects, both inside and outside of the classroom.

To understand what they are discovering in their sensory exploration, young children form basic concepts about their world. These cognitive concepts help them answer questions such as these: How big is it? (size), What does it look like? (shape, color), What kind is it? (classification), and How many are there? (number). Once they can answer these questions, they are able to apply this information to the world around them, finally making sense of their discoveries. Thus, to promote children's cognitive development, teachers must provide children with all sorts of materials and opportunities, as well as the motivation for this sort of playful exploration.

Because cognitive development involves science and math, teachers must find ways to overcome their own reluctance about science and math in case they feel unprepared in these fields. Science for preschool children is simply *a process for finding out.* Math provides *the basic concepts to be used in this process.* Together they equip young explorers with the necessary tools for making sense of their world. An exciting prospect, isn't it?

HELPS CHILDREN DEVELOP CURIOSITY ABOUT THEIR WORLD THROUGH SENSORY EXPLORATION

Preschool children are born explorers. Even as infants, they come with all the necessary equipment to be great discoverers: inquisitive eyes, nose, mouth, tongue, lips, ears, fingers, and toes. In addition to such an array of sensory apparatus, each child also starts out with a strong natural drive or curiosity to put this equipment to good use. They want to find out about everything. Children are forever trying to poke, pry, bite, chew, lick, rub, pinch, sniff, stare at, listen to, or examine playfully in great detail any object or situation they come into contact with. As noted in Chapter 3, we call this initial investigation of new things *manipulation.*

This is how youngsters learn about themselves and their world. They have to touch and test and pull things apart. They may also throw or drop breakable objects, not to be naughty, but to find out what happens when objects hit the floor. Young children are true scientific explorers of their environment. As Humphryes (2000) tells us:

> Children between the ages of birth and six are sensorial explorers; they take in knowledge best through their senses. They gain better understanding when they involve themselves in activities that bring them into *direct* contact with the natural world. (p. 16)

Yet some 3-, 4- and 5-year-olds seem to make no use of their sensory equipment in exploring the world around them. They don't seem to notice anything new or different in the classroom. In fact, they show little interest in their surroundings. Since we know they were born with a great natural curiosity, we can only surmise that somewhere along the way they lost it.

Perhaps their curiosity was mistaken for mischief by the adults in their lives, and they were punished for it. Perhaps adults never took the time to answer their questions or to support their exploratory activities. Whatever the reason, it is now up to you, the teachers, assistants, and student teachers in preschool classrooms, to reawaken children's curiosity and sense of wonder if they have lost it or to direct it toward exploring their environment if they have not.

Assessing Children's Curiosity

What about the children in your classroom? Do they still retain their natural sense of wonder? Do they make comments or ask questions about new materials? Take a moment to observe their actions when they first enter their new environment. Listen also

Take a moment to observe the curiosity of each of your children when they see new materials. How does each respond?

to the questions they ask. The Children's Curiosity Checklist, in Figure 5–1, will help you to observe and assess the curiosity displayed by each of your children. Then you can begin planning activities to promote this important characteristic.

You should soon be able to identify those children with a drive to explore and those who seem to have little interest in the new things around them. It is up to you to provide new and intriguing materials and activities. Then be sure to find ways to motivate uninterested children in as many of these activities as possible.

You might begin by bringing in several pieces of tree bark you have found: a piece of sycamore bark (this tree sheds its bark periodically); a piece of maple bark; a piece of shagbark hickory bark; or any one of a number of other tree barks (e.g., white birch, willow, cottonwood, or pine). Do not peel the bark from a tree to cause damage but instead look for pieces of bark shed naturally or from a broken branch. Place each of three different barks on a piece of colored backing paper on top of the room dividers or other flat surfaces in different parts of the room. Then wait to see what happens.

Children's Curiosity Checklist

Child's Name_____Date_____

_____ Notices new materials

_____ Investigates new objects

_____ Asks "what," "where," "when," and "how" questions

_____ Wants to know "why" about things that happen

_____ Uses senses (sight, hearing, smelling, touching, tasting) to explore things

_____ Likes to do experiments

_____ Can compare one object with another

_____ Uses science tools (magnets, magnifying glasses, binoculars)

_____ Uses math tools (balance, tape measure, abacus, cash register, timers, counters)

_____ Plays matching, counting games

_____ Makes collections, charts, records

_____ Is involved with classroom pets, aquarium, plants, insects

_____ Chooses books about science, counting, animals, plants, ecology

---

Figure 5–1   Children's Curiosity Checklist

Permission is granted by the publisher to reproduce this checklist for evaluation and record keeping.

Does anyone notice one of the bark pieces? More than one? If someone points out one, ask them if they can find any others. Be sure to keep track on your checklist of each child who notices these new items, asks questions about them, or handles them. When several children have shown this interest, gather these youngsters into a small group in your science discovery center along with one or two other children who have shown little interest. Then try to extend everyone's curiosity with a few *sensory* questions.

Sensory Questions

Sensory questions ask what things look like, feel like, smell like, taste like, and sound like. They are not questions with a right or wrong answer. Instead, they should engage children in using their senses to explore new things.

Show them one of the bark pieces and ask, "What does this look like to you?" (sight). Accept any answers they give, but keep on asking questions. "What does it feel like to you?" (touch). Pass the bark around. "What does it smell like?" (smell). "What does it sound like when you tap it?" (sound).

Repeat the answers the children give. You might even want to write down what each child says on newsprint or a chalkboard. "Tracy says it looks like a piece of wood. How can you tell, Tracy? You say wood is brown like that and sort of rumply on top. Yes. Ben says it's a scrap of wood. How can you tell, Ben? Oh, your mom collects scraps of wood and leaves for her garden. Okay Ramon says it feels like wood and smells like wood, but it's really tree bark. Is tree bark wood? How can you tell, Ramon? You're right, Ramon, we do have wood with bark on it right over in our woodworking center. Yes, our tree stumps. Good for all of you for using your eyes, and fingers, and even your noses to find out what it was."

Questions and responses like this start the cognitive thinking processes in yourself and your children. If you do not hear children asking such sensory questions about the new objects you bring into the classroom, start asking them yourself. Your job is to reawaken children's natural curiosity and encourage them to find out things for themselves. But you may need to serve as a behavior model of curiosity to get them started.

Have you retained your own childlike sense of curiosity? If not, you must first reawaken this sense of wonder in yourself. Look around the room when the children are not present and try to see the classroom from their perspective. Get down on your knees for a better view. What is one thing you notice that might attract the attention of a 4-year-old?

Assume that one of the things you notice is wood shavings and curls under the woodworking table. Now pretend you are a new child visiting the room for the first time. What would you want to know about such things if you had never seen them before?

What are they?

What do they feel like?

Where did they come from?

What are they for?

If you are a curious child, you would probably go over and pick up some of the shavings. You might crush one in your hand to see what it feels like or maybe put some on your head for curls and look at yourself in the dramatic play area mirror.

Have any of your children tried doing this? What happens to the wood shavings on the floor? Are they usually swept up and thrown away? Ask your children what they could be used for in the classroom. If the children are learning about recycling things (and they should be), they will be able to suggest some creative uses for such scraps. Does anyone make any of these suggestions?

Put them in the collage basket for art.

Put them in our terrarium.

Put them in the guinea pig's cage for floor covering.

Questions and responses like these start the cognitive thinking processes in yourself and your children. If you do not hear such questions in the classroom, then ask them yourself. What other kinds of questions are the children asking? Get into the habit of writing them down on the Children's Curiosity Checklist you are recording for each child.

For example, Ramon asks, "Why do we always have to have orange juice for snack time?" Later he wants to know, "Where is Mrs. Appleton? Isn't she coming to our room anymore?" And still later, "Is this a piece of bark, too? I found it under the woodworking table. But it doesn't look like the other bark."

From this record of Ramon's questions and checklist responses, you begin to realize that he is a curious boy who remembers things, notices changes as well as new materials, and wants to find out about them. He is even able to make comparisons about new objects with something he has seen previously. You will want to provide Ramon with further opportunities to explore, or you may want to team him as a model with another child who has not shown this curiosity.

Shelley, on the other hand, asks only, "Can I play with the baby buggy now?" a permission question, not a sensory question. She does not seem to notice the tree bark displayed on the science table as Ramon did, nor does she comment on the new arrangement of the dramatic play area.

The questions children ask tell us many things about them. First of all, they tell us if the children are curious. Children who are not curious ask few how, why, or where questions, or they may not ask any questions at all. If their questions contain few sensory terms, we realize they are probably not engaged in sensory exploration. Then it is up to us to reawaken their curiosity by helping them start thinking in terms of sensory questions. We may need to start the questioning process for such children. Children closely imitate the adult models around them. If we are successful in our own questioning, many of the children may soon copy us.

Open-ended sensory questions are the most valuable. They require children to think and imagine and explore with their senses to come up with an answer. The answers to open-ended questions are never right or wrong; they are merely possibilities. They ask a child to look at an ordinary situation from a new perspective—from the point of view of a scientist trying out and testing the object or idea. You do not need to know the answers to these questions at the outset. Instead, you should become familiar with the method scientists use to find out answers. Then together you and the children can be scientists searching for answers to questions about the fascinating objects and ideas in the world around you.

Scientific Inquiry: The Guessing-Game Method (A Higher-Level Thinking Process)

How do you find out the answers to the questions you and the children have posed? Scientists also begin their explorations of new things or ideas with questions. Then they follow a particular sequence of problem-solving steps to find out the answers. Sprung, Froschl, and Campbell (1985) suggest the following steps:

1. State a question or problem.
2. Predict the answer.
3. Conduct experiments.
4. Observe results.
5. Make conclusions.
6. Document final results.

You and the children in your care can have an exciting time following this same sequence. Conducting a scientific inquiry is like going on a treasure hunt. Maybe you'll find something, but maybe you will not. Whatever happens, it is the hunt itself that makes the project worthwhile. In other words, it is the *process* of questioning and trying to find out that is most important, and not the *product* or answer. Translated into early childhood terms, the scientific inquiry includes the following steps:

1. Ask the question you want answered.
2. Guess what the answer may be.
3. Decide how to find out and try it.
4. Watch what happens.
5. Talk about what happened and whether your answer turned out right or wrong.
6. Record what you did and what happened.

What scientific inquiry can turn out to be for young children is a wonderful guessing game, just the type of fun activity that they would invent for themselves if scientists had not already done so. This is another reason that you as a teacher of young children need to be alert to children's curiosity about things. It could lead you all on a discovery trip you would not want to miss.

One day Jessica asked her teacher, "Why is our aquarium getting all dirty on the inside?" The teacher could have responded with, "Oh, I guess it needs to be cleaned." But she realized that this was an excellent opportunity for all of them to learn something new through sensory exploration. Although the teacher knew how to take care of an aquarium, she was not sure what was making the glass dirty. Finding out could be a scientific adventure for all of them.

The teacher talked with the children about Jessica's question. Most of them said they thought that the fish were making the aquarium dirty. They all agreed that they would like to find out. The teacher then asked, "What would happen if we took a glassful of water out of the aquarium and let it sit on the shelf? Would the glass get dirty like the inside of the aquarium?"

Some children thought that maybe it would. She asked them why they thought this, but they did not know. Other children, however, were very insistent that the water glass would not get dirty because there would not be any fish in it. The teacher was excited to hear this comment because it told her that these children were really thinking. Whether right or wrong, they had a reason for their answer involving cause and effect, a new concept for many preschoolers.

The teacher wrote down the steps for finding out on a large sheet of newsprint. She left space under each step to record what the children said and did. Although these were preliterate children who did not yet read or write, they were fascinated to see the teacher writing down what they said and then reading it back to them.

1. *Our question:* Why is our aquarium getting dirty on the glass inside?
2. *Our guess about the answer:* The fish are making it dirty.
3. *How can we find out?* Put some aquarium water in a glass without any fish.

4. *Watch what happens. Use your senses.* The glass began to get dirty in seven days. The "dirt" spread over the glass. Jessica says the dirt felt greasy when she touched it. She says it smelled bad, too. Ramon says the magnifying glass made the dirt look green.

5. *Talk about what happened. Did we guess correctly?* The glass got dirty without any fish in the water. The fish didn't make the glass get dirty. We didn't answer the question on why it got dirty.

6. *Record what we did and what happened.* Listen to our tape: "Aquarium Water Experiment."

After the experiment was finished, the teacher put a blank tape in the cassette player and had every child who wanted to speak into the microphone and tell what they did and what happened. Then she recorded the date and time, and afterward she labeled the tape "Aquarium Water Experiment."

The children may not have been able to read the words the teacher had written, but they understood what had happened. They were excited to contribute to the tape recording, and afterward they listened to the tape every chance they got.

"Did we learn anything from our experiment?" the teacher asked. Children made such comments as these:

The glass got dirty anyway.

The fish didn't make the glass get dirty.

The water smelled bad.

The aquarium is still dirty and we need to clean it.

We still don't know why the glass got dirty.

Don't be too concerned if you do not find out all of the answers. At this stage of their development, children are more interested in the *process* of finding out rather than the results. Finally, Ramon asked, "Why is the dirt so green and slimy? I think the water is polluted." Four-year-old Ramon, with his inquisitive nature and remarkable vocabulary ("green and slimy" and "water is polluted"), was leading them all on a further science adventure. What should they do next?

The teacher brought in a new book that might help them find out more: *Pet Care Guide for Kids: FISH* (Evans, 1993). Brightly illustrated with color photographs of fish as well as children setting up various types of aquariums, the book was an instant hit. Although the children could not read it, they could follow the illustrated steps for aquarium care quite easily. The teacher read the words aloud.

Because their classroom tropical aquarium had been started the previous year, these particular children had not participated in the setup process and selection of the fish. No wonder they had shown little interest in the fish tank until Jessica asked her question about the tank getting dirty. Children must have hands-on experiences like this one from the beginning if they are to learn.

Where will their further explorations take them? The sensitive teacher will follow the lead of the children, listening carefully to what they are saying and asking and then guiding them to find their own answers by using the "guessing-game method" of scientific inquiry. With children like this, such inquiry will surely take them in the direction of learning about topics like these:

How water gets polluted

What makes algae grow

How to keep a "balanced" aquarium

How many fish to have

How much food to feed the fish

Using snails and algae-eating fish

The list of topics is almost endless when we allow and encourage curious children to take the lead with hands-on exploration of things they can see, smell, hear, taste, and touch.

Equipment and Materials in the Classroom

To arouse children's curiosity, they need something to be curious about. Children will often bring in an interesting item from home or something they have picked up on the way to the center. This can be the beginning of their exploration, especially if you display it attractively as a center of attention.

At the outset, however, it is often up to the adult classroom worker to bring in new materials to stimulate children's curiosity. Set up a special table or countertop to feature a new or unusual item that you or the children bring and label it the "Discovery Center." Feature a new item every week, placing it on an attractive backing as you did the bark. Add science tools for children to use in exploring the new item: a magnifying glass, a balance for weighing, a magnet, a measuring tape.

Once you have captured the children's interest in a new object, be sure you are prepared to help children follow up their exploration. For instance, if other children are as intrigued as Ramon was by the bark you brought, you can take them outside to explore living trees by touch. Then they may enjoy doing a bark rubbing by taping light paper against the tree and rubbing the side of the crayon over it.

Before they do the rubbing, ask them a guessing-game-method question. Ask them to guess (predict) what the rubbing will look like? Does anyone guess that it will look like the bark underneath? Because everything in their world is new to them, many are not really sure what will happen when they do something. After their rubbings are finished, have them check to see whether they guessed correctly. Prediction questions are excellent stimulators for young children's thinking.

The bark-rubbing activity may start a flurry of art rubbings back in the classroom. If you have set up your art area for children's free access to materials as suggested in Chapter 3, then be prepared to have rubbings made of all sorts of classroom objects.

Feature a new item every week in the Discovery Center to stimulate children's curiosity.

To continue the children's use of exploring through touch, bring in a piece of driftwood or a seashell—but only if your community is near a water area where such items are common. It is essential to begin with something familiar to the children. Keep the item in a bag and ask a child to insert a hand in the bag and try to guess what the object is by feel. Ask children to bring in their own "secret objects" in bags and challenge the others to guess what they are touching.

Field Trips Around the Building

The immediate environment of the center offers unlimited opportunities for children to explore and discover. Take the children on an outside walk around the building. Give them each a paper bag for collecting anything that strikes their fancy. Take a tape recorder with you to record the sounds of the environment and any questions or comments the children make. Take a camera to record the scenes. Humphryes (2000) suggests:

Observation excursions are fun with all ages of children. While out in a natural setting like your backyard or playground, ask the children to observe one selected item, such as a stream, a one-square-foot microcosm (use a string to mark this), or a cloud, for five minutes. Then ask them: Is it alive? How do you know? What does it feel like? Does it move? What does it do? If you kept it, what would happen? If you stepped on it, what would happen? (p. 17)

What will you find out? Once again you will learn who are the curious children. You will also find out whether you yourself are tuned in to children and their interests. Was it a child who pointed out the dandelion growing from the crack in the sidewalk, or was it you? Once again you may have to get down on your knees to look at the world from the perspective of a 3-year-old before you can become a behavior model for exploring.

Field trips need not be elaborate, all-day, long-distance affairs. Brief ventures out or around the building are best because this is the environment the children are most directly involved with and want to find out about. Their own personal environment is always more meaningful to children than a visit to a remote and distant spot they may never see again. Sometimes adults do not understand the young child's point of view when it comes to field trips.

A trip to the basement of the center building may be more exciting to them than a trip to the zoo. After all, a basement is more immediate—and more mysterious! Most adults have little interest in basements, but think what young children can learn about heat and water and electricity!

One class made exciting discoveries all year long on their monthly "field trip to a tree." They chose a horse chestnut tree on the playground and visited it once a month throughout the fall, winter, and spring. They took photographs, made bark rubbings, pressed leaves, collected horse chestnuts, made necklaces of the nuts, recorded on tape the sound of wind in the leaves, and learned about the birds that nested in the tree.

Book to Read

Their teacher also brought in a fascinating nonfiction book called *The Tree* (Jeunesse & de Bourgoing, 1989), a story for young children about a horse chestnut tree. She realized that this small sturdy book with laminated pages was just right for carrying along on field trips. It had one large illustration per page, with a transparent overlay between pages showing another aspect of the nut, leaf, or tree. The text began with a "scientific inquiry question," just the way the children usually started. Page one, a clear overlay showing a large green chestnut burr asked, "What is hidden inside the green and prickly covering?" The children had to guess. Then they turned the overlay to reveal a shiny brown horse chestnut on the next page. The book traced the tree's seasonal growth one page at a time. Best of all, it also showed the tree in summer, when the children would not be able to visit it with the class.

What else can you do on a field trip? If the children have not already begun to do so, you can start by asking exploratory questions involving the senses: "Close your eyes and what do you hear?" "Does anyone smell anything different?" or "Put your hand on this. What does it feel like to you?" Take photos. Make rubbings. Make a tape recording of the sounds. Take something back with you to the classroom to help children remember, and clarify, and try to understand what they have seen and done. Have children empty their collecting bags when they get back. Have them talk about what they collected. Perhaps they would like to display the objects by making a collage of them or dictating a story about them. If a new interest emerges out of the experience, plan to follow it further with the children using the guessing-game method.

HELPS CHILDREN DEVELOP BASIC CONCEPTS
ABOUT THEIR WORLD BY CLASSIFYING, COMPARING,
AND COUNTING OBJECTS IN IT

As young children begin to explore the world around them, they need to establish some sort of order out of all the incoming data. To make sense of the new information, they need to develop basic concepts about their discoveries. How do they do this? Lind (1996) tells us:

> Concepts are acquired through children's active involvement with the environment. As they explore their surroundings, they actively construct their own knowledge. (p. 17)

As they learn to sort the things they find into categories, compare them with one another, and count them, children develop the basic cognitive concepts that make the world around them meaningful. To keep track of each child's development of basic concepts use the checklist in Figure 5–2, Cognitive Concepts Checklist.

Sorting and Classifying Objects that Are Alike

Adults often assume that preschool children know intuitively how things are alike and what makes them different. This is not usually the case. Young children see objects in general before they notice specific details. You can help them develop perceptual and

---

Cognitive Concepts Checklist

Child's Name_____**Date**_____

_____ Sorts out from a collection the objects that are alike

_____ Matches unit blocks on the floor with block outlines on shelves

_____ Identifies the biggest and the smallest from a collection of toy dinosaurs, trucks, animals, or people figures

_____ Identifies the following shapes by finding examples in the classroom of: circles, squares, rectangles, triangles

_____ Identifies the following colors by pointing out clothing the children are wearing in red, yellow, blue, green, orange, brown

_____ Counts to 10 or to 20 accurately

_____ Counts the number of children present accurately

_____ Counts out accurately different numbers of items according to written numerals

---

Figure 5–2   Cognitive Concepts Checklist

Permission is granted by the publisher to reproduce this checklist for evaluation and record keeping.

thinking skills through activities that encourage them first to find which objects in a group are the same. They will be looking at the items in general and not for specific details.

You need to provide many concrete, three-dimensional games and materials (never workbooks or ditto sheets) in the manipulative/math center that call on children to sort out the items that are alike. Plastic sorting chips, disks, cubes, beads, bears, animals, or fruit are a few of the collections available. Or bring in your own sorting collections of buttons, seashells, or nuts, along with a basket to hold the collection and several plastic bowls for sorting.

At first let the children sort out things that are alike using their own rules. You don't have to mention color, size, shape, or kind. Later, when you are introducing these concepts, challenge them to sort items by a certain concept, say color or size. After a field trip around the building or to a park, children can sort out all the similar items they have collected in their paper bags. Ask them what makes their items alike.

Look around the classroom for other items children can sort for likeness. What about the figures of people in the block center? How will they sort these? By children or community helpers? Or maybe by families? Science collections of seashells, leaves, bark, or rocks can also be sorted. Have children sort small items that are alike into egg carton sections and cover the cartons with clear wrap for display. Leaves that are alike can be pressed between sheets of clear contact paper. Bark pieces that are similar can be placed in a pocket wall chart or fastened to a bulletin board.

By now you should be talking with the children in terms of the categories for sorting, not merely "sorting for likeness." "Josh, can you sort out all the *arches* on the block shelves?" or "Juanita, can you bring me a basket of plastic fruit from the house area food cupboard?"

Sorting should eventually lead into matching for your youngsters. From the start they should be able to match the unit blocks on the floor with the ones on the shelves or by the block outlines you have mounted on each shelf. Many programs keep their manipulative areas stocked with commercial matching games year-round. But you may want to wait before putting out matching boards or lotto games until everyone has learned to sort by likeness.

Comparing Objects by Size, Shape, Color, and Number

Size.   Children's brains seem to pay special attention to the relationships between things. The concept of size is one of those relationships. Learning to understand the property of size helps children make sense out of the new things they are discovering.

There are various orders of size, usually thought of in terms of opposites: big-little, large-small, tall-short, long-short, wide-narrow, thick-thin, fat-thin, or deep-shallow. Direct comparison of objects based on these aspects seems one of the best ways for youngsters to learn size.

Most young children can relate to only one aspect of an object at a time when they are comparing. First they must learn a single concept, say the concept of big, through many games and concrete activities—never with worksheets. Next they can contrast that concept with the concept of little. But don't confuse them by bringing in

"Josh, can you sort out all the arches on the block shelves?"

the concepts of thick-thin or short-tall all at the same time. Give them plenty of time to learn the concept of big as contrasted with the concept of little through all sorts of real, three-dimensional materials before moving on to another pair of opposites.

It makes sense to start with objects in the classroom environment that children can compare and contrast in size. Children need to handle the objects, play with them, and use them in different situations. For instance, can they compare the plastic animals from the accessory shelves in the block center?

Because children seem especially attracted to dinosaurs, why not start with them. Does your collection of plastic dinosaurs show differences in size? Sets of "museum dinosaurs" make this differentiation. Read a dinosaur story to a small group while they hold some of the plastic dinosaurs. Can they tell which is the biggest animal? The smallest?

Books to Read

Bernard Most's (1994) *How Big Were the Dinosaurs?* shows a large picture of a different dinosaur on every page, along with comparisons or measurements the children can relate to. It shows Triceratops with a head bigger than a front door. It takes two hori-

Maybe a child would like to build a home for his biggest dinosaurs in the block center.

zontal pages to show how Supersaurus is longer than a supermarket aisle. Children love to roll these exciting-sounding names around their tongues, and you should have no trouble saying them just as easily from the pronunciation guide following each name. All of the dinosaurs in this book are big, but point out how they are big in different ways.

The concept of little comes in different sizes too. Read Most's (1989) *The Littlest Dinosaur* to acquaint your children with a whole new collection of these beasts, from little Coloradisaurus (kol-or-ADD-ee-saw-russ), only as long as a seesaw, to tiny Mussaurus, smaller than a teddy bear. If this book interests them, follow up with the more dramatic story of *The Smallest Stegosaurus* (Sweat & Phillips, 1993), an exciting and dangerous adventure among the large dinosaurs of his swampside home. Maybe the children would like to build a home for their plastic dinosaurs in the block center or paint a swamp floor mat for them to tromp on.

It is important for children to act out the concepts they are learning, as well. They can pretend to be big or little dinosaurs wearing capes made from different colored cloth or construction paper, with scales marked on them.

Some teachers may think that bringing dinosaurs into the classroom like this can create an out-of-control situation. But children can learn that only certain dinosaurs were fierce. Others were meek and mild. We as teachers need to plug into children's strong interests like this to help them learn appropriate classroom behavior as well as new concepts.

In the wonderfully illustrated *Dinosaur Roar!* (Stickland & Stickland, 1994), each double page shows two dinosaurs portraying opposite characteristics. One roars, but the other squeaks. A little one is fierce, but a big one is meek. Your child "dinosaurs" can also act out these new words and concepts to make them meaningful.

Commercial dinosaur games also include wooden *dinosaur dominoes* in which children must match the dinosaur domino blocks that are alike as they play the game (Constructive Playthings, 13201 Arrington Road, Grandview, MO 64030). What other classroom objects can teach children size concepts in your program?

Shape.   Research shows that children develop concepts in a certain sequence. The concept of shape is one of the earliest to be formed. Young children begin to discriminate objects on the basis of their shape quite early. Be sure to focus on this one concept alone when you first present the idea of shape. Then give children plenty of time and opportunity to make the concept a part of their thinking process before going on to the next concept. In every instance, activities should involve familiar concrete objects at first, not drawings on ditto sheets or in workbooks.

Young children learn through exploring with their senses, but the way they do it is far different from adult scrutiny of a new object. As we have noted, children learn through play. They try out a new object or new concept in a playful way to see what it will do or what they can do with it. Be sure your shape activities provide children with all kinds of hands-on play opportunities for this learning. For children to learn about circles, squares, rectangles, and triangles (the basic shapes), they will, for example, need to play circle games, sing square songs, make triangle hats, and have shape-hunting contests, lotto games, and puzzles. They can sort and pick up unit blocks on the basis of their shapes or mold clay circles and squares and saw wood into different shapes.

Present one shape at a time, for instance, the circle, by filling the classroom with circles. Put paper circles of different sizes, but all the same color, as well as circular cookie cutters and play dough in the art area. In the manipulative area, put out games, puzzles, table blocks, stringing beads, and plastic wheels and gears featuring circles. At the writing table, supply circular forms to be traced, circle peel-offs for decorating envelopes, and the magnetic alphabet letters that are mainly circular in form. Place hula hoops in the large motor area for children to dance in. Place large vinyl adhesive circles on the floor of the block area to see if they will motivate building in circles. Can children find the round cylinder blocks that have circles on their ends?

Computer Programs

Many young children's computer programs feature shapes, although not one shape at a time. They are a good follow-up after children have learned about all the shapes. Plan to introduce new programs one at a time to two children at once seated at the computer. For preschool children, cooperative learning like this is the best way for them to make use of the computer as they learn to take turns, talk together, and teach

each other how the programs work. Stay nearby until you think the children can work the shape program on their own.

Obviously, you need to be familiar with the software yourself to help children access the particular shape activity. Most software these days contains multiple games and activities. Be sure to use only one program at a time until all of the children can operate it. Plan extension activities involving shapes in other learning centers whenever shape programs are in use. The following programs are all CD-ROM software available from Library Video Company, P. O. Box 580, Wynnewood, PA 19096; phone 1-800-843-3620.

Award-winning *Millie's Math House* has playful animal characters interacting in seven games, including building Mouse Houses with squares, triangles, circles, and rectangles; learning about sizes as Little, Middle, and Big try on shoes; decorating cookies with up to 20 jellybeans; counting from 0 to 30 critters in the Number Machine. *Fisher-Price Ready for School: Preschool* teaches letter and number recognition, sorting, sequencing, and more. *Dr. Seuss Preschool* presents valuable lessons in math, reading, and fun with the wacky characters he created. *Disney's Mickey Preschool* teaches counting, ABCs, colors, opposites, and more. The popular *Jumpstart Preschool* includes games that teach numbers, letters, shapes, and colors.

Most computer shape games are good beginning programs for preschool children because they use only one or two keys or a mouse. Computer programs may seem as abstract as ditto sheets, but the children's use of keys to move objects makes them just as valuable as three-dimensional classroom materials. Nevertheless, teachers should also include concrete materials as follow-up learning experiences. Simple shape-finding field trips with a small group of children can also support the classroom shape activities. One program took its children down a city street to search for circles. They took photos of stoplights and street signs. Then the children wanted to go into a used car lot. While such a site held little interest for the adults, it was a new world for the youngsters to explore. The teachers were surprised to find these youngsters more interested in the car wheels than the cars. This should not have been surprising, since young children tend to focus on things at their own eye level. Back in the classroom, the youngsters found circle blocks to use for the snap-block cars they built.

Color.   Although young children seem to talk about colors first, research shows that they develop the color concept shortly after that of shape. Children also name the colors before truly understanding what they mean. You can help them to clarify color concepts just as you did with shapes by starting with one color at a time and providing them with all kinds of games and activities relating to that color. One color at a time, start with the primary colors of red, yellow, and blue, since young children seem to recognize these colors most easily. Then, one at a time, introduce the secondary colors of green, orange when Halloween comes, and pink for Valentine's Day.

To introduce colors successfully, you can relate each color to the children personally in terms of their clothing, shoes, socks, or hats. As you feature each color, check to see which children are wearing that color. Ask if anyone can wear that color tomorrow. Have a color finding search throughout the classroom, looking for that particular color among the block people, animal figures, dinosaurs, dolls, and dress-up clothes. Bring in different color stickers for the children with the color to wear and to attach to the dolls and toys displaying that color.

Books to Read

One classroom used the book *Red Day Green Day* (Kunhardt, 1992) to begin the children's color quest. It is the story of Andrew, who must find and bring a colored item to school for every color day that the teacher announces. He wears red pants for Red Day and brings orange Jell-O for Orange Day. When the color days finally end, Andrew contributes one more thing to the class: his beautiful drawing of all the colors in a rainbow. Color songs, color dances with scarves, guessing games, pegboards, color lotto, food colors in water, and cutting colored construction paper are other activities you can use.

Children with disabilities can learn color concepts along with the other children. Set up the activities as you do everything in your classroom so that children with physical and mental impairments can participate. A child in a wheelchair, for instance, may not be able to do a color dance on her feet, but she can listen to you read the book *Color Dance* (Jonas, 1989) and afterward do her own "color dance" on the wall or ceiling by shining flashlights covered with colored cellophane to the music you play for the other children to dance on their feet.

Feature color concept books in the book area as each color is introduced. *Red Is Best* (Stinson, 1982) gives a fine introduction to this color. Most picture books feature several colors and may be better used after children have learned most of the colors. *Who Said Red?* (Serfozo, 1988) features red, green, blue, and yellow as a girl and boy look for objects displaying these colors outside their house. Another favorite, *My Crayons Talk* (Hubbard, 1996), blasts off with hilarious double-page drawings by the little girl narrator whose crayons can't keep still. Can your children choose a crayon of their own to fill in a page with its own "talk"?

What about mixing colors? Children often learn by accident that mixing two colors together makes a new color. You can set up your easel with only two jars of different primary colors for children to experience this surprising occurrence. On another day, you can put out muffin tins with water and two food colors, then two finger-painting colors at the same table, or two different crayons with paper. What colors will they be? Red and yellow mixed together make orange, red and blue make purple, and blue and yellow make green, the most dramatic change of all.

Light from flashlights, covered with colored cellophane (red, yellow, and blue) can also be mixed together by shining their colored lights on the wall. Have the children predict (guess) what the new color will turn out to be before they start color mixing. The youngest children may not know the names of the secondary colors, but they can guess something.

To support and enhance this learning, children can also flip the color overlay pages of the little book *Colors* (Jeunesse & de Bourgoing, 1989) to see a frog change from blue to green or a squirrel from red to brown. Real creatures can also change colors before the children's eyes. If your classroom includes a salt water aquarium, the youngsters may witness changes in salt water tropical fish from bright to darker colors when it gets dark. Lizards are the champion change-artists, the best known being the chameleon who camouflages itself by changing to the colors of its background.

Computer Programs

Some unique CD-ROM computer programs from Library Video Company (1-800-843-3620) featuring colors include *Green Eggs and Ham*, an animated interactive depiction of Dr. Seuss's classic story, with an activity that challenges children to "Color Match with a Mouse in a House" as they search for brightly colored foods hidden in the kitchen. *Buddy Brush and the Painted Circus* and *Buddy Brush and the Painted Playhouse* incorporates creative and artistic fun with skill building activities such as color identification. In *Jumpstart Artist* young children learn the basics of painting, drawing, crafts, and collages. *The Land Before Time Animated Preschool Adventure* includes shape, pattern, and color recognition games as well as counting and letters. *Shades and JB's Essential Colors & Shapes* introduces children to early color and shape recognition.

Number.   Children encounter the spoken form of numbers long before they understand their meaning. Many can count accurately to 10 or even 20 without having the slightest idea of what 6 or 13 means. They are counting by rote, in other words, repeating a memorized series of number words in a given sequence. This is how learning to count begins. Nursery rhymes such as "One Two, Buckle My Shoe" encourage this skill. So do the following counting books:

Coconut Mon (Milstein, 1995)

Counting Crocodiles (Sierra, 1997)

One Duck Stuck (Root, 1998)

One Lonely Sea Horse (Freymann & Elffers, 2000)

Ten Terrible Dinosaurs (Stickland, 1997) (counts down)

Warthogs in the Kitchen, A Sloppy Counting Book (Edwards, 1998)

Counting in other languages is fun for young children, too. Whether or not you have bilingual children, everyone can learn number names in another language. Perhaps a parent or relative can visit the class and help them to chant the numbers in another language. The picture book *Moja Means One* (Feelings, 1971) introduces the numbers 1 through 10 in Swahili. Another series of counting books illustrates these same numbers in *Count Your Way Through Africa* (Haskins, 1992), *Count Your Way Through China* (Haskins, 1987), *Count Your Way Through the Arab World* (Haskins, 1991), and many others (representing Canada, Germany, India, Italy, Japan, Korea, Mexico, and Russia).

Once children have learned the number names and number order from 1 to 10, they are ready to count things. It may still not be clear to them that 3 means three objects and 7 means seven things. They need to learn the concept of one-to-one correspondence—that is, that each number represents one thing. They can start by counting their fingers. Then they can count the small group of children in each curriculum area. Are they accurate? From there they can practice counting dolls, toys, or

One girl challenged her friend to count all the beans in her container.

any other three-dimensional object that is meaningful to them. Be sure they touch each object they count. Unglaub (1997) notes: "Teaching a child to count isn't teaching her to understand math unless you teach her to touch another object for each additional number (2, 3, etc.)" (p. 48). Children also need to understand that the last number they say represents the total number of objects they counted.

Soon children will go beyond 10 to 20 in their counting. Have the children help you take attendance every day by touching each child in the morning circle as they count. At this point give the youngsters all sorts of counting opportunities. This is not a chore for them; they love it. They may want to count their science collections, for example. How many nuts, shells, leaves, or stones do they have?

One class became so engrossed in counting things that they insisted on counting the ants in the class's ant farm. How could they possibly keep track of all the busy little creatures as they scurried around? Every time children started a count, they lost track of either the ants or the numbers. The teacher suggested that they "tally" each ant that was visible by making a mark. Soon children were going around with pencils and file cards recording a mark for each ant and then counting up the marks. Most preschool children are not at the level of tallying by 5s, but a few may want to attempt it.

Books to Read

To support their counting efforts, this teacher brought in two humorous ant storybooks dealing with counting. *Amazing Anthony Ant* (Philpot & Philpot, 1994) is a cleverly illustrated rhyming story that can be chanted or sung to the tune of "When Johnny Comes Marching Home." The story is about the ants marching one by one and two by two, with Anthony stopping to tie his shoe. *One Hundred Hungry Ants* (Pinczes,

1993), on the other hand, has a long line of ants going to a picnic, with the littlest ant stopping them and dividing the line of ants into two lines, into four lines, and so on, to help them get there quicker. They spend so much time dividing their lines that when they get there, the picnic is gone.

If your children like to tally, give them each a file card and a paper punch. They can punch one hole for every car or truck or bicycle that goes by the window. Another day, paste a picture of the kind of vehicle on each card and take the children out for a vehicle-tallying field trip. Don't forget to have them count up their final tally.

Then begin reading counting books in which number names and number symbols are illustrated by numbers of objects. In the simple book *Joe Can Count* (Ormerod, 1986), a little African American boy counts different animals from 1 to 10 with his fingers. The book *Feast for 10* (Falwell, 1993) shows an African American family going from 1 to 10 by shopping for food items, preparing the meal, and finally having 10 hungry people sitting down to eat.

This may be the time for you to change the signs in the learning centers that regulate the number of children allowed in each. Put number symbols beside the stick figures you may be using. Later, remove the stick figures altogether and use only numerals. Can the correct number of children go to each of the centers? Try it and see. Have someone count how many children are in each center and see if this number agrees with the number sign in the center. As you can see, learning to count is important for children. As Unglaub (1997) explains: "Why is the ability to count rationally so important? If unable to count rationally, the child is not ready to start more formal activities with numbers that lead to mathematical concepts." (p. 48)

Once children have learned to count and you have introduced true number symbols, be sure to give children many opportunities to play with numbers using concrete materials and three-dimensional numbers. Toy cash registers, toy money, stepping-stone numerals, plastic numbers, and computer number games (as discussed under "Shapes") are appropriate activities.

Be aware that when using the computer, young children often confuse the concept of letters and numerals. If the youngsters have been using only letter keys on the computer, you may have to help them locate and learn the number keys when they are ready to use number programs. Some teachers have reproduced their own giant computer keyboards on linoleum, with keys large enough for children to stand on. They give each child a letter or number card and ask them to stand on the key with their letter or number. As they become more familiar with the keys, the teacher then calls out a letter or number for children to see who can find it and stand on it.

HELPS CHILDREN APPLY BASIC CONCEPTS ABOUT THE NATURAL WORLD THROUGH HANDS-ON EXPERIENCES

As young children develop their cognitive abilities through scientific inquiry, they need to learn to apply these concepts to the natural world around them. Preschool is the right time and proper place to awaken young children's awareness of Earth's precious gifts: the air they breathe, the water they drink, the food they eat, the plants and animals they depend on, and the beauty around them. They also need to learn that the world around them deserves proper use and protection from abuse. Holt (1992) notes:

> We should emphasize the environment and the role humans play in consuming, or protecting Earth's riches. Each child's interactions with the world affect not only the child but the world. . . . Concepts of balance, harmony, cooperation, and interdependence can be found in any nature study. Teachers should make certain that these ideas are emphasized: These are ways in which all forms of life coexist and support each other naturally. It is an emphasis long overdue. (pp. 132–133)

Following a Broad but Simple Concept

In making year-long science plans for preschool children, teachers should start with a broad but simple concept that can last much of the year and take the class in a variety of directions depending on their interests. This concept should involve one of the gifts that the Earth gives us, so that children can in turn look for ways to protect that gift and to show their appreciation. For example, some programs focus on this broad but simple concept: *We use water.* To get them started with their science planning, one teacher started out by asking her co-teachers and the children to think of all the uses we make of water. "We drink water" was the first use. Sometimes children's long drink of water is also for looking and for listening to the splash. "We wash our hands in water." But we know that children are doing more than just getting their hands clean. They are fascinated by water. They love its sound and its feel. Wise teachers use children's intense interests to provoke further thinking.

Another teacher started her science activities for the year by bringing in a container of bottled water from the supermarket for her Discovery Center. This in turn stimulated the children to wonder and talk about other kinds of water. They filled a glass of water from the tap and visually compared the bottled water with the glass of water. They looked the same. The teacher then asked a small group who had gathered around the display table, "How else can we tell if there is any difference between bottled water and tap water?"

After one child suggested smelling the two types of water, everyone wanted a turn. All decided there was a difference that was hard to put into words, but they agreed that the tap water smelled stronger. Next, of course, everyone had to taste the two. Most of the children liked the bottled water better. The teacher recorded the results on newsprint after each child's name.

When the teacher asked what other kinds of water are around us, someone mentioned pond water in the nearby park, which eventually led to a picnic and field trip to the park. While at the pond, the children became excited when they saw mallard ducks swimming around. They wanted to feed the ducks with their sandwiches. But a park attendant told them that too many people feeding too much bread to the ducks was making the pond polluted. He said that ducks were healthier when they fed on underwater plants like they were supposed to.

Underwater plants? Could they find any? This got the children wondering about what else grew in the water. As they walked around the pond, Anthony found some tadpoles and collected them in a jar of greenish pond water. Tracy saw some under-water plants near shore, and the teacher let her pick a few stems and leaves. But other children found discarded paper cups and plastic trash on the shore and put them in their collecting bags. They talked to a man fishing from the shore, but he told them that he didn't catch much anymore because the pond was so polluted.

Back in the classroom the children decided to make a collage out of the trash they had collected by gluing it to a poster board and then displaying it on the wall for all to see. The collage said: *LITTER IS NOT BEAUTIFUL* and *PLEASE DO NOT LITTER IN THE PARK*. Tracy put her stems into Anthony's jar of pond water for the tadpoles to rest on and to see if they would grow.

Next, the children wanted to know what else uses water. Andrea told them that Whiskers, the classroom guinea pig, drinks a lot of water. She was the guinea pig attendant for the week. They wanted to know how much water. So Andrea started recording with a paper punch and file card each time she filled its drinking bottle. Then children began talking about how much water their pets drank at home. The teacher set up a chart for recording their pets' names and how much water they drank every day. Everyone was surprised when Jasmine announced that her pet was a plant, a geranium, and that it too drank water.

"How can you tell?" they asked. "That's a good question," replied the teacher. "How can we tell if a plant drinks water?" she asked. "Give it a glass of water!" laughed one of the children. The next day the teacher brought in a white flower (a carnation) and a stalk of celery. The children helped her set up a water-drinking plant experiment by pouring about an inch of water into two glasses and mixing it with red ink. The teacher then trimmed the stems of the flower and celery and stood each one in a glass of the red liquid. "What do you think will happen?" she asked. The children tried to guess, but they really were not sure.

They watched the two plants closely all morning, but nothing happened. Then Jasmine noticed a change. The liquid was going up into the flower and celery! They were turning red! By the end of the day, both had turned a definite pinkish-red color. "Do plants drink water?" the teacher asked them. "Yes!" was the loud reply. "And what if the water is polluted with red ink?" she wanted to know. A vigorous discussion followed. Preschool children like this can begin to think seriously about what is happening to water, one of the Earth's priceless gifts. But the children were not finished with their inquiry into using water. As the days and weeks went by, they asked and tried to answer other questions:

How does water get polluted?

How can we stop pollution from getting into water?

How can we get pollution out of water?

They learned that the green in the pond water was actually tiny plants called algae. Although algae was not pollution, too much algae was a sign of pollution in the water, perhaps from lawn fertilizer or from bread thrown to the ducks. They also learned that too much algae could make fish die. They remembered the algae that grew on the inside of their aquarium and how they found ways to get rid of it.

From the book *My First Green Book: A Life-Size Guide to Caring for Our Environment* (Wilkes, 1991), they used ideas about making a natural filter in a flower pot with blotting paper, sand, and gravel to make Anthony's green pond water clean. Some of the green came out. They also tried using an aquarium pump and filter to clean the water; and finally they added one of their aquarium snails to help clean their pond water.

Their interest in watching the snail eat algae on the sides of their aquarium led this group of curious explorers on still another field trip to the lot in back of their center to find out more about garden snails. The teacher had read them the book *The Snail's Spell* (Ryder, 1982), a story showing a little girl who imagines herself to be 2 inches long like a snail and who then experiences life in a garden.

They did not find any snails in back of the center. Instead, some found carpenter ants, some found beetles, and Cayla found a butterfly chrysalis. That started a whole new direction of exploration. It is obvious that one thing leads to another in preschool science. This means that adult classroom workers must be alert in seeking out and following the children's interests. Meanwhile, they will be integrating these new interests into the broad general concepts the class is pursuing. Detours like a butterfly-hatching activity should be not only expected but also welcomed.

The children collected Cayla's caterpillar chrysalis on a plant stalk, along with some plant leaves. They placed these in a cage in the classroom. The teacher brought in a calendar for Cayla to mark off the days that it took the caterpillar to grow into a butterfly.

Books to Read

During the long wait for the butterfly to hatch, the teacher read them several books about butterflies: *The Very Hungry Caterpillar* (Carle, 1971), showing a caterpillar's eating spree day by day before it becomes a chrysalis; *Where Butterflies Grow* (Ryder, 1989), a beautifully detailed story about a black swallowtail caterpillar's life; and *The Butterfly Hunt* (Yoshi, 1990), a story about a boy involved in an exciting adventure to catch a certain yellow butterfly for a pet. When he finally succeeds, he does something surprising: He sets it free—"And forever and ever the butterfly was his very own."

When Cayla's butterfly finally hatched from its chrysalis, the children watched in fascination as its wings opened up in all their beauty. Then they took it outside and set it free.

By now the teacher of this class was aware that the children were seriously interested in the natural world outside their classroom, and wanted to hear other stories about children like themselves who helped to save and protect the life around them. She read them *Island Baby* (Keller, 1992) about the little Caribbean island boy who helped his grandfather with injured birds in his bird hospital, and finally rescued and helped to heal a little flamingo with a broken leg. This sent the children off on several bird-watching expeditions, finally resulting in their rescuing and raising a baby robin.

Plants need rescuing, too, the children learned when the teacher read them *Fernando's Gift* (Keister, 1995) in English and Spanish, about a little Costa Rican boy who lived in the rain forest where many wonderful old trees were being cut down. When his friend Carmina discovers that her favorite climbing tree has been cut down, Fernando is able to give her a plant gift from his father's plant nursery, and the two of them ride to a safe place in the jungle to plant it. Of course the teacher then had to take the children on a field trip to a nearby plant nursery where they purchased their own "climbing tree" and planted it outside the classroom window.

The teachers of this class, as well as most early childhood teachers who truly look for and follow the interests of their children, ended up becoming "guessing-game scientists" themselves. According to Holt (1992):

> It is a style that leads a person to wonder, to seek, to discover, to know, and then to wonder anew. It is a style in which good feelings of joy, excitement, and beauty accompany these mental and physical interactions with one's world. Not only children but adults can experience science. It is a way of life. (p. 118)

SUMMARY

This chapter looks at ways to promote children's questioning, exploring, and problem-solving skills to develop their thinking skills. Early childhood classroom workers need to be aware of how children use their senses to explore the world around them and need to set up classroom activities to promote such exploration. Using children's natural curiosity, or reawakening it if they seem to have lost it, should be the classroom workers' goals in the cognitive development of young children. Bring in new materials, pose questions about them, take children on nearby field trips, and make photo, tape, and written records of happenings. Be sure to record the questions that children are asking so that you will know what direction to take next in planning cognitive activities.

Help children develop cognitive concepts such as that of size, shape, color, and number, using them to classify and compare objects in the classroom. Children can then apply these concepts to the exploration they are already doing as they collect, compare, and record interesting materials in their environment. Interact with the children yourself to stimulate their curiosity and encourage them to think and solve problems. Help them to become guessing-game scientists.

Ask open-ended sensory questions and listen to the way the children answer them. This should give you clues as to what direction you should take next with individuals and the group in providing them with new cognitive activities or extending the present ones. Read books and provide computer games for children to play in order to reinforce the concepts they are learning. Help children to appreciate the beauty of nature around them and to understand the Earth's rich gifts of air, water, food, plants, animals, and beauty, as well as how they can protect and preserve these treasures.

LEARNING ACTIVITIES

1. Read Chapter 5, Advancing Cognitive Skills, and write out answers to Question Sheet 5.

2. Meet with your trainer or instructor and discuss answers to Question Sheet 5.

3. View one of the videotapes listed and make 10 file cards with ideas for developing young children's cognition.

4. Read one or more of the references cited or suggested readings and add 10 cards to your file, with specific ideas for helping children develop cognitive skills. Include the reference source on each card.

5. Observe and record several of your children's actions using the Children's Curiosity Checklist in

Figure 5-1. Bring in a new material or find another way to improve their curiosity. Record what you did and the results.

6. Take a small group of your children on a brief field trip to a nearby area. Follow up with a classroom activity to clarify concepts or support learning. Record the results.

7. Help the children learn a new concept using ideas from this chapter. Write down questions they ask and how they learned the answers. Record how you know what concepts children learned from this activity.

8. Help children investigate a science interest using the guessing-game method of scientific inquiry. Record what happens.

9. Support children in their investigation of an environmental issue concerning plants, animals, insects, fish, birds, butterflies, water, or air. Record what happens.

10. Complete the Chapter 5 Evaluation Sheet and return it to your trainer or college supervisor.

QUESTION SHEET 5

1. Why is it important to help children develop cognitive skills during the preschool years?

2. How do children use their senses to explore the world around them?

3. What can we do to reawaken the curiosity of children who seem to have lost their sense of wonder?

4. How can field trips to nearby locations promote cognitive development?

5. How can you follow up on children's science interests with materials in the classroom? Give specific examples.

6. What do the concepts of size, shape, color, and number have to do with children's cognitive development?

7. How would you help children to learn a new idea such as the concept of circle?

8. How can children in your classroom learn the meaning of numbers (i.e., one-to-one correspondence)?

9. Why is it important for young children to learn counting?

10. Why is it important for children to learn sorting and classification skills? How can they do it in your classroom?

11. Give an example of several broad but simple science concepts you might follow throughout the year.

12. How would you begin planning a study of the concept "we use water"? Why?

13. How can you get young children deeply involved in an environmental issue?

14. What would you do if an unexpected event (e.g., finding a butterfly chrysalis) interrupted your science plans for the day? Why?

15. What is an example of a question children might ask about the environment that you do not know the answer to? How would you handle this? Be specific.

REFERENCES

Evans, M. (1993). *Pet care guides for kids: FISH.* New York: Dorling Kindersley.

Holt, B. G. (1992). In M. Rivin (Ed.), Science is a way of life. *Young Children, 47*(4), 4–8.

Humphryes, J. (2000). Exploring nature with children. *Young Children, 55*(2), 16–20.

Lind, K. K. (1996). *Exploring science in early childhood: A developmental approach.* Albany, NY: Delmar.

Sprung, B., Froschl, M., & Campbell, P. B. (1985). *What will happen if . . . Young children and the scientific method.* Beltsville, MD: Gryphon House.

Unglaub, K. W. (1997). What counts in learning to count? *Young Children, 52*(4), 48–49.

Wilkes, A. (1991). *My first green book: A life-size guide to caring for our environment.* New York: Knopf.

SUGGESTED READINGS

Baroody, A. J. (2000). Does mathematics instruction for three-to-five-year-olds really make sense? *Young Children, 55*(4), 61–67.

Charlesworth, R. (1996). *Experiences in math for young children.* Albany, NY: Delmar.

Copely, J. V. (2000). *The young child and mathematics.* Washington, DC: National Association for the Education of Young Children.

Desrochers, J. (2001). Exploring our world: Outdoor classes for parents and children. *Young Children, 56*(5), 9–11.

Evans, M. (1992). *Pet care guides for kids: GUINEA PIGS.* New York: Dorling Kindersley.

Jaelitza. (1996). Insect love: A field journal. *Young Children, 51*(4), 31–32.

Moomaw, S., & Hieronymous, B. (1995). *More than counting: Whole math activities for preschool and kindergarten.* St. Paul, MN: Redleaf Press.

Moran, M. J., and Jarvis, J. (2001). Helping young children develop higher order thinking skills. *Young Children, 56*(1), 31–35.

Patton, M. M., & Kokoski, T. M. (1996). How good is your early childhood science, mathematics, and technology program? Strategies for extending your curriculum. *Young Children, 51*(5), 38–44.

Perry, G., & Rivkin, M. (1992). Teachers and science. *Young Children, 47*(4), 9–16.

Seefeldt, C., and Galper, A. (2002). *Active experiences for active children: Science.* Upper Saddle River, NJ: Merrill/Prentice Hall.

Shantal, R. (1998). Age-appropriate ecology: Are you practicing it? *Young Children, 53*(1), 70–71.

Shaw, J., & Blake, S. (1998). *Mathematics for young children.* Upper Saddle River, NJ: Merrill/Prentice Hall.

Thatcher, D. H. (2001). Reading in math class: Selecting and using picture books for math investigations. *Young Children, 56*(4), 20–26.

Tomich, K. (1996). Hundreds of ladybugs, thousands of ladybugs, million and billions and trillions of ladybugs—and a couple of roaches. *Young Children, 51*(4), 28–30.

Wilkes, A. (1990). *My first nature book: A life-size guide to discovering the world around you.* New York: Knopf.

Winnett, D. A., Rockwell, R. E., Sherwood, E. A., & Williams, R. A. (1996). *Discovery science: Explorations for the early years, Grade pre-kindergarten.* Menlo Park, CA: Addison-Wesley.

Ziemer, M. (1987). Science and the early childhood curriculum: One thing leads to another. *Young Children, 42*(6), 44–51.

CHILDREN'S BOOKS

Carle, E. (1971). *The very hungry caterpillar.* New York: Crowell.

Edwards, P. D. (1998). *Warthogs in the kitchen: A sloppy counting book.* NewYork: Hyperion.

Falwell, C. (1993). *Feast for 10.* New York: Clarion.

Feelings, M. (1971). *Moja means one.* New York: Dial.

Freymann, S., & Elffers, J. (2000). *One lonely sea horse.* New York: Scholastic.

Haskins, J. (1987). *Count your way through China.* Minneapolis, MN: Carolrhoda Books.

Haskins, J. (1991). *Count your way through the Arab world.* Minneapolis, MN: Carolrhoda Books.

Haskins, J. (1992). *Count your way through Africa.* Minneapolis, MN: Carolrhoda Books.

Hubbard, P. (1996). *My crayons talk.* New York: Henry Holt.

Jeunesse, G., & de Bourgoing, P. (1989). *Colors.* New York: Scholastic.

Jeunesse, G., & de Bourgoing, P. (1989). *The tree.* New York: Scholastic.

Jonas, A. (1989). *Color dance.* New York: Greenwillow.

Keister, D. (1995). *Fernando's gift.* San Francisco: Sierra Club.

Keller, H. (1992). *Island baby.* New York: Mulberry.

Kunhardt, E. (1992). *Red day green day.* New York: Greenwillow.

Milstein, L. (1995). *Coconut mon.* New York: Tambourine.

Most, B. (1989). *The littlest dinosaurs.* San Diego: Harcourt.

Most, B. (1994). *How big were the dinosaurs?* San Diego: Harcourt.

Ormerod, J. (1986). *Joe can count.* New York: Mulberry.

Philpot, L., & Philpot, G. (1994). *Amazing Anthony Ant.* New York: Random House.

Pinczes, E. J. (1993). *One hundred hungry ants.* Boston: Houghton Mifflin.

Root, P. (1998). *One duck stuck.* Cambridge, MA: Candlewick.

Ryder, J. (1982). *The snail's spell.* New York: Puffin.

Ryder, J. (1989). *Where butterflies grow.* New York: Dutton.

Serfozo, M. (1988). *Who said red?* New York Macmillan.

Sierra, J. (1997). *Counting crocodiles.* San Diego: Harcourt.

Stickland, P. & Stickland, H. (1994). *Dinosaur roar!* New York: Dutton.

Stickland, P. (1997). *Ten terrible dinosaurs.* New York: Dutton.

Stinson, K. (1982). *Red is best.* Toronto, Canada: Annick Press.

Sweat, L., & Phillips, L. (1993). *The smallest stegosaurus.* New York: Puffin.

Yoshi. (1990). *The butterfly hunt.* Saxonville, MA: Picture Book Studio.

VIDEOTAPES

South Carolina Educational Television. (Producer). *How young children learn to think: Piaget's theory.* Washington, DC: National Association for the Education of Young Children. (#809).

Indiana Steps Ahead. (Producer). *Exploring science and nature.* Washington, DC: National Association for the Education of Young Children. (#884; in Spanish #884S).

South Carolina Educational Television. (Producer). *Sensory play: Constructing realities.* Washington, DC: National Association for the Education of Young Children.

South Carolina Educational Television. (Producer). *Sharing nature with young children.* Available from the National Association for the Education of Young Children, Washington, DC.

CHAPTER 5 EVALUATION SHEET
ADVANCING COGNITIVE SKILLS

1. Student _____

2. Trainer _____

3. Center where training occurred _____

4. Beginning date _____ Ending date _____

5. Describe what student did to accomplish General Objective.

    _____

    _____

6. Describe what student did to accomplish Specific Objectives.

    Objective 1 _____

    _____

    Objective 2 _____

    _____

    Objective 3 _____

    _____

7. Evaluation of student's Learning Activities

    _____

Comments:

    _____

    _____

    _____

    _____

    _____

    _____

    _____

    _____

Permission is granted by the publisher to reproduce this page for evaluation and record keeping.

Advancing
Communication Skills

GENERAL OBJECTIVE

To promote children's communication skills through listening, speaking, emergent reading, and emergent writing

SPECIFIC OBJECTIVES

_____ Talks with individual children to encourage listening and speaking

_____ Uses books and stories to motivate listening, speaking, and emergent reading

_____ Provides materials and activities to support emergent writing

Communication skills, the ability to listen, speak, read, and write, are a most important aspect of young children's development in the preschool classroom. We understand that the drive to communicate is inherent from birth in all human beings. We also know that children strive endlessly to accomplish this goal of communication with the others in their environment, unless they are impaired, neglected, or somehow thwarted. And we know that poor development of communication skills during the early years can affect children's thinking and learning abilities throughout life.

New Brain Research

New brain research shows us the importance of early child–adult interactions from birth on. A baby's early communication efforts help to wire her brain for the spoken and written language to follow. Communication involves both receiving and expressing information. Willis (1998) notes:

> Babies enter the world communicating. While it may be several months or even a year before babies utter their first meaningful words, they are communicating (nonverbally) within a few hours of birth. By six months of age, a child has become a language specialist, focused on the sounds he hears most frequently. (p. 64)

By 20 months of age children may have a sizable vocabulary—that is, if their caregivers talk to them, cuddle them, and interact with them. Recent research shows that youngsters whose mothers talk to them frequently average 131 more words than children whose mothers are less verbal (Begley, 1997).

Language modeling behavior by the adults around them is the key factor in children's learning to communicate. Youngsters from highly verbal homes often speak early and well, whereas children from homes where nonverbal communication is the norm are often delayed in learning to speak fluently. In other words, all young children need to hear language spoken around them to learn to speak it themselves.

It is your role then, as a teacher, assistant, volunteer, or student teacher in a preschool program, to promote children's communication skills in some of the following ways.

TALKS WITH INDIVIDUAL CHILDREN TO ENCOURAGE LISTENING AND SPEAKING

For children to learn to speak they need to learn to listen to the speaking going on around them. How do they learn to listen? Their teachers must make it a point to model and teach active listening themselves. Are you a good listening model for your children?

Becoming an Active Listener

Active listening takes more than merely stopping your own talking while another person speaks. Here are some points to consider:

1. Quiet your mind's flow of thoughts.
2. Receive and process the incoming speaking.
3. Concentrate on the key points of what is being said.
4. Get involved emotionally with what you hear.

You may believe you are already a good listener, but Jalongo (1995) found that according to recent studies, "American adults listen at only 25% efficiency; most adult listeners are preoccupied, distracted and forgetful nearly 75% of the time" (p. 13). If we expect children to listen to us, then we must make a concerted effort to model good listening behavior ourselves.

To practice good listening you should first face the person who is speaking and then make and keep eye contact. If a child is speaking to you, squat down or sit down next to her rather than leaning over her. Then really listen to what is being said. Let her finish; don't interrupt. When you reply, try to repeat something she said. This lets the child know you have heard her. Besides serving as a model for a child to emulate, your listening to a child like this helps him or her to feel valued as a person.

Your response should also encourage the child to continue talking. You might suggest, "Tell me more about that funny puppy you saw on the way to the center this morning." If your concentrated listening and sincere response show that you are genuinely interested in children's communications, they will be motivated to listen more carefully themselves.

Helping Children Become Active Listeners

If children pay little attention to what you are saying to them or do not seem to hear what you say, they may need to be screened for hearing impairments or attention deficits. Do not wait until they enter elementary school. The earlier such deficits can be identified, the sooner they can be corrected. Be sure children and their parents are referred to appropriate professional assistance without delay.

Many teachers spend more time talking to groups than to individuals. Yet to involve children in learning to listen you need to spend time talking individually with each child every day. Make listening and speaking to individuals an important part of your daily routine. Keep a list of children's names handy and check it off each time you speak with an individual. Did you miss anyone? Be sure to catch up with them the next day.

What kinds of adult speaking can individual children expect to hear in your classroom?

Greeting each child when he or she arrives

Talking to a child in a learning center

Talking on a pretend telephone to a child

Making an audiotape for a child

Reading a book to a child

Helping a child start or complete a project

Conversing with individual children at the lunch table

Giving verbal support to a child who needs it

Having a private conversation with a child about something of interest

Saying good-bye to each child at the end of the day

Remember that children 3 to 5 years old are at the beginning of their language development and may not understand everything you say. Kratcoski and Katz (1998) suggest the following teacher communication behaviors to help facilitate child language understanding:

Use simple sentences.

Speak slowly and clearly.

Vary your tone/expression to emphasize key words.

Pause between sentences.

Use concrete vocabulary.

Try to "comment" more than "question" (p. 31).

Children can also learn from simple listening games. Make up your own or play "What Do the Animals Say?" with a small rather than large group at a time. (The larger the group, the less individual children seem to hear or understand.) To play this game you tell the children, "Listen carefully to what each animal says, and if you think the animal is wrong or trying to fool you, say 'Gotcha!'" You can pretend to be as many animals as you want, making a correct sound for all but one:

"The dog says *ruff-ruff!*"

"The cat says *meow!*"

"The mouse says *squeak-squeak!*"

"The horse says *meow!*"

This game has dozens of variants. Play a different one every day with sounds of motor vehicles, musical instruments, carpenter's tools, or people walking, for instance. If children enjoy the animal sounds game, read them *Mice Squeak, We Speak* (De Paola, 1997) to give them more ideas for their games. To check on your own listening and speaking skills, do a self-analysis using the Teacher Listening and Speaking Checklist, Figure 6–1.

TEACHER LISTENING AND SPEAKING CHECKLIST

_____ Makes eye contact with speaker at speaker's level

_____ Listens by quieting the mind's flow of thoughts

_____ Concentrates on key points of what is being said

_____ Gets emotionally involved in what is being said

_____ Repeats something that is said to the speaker

_____ Listens attentively to the speaker's reply

_____ Listens to an audiotape a child has made and makes comments

_____ Greets each child individually when child arrives

_____ Converses with individuals in learning centers

_____ Talks to individuals on pretend telephone

_____ Converses with individuals at lunch table

_____ Says good-bye to each child at end of the day

_____ Speaks slowly and clearly

_____ Uses simple sentences, good grammar

_____ Uses more comments than questions

Figure 6–1   Teacher Listening and Speaking Checklist

Permission is granted by the publisher to reproduce this checklist for evaluation and record keeping.

Soundproofing the Room.   Children need to hear words and how they are used to use them themselves. Make sure your classroom is full of talking, but not loud talking. Listen for it. If you hear only noisy sounds or shouting, it may be a sign that your room needs soundproofing. Youngsters should be able to hear one another without raising their voices. If they cannot, you should improve the room's sound absorption. Install carpeting on the floor and sound-absorbent tiles on the ceiling. Hang floor-length drapes at the windows and colorful picture rugs or cloth hangings on the walls.

If you do not have the authority to install carpeting or ceiling tiles, you can still help to soundproof the room. Use area rugs on the floor and draperies on the walls. Cloth absorbs sound better than cardboard or wood. Think of ways you can include cloth rather than cardboard in different parts of the room. For example, use colored cloth backing for the signs that label each curriculum area. Cover your bulletin board with colored burlap. Make your jobs-chart out of cloth with pockets for each child's job card. Fasten cloth curtains to the backs of room dividers. Bring in several bright pillows for the book and housekeeping centers. Now your children should be able to hear clearly and speak without shouting. But as Selman (2001) points out:

> Talking involves communication—speaking with and to someone, getting feedback, and composing language in response to that feedback. Talking with someone implies a continuous exchange—a dialogue. (p. 15)

Helping Children Become Speakers

For verbal communication to occur with preschool children, two factors seem to operate. First, there must be a stress-free environment that allows but does not force them to communicate. Children need to feel support from those around them in order to express themselves in their very personal but still imperfect mode of communication. Second, there must be a necessity for language. Children must have the need to communicate in the classroom.

Stress-Free Environment.   For many children, verbalizing is a new and untried skill outside their homes. They need not only opportunities to become proficient in speaking but also encouragement to continue. Children usually respond well to anything closely associated with themselves. Try playing name concept games to put them at ease.

"I'm thinking about someone with white-and-blue sneakers and a black T-shirt with a tiger on it. Guess who I'm thinking about? Robbie, right! Now you tell me who you are thinking about, Robbie, and see if I can guess."

Give children positive feedback for their verbal skills just as you would for their block buildings or paintings. "I like the way you said my name, Breanna. Breanna is such a nice-sounding name, too."

A stress-free environment also means that you accept the children as they are, which means you accept their language no matter how poorly pronounced or how ungrammatical. Language is a very personal thing. It reflects not only the child's early stage of development but also his or her family. Therefore, you must be especially careful not to correct children's language in a way that shows a lack of respect for them or their parents. Try to avoid telling them they are saying a word incorrectly. You may wonder, then, how they are going to learn the correct pronunciation. They will learn it by hearing you use words correctly and by imitating and practicing new words in the many interesting language activities you provide.

A stress-free environment also means that your classroom is free from stressful situations for young children. They should not be forced to perform verbally, creatively, or in any other way. Offer them interesting opportunities and warm encouragement, but do not force a shy or unsure child to speak.

Finally, in a stress-free language environment, you talk to children with *responsive language* that conveys respect for them, rather than with *restrictive language* that conveys disrespect and teacher control. Researchers who observe teachers and caregivers of young children have noted that the manner in which they talk to youngsters tells a great deal about the way they treat children in general. As Stone (1993) notes, "Responsive language is language that conveys a positive regard for children and a respect for and acceptance of their individual ideas and feelings" (p. 13).

Teachers who use responsive language in the classroom give reasons for the statements they make. For example, they may say, "It's too wet to go out now. We'll wait till the grass dries," rather than, "We're not going out now. Why? Because I said so." They encourage children's independence and choice-making rather than teacher control. For instance, they may say, "Everyone can choose the activity area he or she wants to play in. Just take one of the area necklaces," instead of the restrictive, "Beth, you and Greg work at the art table now."

Classroom workers who speak in responsive terms use "nurturant control" such as, "I need each of you to put your toys back on the shelf so that we can go outside," rather than the restrictive, "No one is going anywhere until this room is clean." Stone (1993) further defines restrictive language as "language that involves teacher control through such power-assertion methods as issuing unnecessary or disrespectful commands, threats, punishments, and criticisms" (p. 13).

When rules and limits are verbalized, teachers who use restrictive language may say, "No yelling in the room," instead of the responsive, "Let's speak softly." They may comment on children's beginning art products with the restrictive, "You didn't try very hard, Ethan. That's just a scribble," instead of, "You really enjoyed using all those colors, Ethan."

How do you talk to children? Do you treat them as full-fledged human beings to be respected or as inferior little beings who are too young to know much? Your feelings and attitudes toward the children are expressed more clearly than you may realize in the language you use around the youngsters. Think twice before beginning your sentences with words and phrases such as *don't, stop, no,* or *not that way.* Think of ways you can convey the same meaning respectfully.

Your use of restrictive language, whether directed toward one child or to all of them, makes the classroom a stressful environment for everyone. Listen to yourself talk to the children. Is your language responsive or restrictive? Turn on the cassette recorder and make a tape of your speaking mode to find out. If you decide to change your method of speaking to a more responsive style, note the children's reactions. Are they also more responsive, positive, and happy? Nonverbal children are much more

How do you talk to the children? Do you treat them as full-fledged human beings to be respected?

likely to begin their own tentative classroom speaking when they hear how sensitively the teacher speaks to them.

Confidence.   The so-called nonverbal child is frequently one who lacks confidence to speak outside the confines of the home. At home he may be a regular chatterbox. To assure yourself of the child's verbal ability, you may want to talk with the parents to learn how much their child communicates verbally at home. It is not necessary to tell parents that their child is not speaking in school. The pressure they might put on the child to speak in school could well have adverse effects.

Your principal task with shy or uncommunicative children is to help them feel comfortable in the classroom. All classroom workers need to be aware that overt efforts to get such children to speak before they are at ease in the classroom may well be counterproductive. Instead, the staff should direct their efforts toward accepting the children as they are, using smiles, nods, and words of acceptance for their positive accomplishments when appropriate and leaving the child alone when necessary.

It takes a great deal of patience and forbearance on the part of an early childhood classroom staff to allow shy children to become at ease in their own good time, but this is often the only successful method. Weeks and even months are sometimes necessary for the extremely sensitive child to respond. If you have persisted in your support-without-pressure approach, you will be rewarded one day by a smile and even a whispered sentence. Do not make a fuss when shy children say their first words. Accept their speaking matter-of-factly, just as you have always accepted them.

Book to Read

The children's picture book *Chatterbox Jamie* (Cooney, 1993) tells a typical story about little Jamie who chatters on and on to his mother and father about going to nursery school until at last he gets there. Then he is so uneasy about being left by his parents that he doesn't say a word. "But Jamie stood still like a robot with its power turned off; no words came." If you have children like Jamie who are talkative at home but nonverbal in class, try reading them a story like this. They may identify with Jamie and finally begin to talk in preschool just as he does.

Necessity.   Do children have the need to communicate in your classroom? You can provide opportunities for communication to take place. Remember, you are the role model. You need to communicate verbally yourself whenever possible. Set aside a time of day when you greet the children and they greet one another.

Have a small group or a circle time in which the children have a chance to tell about something. A shy child might talk through a hand puppet at first. You can demonstrate how, but don't force the issue if the child does not want to use the puppet. Give the children a chance to pretend in the dramatic play area or with blocks or water. Ask one child to help another with a new tool or piece of equipment. Give children oral messages to carry to someone else in the room. Have them ask someone a question and return to you with the answer. Sit with the children at snack or lunchtime and start a conversation about something of interest to them.

Conversations.   If children feel confident, they will probably converse with others. However, if they feel more comfortable talking with adults than with other children, as many preschoolers do, their lack of peer conversation may be one of socialization rather than language. Be sure to eat with children at lunch time or snack time, especially with shy or nonverbal children. This will give you an informal assessment of which children converse spontaneously and which ones do not. Try engaging each child at your table in conversation, but without pressure. Then give them something to talk about with one another. Perhaps the shy child will tell a tablemate what he is going to do when he gets home.

In addition to giving support without pressure, your task will also involve easing the shy child into social situations with one or two other children, perhaps through role play. You may need to be nearby in the beginning, but you can withdraw when you see the child playing comfortably with the others.

Toy telephones can help promote conversational language. Be sure to have at least two phones, one for the caller and one for the receiver. For children who need special practice in speaking, you should put in a pretend call yourself and talk with them every day if necessary. Other children will see you doing this and soon begin calling on their own. To make it more realistic, keep an old telephone directory in the area and pretend to look up the number.

An important but frequently overlooked element in stimulating children's conversations in early childhood classrooms is the mix of children. Is your classroom composed of a single age group, such as all 3-year-olds or all 4-year-olds? Or are these two age groups combined? Because children learn so much of their language through imitation of others, it is helpful for them to be around children a bit more advanced than themselves. The language of 3-year-olds will develop much faster with 4-year-olds in the same classroom.

To promote spontaneous conversation between yourself and the children, you need to be an active communicator with responsive, not restrictive, speaking habits. This means you are a person the children are able and willing to approach. You may have to take the initiative with shy children. They may lack the confidence to approach you on their own. Try stationing yourself in a particular learning center near these children to create opportunities for conversation. If the children do not respond, you may need to talk on your own awhile, describing what is going on in the area and wondering what else is going to happen. In most cases, they will eventually join in the conversation.

Observers of teacher behavior note that teachers usually respond mainly to the children who talk the most. Quiet or inarticulate children—those who truly need conversational practice—are frequently ignored. You must therefore make a special effort to ensure that you do not unintentionally overlook such children. Remember, patience, not pressure, should govern your approach.

Bilingual Children

Bilingual children are fortunate to attend a preschool program that recognizes their home language as well as English because they will have the opportunity to become fluent in both languages during their period of natural language acquisition. At no other time in their lives will they be able to acquire another language so easily.

To learn a second language, they must hear and practice it, and you must provide opportunities for them to do so. These should not be formal teaching lessons. Young children from birth to age 6, acquire native and second languages in a most informal and spontaneous way—by hearing it spoken around them, by trial and error in speaking it themselves, and by subconsciously extracting the rules of the language—not through formal grammar teaching.

If most of the children speak English as a first language, but a few speak, say, Spanish, you or one of your co-workers should also speak both languages. Most of the day you will be speaking mainly English, but spend an hour a day, or a half hour in a half-day program, speaking nothing but simple Spanish. Those children who speak Spanish will respond naturally. Those children whose native language is English will pick up a great deal of Spanish, not by being taught formally, but by hearing it spoken around them.

Read children's books in Spanish, sing songs in Spanish, do painting or build with blocks making comments in Spanish, and have a wonderful time during your "Spanish hour" every day. By the end of the year, you may have many so-called Anglo children responding in Spanish as fluently as your native Spanish speakers. A second language is a true gift. Everyone will feel good about receiving it: the Hispanic children whose language you have recognized by using it in school and the non-Hispanic children who have learned to say and understand simple phrases in a new language.

Instead of having an instructor or a parent with a second language come into your classroom and "teach" the children to say *hello, good-bye, how are you?* and how to count to 10, ask this person to come into your classroom and spend time with the children, speaking nothing but the second language. Don't use a translator. The children will be able to pick up enough nonverbal cues to understand—perhaps better than you do! Eventually, they will be able to reply in the second language. You may want to start by sharing picture books in the second language with the children. Here are some favorite books written in English that also appear in a Spanish edition (available from Lectorum Publications, 205 Chubb Ave., Lyndhurst, NJ, 07071; 1-800-345-5946):

Amazing Grace (La asombrosa Graciela) (Hoffman, 1991)

The Grouchy Ladybug (La mariquita malhumorada) (Carle, 1977)

I Had a Hippopotamus (Yo tenia un hipopotamo) (Lee, 1996)

Is Your Mama a Llama? (Tu mama es una llama?) (Guarino, 1989)

A Pocket for Corduroy (Un bolsillo para Corduroy) (Freeman, 1978)

The Rainbow Fish (El pez arco iris) (Pfister, 1992)

Stella Luna (Stellaluna) (Cannon, 1993)

The Very Hungry Caterpillar (La Oruga Muy Hambrienta) (Carle, 1981)

Be sure to have both English and Spanish editions available for the adults in the classroom to read to the children.

Adults tend to think about learning a new language in adult terms; because it is so difficult for adults, what must it be for a little child! Just the opposite is true, however, for the young child. It is much easier for a preschooler to learn a second language than it is for an adult because the brain of the preschooler is programmed to learn languages, even more than one at a time. Thus, young children can learn a second language just as naturally as they learn their native tongue as long as they hear it spoken around them.

Besides the many English language activities you provide for your children, you should also plan specific activities using the second language, such as name chants and songs. The children can speak daily on the toy telephone with another second language speaker. A bilingual puppet can be part of your daily activities, talking to individuals and groups in both languages. Children can also learn to greet one another and say good-bye in the second language.

Dramatic play is one of the best vehicles for children's language development because natural conversation occurs. Be sure you allow enough time in your daily schedule for bilingual children to become involved in pretend play using a second language. If they seem shy, help them take on a role by playing alongside these children until they feel comfortable with the other youngsters.

USES BOOKS AND STORIES TO MOTIVATE LISTENING, SPEAKING, AND EMERGENT READING

During the 1980s and 1990s, it became evident to educators that more and more preschool children were entering elementary school already able to read. What was happening? Were more parents teaching their children to read? Were children learning

Some children seem to emerge into reading by following the pictures in picture books over and over.

from television? Educational researchers found something quite different. They learned that when conditions were right, some young children were actually teaching themselves to read just as they taught themselves to talk.

This process is now called *emergent literacy*. Some children seem to "emerge" naturally into reading and writing by following the print in picture books, interacting playfully with the "print" in their environment, subconsciously extracting the rules about reading and writing, and then trying out reading and writing through trial and error until they get it to work for them. Educators also realized that learning to communicate is a holistic process encompassing listening, speaking, reading, and writing together, not separately. They also realized that this process starts for children at birth.

If children's environment is filled with print materials (picture books, newspapers, magazines, television, computer programs, fast-food restaurant signs, and labels on cereal boxes, toys, and T-shirts), many children try to figure out what this print says.

If people around them tell them what the signs say and if the adults in their lives are readers themselves who read to the youngsters, then some of these children will manage to extract the rules for reading on their own before they enter school. As West and Egley (1998) note: "Young children may first learn about print by using objects with print on them, such as cereal boxes, clothing labels, and toy packages" (p. 43).

To support all children in acquiring these skills, a new philosophy for teaching reading and writing in elementary school has thus emerged. No longer are the children taught to read through basal readers, the *Dick-and-Jane*-type books. Instead, they use real children's literature like the books discussed here. Classrooms are encouraged to develop a "print-rich environment" in which written communication is evident everywhere: recipe charts, posters, letters, curriculum area signs, words to songs, rules charts, labels for objects, children's name tags, alphabet games, computer software, sign-up sheets, magazines, newspapers, and books.

Preschool teachers need to become aware of their children's emergent literacy, because it is happening whether or not they notice. Emergent reading in preschool, however, *does not involve the formal teaching of reading and writing.* Instead it encourages teachers to set up a print-rich environment with activities for children to accomplish on their own. And it involves *reading to children.* The most important experience a preschool child can have, in fact, is a happy adventure with storybooks.

If preschoolers are to meet with success and enjoyment in learning to read, they need to have a pleasant encounter with books at the outset. It is hoped that a child's acquaintance with books will begin in the home long before the child enters a classroom. The books and activities you provide will be a follow-up and extension of the story reading that occurs at home. But for some children, the experience in your classroom will be their initiation into the exciting world of books and reading. You will want to make it a joyful one.

When children see their teachers and parents reading, they begin to internalize the idea that reading is something important that the adults around them like to do. It is something they themselves will want to learn as soon as they can.

Adults who read to a preschool child are saying something else very important: "I like you enough to take time out of a busy day to share something nice with you." It creates a good feeling for all concerned.

Books to Motivate Listening

To acquire speaking skills, young children need to be able to listen and to hear, as previously discussed. One of the best ways to promote good listening skills in young children is to read them books that attract their attention. What kinds of books are these? They are picture books, of course, but to attract children's initial attention, these books should have enticing pictures on the cover.

An elephant, bear, flamingo, and lion look on with eyes popping and feet dancing at the sight of two boys and a girl painting the cover sign that reads, *Going to the Zoo,* the title of Paxton's (1996) exciting zoo adventure. *Noisy Nora,* Wells's (1997) endearing mouse girl with the mischievous eyes and foot reaching backward to knock over a chair, invites the reader to come in and see what new tricks she is up to in this book. But how will children respond to *Here Come the Aliens!* (McNaughton, 1995), a story about a bunch of bumpy, grumpy, bizarre space creatures floating through the black of outer space? Just what today's youngsters ordered, you will soon discover.

As you choose books for your children, look for books with intriguing covers and appealing characters. The children may not be able to read the title at first, but later they will know it well from repeated use. *Silly Sally* (Wood, 1992) shows an upside-down Sally with her tongue sticking out and her orange curls flying. The youngest children simply love Silly Sally, who goes to town walking backward upside-down through a field of yellow buttercups. They'll want this story repeated so many times they'll soon be "reading" it themselves—about the silly pig who dances a jig, the silly dog who plays leapfrog, and the silly loon who sings a tune. The story not only mesmerizes children with its rhyming cadences and loony characters but also entices everyone into dramatizing the action.

Preschool listeners also like book action that is exciting, fast-paced, and fun, with only brief text on each page. Books with longer texts are for older children. Three- and 4-year-old listeners want you to get on with the story and keep turning the pages. If you stop on a page for too long, they often lose interest. In *Zoom! Zoom! Zoom! I'm Off to the Moon!* (Yaccarino, 1997) a few exciting words embedded in each double-page illustration keep the action so fast paced the reader must keep a finger in the page ahead to turn it on time.

The words themselves also attract preschool story listeners. They like words with distinctive sounds to be repeated now and then in the story. Words like *slobber, dribble, gobble, munch,* and *vamoosed* from *Here Come the Aliens!* keep children coming back for more; or the monkeys with their *scritch, scritch, scratchin'* and the big black bear *a-huff, huff, a-puffin'* repeated three times in *Going to the Zoo,* soon entice your listeners to join in.

Remember that children's first level of learning on their own is *manipulation* (see chapter 3). Is children's wordplay actually manipulation? Yes. Just as they play with blocks, toys, and each other, children also play with words. Youngsters make up non-sense words, repeat word sounds, mix up words, say things backward, make up chants, and repeat rhyming words. Most people pay little attention to this activity because it seems so inconsequential. What we have not seemed to realize is that through this playful activity, children are once again at work creating their own knowledge. This time the content is language rather than cognitive concepts, and this time the child is manipulating the medium (words) with his voice rather than his hands. Preschool teachers should feel a great deal of relief when they realize that it is playful activities like this that help children emerge into literacy. As Klenk (2001) notes:

> Play-based literacy offers a much-needed reasonable response to the increasing expectations placed on young children (and their teachers) for literacy achievement. While these experiences do not hinge on formal instruction, they are authentic and purposeful.

Storybooks that help children play with words often become their favorites. In addition to the books described previously, the following contain words or phrases with distinctive sounds that children enjoy:

The Beastly Feast (Goldstone, 1998)—"antelope bring cantaloupe"; "mosquitoes bring burritos"

BOOK SELECTION CHECKLIST

Title _____ Author _____

Publisher _____ Date _____

_____ Illustrations attract attention

_____ Title sounds intriguing

_____ Characters that children can identify with

_____ Action exciting, fast paced, fun

_____ Text is brief (a sentence or two per page)

_____ Words have distinctive sounds

_____ Words or phrases are repeated

Figure 6–2   Book Selection Checklist

Permission is granted by the publisher to reproduce this checklist for evaluation and record keeping.

Boodil My Dog (Lindenbaum, 1992)—"Boodil," "suspicious," "party poopers"

Pigs in the Mud in the Middle of the Rud (Plourde, 1997)—"budge-smudge"; "scatter-smatter"; "shuffle-smuffle"; "charge-smarge"

The Listening Walk (Showers, 1991)—"twick," "dup," "brack-a," "chrroooofff"

As you read these books to children, note how attentively they are listening—waiting for their favorite word. Then they often go into spasms of laughter or repeat the word over and over. This *repetition* is the next stage in children's interaction with new things, you remember. When children ask you to "Read it again, teacher," be sure that you comply.

Children's level of language learning requires that words and stories be repeated again and again for real learning to take place. They will soon know their favorite stories so well that you won't dare skip a word when reading. Does this really matter? Jalongo and Ribblett (1997) have this to say about it:

Educators now know, based on emergent literacy research, that an important break-through in the literacy process occurs when a child knows a few books so well that she can tell if any portion of the text has been skipped or altered. (p. 15)

As you choose books for preschool children, keep in mind the criteria listed in Figure 6–2 to help in your selection.

Reading Books to Children

Until recently, picture books in preschool programs were seriously *underused* by teachers. All too often the books were relegated to bookshelves for children to look at on their own. Instead of reading books, teachers used filmstrips, cassettes, or videotapes of books.

Teachers need to know that these abstract representations are not the same as an actual teacher reading a real book to a live child. *Reading books to the children in your program may be the single most important activity that you engage in.* Plan your daily schedule to allow children to choose and look at books on their own sometime during the day. But you or one of your co-workers should be responsible for reading at least once a day to the children.

You may choose to read to an individual child or a small group at a time while the rest of the children engage in another interesting activity. Be sure the others also have their turn to hear the story later on. Children need to sit near the reader to see the pictures, to become personally involved in the story, and to enjoy the sense of closeness that develops with the teacher and other children while the story is being read. Keeping the group small makes it easier to accomplish this closeness. Make story reading a personal experience for your children by reading to both individuals and small groups.

The reader should sit at the children's level rather than on a teacher's chair above them while they sit on the floor. You may also want to invite a guest story reader from time to time. Parents, grandparents, retired teachers, or librarians make excellent readers. Older children may enjoy participating too.

Although individual children will readily come to you with books to be read, you also should approach particular children with a book you have picked out especially for them. A child you have previously identified as needing help in speaking can benefit by having stories read on an individual basis. To be a successful story reader, you will want to keep these hints in mind:

1. Know your book well.
2. Start with an attention-getting device.
3. Make your voice as interesting as possible.
4. Help children get involved through participation.

Know Your Book Well.   If you have chosen your book on the basis of the information in the Book Selection Checklist (see Figure 6–1), then you are already well acquainted with it. If not, skim through the pages and note these features:

1. Sound words for which you can make the sound rather than reading the word
2. Places where you might substitute the listener's name for the name used in the book
3. Picture details you might ask a listener to look for if you are reading to one or two children
4. Places in the story where you might want to pause and ask your listeners to guess what comes next

In other words, be sure to read the book to yourself before reading it to the children.

Start with an Attention-Getting Device.   Your story reading will not be successful unless you have your listeners' attention. You will not want to stop to reprimand disruptive children. It is better if they are all ready and eager for you to begin. You can help them become ready by beginning with an attention-getting device.

One of the simplest and most effective devices is to use the cover of the book. You might, for instance, ask the children something about the cover illustration. Here are some examples:

1. "Today our story is *Noisy Nora*." "Do you see Nora making noise?" "What does it look like she is doing?" "What do you suppose might happen?"

2. "The name of this book is *Zoom! Zoom! Zoom! I'm Off to the Moon!*" "What has this boy got on his head?" "Why do you suppose he is wearing that?" "Shall we open the book and find out?"

3. "What is *Silly Sally* doing on the cover of this book?" "Did you ever try to do that?" "What do you think will happen to Sally?"

Make Your Voice as Interesting as Possible.   Do you enjoy reading aloud to children? Your voice often reflects your feelings. If you are enthusiastic about story reading, the children will know it by the tone of your voice. They love to have the teacher dramatize the story by making her voice scary or whispery or deep. Can you do that? Most of us don't know until we try. Even then, we're not sure how we come across. Turn on the tape recorder during story reading time and record your voice. Then play it for yourself later when you're alone. Do you like the way you read the story? Practice alone with a tape recorder until you have developed the voices you think enhance the story the most.

Help Children Get Involved Through Participation.   Young children enjoy stories better if they are a part of them. You, the story reader, can get children directly involved in a number of ways. For instance, you might ask your listener to say the next word. In *The Beastly Feast,* short simple sentences are illustrated by large vibrant animals bringing food to the feast. When your listener hears and sees that "bears bring pears" and "parrots bring carrots," have her say the word to complete the line "flies bring _____," as you point to the picture of the pies. Or have her count down from 5 in *Zoom! Zoom! Zoom! I'm Off to the Moon* on the page where the rocket blasts off. Or have her guess where *Noisy Nora* is hiding when she says she is leaving home.

Be careful, however, with a large group. Child participation often disrupts the group because everyone wants a turn to say the answer. Avoiding that problem is another advantage for reading to small groups and individuals. With a small group you can keep control of what happens by calling on a particular child by name, instead of opening it to everyone.

For groups who are not used to sitting still and listening to a story, you may not want to interrupt the flow of the story with individual involvement at first. You must decide whether your priority for the children is to complete a story without interruptions or to get the children involved by offering them opportunities to participate.

Books to Motivate Speaking

Can picture books motivate other kinds of speaking? They can if you choose them knowledgeably. Look for books with a character on the cover who speaks as the story progresses. If the children enjoy the book and want you to read it again, you can in-

An exciting approach for motivating children's speaking is to have each child hold a character doll and speak for the character as you read the story.

volve them in speaking for the character. Start with simple stories where a single character repeats words throughout the story. An animal character is often a good one to begin with because children are so attracted to talking-animal stories.

Use a Puppet

Also try using an animal puppet or stuffed animal toy for the child to speak for the character. Hiding behind a puppet who talks is a good way to involve even the shiest children. Animal puppets can be made by you or the children from small paper bags with the bag bottom as the face. Paint or glue on eyes, nose, mouth, and animal ears. Socks also make good puppets, with peel-off circles as the eyes and nose. The puppeteer opens and closes his hand within the end of the bag or sock while he speaks for the puppet. Hot-pad gloves in the form of jungle animals make excellent puppets as well. Some toy stores and children's book stores now sell stuffed animal toys or puppets to accompany particular books. Educational supply companies also stock toys and puppets to accompany children's books. (See Book Toy Distributors at the end of this chapter.)

An exciting approach for motivating children's speaking is to have a child hold a character doll or wear an animal puppet and speak for the animal as you read the story. Ask for a volunteer to be the talking animal. You will quickly have more volunteers than you need, so start with a small group of children. Yes, they will want the story repeated until everyone gets a chance to be "the grouchy ladybug" or whomever. Children need the *repetition* to practice this "book language." Be sure to congratulate all of your animal speakers, pointing out what you liked about their speaking. Books you should consider purchasing or borrowing from a library for this important language activity include the following:

Am I Beautiful? (Minarik, 1992)—(Have a hippo puppet who repeats, "Look, at me. Am I beautiful, too?")

Brown Bear, Brown Bear, What Do You See? (Carle, 1992)—(Have bear puppet ask this question)

Do You Want to Be My Friend? (Carle, 1971)—(Have a mouse puppet who says, "Do you want to be my friend?")

Does a Kangaroo Have a Mother, too? (Carle, 2000)—(Have any puppet ask this question about various animals)

The Grouchy Ladybug (Carle, 1977)—(Have a ladybug puppet who repeats, "Do you want to fight?" and "Oh, you're not big enough.")

Is Your Mama a Llama? (Guarino, 1989)—(Have a llama puppet who repeats, "Is your mama a llama?")

Polar Bear, Polar Bear, What Do You Hear? (Carle, 1992)—(Have polar bear puppet ask this question).

Some talking-animal books have the other animal characters responding to the main character with a distinctive saying. For these stories, have children volunteer to be the other animals who speak when it is their turn. It is not necessary for each of them to have a puppet unless you have a large supply. You can point to children if they forget their turns. In the cumulative tale *Hattie and the Fox* (Fox, 1992), Hattie, a big black hen, spies different parts of an animal hiding in the bushes, but when she tells the other animals, they all respond with the same saying: "Good grief" (goose); "Well, well" (pig); "Who cares?" (sheep); "So what?" (horse); and "What next?" (cow). If you, as Hattie, read the story to a group of five children, then each child will have a chance to speak several times for each animal before Hattie's parts turn into a whole fox.

The Very Quiet Cricket (Carle, 1990) tries to answer the insects who greet him, but nothing happens when he first rubs his wings together. Choose a child to be each of the insects and point to them when it is their turn to say "Welcome" (cricket), "Good morning" (locust), "Hello" (praying mantis), "Good day" (worm), "Hi" (spittlebug), "Good afternoon" (cicada), "How are you?" (bumblebee), "Good evening" (dragonfly), and "Good night" (mosquitoes). The children need to be very quiet on the last page of this story, when the cricket finally gains his voice, for this book actually chirps!

In Carle's *The Very Busy Spider* (1984), various animals approach the spider asking in whole sentences whether she wants to do different things (e.g., "Want to go for a ride?"). Your children can be the horse, cow, sheep, goat, pig, dog, cat, duck, rooster, and owl who ask the questions. Children with visual impairments may want to sit on your lap to feel the textured spider web as it grows.

Once children are used to speaking for the characters, they are ready for the next step in their development of communication skills: taking on a character's entire role through simple playacting. Look for books showing people characters on the cover who seem to be speaking to one another. For example, *I'm Calling Molly* (Kurtz, 1990) shows a little African American boy talking on the telephone to a little Anglo American girl. It is a story about Christopher and his next door neighbor to Molly, who won't come over to play because she is playing dress-up with Rebekah. If your children show strong interest in the story, this may be a book to involve them in a simple type of playacting called "story reenactment."

Just as preschoolers enjoy taking on the spontaneous roles of mother, father, doctor, and nurse in the dramatic play area, they can also enjoy playing the roles of favorite book characters. In story reenactment, children play character roles while you read the story. More than one child can play the same role at the same time. For example, if you have two or three Christophers calling on the phone for Molly, give each of them a chance to make their calls. If you have several Mollys, let them each have their say. The children can dress up for their parts or play them with pretend props. They can copy the characters' actions and words just like they are in the book or make up their own. The children who do not want a role can be the audience. This informal drama is for the children themselves and not an outside audience. If all goes well, they will want to repeat the story reenactment. Ishee and Goldhaber (1990) tell us:

> Many repetitions help children. For many children it is necessary to watch a play numerous times before making the first gesture of pretense within the play. For others, repetition allows an opportunity to elaborate and expand on the story as pretended. (p. 74)

Simple stories that children want repeated are the best ones for story reenactment. *On a Hot, Hot Day* (Weiss, 1992) has a Hispanic mother in the city talking to her child Angel during each of the four seasons. Several children can play the roles of Mama and Angel at the same time, saying "Think cool" in the summer as they twirl around in the spray from the fire hydrant; "Sip slow" on a rainy fall day as they sip hot cocoa in a luncheonette; "Bundle up" in the winter as they shake snow from their coats; and "Breathe deep" in the spring as they sniff the plants on the windowsill. Give each Mama and Angel a chance to say their lines and do their actions separately before continuing.

Simple folktales also make fine story reenactments. Children may already know *The Three Billy Goats Gruff* (Galdone, 1973), but what about *Zomo the Rabbit* (McDermott, 1992) from West Africa, who is not big and not strong, but very clever? Children can reenact the roles of the Sky God, whom Zomo goes to seeking wisdom; Big Fish, whom Zomo causes to dance in order to shake off his scales; Wild Cow, whom Zomo catches to get her milk; and Leopard, whom Zomo trips to get his tooth. Folk stories with three tasks like this are easy for children to remember and reenact with gusto.

Books to Motivate Emergent Reading

Research has found that the best books to promote emergent reading in young children are *predictable books,* that is, picture books that "contain selections with repetitive

1. Text has repetitive and rhyming words, lines, episodes
2. Text is brief, fast-paced, and fun
3. Text has cumulative episodes
4. Pictures clearly illustrate words, lines, and episodes
5. Books may have audiotapes available

Figure 6–3   Predictable Books for Preschoolers

structures which enable children to anticipate the next word, line, or episode" (Bridge, 1986, p. 82). This makes sense when we remember how important repetition is in the early childhood learning process.

For preschoolers, these books also need to be simple, fast-paced, and fun. Some may have episodes that are repeated in a cumulative fashion as new episodes are added. Other helpful books have rhyming words that children can remember. Still other helpful features are pictures that clearly illustrate words or sentences. Then when children hear these stories read aloud again and again, they remember what is coming next—what word, what line, or what episode. Eventually they will be able to connect that written word, line, or episode in the book with the spoken word, line, or episode. Finally, they will be able to look at the written word, line, or episode in the book and say it themselves.

Are we saying, then, that you should begin "teaching" your preschool children to read? No. We are saying that you should read predictable books to them and provide them with such books to explore for themselves. To stimulate emergent reading in your children, you should fill your classroom with print materials and make frequent references to what those materials say. The children themselves will take it from there.

To select predictable books from the wide array of children's books available, consider the criteria in Figure 6–3, Predictable Books for Preschoolers. Children's fingerplays, chants, and songs also make excellent predictable books because children already know the rhyming, repetitive words and are accustomed to saying or singing them. More of these fine chanting books are being published each year. Be on the lookout for them. The purpose of such books is not to teach children the chants but to show them what their already familiar chant looks like when it is written in words and illustrated in pictures.

More than one version of certain chants are sometimes available. For example, *This Old Man* (Jones, 1990) shows the traditional fingerplay with a grandfather playing knick-knack for his granddaughter, but every other page has a hole in the middle to look through and predict what's coming. Children quickly spot a drum through the first hole and thus can say the word in unison before turning the page. When the page is turned the word *DRUM* appears in large capital letters. In *Knick Knack Paddywack* (Moss, 1992), a lively old man plays not only knick-knack, but also bip-bop, bim-bum, jig-jug, and a half dozen more catchy words, before he blasts off into outer space. Which one should you choose? Buy both of them. Your children will be doubly enchanted.

The Itsy Bitsy Spider (Trapani, 1993) is an expanded but very popular new version of the well-known fingerplay and song, as mentioned in Chapter 4. After climbing up the waterspout and being washed out, the spider climbs up the kitchen wall, the yellow pail, the rocking chair, and the maple tree in colorful double-page pictures that clearly illustrate the spider's adventures. Read the story to individuals or a very small group so that children can find the spider and predict what will happen next.

The House That Jack Built (Stow, 1992) tells the traditional cumulative tale in a lush Caribbean setting, showing Jack's cottage, all of the animals, the man all tattered and torn getting married to the maiden all forlorn, and so on. Young children enjoy working their way forward and backward through the story that starts and ends with the house that Jack built. Its catchy rhythm and ageless rhymes will have youngsters tapping and clapping as they follow the words and guess what comes next.

Miss Mary Mack, a Hand-Clapping Rhyme (Hoberman, 1998) makes a fine predictable book because the last word on every line is repeated three times: "Miss Mary Mack, Mack, Mack; All dressed in black, black, black . . . " This traditional jump-rope rhyme about the elephant who jumps so high he reaches the sky and doesn't come back till the Fourth of July can be chanted or even sung to the tune on the end page.

Audiocassettes are available for some predictable books. Use them to give children an opportunity for exploring books on their own. Youngsters can use a headset to listen to the tape as they turn the pages of the book. Some tapes include page-turn signals to help them know when to continue. You may need to help individuals get started using tapes like this. Book tapes should not, however, replace your own reading to children. Youngsters need your personal touch and encouraging comments or questions.

PROVIDES MATERIALS AND ACTIVITIES TO SUPPORT EMERGENT WRITING

Just as preschool children can emerge into reading, they are also able to emerge into writing if the environment is conducive. This means you should set up a writing area, as suggested in Chapter 3, stocking it with all sorts of enticing writing implements. Felt-tip pens in a rainbow of colors are the favorite writing tools for preschoolers in their early scribbling efforts.

This is a *manipulation* phase for the youngsters, when they first try out things on their own. They are playing around with using writing tools and making marks on paper. Some of their scribbles may be for drawing, while underneath they make writing scribbles "to tell what the picture is about." You should support them with encouragement and acceptance (e.g., "Oh, Marissa, you really like to make your scribbles in different colors, don't you?"). Children may want to tell you what their scribbles say. But just as often they may ask you what they say because you know how to read and they don't!

Have a bulletin board nearby where children can display their writing products just as they do their art. You will easily recognize children's progression to the *mastery* level of prewriting, when they fill paper after paper with row after row of scribbles, much like lines of writing.

Children's early writing efforts are for fun as they explore this new medium spontaneously. At some point, however, they may want to communicate something even in scribbles. Using the materials in the writing center, you can help them make signs for their block buildings, write a letter to someone, write their scribbled names on a sign-up sheet for the computer, or sign out for a book to take home overnight. Children who use such "mock writing" in meaningful ways are progressing to the *meaning* level of exploratory play. Their scribbles may even begin to look like real letters.

Some children may start "writing" their own stories. You can encourage such efforts by mounting scribble stories on the wall in the writing area. Other children may tell you, "You write it. I don't know how to write." You can answer, truthfully, "I used to know how to do scribble writing, but I forgot. So you'll have to write it for me."

Not all children will reach this level, nor should you expect them to. Encourage children to use the writing area in any way they want, just as they do the art area. Yours will be a supportive and facilitating role, not a direct teaching role. That will come later in elementary school. Instead, provide the paper and writing tools for their own private efforts and congratulate them on the results.

Writing Opportunities

Books to Read

In addition, you should provide opportunities to motivate children's writing, just as you do their speaking, listening, and reading. For example, read books to the children in which the characters communicate by writing. *Like Me and You* (Raffi, 1985) is a simple multicultural story with a picture on every page showing a child from a different country mailing, receiving, reading, and writing pen pal letters. The words tell where each child lives and culminate in the Raffi song "Like Me and You."

Bring in some picture postcards and have interested children "write" to one another and "mail" the cards in each other's mailboxes made from shoe boxes. Another time they may want to write to children in the class next door. Some children may be able to print cards with real letters to their mothers on Mother's Day.

Read *Good Morning Franny Good Night Franny* (Hearn, 1984) about Franny, a city girl in a wheelchair who becomes friends with Ting, an Asian girl who knows only a few English words. Franny writes "good morning" and "good night" in Ting's notebook for the little girl to practice. Later, when Ting moves away, Franny finds these same words written on the sidewalk as a message to her. Your children can write scribbled messages to one another to be placed in their classroom mailboxes. Another time take the children outside and, with permission, have them write or draw on the sidewalk or blacktop with sidewalk chalk. Colored chalk and individual chalkboards can be an added attraction in the writing area at this time.

Some children may eventually be able to print cards with real letters to their mothers on Mother's Day.

Bunny Cakes (Wells, 1997), Max Bunny's hilarious misadventures in trying to buy ingredients for a birthday cake for Grandma, is a perfect preschool writing story. Illustrations on every page show what Max's older sister Ruby prints as the name of the ingredient she wants Max to show the grocer each time he goes to the store. Underneath the printed name, Max scribbles the name of the ingredient he wants, "Red-Hot-Marshmallow Squirters," but somehow the grocer fails to understand until Max finally draws a picture of the squirters. Have children "write" down their own favorite food on note paper, as Max did. Can you read what they have written?

If children know how to regulate their own turns in the learning centers with name tags or necklaces, have them use a sign-up sheet for a change. A small clipboard with a pencil attached can be fastened at the entrance to each area. The number of children allowed in the area can be noted on the clipboard tablet. Other sign-up sheets can be used for taking turns with the computer, the tricycle, the cassette player, and other popular items. Children can write their names under one another's however they wish—in a scribble, with printed letters, or in a symbol. Most children can identify their own scribbles quite well.

Bring in letter stampers and stamp pads. Can anyone stamp the letters of her name?

Alphabet Letters

Besides scribbling, preschool children will soon begin trying to print alphabet letters, usually the letters of their names. Some children have already started printing their names at home. Others may know only the first initial. Should you teach these children the ABCs? The answer is "not really." They will teach themselves the letters they need to know if you provide them with developmentally appropriate materials and opportunities. Have a shaving cream day in the writing center, for instance, and let children try printing their names or initials in the shaving cream with their fingers.

Put out three-dimensional wood or plastic or magnetic alphabet letters in the writing center. Children can play with them to find their own name letters or to match letters that are the same. Bring in letter stampers and stamp pads. Can they stamp the letters of their names? Also, you can have alphabet books available here and in the reading area. Today's alphabet books are anything but traditional. Your children will marvel at or chuckle over some of the popular ones:

A Is for Salad (Lester, 2000)

Alligator Arrived with Apples: A Potluck Alphabet Feast (Dragonwagon, 1987)

Chicka Chicka Boom Boom (Martin & Archambault, 1989)

Eating the Alphabet: Fruits & Vegetables from A to Z (Ehlert, 1989)

The Handmade Alphabet [For "signing"] (Rankin, 1991)

The Icky Bug Alphabet Book (Pallotta, 1988)

K Is for Kiss Good Night: A Bedtime Alphabet (Sardegna, 1994)

A manual typewriter in the writing area is another source for letter play with children. They may start by pretending to be typists, but soon children begin hunting for the letter keys to spell out their own names. A typewriter like this also makes a good introduction to the computer. When you plan to bring a computer into the classroom, start with a typewriter if you can. Children can practice pressing keys and will soon learn that pressing only one key at a time is the way to print a letter, while pressing several keys at once makes the keys jam.

Book to Read

If your children are using a typewriter be sure to read them the book *Click, Clack, Moo Cows That Type* (Cronin, 2000) a hilarious story about Farmer Brown's cows that spend all day in the barn typing! When he goes to check out the sounds, he finds a note addressed to him: "Dear Farmer Brown, The barn is very cold at night. We'd like some electric blankets. Sincerely, The Cows." The upset farmer declares "No way," but soon the hens are also having the cows type a message asking for electric blankets for them, too. Finally, they all agree to exchange the typewriter for the blankets. The duck is assigned to carry the typewriter to the farmer, but guess what happens along the way? Can any of your children type a message?

Computer Programs

The computer is a powerful addition to the self-teaching tools of an early childhood classroom. Because of its interactive nature, the computer allows children to explore and experiment with programs through trial and error. Children learn that pressing a key causes something to happen. If they press the correct key, then the program responds the way it should. If the key is wrong, either the program does not respond or it signals an error.

Some early childhood programs have a serious problem in using computers: No one on the staff feels comfortable with a computer. As a result, the machine stands silent and unused except for children's pretend play. If this is the case in your program, find a volunteer who will act as a computer aide. Often a knowledgeable parent, teacher, or student from a local high school, college, or university will volunteer to spend enough time to get the children started.

Your staff, along with the children, can watch, learn, and practice how to use the programs. They will see that it is best to start with a small group of children at a time, with two children seated as the computer operators and the others standing behind them as observers, as mentioned previously. Having two child operators at once helps children learn from one another and teaches them keyboard turn-taking skills. Place two computer necklaces in the area to regulate numbers of children. Adults should allow the youngsters to learn on their own as much as possible.

One of the first programs should be a simple but interesting alphabet game, using all the letter keys on the keyboard. Children often start by pressing any key to see what happens. Later they search for particular letters to make their favorite graphics appear. In this way they learn alphabet letters and the keyboard at the same time.

The levels of playful exploration are the same with computer programs as with blocks and paints. Children first *manipulate* the keys to learn what will happen. Then, they gain *mastery* of the letters by repeating them over and over. Finally, they apply *meaning* by making up their own games with computer graphics.

One or two alphabet programs are all they need to get started. Let children play with them for as many days or weeks as necessary before introducing other software. Choose from among beginning programs such as these CD-ROM programs from Video Library Company (1-800-843-3620):

Alphabet Express: Preschool	*Blue's ABC's Time Activities*
Alphabet Play with the ABC's	*Curious George Pre-K ABC's*
Alphabonk Farm	*Disney's Mickey Preschool*
Arthur's Preschool	*Dr. Seuss' ABC*

At the same time, you can have three-dimensional alphabet games available, along with alphabet books, songs, and circle games. Play games in which children represent a letter from their name by making some sort of movement or sound. Invent your own alphabet games or let children contribute. Observe your young computer operators closely and you will note that the most accomplished users have already invented an "I Caught You" or "I Stopped You" game by pushing a key to stop their partner's computer graphic from completing its movement.

Once again we realize that the young child's brain is programmed to learn beginning communication skills through playful exploration and trial and error. Let us assist in this endeavor by filling our classrooms with interactive learning materials and fun activities for children to accomplish on their own.

SUMMARY

This chapter discusses children's verbal and literacy skills, giving suggestions on how teachers can help youngsters develop verbal communication by helping children become active listeners, soundproofing the room so that children can hear themselves speak, providing a stress-free environment to support children's confidence in speaking, giving children reasons to communicate, and supporting children's conversations. Teachers need to evaluate their own language for their use of responsive rather than restrictive speech. Suggestions and books for supporting bilingual children, especially Spanish speakers, are included.

Books to motivate children's listening, speaking, and emergent reading are discussed, along with a book selection checklist. Directions on how best to read books to children, how to help them reenact stories dramatically, and how to use book puppets are given, with special emphasis on "predictable books" to encourage emergent reading. Emergent writing is presented through use of three-dimensional materials in the writing area, as well as alphabet books and the appropriate use of computer programs.

LEARNING ACTIVITIES

1. Read Chapter 6, Advancing Communication Skills, and write out answers to Question Sheet 6.

2. Meet with your trainer or instructor and discuss answers to Question Sheet 6.

3. View one of the videotapes listed and make 10 file cards with specific ideas for developing children's speaking, listening, prereading, or prewriting skills.

4. Read one or more of the references cited or suggested readings and add 10 file cards to your file, with specific ideas for helping children develop communication skills. Include the reference source on each card.

5. Work with a shy or nonverbal child, using suggestions in this chapter to help but not pressure him or her to speak.

6. Review 10 of the children's books discussed in this chapter, making a file card for each. Read several of these books to individuals or a small group. Record the results.

7. Do a story reenactment with children based on a favorite book. Record the results.

8. Bring in a new predictable book for the children and read it to them, extending the experience with a puppet or activity and record the results.

9. Use an alphabet computer program (or alphabet book and activity) with the children. Observe and record how children use this program independently.

10. Complete the Chapter 6 Evaluation Sheet and return it to your trainer or college instructor.

QUESTION SHEET 6

1. How does the drive to communicate assist children in their language development?

2. What does the new brain research have to say about how children develop communication skills?

3. How can you as teacher become an active listening model for the children?

4. How can you help children to become active listeners?

5. What can you do to make the environment stress-free so that children gain confidence to speak?

6. What are responsive language and restrictive language? Give examples. How should they be used and why?

7. How can you help but not pressure children to participate in conversations?

8. In what different ways can the use of puppets promote language skills?

9. How can you help children who speak a language other than English? Be specific.

10. Describe emergent reading and tell how you would use a predictable book to encourage emergent reading in children.

11. Describe how you would choose a book and then read it to an individual or small group based on information from this chapter.

12. Should you use book audiotapes with children? Why or why not?

13. Describe how you would involve preschool children in learning to write.

14. How should alphabet letters be used in an emergent writing program?

15. What problem do many preschool programs face in using the computer with children? How would you overcome this problem?

REFERENCES

Begley, S. (1997). How to build a baby's brain. *Newsweek,* Spring/Summer, 28–32.

Bridge, C. A. (1986). Predictable books for beginning readers and writers. In M. R. Sampson (Ed.), *The pursuit of literacy: Early reading and writing.* Dubuque, IA: Kendall/Hunt.

Ishee, N., & Goldhaber, J. (1990). Story re-enactment: Let the play begin! *Young Children, 45*(3), 70–75.

Jalongo, M. R. (1995). Promoting active listening in the classroom. *Childhood Education, 72*(1), 13–18.

Jalongo, M. R., & Ribblett, D. M. (1997). Using song picture books to support emergent literacy. *Childhood Education, 74*(1), 15–22.

Klenk, L. (2001). Playing with literacy in preschool classrooms. *Childhood Education, 77*(3), 150–157.

Kratcoski, A. M., & Katz, K. B. (1998). Conversing with young language learners in the classroom. *Young Children, 53*(3), 30–33.

Selman, R. (2001). Talk time: Programming communicative interaction into the toddler day. *Young Children, 56*(3), 15–18.

Stone, J. (1993). Caregiver and teacher language—Responsive or restrictive? *Young Children, 48*(4), 12–18.

West, L. S., and Egley, E. H. (1998). Children get more than a hamburger: Using labels and logos to enhance literacy. *Dimensions of Early Childhood, 26*(3 & 4), 43–46.

Willis, C. (1998). Language development: A key to lifelong learning. *Child Care Information Exchange, 121,* 63–65.

SUGGESTED READINGS

Armington, D. (1997). *The living classroom: Writing, reading, and beyond.* Washington, DC: National Association for the Education of Young Children.

Beaty, J. J., & Pratt, L. (2003). *Early literacy in preschool and kindergarten.* Upper Saddle River, NJ: Merrill/Prentice Hall.

Bobys, A. R. (2000). What does emerging literacy look like? *Young Children, 55*(4), 16–22.

Clements, N. E., & Warncke, E. W. (1994). Helping literacy emerge at school for less-advantaged children. *Young Children, 49*(3), 22–26.

Collins, N. L. D., & Shaeffer, M. B. (1997). Look, listen, and learn to read. *Young Children, 52*(5), 63–68.

Elster, C. A. (1994). "I guess they do listen:" Young children's emergent readings after adult read-alouds. *Young Children, 49*(3) 27–31.

Fields, M. V., & DeGayner, B. (2000). Read my story. *Childhood Education, 76*(3), 130–135.

Hayes, L. F. (1990). From scribbling to writing: Smoothing the way. *Young Children, 45*(3), 62–69.

Jacobs, J. S., & Tunnell, M. O. (1996). *Children's literature briefly.* Upper Saddle River, NJ: Merrill/Prentice Hall.

Jalongo, M. R. (1996). Teaching young children to become better listeners. *Young Children, 51*(2), 21–26.

Machado, J. M. (1995). *Early childhood experiences in language arts: Emerging literacy.* Albany, NY: Delmar.

Moore, L. M. (1998). Language learning and some initial literacy skills through social interactions. *Young Children, 53*(2), 72–75.

Neumann, S. B., & Roskos, K. A. (1993). *Language and learning in the early years: An integrated approach.* Ft. Worth, TX: Harcourt.

Novick, R. (2000). Supporting early literacy development. *Childhood Education, 76*(2), 70–75.

Oken-Wright, P. (1998). Transition to writing: Drawing as a scaffold for emergent writers. *Young Children, 53*(2), 76–81.

Perrotta, B. (1994). Writing development and second language acquisition in young children. *Childhood Education, 70*(4), 237–241.

Roskos, K. A., & Neumann, S. (1994). Of scribbles, schemas, and storybooks: Using literacy albums to document young children's literacy growth. *Young Children, 49*(2), 78–85.

Riojas-Cortez, M. (2000). It's all about talking: Oral language development in a bilingual classroom. *Dimensions of Early Childhood, 29*(1), 11–15.

Schickedanz, J. A. (1999). *Much more than the ABCs: The early stages of reading and writing.* Washington, DC: National Association for the Education of Young Children.

Wasik, B. A. (2001). Teaching the alphabet to young children. *Young Children, 56*(1), 34–40.

Wright, J. L., & Shade, D. D. (Eds.). (1994). *Young children: Active learners in a technological age.* Washington, DC: National Association for the Education of Young Children.

CHILDREN'S BOOKS

Cannon, J. (1993). *Stella Luna.* San Diego: Harcourt Brace.

Carle, E. (1967). *Brown bear, brown bear, what do you see?*

Carle, E. (1971). *Do you want to be my friend?* New York: Crowell.

Carle, E. (2000). *Does a kangaroo have a mother, too?* New York: HarperCollins.

Carle, E. (1977). *The grouchy ladybug.* New York: Crowell.

Carle, E. (1992). *Polar bear, polar bear, what do you hear?*

Carle, E. (1981). *The very hungry caterpillar.* New York: Putnam.

Carle, E. (1984). *The very busy spider.* New York: Philomel.

Carle, E. (1990). *The very quiet cricket.* New York: Philomel.

Cooney, N. E. (1993). *Chatterbox Jamie.* New York: Putnam's.

Cronin, D. (2000). *Click clack moo cows that type.* New York: Simon & Schuster.

DePaola, T. (1997). *Mice squeak, we speak.* New York: Putnam's.

Dragonwagon, C. (1987). *Alligator arrived with apples, A potluck alphabet feast.* New York: Macmillan.

Ehlert, L. (1989). *Eating the alphabet: Fruits & vegetables from A to Z.* San Diego: Harcourt Brace.

Fox, M. (1992). *Hattie and the fox.* New York: Macmillan.

Freeman, D. (1978). *A Pocket for Corduroy.* New York: Viking.

Galdone, P. (1973). *The three billy goats gruff.* New York: Clarion.

Goldstone, B. (1998). *The beastly feast.* New York: Holt.

Guarino, D. (1989). *Is your mama a llama?* New York: Scholastic.

Hoffman, M. (1991). *Amazing Grace.* Glenview, IL: Scott Foresman.

Hearn, E. (1984). *Good morning Franny good night Franny.* Toronto, Canada: The Women's Press.

Hoberman, M. A. (1998). *Miss Mary Mack.* Boston: Little, Brown.

Jones, C. (1990). *This old man.* Boston: Houghton Mifflin.

Kurtz, J. (1990). *I'm calling Molly.* Morton Grove, IL: Whitman.

Lee, H. V. (1996). *I had a hippopotamus.* New York: Lee and Low.

Lester, M. (2000). *A is for salad.* New York: Putnam & Grosset.

Lindenbaum, P. (1992). *Boodil my dog.* New York: Holt.

Martin, B., & Archambault, J. (1989). *Chicka chicka boom boom.* New York: Simon and Schuster.

McDermott, G. (1992). *Zomo the rabbit: A trickster tale from West Africa.* San Diego: Harcourt Brace.

McNaughton, C. (1995). *Here come the aliens!* Cambridge, MA: Candlewick.

Minarik, E. H. (1992). *Am I beautiful?* New York: Greenwillow.

Moss, M. (1992). *Knick knack paddywack.* Boston: Houghton Mifflin.

Pallotta, J. (1988). *The icky bug alphabet book.* Watertown, MA: Charlesbridge.

Paxton, T. (1996). *Going to the zoo.* New York: Morrow.

Pfister, M. (1992). *The rainbow fish.* New York: North-South Books.

Plourde, L. (1997). *Pigs in the mud in the middle of the rud.* New York: Blue Sky/Scholastic.

Raffi. (1985). *Like me and you.* New York: Crown.

Rankin, L. (1991). *The handmade alphabet.* New York: Dial.

Sardegna, J. (1994). *K is for kiss good night: A bedtime alphabet.* New York: Doubleday.

Showers, P. (1991). *The listening walk.* New York: Harper.

Stow, J. (1992). *The house that Jack built.* New York: Dial.

Trapani, I. (1993). *The itsy bitsy spider.* Boston: Whispering Coyote.

Weiss, N. (1992). *On a hot, hot day.* New York: Putnam's.

Wells, R. (1997). *Bunny cakes.* New York: Dial.

Wells, R. (1997). *Noisy Nora.* New York: Dial.

Wood, A. (1992). *Silly Sally.* San Diego: Harcourt.

Yaccarino, D. (1997). *Zoom! Zoom! Zoom! I'm off to the moon!* New York: Scholastic.

VIDEOTAPES

Apple Computer (Producer). *The adventure begins: Preschool and technology.* Washington, DC: National Association for the Education of Young Children. (#827).

Davidson Films (Producer). *Nourishing language development in early childhood* (A. S. Honig). Washington, DC: National Association for the Development of Young Children. (#859).

High/Scope (Producer). *Language and literacy.* Ypsilanti, MI: Author. (Also available from Redleaf Press, St. Paul, MI.)

Resources and Instruction in Staff Excellence (Producer). *Developing the young bilingual learner.* Washington, DC: National Association for the Education of Young Children. (#801).

State of Indiana (Producer). *Far ago and long away: Innovative storytelling.* Washington, DC: National Association for the Education of Young Children. (#840; in Spanish #840S).

BOOK TOY DISTRIBUTORS

Demco Kids & Things
P. O. Box 7488
Madison, WI 53707
(1-800-356-1200)

Llama puppet *(Is Your Mama a Llama?)*
Ladybug glove puppet *(The Grouchy Ladybug)*
Elephant puppet *(The Grouchy Ladybug)*
Kangaroo puppet *(Does a Kangaroo Have a Mother, Too?)*

Constructive Playthings
13201 Arrington Rd.
Grandview, MO 64030
(1-800-448-4115)

Spider puppet *(The Very Busy Spider)*
Ladybug puppet *(The Grouchy Ladybug)*
Bear puppet *(Brown Bear, Brown Bear What Do You See?)*
Hippo puppet *(Am I Beautiful?)*
Elephant puppet *(The Grouchy Ladybug)*

Lakeshore Learning Materials
2695 E. Domingues St.
P. O. Box 6261
Carson, CA 90749
(1-800-421-5354)

Caterpillar/Butterfly *(The Very Hungry Caterpillar)*
Storytelling doll *(This Old Man)* Storytelling doll *(Joseph Had a Little Overcoat)*

CHAPTER 6 EVALUATION SHEET
ADVANCING COMMUNICATION SKILLS

1. Student _____

2. Trainer _____

3. Center where training occurred _____

4. Beginning date _____ Ending date _____

5. Describe what student did to accomplish General Objective.

   _____

   _____

6. Describe what student did to accomplish Specific Objectives.

   Objective 1 _____

   _____

   Objective 2 _____

   _____

   Objective 3 _____

   _____

7. Evaluation of student's Learning Activities

   _____

Comments:

   _____

   _____

   _____

   _____

   _____

   _____

   _____

Permission is granted by the publisher to reproduce this page for evaluation and record keeping.

Advancing Creative Skills

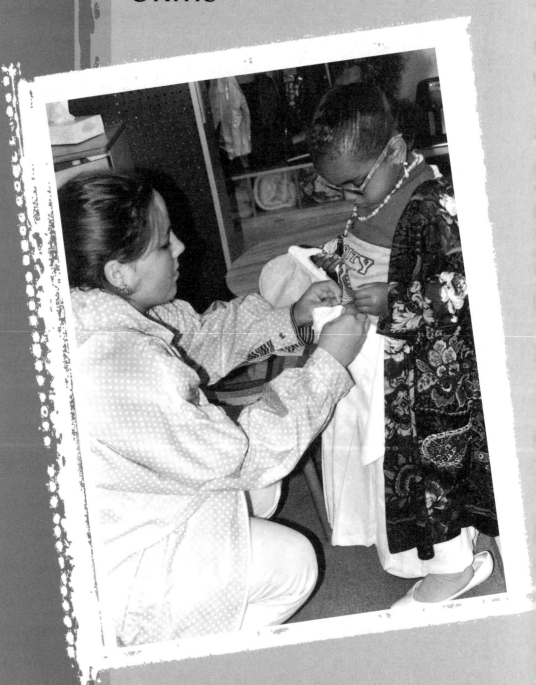

GENERAL OBJECTIVE

To promote children's creativity through playful expression and freedom of activity

 SPECIFIC OBJECTIVES

_____ Gives children the time, opportunity, and freedom to do pretend and fantasy role play

_____ Provides a variety of art materials and activities for children to explore on their own

_____ Encourages children to create and have fun with music

When we speak of a person with **creative skills,** we generally mean someone who has original ideas, who does things in new and different ways, and who uses imagination and inventiveness to bring about novel forms. Can young children be creative in these ways?

Not only can they be, but they are. Creativity seems to be intuitive in young children, something they are born with. From the very beginning they have the capacity to look at things, to hear, smell, taste, and touch things from an entirely original perspective—their own. After all, preschool children are new and unique beings in a strange and complex world. The only way they can make sense of things around them is to explore with their senses—to try them out, to see what makes things the way they are, to see if they can be any different.

Young children bring to any activity a spirit of wonder, great curiosity, and a spontaneous drive to explore, experiment, and manipulate in a playful and original fashion. This is creativity. It is the same impulse that actors, artists, writers, musicians, dancers, and research scientists have.

You may respond that not all children behave like this. Some show little creativity or little interest in creative activities. As we noted in the chapter on cognitive skills, some children show little interest in anything new. Some will not engage in any activities unless directed by the teacher. These are the children who need our special assistance in rediscovering the creativity they were born with.

Acceptance and Encouragement

Creativity flourishes only where it is accepted and encouraged. Infants, toddlers, and preschoolers who have been dominated by the adults around them and not allowed to do anything their own way may not show much creativity. They have already learned the sad lesson that experimentation only gets them into trouble. Children who have been the victims of neglect, lack of love, harsh discipline, or overprotection seem to lack the spark of creativity as well.

It is extremely important for teachers, assistants, volunteers, and student teachers in preschool programs to help rekindle that spark. It is imperative that young children be able to use the creative skills of pretending, imaginative thinking, fantasizing, and inventiveness in learning to deal with the complex world around them. Strange as it may seem, these are the skills that will help them most in problem solving, getting along with others, understanding their world, and eventually, doing abstract thinking. Promoting creativity is, in fact, a most effective way to promote cognitive development.

Freedom

The key to setting up an environment that promotes creativity is freedom. Children must be free to explore, experiment, manipulate, invent, and pretend spontaneously. Having an adult show them how or tell them what to do defeats this purpose. Adults do not see things or use things as children do. Young children need the opportunity to work out many ideas on their own and in their own way, without adult direction or interference.

GIVES CHILDREN THE TIME, OPPORTUNITY, AND FREEDOM TO DO PRETEND AND FANTASY ROLE PLAY

Traditional early childhood dramatic play usually takes place in the dramatic play learning center, where the setup often includes a child-size version of a kitchen with wooden table, chairs, stove, refrigerator, and cupboards. Or it may be a child-size store with shelves of boxes and a checkout counter, or a doctor's office, or a restaurant. Children play roles they have seen enacted by their parents, community helpers, or people from the field trip sites they have visited. They learn how it feels to be someone else as they pretend to be a mother, father, doctor, or police officer. (For more about dramatic play, see Chapter 9.)

Another type of dramatic play that may be even more conducive to young children's development of creativity is fantasy role play. Fantasy role play involves the children in pretending to be a fictitious storybook hero or to be themselves in a fantasy setting. It can start with a realistic situation and catapult the children into an adventure that may carry them to the stars and back. A good method for involving young children in such rich pretending is to read them a picture book featuring fantastical situations and then provide props for their own role play.

Picture Books as Motivators

Most teachers and many children are familiar with the classic fantasy *Where the Wild Things Are* (Sendak, 1963), and they may have already held a classroom "wild rumpus" dance to weird music. Children can also pretend on their own if the teacher encourages them with comments like "If you were Max, what else would you do in the Land of the Wild Things?" They can close their eyes and imagine being Max, after you have read them this story.

You can also help extend their pretending by making Max and wild-things costumes for fantasy role play. You can photocopy pictures from the book onto overhead transparencies and then project these transparency pictures as child-size figures onto newsprint or poster boards to be traced around, colored in, and cut out. To make the life-size figures into costumes, tape the figures to plastic trash bags and cut out holes for arms and heads. Or children can make their own wild-things masks. Children love to be wild-things monsters stomping around, but be sure there is also a Max with a magic trick for taming them. Not all children require costumes for pretending, but many youngsters need some kind of prop to get them started.

Along the same line but without the fanciful creatures is *The Salamander Room* (Mazer, 1991). Brian finds an orange salamander in the woods and brings it home to live. When his mother challenges him with questions about where it will sleep, what it will eat, and who it will play with, Brian imagines an entire forest appearing in his room, page by page, with the ceiling opening to the sky while Brian lies in his own bed. After reading it, the teacher can ask other questions such as "What do you think Brian will do in the morning?" or "What if the salamander decides to go back to the forest?"

Children who enjoy such stories will want to talk more about them after you finish reading and then may want to pursue a similar imaginary adventure of their own. You can support their pretending by having a "prop box" on hand filled with items to motivate fantasy role play. Paste the dust jacket cover of the book on the box to identify it. A prop box for *The Salamander Room,* for example, might contain miniature plastic forest animals, birds, insects, and amphibians from a toy store, museum shop, or school supply company, as well as small branches from trees, pinecones, pebbles, and stones of different sizes. Children can pretend with miniature items in the block area or sand table just as easily as they do with costumes and child-size props.

In *James in the House of Aunt Prudence* (Bush, 1993), little James is dropped off to spend the day with his Great-Aunt Prudence in her elegant but mysterious Victorian house. When she leaves after serving him tea and macaroons, a huge bear arrives to carry James on its back in an adventurous romp through every room of the house, with a wicked Mouse King, flying bats, monkeys on gigantic insects, and an enormous red octopus in hot pursuit. People step out of portraits on the walls to join in the mêlée, until James's aunt finally reappears and sets them all straight. The teacher can ask listeners questions such as, "What do you think might happen when Aunt Prudence leaves the room again?" A prop box for this story could contain homemade head bands with animal ears or insect antennae, paper bat wings, cloth capes, and a plate with pretend macaroon cookies.

In *Going Home* (Wild, 1993) a Hispanic boy named Hugo can't wait to go home from the little hospital next door to the zoo. Two other children, Simon and Nirmala, share the children's ward, which is decorated with zoo posters. Then something happens. From outside the window Hugo hears the zoo elephant shrieking a message to him, so he puts on his slippers and goes for a ride across the plains of Africa. When his mother and sister come to visit him, Hugo gives his sister a paper elephant with floppy ears he has made. For each visit from his family, Hugo gives his sister a souvenir from one of his adventures: a howler monkey finger puppet from the Amazon and a snow leopard mask from the Himalayas. When he finally gets to go home, Hugo tells the other two children about wearing magic slippers for their own adventures with the zoo animals. "What adventures do you think Simon and Nirmala might have?" you could ask. This prop box can contain a pair of magic slippers and either miniature zoo animals or hot-pad animal puppets for your children's pretending. If this story really catches on, the children may want to make their own paper animals.

Children are fascinated with animals, all kinds of animals; but pretending about animals is easier if the animals are pets the children know personally. If guinea pigs are your classroom pets, you might start by reading the story of *John Willy and Freddy McGee* (Meade, 1998), two little pet guinea pigs that escape from their cage and explore the house where they live, because life in a cage is so BORING. They find that life outside the cage may be fun but it is also dangerous when the house cat starts chasing them. They finally hide in the ball tunnels inside the pool table until the cat drives them out by knocking balls into the holes.

Would your children like to continue the adventures of John Willy and Freddy McGee by pretending to be guinea pigs who escape into your classroom or into a pretend jungle? Your prop box could contain headbands with guinea pig ears and cat ears if children want to take the roles themslves. Or your might purchase from Demco (1-800-356-1200) guinea pig puppets or make your own puppets. Puppets can be made from paper bags, socks, and hot-pad gloves. You will also want jungle animal puppets such as a lion, elephant, giraffe, and boa constrictor to interact with the guinea pigs during their jungle adventure. You can turn your dramatic play center into a setting for animals if you make it into a jungle camp, or a pet store, or an animal hospital, or a museum.

Both boys and girls should be encouraged to take on fantasy roles from the books you read. In *Abuela* (Dorros, 1991), a little Hispanic girl named Rosalba and her grandmother from New York City start out for the park, but they end up sailing above the city and out to the Statue of Liberty in Rosalba's vivid imagination. When they return to the park, her Spanish-speaking grandmother says, "Vamos . . . " ("Let's go"), and they go off to another adventure into a rowboat, on the last page. A prop box for this fantasy can contain miniature people, boats, planes, cars, and table blocks for creating a city. The sand table can make a fine city park with a hand mirror for a pond.

In *Tar Beach* (Ringgold, 1991) an African American inner-city girl does some pretend flying of her own. Cassie accompanies her family to the rooftop of their apartment building during hot summer nights for a picnic, with blankets and picnic food, on the "tar beach." Later as she and her brother lie on their blankets looking up at the stars and the lights from nearby buildings, Cassie imagines herself flying over the city to see the sights.

Children love to pretend with character dolls such as Cassie from Tar Beach.

Character dolls accompany a number of books such as *Tar Beach, Abuela,* and *Legend of the Bluebonnet* (DePaola, 1983), a folktale about a Native American girl who sacrifices her most precious possession—her doll—to bring the necessary rain for her people. Children love to play with character dolls such as these, inventing their own adventures. Be prepared to have Cassie and Rosalba fly around your classroom and tell about the imaginary sights they have seen.

Guided Fantasy

Read *Dinosaur Days* (Manning, 1993) one day at a time to see what your children might imagine themselves doing "if on Monday a pudgy green dinosaur slipped from the cupboard, slurped up your orange juice, and squished flat your toast." Children do not always have to act out their fantasies in a physical way. Have them close their eyes and create the fantasy in their heads. This type of imagining is called *guided fantasy*. You should do it, too, and then talk about the images all of you created in your mind's eye before reading what happens next on Tuesday. Edwards (1990) tells us:

> Guided fantasy provides adults and children with opportunities to create symbols and images that are flexible and original in thought. Guided fantasies are fluent and ever-changing. In the process of pretending and imagining, people can invent and elaborate on images that are as original and individual to them as their fingerprints. (p. 12)

Other books can also motivate this imagining. In *Space Travelers* (Wild, 1992), Zac and his mother are homeless people who sleep at night in a rocketship climber that stands in the middle of the park. Every night Zac zooms in his imagination to outer space. Your children can pretend to be Zac and zoom along too. What will they see? Or they can pretend to be the little UFO being who lands his spaceship on Earth and befriends a little boy creature in *UFO Diary* (Kitamura, 1989).

Guided fantasy can also take place outside when children look up at the clouds and imagine them to be different objects. Yohance, the Caribbean island boy in the book *Yohance and the Dinosaurs* (Obi, 1996) sees dinosaurs and lizards in the clouds above his island home every time he looks. When he waves his arms his imagination takes off and a Triceratops gives him a ride. Read this book outside on a day when puffy clouds fill the sky, and see where your children's imaginations take them.

Music can stimulate guided fantasy, too. Play different instrumental recordings as children close their eyes and float away in their minds. Where do they go? Talk about it. Because children love to pretend, you can use guided fantasy to introduce any idea, topic, or new experience. For instance, you can ask children in the art center to pretend to be a lump of clay turning into any object they choose, or to be the colors blue and yellow getting ready to mix together to create something new and wonderful. In the music center a small group of children might pretend to be tom-toms and flutes dancing a rain dance. Can someone imagine he is the thunder? In the science center children can pretend to be explorers in an Amazon rain forest discovering new insects.

> Once the children begin to understand guided fantasy, you can design fantasy journeys for all areas of the creative arts. . . . Each child gets to be the artist, musician, sculptor, and dancer in every experience, and the source of every creation comes from within the child. (Edwards, 1990, p. 17)

You and the children may want to record these fanciful adventures on a tape recorder or in personal journals with dictated stories and child illustrations. Guided fantasy also makes an excellent transition activity. Whenever children are finished with one activity and waiting to start another, try using guided fantasy, and take them on an exciting adventure of the mind. You can get them started but then let them add the details as they imagine who they are and where they are going.

PROVIDES A VARIETY OF ART MATERIALS AND ACTIVITIES FOR CHILDREN TO EXPLORE ON THEIR OWN

When most teachers think of creativity, the art area comes to mind first. Unfortunately for young children, this is often the least creative area in the entire classroom, because it is entirely adult-directed. Nothing happens spontaneously. Adults get out the art supplies, set up activities on tables, instruct the children on how to use them, and then stay at the tables to make sure the youngsters follow directions. This is not creative art. It is more of an exercise on following directions. Structured activities like these should not be banished from the classroom, since they are appropriate for promoting manipulative and direction-following skills. But teachers and children should not confuse them with creative art.

As mentioned previously, the key to creativity is freedom. Children need to be free to explore, experiment, invent, and pretend with art materials just as they do with blocks or dress-up clothes. Adults rarely consider it necessary to remain in the housekeeping corner to make sure the children dress up "properly" or play roles "correctly," yet this kind of supervision occurs all too frequently with art. As Fox and Diffily (2000) insist:

> Easy access to a variety of art materials and people who encourage exploration of those materials is essential to the creative process. Equally important is the children's freedom to select the topics and to stay with an activity until they determine it is finished. (p. 6)

Process Versus Product

We need to step back and think about our primary purpose for having art in the classroom. Is it to have children paint a nice picture or make a lovely collage to take home to Mother? If this is true in your classroom, then you have confused the product of art with the process. Most preschool children do not yet have the skills or the development level to turn out an accomplished art product. Our goal should instead be to assist children in becoming involved in the creative process, because it is this process that is most important in young children's development.

We should not be faulted for making the mistake of focusing on the product. It is much easier to see a painting than a process. Moreover, no one ever told us this was not the proper way to "teach" art. After all, isn't everyone more concerned with the picture than the painting of it? Not everyone.

Take a look at the children in your classroom who are involved in painting. The only thing that seems to matter to them is the experience, that is, the process. They focus on their product only after adults have made a fuss about it, after they have learned that this is what pleases adults. Before that, they seem more interested in things like smearing the paint around, slapping one color on another, moving the brush back and forth, and covering everything they have painted with a new color. This is the process of art—and this type of experimentation is how creativity is born.

Easel Activities

How can you set up your art activities to promote children's freedom to create? First of all, you need to have one or two easels that are kept out and ready for use every day. Large sheets of easel paper should be nearby for extended use. Children can choose to easel paint during the free-choice period by selecting an "easel necklace" or easel apron, for instance. No teacher direction or assistance should be needed. Children learn to handle the brush and control the paint by themselves.

Observe beginners and you'll see how they manage. New painters spend a great deal of time trying out which hand to use, the best way to hold the brush, how to get paint from jar to paper, how to move paint around on the paper, and how to control the drips. In other words, they are "manipulating the medium" rather than painting a picture.

Observe beginners and you'll see how they spend a great deal of time trying out how to get paint from jar to paper, and how to use the brush.

To help children manage this new medium, be sure to have short "chubby brushes" or beginner's brushes for easel painting. Some easel brushes are the right thickness for pudgy fingers, but too long for preschoolers to manipulate easily. You might want to put out only one or two colors of paint, until children are ready to handle more.

Art Supplies

Store commonly used art materials within children's reach. Have paper, paints, brushes, crayons, felt-tip markers, paste, scissors, and construction paper available for free use when the children arrive. Keep art supplies on low shelves next to the children's tables or work space to make it easier for children to see and select from what is available and later to return items to their shelf space when they are finished. Be sure to mount cutouts or tracings of the art items on nearby shelves for children's easy return to the proper space.

You will want colored construction paper, white drawing paper, brown paper bags, paste, glue, scissors, crayons, felt-tip pens, colored chalk, finger paints, yarn pieces, Popsicle sticks, pipe cleaners, and a basket of collage scraps. Let children know they are free to select from the materials to use at the art tables, as they wish.

At other times, you may want to set up the art activity before the children arrive, and let them "play" with it creatively during free-choice periods. Take play dough, for example. In the beginning, you may want to mix the dough and have it ready for the children to explore and experiment with when they come in. Perhaps you'll put out rolling pins and cookie cutters for the children to use by themselves. You can do this for a number of days with different implements, once the children's interest for rolling pins and cookie cutters has waned.

After children have exhausted the possibilities for manipulating the tools and dough, you can involve them in the fun of measuring and mixing the dough themselves before they play with it. Another time you can have them add food coloring of varying colors for an entirely different effect.

At another time, put out colored chalk, dishes of water, and brown paper grocery bags. Children can experiment by drawing on the bags with or without water, for different effects. The chalk can be dipped in water each time the child draws. Another day bring in chalkboards for the children's chalk drawing experiments.

No matter what art materials you use, arrange them so that the children can be creative with them on their own. Collage scraps, paste, and backing paper can be waiting for children on one of their tables. What they do with them is up to them. Another day have food coloring, medicine droppers, and jars of water waiting.

Finger painting can be done on smooth paper, on tabletops, on large plastic trays, or on large sheets of butcher paper on the floor. Children can start with shaving cream to get used to the messiness of finger painting but still be able to clean it up easily. The point is to set up art activities so that children can work creatively on their own. Occasionally you may have to get involved to get the children started, but then you can withdraw and let them finish by themselves.

The same principles apply to mixing paint. Let children experiment on their own with two colors at first. Yellow and blue make green; yellow and red make orange; blue and red make purple. After experimenting with each of these pairs of colors for a long while, put out three colors for mixing, and then later, four.

Acceptance of Art Products

If freedom is the most important aspect of creativity, then acceptance is the second. You must accept unconditionally whatever the child produces, just as you accept the child unconditionally. Not all children may live up to the standards you expect, but that does not mean you don't accept them and value them as human beings.

The same is true of their creative products. A smudge of brown covering an easel paper may mean a breakthrough to a child struggling to conquer the medium of drippy paint and awkward brushes. You must accept it for what it is—not a painting,

Be sure to accept a beginner's art work for what it is: not necessarily a picture but a process.

but a process, the results of a difficult struggle with the medium. In addition, you must accept it honestly. What should you say? How about: "You surely used a lot of paint in your work today, Charles!" That is an honest appraisal of what happened, and the child can accept that.

On the other hand, a child may have done a representational drawing and want your reaction to it. If you are not sure what to say because you are not sure what the drawing represents, you can respond by commenting on the artistic elements of the drawing. Its color, its patterns, its shape, the lines used, the texture of the painting, and the placement of the painting on the paper are all good possibilities. To ask a child "What is it?" may be insulting when the child knows the red blob is a fire engine. Instead, you might say "I like the way you used the red color. What do you think?" or "I really can see that picture. The color is bright and beautiful."

Some teachers ask children "Do you want to tell me about your picture?" This is certainly a nonjudgmental comment and may elicit information about the picture that you can follow up on. However, what the child is showing you may not be a picture at all, but the results of the artistic process she was following. She will probably not be able to articulate that. Furthermore, children don't always want to talk about their paintings and drawings. Showing them to you may be only an indication that they are done and want you to see what they did.

To other children, their art is private. They may not want to talk about it or even show it to you. That is their choice. You should, however, give them the opportunity to hang their work on the wall where art is displayed. Let the child place it where she wants, or you may give her the choice of mounting it first on backing paper to show it off better.

Book to Read

The perfect book to read about the picture an animal-child paints in school and what he should do with it is *Peter's Picture* (Gorbachev, 2000). As Peter carries his wonderful picture home, various animals stop him with silly ideas of what he should do with the picture. But his father knows just the right thing, and goes down to the basement and makes a beautiful frame for it.

Stages of Art Development

You will become more appreciative of children's art if you understand the various developmental stages children go through in drawing when they are allowed to express themselves spontaneously. From 2 to 3 years old, children mainly scribble, which is an important stage that should not be discouraged if we want children to develop drawing skills. Scribbling is to drawing what babbling is to speaking. All children everywhere make these same markings, in the same way, at approximately the same age (Kellogg, 1969).

Sometime between 2 and 4 years old, the scribbles take on outline shapes such as circles, ovals, squares, triangles, and crosses. Between 3 and 5, children begin to make designs from the shapes they have been drawing. Although there are an unlimited number of possibilities, children usually draw only a few favorites over and over, such as "radials" and "suns." Between the ages of 4 and 5, their designs often take the form of a person. These "tadpole people" grow out of "suns," with the rays of the sun becoming the arms, legs, and hair of the person, and the circle becoming the face and the body. All children everywhere seem to make their first people this way.

By age 5, many children are at a pictorial stage, creating representational drawings (see Figure 7–1). Whether they continue developing talent in art during their elementary school years depends as much on freedom and acceptance as it does on inborn skill.

It is important for you and the children's parents to know about the stages of art development in young children so that the next time a 3-year-old shows you a page of art scribbles, you will not be tempted to dismiss it as "only scribbles." Instead, you will know it is the child's first exciting step in the developmental process of learning to draw.

To demonstrate that you really do accept children's artwork, whether scribbles or pictures, you can make a collection of each child's paintings over a number of weeks or months. You can display children's paintings attractively in your room on backing paper or in frames. You can also take photos of each child working at an easel, as well as photos of his completed work to be included in a scrapbook about the child.

1. *SCRIBBLE*
     UNCONTROLLED
   Marks made on paper for enjoyment. Child has little control
   of eye and hand movement. No pattern.

     CONTROLLED
   Control of eye and hand. Repeated design.

     NAMED SCRIBBLE
   Child tells you what s/he has drawn. May not be
   recognizable to adult.

2. *SHAPE AND DESIGN*
   Child makes shapes such as circles, squares, ovals, triangles.

   Child's muscle control is increasing and s/he is able to place
   shapes and designs wherever s/he wants.

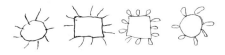

3. *MANDALA*
   Child usually divides circle or square with lines.

   SUNS
   Formed from oval, square, or circle with short
   lines extending from the shape. The extending
   lines take many variations.

4. *RADIALS*
   Lines that radiate from a single point. Can be part
   of a mandala.

5. *HUMANS*
   Child uses SUN design and develops a face by adding
   human features. . . a "sun face."

   Child elongates several lines of the SUN design to create
   arms and legs.

6. *PICTORIALS*
   Child combines ALL stages to make recognizable designs
   or objects.

Figure 7–1   Stages of Art Development

Source: From C. B. Helm, 1993, by B. Helm. Reprinted with permission of B. Helm.

Computer Art Programs

Preschool children experience as much enjoyment and learning through computer art programs as they do with paper and paints. They do not start with representational pictures in either medium, you remember, but they certainly have as much fun manipulating colors and lines on the computer screen as they do on an easel. Be sure to have a printer so that they can save and print out their computer art. But many children are just as happy to erase their colors, lines, or whole screens of scribbles. Thus we see clearly that it is the process and not the product of art that is most important to youngsters.

Painting is different from drawing, whether it is done with a brush, a finger, or a computer mouse. While drawing is concerned with lines and shapes, painting is more fluid in terms of colors and the tools used. Different computer programs, in fact, feature different forms of art. Instead of a keyboard, most computer art programs use an attached tool for painting such as a touch pad, touch screen, or mouse.

Just as they do with a brush and paper, children play around with the computer tool to move the colors or lines on the screen. Through this kind of exploratory manipulation, they teach themselves how to hold the painting tool or their finger, and they learn what happens when they move it certain ways. It may take many days or even weeks of playing around before some children gain control of the computer tool.

Then they practice making colored scribbles on the screen over and over, just as they do with real paint and a brush. Colors do not matter so much at first. They seem to use whatever color is at hand just as they do with beginning easel painting. In fact, children progress through the same developmental stages in computer art that they do with paper and paint art. But be sure to have two children at a time using a program just as you did with number and letter programs.

A number of computer programs feature coloring books that call for manipulative rather than creative skills. Instead of these types of programs, look mainly for programs that start with a blank screen for children to paint or draw on. Some disks include drawing, painting, and coloring books.

Be sure to have easels and paints out and ready for use when computer art programs are in use. Real finger painting should be featured in the art area when computer programs using touch screens or touch pads are in use. Such programs call on children to paint with a finger. Computer art programs to consider include these CD-ROM programs from Library Video Company (1-800-843-3620):

Crayola Magic 3D Coloring Book: Fanciful Friends (5R3617)

Crayola Creativity Pack Volume 4 (5R3505)

Creative Advantage Library (5R2248)

Curious George Paint and Print Studio (5R3208)

Kid Pix Studio (5R2190)

Sesame Street Create and Draw in Elmo's World (5R3494)

ENCOURAGES CHILDREN TO CREATE AND HAVE FUN WITH MUSIC

Children need adult role models to dramatize to them how we want them to behave. This is as true in the creative arts as it is in eating food at the lunch table. The cliché is true: Children will do as we do, not as we say. If you want your children to be creative with music, it is up to you to lead the way.

Your creative actions should be as natural and spontaneous as you want the children's to be. In other words, don't direct the children to watch what you're doing and copy you. You will want children to take original actions spurred by your leadership, not to imitate you.

Are you afraid to sing in front of others? Many of us are. Could it have something to do with our own improper introduction to music? We owe it to the children in our care to avoid the same mistake with them. Music is essential for children's development. But not every teacher feels this way. As Snyder (1997) notes:

> Parents and teachers who don't have a musical background may not perceive the value of early music experiences, or may feel awkward and inadequate to engage in musical activities. (p. 165)

As early childhood professionals in the 2000s, we need to know why it is essential to overcome this reluctance to include music as an important part of the curriculum. If you are one who feels inadequate in music, the following information may make you change your position.

New Brain Research Regarding Music

Researchers have found that early exposure to music may be necessary or at least may greatly enhance the development of cognitive processes. "Music is the most direct route to thinking, because it requires neither words nor symbols to be perceived." (Snyder, 1997, p. 165). But early exposure to music is especially essential during the critical period for development of the brain's "music center." This critical period for development takes place during the preschool and beginning elementary years. What Snyder has to say is important news to many early childhood educators:

> Music and other arts that evoke emotional response appear to open the gate to the neuro-cortex and higher level thinking. Music stimulates and motivates critical thinking. (p. 166)

Frank Wilson, a neuroscientist who has registered brain scans of children as they perform certain tasks, reports that when children read words, the language center of the brain lights up on his scanner. But when they sing music, the entire brain lights up like a Christmas tree (Snyder, 1997, p. 168). Hap Palmer, a children's music specialist, found that songs not only stimulate children's oral language development, but young children can even learn to read through singing the words in specially written books accompanied by musical tapes. Davies (2000) reports that because music heightens emotional involvement in learning, it makes it easier to remember information. "Music helps us store and retrieve rich, multisensory memories" (p. 149).

Singing

Now that you know how important it is to involve your children in music, you need to make a concerted effort to do so. How will you begin? You don't need to be able to carry a tune; many of the children can't either. All that matters is that you have fun with sounds and that you get the children involved. If you are having fun, the children will, too. Start with a monotone chant. Make up your own if you don't know any.

Hap-py day,
Hap-py day,
Let's have a
Happy, happy day!

Clap while you are chanting. Some of the children may follow your lead and clap along with you. Repeat the chant a few times, and perhaps some of the children will join in. This isn't done during a formal "music period." Let's not make music formal. It can be done any time you feel like it. Maybe something makes you feel happy. Maybe everyone is busily working and it makes you feel good. You are doing your song or chant because you feel like expressing an emotion. Whether the children respond doesn't matter, but your acting in this spontaneous and creative way sets the stage for children to make up songs or chants when they feel good, too.

What other situations during the day can you convert to songs or chants? How about pickup time?

We're picking up the blocks,
We're picking up the blocks,
Clunk, clunk, clunk, clunk,
We're picking up the blocks.

These words can be chanted or sung to the tune of "The Farmer in the Dell." If the children join in, let them help you invent words for the other items to be picked up.

Children can also act out the words to familiar chants while singing them. If the chants also appear in picture books, teachers can photocopy the book pages, cut out and laminate the people and animal characters, and have children stand them up in the sand table when their verse is sung. Here are some of the books:

Miss Mary Mack (Hoberman, 1998)

Old MacDonald Had a Farm (Rounds, 1989)

Skip to My Lou (Westcott, 1989)

The Wheels on the Bus (Kovalski, 1987)

The Seals on the Bus (Hort, 2000)

What fun children can have acting out the animal antics of seals, tigers, geese, snakes, and skunks in *The Seals on the Bus* as they sing the song to the tune of "The Wheels on the Bus Go Round and Round." Achilles (1999) suggests that individual children can play with the cutout characters in a sandbox while listening to the song on headphones. If you do not have a tape of a particular song, make your own on a blank cassette as the children sing it. As she notes:

> Sandbox theater provides an opportunity for an individual child to manipulate characters while listening to a musical story on headphones. The caregiver prepares the theater by filling a rectangular cake pan with sand and gluing pictures of the characters in a song on tongue depressors. The child moves the characters while listening to or singing the song. (p. 24)

Singing or chanting directions can apply to any number of situations: putting on outside garments, setting the table, washing hands, or getting out cots for the afternoon nap (when you can whisper the chant). You can sing or chant a welcome to the children in the morning or when using their names throughout the day. Here are some beginning lines to familiar tunes just to get you started:

Where is Bobby? ("Where Is Thumbkin?")
Where, oh where, is nice little Lisa? ("Paw Paw Patch")
Joel, Joel, come to lunch. ("Skip to My Lou")
Here comes Joyce through the door. ("This Old Man")

Chanting of nursery rhymes whenever the occasion calls for it is another method of involving the children in rhyme and rhythm. When you see it raining outside, you might chant in a singsong voice:

Rain, rain, go away,
Come again another day,
Josh and Carolyn want to play.

You or the children may want to make up fingerplays to go along with your songs or chants. Chant or sing a song at least once a day, and you'll soon be doing it more often. You'll know it was worth the effort when the children begin singing the songs back to you.

You and the children can enjoy creative movement along with the music you are making. Large motor movements such as walking, jumping, hopping, running, and leaping can be done to music. Once children have learned a song or chant, you or they can begin to make appropriate movements. If the song expresses happiness, have the children make happy movements. How can they do it? Perhaps by jumping or clapping or hopping in a circle as they sing. Ask the children to show with some kind of movement that they feel happy. Each child may express it differently. Using their bodies as well as their voices validates the feeling and increases their enjoyment. (See also Chapter 4.)

Using Recorded Music

Even nonmusicians can provide a quality music program for young children by bringing in tapes or records from lullabies to the classics that children can listen to on headsets in the music center. Some can be instrumentals and others feature vocalists. As Jalongo (1996) notes, "Children respond to different types of music through different types of vocalizations and body movements" (p. 6).

Music can help you set moods in the classroom. Play it softly in the background during the free-choice period, or louder during large motor activities. The songs you sing with the children can come from recorded music. Play them over and over and soon both you and the children will know the songs by heart. Then when you want to calm down the children before naptime, for example, sing (or chant) calming songs with them. Some records or cassettes that children especially like include these from Constructive Playthings. (800-448-4115)

Quiet Places (Hap Palmer)

Rise and Shine (Raffi)

Sea Gulls (Hap Palmer)

Singable Songs for the Very Young (Raffi)

Songs Children Love to Sing (Ella Jenkins)

You'll Sing a Song and I'll Sing a Song (Ella Jenkins)

Books to Motivate Music

Song picture books can also be used to motivate singing, chanting, and fingerplays. Whether you read the book first and then sing (or chant) the song makes little difference. Children seem to be captivated by the rhythm, rhyme, and funny words of these game songs. That's why they like books such as these:

Fiddle-I-Fee, A Farmyard Song for the Very Young (Sweet, 1992)

I Know an Old Lady Who Swallowed a Fly (Westcott, 1980)

The Itsy Bitsy Spider (Trapani, 1993)

Manipulating the Music Medium

What other kinds of musical experiences do the children have in your classroom? Children need to play with music as they do with blocks, trying out different combinations, breaking them up, and starting all over. And again, as with art, it is the process, not the product, that is important. Songs and dances may be highly satisfying, but if they are not arrived at in fun, they may never be repeated.

Initially, children will do with music and movement just what they do with art: learn to manipulate the medium. This sounds strange when we talk about music, but it is the natural way young children learn any new skill spontaneously. In other words, they need the chance to play with sounds, rhythm, and movement.

You can set up a sound-making table in a noisy area of the classroom. Sound-makers can be a series of small containers, such as empty tuna cans, juice cans, margarine cups and covers, with a collection of seeds, beans, rice, and pebbles the children can place inside the containers to shake. Have a record player or cassette player on the table that the children can use by themselves, along with several records or tapes of rhythmic music. Let them try shaking the containers to music. They may want to record and play back the results.

At another time, use containers as drums. Add a collection of sticks or drumsticks with tape wrapped around the ends to cut down on noise, and let the children practice drumming to music. You can also use metal containers and large spoons with their bowls taped over as drumsticks. Let the children fill a set of jars or glasses with varying amounts of water and tap them with a spoon. Put out a large collection of "junk" items and encourage the children to invent their own music makers. You may call this noise, not music, but don't tell the children that, if you want them to continue creatively.

This stage of music-making compares to the scribble stage in art and the babble stage in speaking. After the children have learned to manipulate the medium with ease, they will want to perform it again and again during the *mastery* stage of exploratory play. Be prepared!

Rhythm Instruments

Sometimes a story can stimulate children to create something of their own. *The Banza* (Wolkstein, 1981) tells the Haitian folktale of a little tiger, Teegra, and goat, Cabree, who are best friends. To seal their friendship, the tiger gives the goat a magic "banza," or banjo, to protect him, saying, "The banza belongs to the heart, and there is no stronger protection than the heart." When the little goat finds herself surrounded by 10 hungry tigers, she plays a song on the banjo that finally frightens all the tigers away.

Your children can make their own magic banjos with shoe boxes and long rubberbands. Help them to cut a large heart-shaped hole out of the cover of the box, just like Cabree's, and to cut four grooves at each end of the cover for holding the four rubberbands, which are stretched lengthwise around the cover and box. Children can paint or decorate their banjos to suit themselves before adding the rubberbands. Have them sing or hum as they strum with their thumbs—but not too hard.

Often teachers think of rhythm instruments in plural, that is, as a rhythm band. Children enjoy making music as loud as they can in a rhythm band. But before you begin having children march around the room in a group playing their instruments, be sure that each child first has a chance to make music with a single instrument on his own. Otherwise, individual instruments may not be heard above the sound of an entire band.

That is why it is important to maintain a music center with a record player or tape player that children can use independently. Rhythm instruments can be hung on a pegboard in the area for use by children during free-choice periods. Encourage children to try out any of the instruments by themselves to see what they sound like. Then have them play their instruments to recordings of background music such as these:

*It is the music maker,
not the listener, who gets the most
out of music.*

And One and Two (Ella Jenkins)
Let's Get the Rhythm of the Band (African-American music)
Modern Tunes for Rhythms and Instruments (Hap Palmer)
Rhythms on Parade (Hap Palmer)
This Is Rhythm (Ella Jenkins)

You can limit the volume on the record player by taping down the knob, if this seems a problem, or have children use headsets with the volume controlled.

After children have had the chance to experiment with the instruments, bring the instruments to circle time and introduce them one at a time to the children. Pass each instrument around and let them give it a try. Then each child who wants to can take an instrument and march around the room with the group to the music of one of the recordings mentioned. Because children often have conflicts about getting a particular instrument when the whole class is involved, have everyone exchange instruments for each march they participate in. Then each child will have a turn with more than one instrument. Later they can practice on their favorite instrument in the music center.

If you bring your own instrument to play, make it one that the children can also try out. Remember, it is the music maker, not the listener, who gets the most out of the experience. Children can strum on your autoharp, for instance, while you press the chord buttons. Have a child sit next to you and strum as you press the chord buttons and sing a song with the group. They can take turns until everyone gets a chance. Other instruments include guitars, ukuleles, and electric keyboards. A small keyboard brings the piano down to size for preschool children.

Blowing instruments such as harmonicas, kazoos, and plastic flutes have always been popular with youngsters. Unfortunately, they are not really safe for a group of children because of possible germ transfer through saliva, unless you carefully clean each instrument with a medicated wipe after every use.

Children do not need outside instruments to make music. They can be an instrument themselves by humming, clapping, or tapping their feet or fingers. You may want to introduce them to rhythm clapping during circle time. Let them clap out name chants— "Here-comes-Bren-da"— with a clap for each syllable. Or children may want to play "Follow the Leader," with clapping patterns in a rap rhythm: One child claps out a rhythm, then the other children try to imitate it. These rhythms can be recorded and played back.

Once you realize that many opportunities for individual play and experimentation with instruments are essential at the preschool level, your music program will take on an entirely different character. In addition you may discover a particular child with an undiscovered musical talent. Sometimes a 3-year-old turns up who is a better autoharp strummer than you! As Jalongo (1996) reminds us:

> Music is particularly important in the early childhood program because, as leading theorist and Harvard professor Howard Gardner has concluded, "Of all the gifts with which individuals may be endowed, none emerges earlier than musical talent." (p. 11)

Other Creative Activities

Every curriculum area in the classroom can promote creativity in children if you set it up so that children can use it on their own. Sand and water tables are sources for imaginative play when interesting accessories are located within the children's reach. Manipulative materials and table toys also promote creativity when children are free to choose materials they want and use them in imaginative ways.

SUMMARY

This chapter focuses on the goal of promoting children's creativity through playful expression and freedom of activity in the areas of fantasy role play, art, and music. Fantasy role play, an activity new to many preschool programs, asks children to pretend to be a fictitious storybook character or to be themselves in a fantasy setting. By hearing you read a picture book with a fantasy theme, children can talk about what happened and then get involved in fantasizing about "what else would happen if . . . " Prop boxes containing costumes or miniature figures help children to extend these stories by pretending on their own, an excellent stimulant for creative thinking.

By encouraging children to experiment with materials and colors in art and then by accepting their artistic products, we support children's continued creative development. Although teacher-directed art has a place in the curriculum in promoting children's direction-following and manipulative skills, it should not be confused with creative art in which the child is in control of manipulating the medium her own way to discover what will happen. However, teachers need to know the stages of children's development of drawing skills in order to support their experiments. These same skills are evident in children's use of computer art programs.

If selected with care, such programs can add a great deal to your children's independent development of creativity.

Music can also promote creativity in children when teachers use it themselves in a relaxed and enjoyable manner. To encourage music production in the preschool classroom, teachers must lead the way by chanting, singing, and providing music-making objects and instruments. Children need to become actively involved in creating their own music, and not merely passive listeners to records and tapes. Rhythm instruments can be made by the children and kept out for their use.

LEARNING ACTIVITIES

1. Read Chapter 7 and write out answers to Question Sheet 7.

2. Meet with your trainer or instructor and discuss answers to Question Sheet 7.

3. View one of the videotapes listed and make 10 file cards with specific ideas for developing children's creativity.

4. Read one or more of the references cited or suggested readings and add 10 cards to your file, with specific ideas for helping children develop creative skills. Include the reference source on each card.

5. Read one of the suggested fantasy picture books with the children. Talk about it afterward and provide props for their fantasy role play.

6. Introduce children to an art computer program and let them experiment with it. Record the results.

7. Make a collection of a child's paintings, drawings, or computer art over a period of time that illustrates the stages of art children go through. Write up or discuss with your trainer how your collection illustrates the stages.

8. Do a singing/chanting activity with children using ideas from this chapter. Record the results.

9. Set up a sound or rhythm instrument activity for individuals or small groups to use. Write up the results.

10. Complete the Chapter 7 Evaluation Sheet and return it to your trainer or college supervisor.

QUESTION SHEET 7

1. What is a creative person like?

2. What seems to kill creativity in children?

3. What can preschool teachers do to keep creativity alive in children? Why should they?

4. How can fantasy role play promote creativity in children?

5. What is "guided fantasy" and how is it carried out with children?

6. What is meant by the expression "confusing the product with the process"? How can this affect children's art?

7. Why should children be allowed to "play" with art materials?

8. Why is it important to accept children's creative products even if they do not seem well done or attractive?

9. Why is it important to understand the developmental stages children go through in teaching themselves to draw?

10. How can computer art programs contribute to children's development of creativity? Be specific.

11. How can you get the children in your classroom to sing?

12. How can a children's book motivate a music activity?

13. How can rhythm instruments be used creatively?

14. What other ways can children become involved with making music?

15. How can adult instruments be used in preschool music?

REFERENCES

Achilles, E. (1999). Creating music environments in early childhood programs. *Young Children, 54*(1), 21–26

Davies, M. A. (2000). Learning . . . The beat goes on. *Childhood Education, 76*(3), 148–153.

Edwards, L. C. (1990). *Affective development and the creative arts.* Upper Saddle River, NJ: Merrill/Prentice Hall.

Fox, J. E., and Diffily, D. (2000). Integrating the visual arts—Building young children's knowledge, skills, and confidence. *Dimensions of Early Childhood, 29*(1), 3–10.

Helm, C. B. (1993). Unpublished table.

Kellogg, R. (1969). *Analyzing children's art.* Palo Alto, CA: National Press.

Jalongo, M. R. (1996). Using recorded music with young children: A guide for nonmusicians. *Young Children, 51*(5), 6–14.

Snyder, S. (1997). Developing musical intelligence: Why and how. *Early Childhood Education Journal, 24*(3), 165–171.

SUGGESTED READINGS

Beaty, J. J. (2002). *Observing development of the young child.* Upper Saddle River, NJ: Merrill/Prentice Hall.

Clements, D. H., Nastasi, B. K., & Swaminathan, S. (1993). Young children and computers: Crossroads and directions from research. *Young Children, 48*(2), 56–64.

Dighe, J., Calomiris, Z., & Van Zutphen, C. (1998). Nurturing the language of art in children. *Young Children, 53*(1), 4–9.

Edwards, L. C. (2002). *The creative arts: A process approach for teachers and children.* Upper Saddle River, NJ: Merrill/Prentice Hall.

Ferguson, C. J. (1999). Building literacy with child-constructed sociodramatic play centers. *Dimensions of Early Childhood, 27*(3), 23–29.

Jalongo, M. R., & Collins, M. (1985). Singing with young children! Folk singing for nonmusicians. *Young children, 40*(2), 17–22.

James, A. R. (2000). When I listen to the music. *Young Children, 55*(3), 36–37.

Koster, J. (1997). *Growing artists.* Albany, NY: Delmar.

Moravcik, E. (2000). Music all the livelong day. *Young Children, 55*(4), 27–29.

Myhre, S. M. (1993). Enhancing your dramatic-play area through the use of prop boxes. *Young Children, 48*(5), 6–11.

Seefeldt, C. (1995). Art—A serious work. *Young Children, 50*(3), 39–45.

Smith, M. K. (1996). Fostering creativity in the early childhood classroom. *Early Childhood Education Journal, 24*(2), 77–82.

Szyba, C. M. (1999). Why do some teachers resist offering appropriate, open-ended art activities for young children? *Young Children, 54*(1), 16–20.

Wolf, J. (2000). Sharing songs with children. *Young Children, 55*(2), 28–30.

Zimmerman, E., and Zimmerman, L. (2000). Art education and early childhood education: The young child as creator and meaning maker within a community context. *Young Children, 55*(6), 87–92.

CHILDREN'S BOOKS

Bush, T. (1993). *James in the house of Aunt Prudence.* New York: Crown.

DePaola, T. (1983). *Legend of the bluebonnet.* New York: Putnam.

Dorros, A. (1991). *Abuela.* New York: Dutton's Children's Books.

Gorbachev, V. (2000). *Peter's picture.* New York: North-South.

Hoberman, M. A. (1998). *Miss Mary Mack.* New York: Scholastic.

Hort, L. (2000). *The seals on the bus.* New York: Henry Holt.

Kitamura, S. (1989). *UFO diary.* New York: Farrar Straus Giroux.

Kovalski, M. (1987). *The wheels on the bus.* Boston: Little Brown.

Manning, L. (1993). *Dinosaur days.* New York: BridgeWater Books.

Mazer, A. (1991). *The salamander room.* New York: Knopf.

Meade, H. (1998). *John Willy and Freddy McGee.* New York: Marshall Cavendish.

Obi, A. (1996). *Yohance and the dinosaurs.* London: Macmillan Caribbean.

Ringgold, F. (1991). *Tar beach.* New York: Crown.

Rounds, G. (1989). *Old MacDonald had a farm.* New York: Holiday House.

Sendak, M. (1963). *Where the wild things are.* New York: Harper.

Sweet, M. (1992). *Fiddle-I-Fee, A farmyard song for the very young.* Boston: Little, Brown.

Trapani, I. (1993). *The itsy bitsy spider.* Boston: Whispering coyote.

Westcott, N. B. (1980). *I know an old lady who swallowed a fly.* Boston: Little, Brown.

Westcott, N. B. (1989). *Skip to my Lou.* Boston: Little, Brown.

Wild, M. (1992). *Space travelers.* New York: Scholastic.

Wild, M. (1993). *Going home.* New York: Scholastic.

Wolkstein, D. (1981). *The banza.* New York: Dial.

VIDEOTAPES

High/Scope. (Producer). *Creative representation: High/Scope Preschool Key Experiences.* Ypsilanti, MI: High/Scope and St. Paul, MI: Redleaf Press.

Indiana State (Producer). *Dramatic play: More than playing house.* Washington, DC: National Association for the Education of Young Children. (#895; in Spanish #895S).

Video Active Productions (Producer). *Music across the curriculum.* Washington, DC: National Association for the Education of Young Children. (#832).

Video Active Productions (Producer). *Music play: Bah bah be-bop.* Washington, DC: National Association for the Education of Young Children. (#810).

CHAPTER 7 EVALUATION SHEET
ADVANCING CREATIVE SKILLS

1. Student _____

2. Trainer _____

3. Center where training occurred _____

4. Beginning date _____ Ending date _____

5. Describe what student did to accomplish General Objective.

   _____

   _____

6. Describe what student did to accomplish Speciific Objectives.

   Objective 1 _____

   _____

   Objective 2 _____

   _____

   Objective 3 _____

   _____

7. Evaluation of student's Learning Activities

   _____

Comments:

   _____

   _____

   _____

   _____

   _____

   _____

   _____

Permission is granted by the publisher to reproduce this page for evaluation and record keeping.

Building a Positive
Self-Concept

GENERAL OBJECTIVE

To help children improve their self-concept through your attitude and behavior toward them

SPECIFIC OBJECTIVES

_____ Accepts self and every child as worthy and uses nonverbal cues to let children know they are accepted

_____ Accepts diversity in children and helps children to accept one another

_____ Helps every child to experience success in the classroom

Self-concept formation begins at birth and develops throughout a child's preschool years. How children eventually come to feel about themselves is the result of an accumulation of contacts and experiences with other people and with the environment. If most of these contacts have been positive, children should feel good about themselves. If children are accepted by their families, if they have been loved and cared for, shown affection, fed and clothed properly, and provided with a stimulating environment, then they begin to develop a perception of themselves as likable human beings. If they are not neglected or left alone too much, not scolded too harshly or restricted too severely, and not nagged at constantly, then they in turn will tend to like themselves and other human beings.

If, on the other hand, children have accumulated a series of negative responses from other people and the environment, they will come to believe there is something wrong with them. Young children are highly egocentric; they view everything as if they are the source of all happenings around them. If everything they do receives a negative response, they quite naturally assume it is their fault and that they are not good. If the adults around them seldom pay attention to them, they may feel they are not likable.

You and your classroom staff must help the children in your care experience as many positive interactions with people and things as possible. You need to be aware, however, that self-image grows from an accumulation of responses and not from just one or two. You and your co-workers will therefore want to be consistent in your behavior with children so that they receive a clear, ungarbled message of your positive feelings toward them.

ACCEPTS SELF AND EVERY CHILD AS WORTHY, AND USES NONVERBAL CUES TO LET CHILDREN KNOW THEY ARE ACCEPTED

Acceptance is an essential component in the development of a positive self-concept. Most people need to feel that they are accepted by those around them to feel good about themselves. Just as important is their acceptance of themselves as worthy persons before they can wholly accept others. It is therefore critical that children accept themselves and feel acceptance *by* others and *for* others.

Adult Self-Acceptance

This role of acceptance applies to adults as well as children. For you as a teacher to accept the children in your program, you also need to feel good about yourself as a person. Are you accepted by the people who are significant in your life? Do you accept yourself? These may be areas you need to work on before you can be a truly effective teacher. What do you like about yourself? List some of the qualities that you think are most positive. Are any of the following qualities on your list?

Positive Qualities List

My love for children

My dedication to teaching

My ability to stay with a task until it is finished

My ability to establish rapport with children

My sense of humor

Then make a second list. Do not call it your "negative qualities list." Just as with children, we also need to approach things positively. When we use the word "negative" as it concerns ourselves or children, we tend to think in terms of negative, or bad, or wrong. Instead, label this list "Qualities I Would Like to Possess." Are any of the following qualities on your second list?

Qualities I Would Like to Possess

Confidence that I am doing my job correctly

Better organizational skills

Better control over my temper

A nicer sounding voice

Ability to sing comfortably in front of the children

Choose one of the qualities on the second list and try working on it. What will give you confidence that you are doing your job correctly, for instance? Look at your positive qualities on the first list and think about how they can help you to become confident about doing your job. You may decide that if all of the children accept you and you are able to establish rapport with each of them, then you can feel confident you are doing your job. Your acceptance of every one of the children and their reciprocal acceptance of you thus becomes one of the tasks you should focus on in the days and weeks to come.

Adult–Child Acceptance

Your first step in helping a child accept and feel good about herself is to accept the child yourself, totally and unconditionally. This advice may sound obvious to you. Of course you accept the unhappy child—just as you accept all of the children in your classroom. But do you accept her totally and unconditionally? In reality, you may have children you favor above others as well as children you do not like. What about the loud and aggressive child or a child who is never clean, who is overweight, who whines or tattles, or who doesn't speak English? You need to sort out your feelings and change them before you can hope to bring about change in the children's feelings about themselves.

A simple way to start with children is similar to the way you started with yourself: List all the children in your class. After each name, write down as frankly and honestly as possible, a positive quality you like about each child and why. Also write what you would like to see changed in each child and why. Then write down your reaction to the child in the classroom. For example:

Marie

What I like: Her quiet way of playing

Why: I like quiet children.

Changes needed: Her uncleanliness

Why: I dislike dirtiness.

My reaction in class: I leave her alone.

Joshua

What I like: When he plays without disrupting others

Why: I like children to be friendly toward each other.

Changes needed: His negative attitude

Why: I don't like the way he acts toward others.

My reaction in class: I scold him when he misbehaves.

When you have finished, go back through the list and ask yourself the following questions, for each child: Do I really accept this child totally and unconditionally? Do my daily reactions convey to the child that I accept him as he is? If not, you may need to change the way you react toward the child so that he knows you accept him.

This does not mean that you must accept disruptive or destructive behavior from a child. You accept the child, not the behavior. You should accept every child as a valuable individual despite the child's appearance or behavior. This acceptance means that you will help each child overcome inappropriate behavior through your behavior toward that child and your respect for him or her as an individual. If you find from your list that you do not do this with certain children, then you need to begin changing your own attitude toward them.

You can start by listing, for three days, positive behaviors that you notice about a child whom you have not accepted totally. Keep a pen and pad handy during the day and make a special effort to observe and record positive things about the child. These notes, like your original set, are for your eyes only or for sharing with your trainer. You should keep them in a private place to be disposed of when you finish. Marie and Joshua are children you have not accepted fully according to your reactions toward them. You might start observing and recording positive behaviors for each of these children.

Starting with Joshua, what did you find? You might have noticed that on the first morning Joshua said "Hi" to Michael when he came in, that he put his jacket in his cubby without bothering anyone, and that he ate his snack without disturbing his neighbor.

How did you respond to these positive actions? You waved at him from across the room when he came in and said, "Hi, Joshua!" You watched him put his jacket in his cubby, nodding and smiling at him when he turned around. After snack you smiled and said, "That was a good snack time, Joshua, wasn't it?" You already seem to know by intuition that it is always good to call children by name when you speak to them. This is probably part of your ability to establish good rapport with children that you noted under your positive qualities.

Within a few days of similar observing, recording, and responding, you may find that a change has occurred both in the child and in yourself. When you look for positive behaviors in children, you will find them. We see what we look for. The more positive behaviors you notice, the better you begin to feel about the youngster. This often comes across to the child nonverbally, and he in turn begins to act more positively. In the end, both of you feel good about one another—you because the child's behavior seems to have improved and the child because he senses that you approve of him more than you did previously. Try the previous exercise to see how it works for you.

Books to Read

Gliori's (1999) story *No Matter What* about two foxes, Large and Small, clearly illustrates the idea that no matter what Small fox does, Large fox still loves him. Even if he is a grumpy grizzly bear, or a squishy bug who spills his soup, Large fox still loves him for himself. Another book with the same theme is Baker's (2001) *I Love You Because You're You* also with fox characters: a mother and a small child. The mother speaks in verse to the child telling him how she loves him when he's happy, silly, frightened, sad, angry, wild, and no matter how he feels or what he does. You should also feel the same way about your children.

Nonverbal Cues

In addition to speaking, you should also demonstrate your acceptance of children through nonverbal cues. Children understand more about how you feel toward them by the way you act than by what you say. Your tone of voice, for instance, conveys as much or more meaning than your words. How do you sound to the child that you seem to have trouble accepting totally? Switch on your cassette tape recorder when you are in a learning center with the child. After class, play back the tape and listen to yourself. Ignore everything on the tape but the tone of your voice. Play it low enough so that you cannot even make out the words. Are you satisfied with what you hear? If not, you may want to make a note to yourself about changing the tone of your voice, perhaps making it softer or keeping the scolding tone out of it. This is also another of the qualities from your list that you wanted to develop in yourself.

Another nonverbal cue you should evaluate is your facial expression. How does it look to a child? Do you scowl or frown very much? Do you smile a lot? Try smiling at an unhappy child. Children reflect the people around them. If nobody ever smiles at them, why should they feel happy? Be persistent in your smiling. Eventually you will get a smile in return.

Nearness and touch are also important cues of acceptance to preschool children. Affection is usually expressed through hugs, a hand on the shoulder, an arm around the waist, or sitting or standing close to someone. Most children crave this affection. Those who seem not to, who instead withdraw from touch or contact, may indeed have self-concept problems or may be merely shy. Your nonverbal cues of acceptance with these children may have to be smiles and a friendly voice until they feel better about themselves and become more at ease in the classroom. Do not allow the current exaggerated concern about "good touches and bad touches" to alter your display of affection toward the children in your care. Your "good touches" are necessary for the growth of their positive self-concept.

It is important for all of the adults in the preschool classroom to behave consistently toward all of the children. If you are the head teacher or team leader, it is your responsibility to make sure this happens. If you notice that a classroom worker seems to have a favorite child or seems to ignore another child, you may want to have a team meeting at which all of you do the exercise of listing the children's names, along with your likes, changes needed, and reactions. The harm created by an adult's showing favoritism lies in the nonverbal cues this action conveys to each of the other children. It says, very clearly, "This favored child is somehow more likable than you are" or "You are not as good as this other child."

Your acceptance of and your positive reactions toward all of the children in your class are thus extremely important in promoting their growth of healthy self-concepts. Just as you periodically assess children's feelings about themselves, you must also constantly check on your own feelings about the children. As Eaton (1997) notes:

> Research suggests that an adult's sensitive, personally attentive, genuinely focused relationship with a child increases the child's self-esteem. (p. 44)

Figure 8–1   Self-Concept
Checklist

Child's Name _____Date_____
_____ Looks at you without covering face when you speak to child
_____ Can identify himself or herself by first and last name
_____ Seeks other children to play with or will join when asked
_____ Seldom shows fear of new or different things
_____ Is seldom destructive of materials or disruptive of activities
_____ Smiles, seems happy much of the time
_____ Shows pride in accomplishments
_____ Stands up for rights
_____ Moves confidently, with good motor control

Permission is granted by the publisher to reproduce this page for evaluation and record keeping.

Read *How About a Hug?* (Carlson, 2001) with large pictures illustrating Have-a-Great-Day Hugs, It'll Be Okay Hugs, You-Did-Great Hugs, I'm Sorry Hugs, and many more. Then give your listeners a big hug!

Child Self-Acceptance

How do children feel about themselves in your classroom? A child's self-concept is an elusive thing to pin down. One way to begin assessing self-concept is through observing children and recording their behavior according to a checklist. The Self-Concept Checklist in Figure 8–1 can help you and your colleagues assess a child's self-perception. The behaviors listed should occur consistently; otherwise they may not represent an accurate picture of the child.

It is important at the outset that you try to determine how children feel about themselves. Since they often have difficulty expressing this verbally, you must determine it through observing and recording children's particular responses or behaviors as they interact with other children and in activities. Add this information to each child's records and use it as you make individual plans for the child.

For children who have few check marks, you and your co-workers will need to provide special experiences for strengthening their self-concepts. Perhaps the most critical indicator or a child's self-image is the entry "Smiles, seems happy much of the time." The child who does not smile or act happy demonstrates obvious evidence of troubled feelings. What can you do to help?

Book to Read

Lovell's (2001) book *Stand Tall, Molly Lou Melon* is the story about the shortest girl in class who has buck teeth, a voice like a bullfrog being squeezed by a boa constrictor,

Children need to know what they look like to accept themselves completely.

and is fumble-fingered. Her grandma tells her to walk proud, smile big, and sing loud, so she does, helping all the other children to appreciate her, even the school bully.

Mirrors, Photos, and Tapes

Besides accepting the child yourself, the most important role you can play is helping children accept themselves. Children need to know what they look like to accept themselves completely. A full-length mirror is thus a classroom necessity. Children will use it not only in the dramatic play area but also at odd moments during the day. They are curious about themselves. "Is this what I really look like?" You will find that they use mirrors differently from adults who, after all, already know what they look like. Some children may make faces at themselves or pile on hats and dress-up clothes before they face the mirror. Others may stare at their images for quite a while.

Young children are trying to sort themselves out and find out who they are. Hand mirrors serve the same purpose, giving a close-up view of the face for a child sitting at a table. Keep more than one in the classroom.

A camera is another good tool for promoting the development of a positive self-concept. Take many photos of each child during the program year, when they have just built a block building, completed a science project, or pretended to be a firefighter. Now they can see how they look as builders of tremendous block apartment houses or drivers of zooming fire trucks.

Take photos of the child and his or her parents when you make home visits, once again to demonstrate your acceptance of both the child and the family. Photograph each child doing an art project, perhaps feeding a classroom pet, participating in a field trip, making a puzzle, going down a slide, or talking with a friend. Display the photos in the center or in a personal scrapbook each child may want to make.

Have pictures of individuals laminated and used by the youngsters on an attendance board or job chart. Make photo puzzles by enlarging a photo of each child, gluing it to cardboard, and cutting it into puzzle pieces to be kept in separate manila envelopes in the manipulative area.

A tape recorder may serve the same purpose. Spend time with individuals or small groups, recording each of their voices, playing them back, and discussing them. Children may want to tell something about themselves, their pets, their families, or their homes. Or they may want to tell a story, sing a song, or pretend to be someone else. When they learn to use the tape recorder on their own, they can tape each other's voices.

Self-Concept Name Games

Children enjoy the same feeling about seeing their names as they do about seeing themselves in a mirror or in a photo. Some children may already know how to print their names. Many will know at least the first letter of their name. Use children's printed names in every way you can think of not only to help them learn to recognize their names but also to make them feel good about themselves. "J-o-s-h-u-a—those are my letters. That's me!"

Play "Find Your Name Card" with a small group of children and place their name cards in a pile on a table. Play "Match Your Name Card" with duplicate name cards and the cards on the attendance chart. Bring in sets of alphabet blocks with duplicate blocks of each letter and let individuals try to make their name out of blocks. Take a photo of the completed names. Use children's name cards on their place at the lunch table. Have mats with children's names on them for their seats on the floor at circle time. Also use children's names in familiar songs whenever you can. As Warner (1999) notes:

> Substituting children's names in familiar songs not only will delight children, but also helps them gain a sense of special recognition. Singing "Raul Had a Little Lamb" or "Two Little Blackbirds going to the mall; one named Kelsey and the other named Paul," makes children giggle with pleasure. (p. 21)

Self-Concept Art

Children's art creations of all kinds should make them feel good about themselves as they learn to manipulate the many art media successfully. Actual body, hands, and feet tracings make an especially good personal statement. Have each child lie down on a large piece of butcher paper while either you or another child traces around the youngster. The child can then paint in the outline of herself, coloring on clothes, shoes, face, and hair. Body tracings like this can be cut out and mounted on the classroom wall, with the child's name either on or under the painting. Some programs do body tracings at the beginning and end of the year so that children can compare the differences. Did they grow taller? Did their art skills improve?

Hands and feet can also be traced, colored in, and mounted on backing paper for all to see. Some programs do hand and feet stampings, instead, using water-soluble paints in a shallow pan. Children dip each hand or foot in the paint and stamp it on a white background. This art creation can be separate for each child or a group mural. Children can also do "sneaker rubbings" by fastening a piece of white paper to the bottom of each sneaker and rubbing the side of a crayon over it until the pattern appears. Children can then cut out and mount the shoe bottoms.

Face tracings are sometimes done by the teacher, tracing lightly on tissue paper held against a child's face. Afterward these are colored in and cut out by each child. Wait until every child's personal art has been completed before displaying it in class so that no one feels left out.

Self-Concept Picture Books

Children can learn to accept themselves and others through stories about children who have the same concerns as they do. *I Want to Be* (Moss, 1993) is a prose poem set to Jerry Pinkney's elegant art about the answers an African American girl gives when people ask her what she wants to be. At first the girl does not know what she wants to be. Then she tries on a grass mustache and a dandelion beard, and soon her imagination takes over. She whirls and twirls into scene after scene of her dreams "to be."

I CAN (Winter, 1993) is a simple story of a preschool Anglo boy and his little sister at home. Each page shows one of the boy's accomplishments (I can dress myself) opposite his sister's struggle to imitate him (She can't). In *You're Just What I Need* (Krauss, 1998), a little girl covers herself with a blanket on her mother's bed, and her mother plays a hide-and-seek game of pretend with the bundle, wondering what it could be? A bundle of laundry? No. A bundle of carrots? No, no. A monkey? No, no, no. Finally the little girl pops out and shouts, "It's me!" And the mother holds her close and says, "You're just what I need."

Am I Beautiful? (Minarik, 1992) is about another mother–child situation, only this time about animals, as a baby hippo wanders around watching different animals admire their babies and asking them "Am I beautiful, too?" Each of them tells him to run along and ask someone else. He finally gets the answer he is waiting for when he asks his own mother.

ACCEPTS DIVERSITY IN CHILDREN AND HELPS CHILDREN TO ACCEPT ONE ANOTHER

The children in your classroom will probably reflect the multicultural, rich, poor, gifted, differently abled, fascinating tossed salad of humans that makes America an exciting place to live. If you as an early childhood professional cherish each youngster as a worthy and special person, the children in your care will follow your lead in

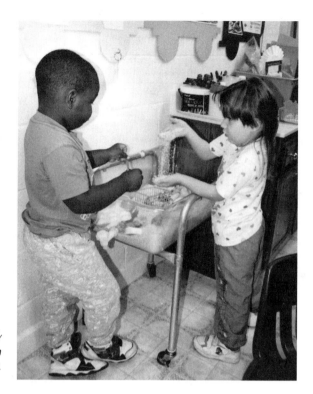

Teachers need to accept diversity in children and help children accept one another.

accepting each of their classmates as well. To assist you in this acceptance, keep in mind the following guidelines:

1. Stress similarities but honor differences.
2. Build on each child's strengths.
3. Have high expectations for everyone.

First of all, as previously mentioned, you must accept the child as he or she is: his looks, his language, his culture, her clothing, her disability, her voice. You show your acceptance by your tone of voice, your smile, your words, your actions. Greet each child cheerfully every day. Help each one to feel at home in your classroom.

Stress Similarities but Honor Differences

Although you may note that certain children have different skin colors, hair styles, languages, or disabilities, each is a child like the others, with similar needs for your attention, affection, and support. There is no need for you to treat any child as different or to behave differently toward any child.

You are the behavior model the children look to for a cue as to how they should behave toward a child they perceive as different. If the children see that you behave toward that child just as you do toward them, they will feel safe in doing the same. For instance, if the children discover that Alberto doesn't speak the same way they do, you can agree with them, pointing out matter-of-factly: "Many people in the world speak different languages. Would you like to learn some words from Alberto's language?"

In other words, you should behave the same way with every child. The child who is overly aggressive and the child who is overweight also need your acceptance. The child with leg braces and the child with a hearing aid are children first of all, not disabled children. They need to feel they are not different from the others, because "feeling different" usually means "feeling inferior" and often invites teasing and ridicule from other children.

Books to Read

Read, first for your own benefit and then for your children, the light-hearted picture book, *KIDS* (Anholt & Anholt, 1992), an exuberant introduction to dozens of "happy kids, grumpy kids, skinny kids, dumpy kids," in a rhyming, rollicking romp through childhood. From "What do kids do?" and "Where do kids hide?" to "What are nasty kids like?" the answers show individual children doing and being, wondering and wishing just the sort of things your children can identify with. Can they pick out the picture of the kid who is most like them?

Another area in which children can find similarities is food. Although different children and families may eat different kinds of food, they all have to eat. In the book *Everybody Cooks Rice* (Dooley, 1991), a big sister finds out that everyone in her multiethnic neighborhood eats some kind of rice, when she has to track down her brother Anthony because it's time for dinner. You can bring in chopsticks and have the children cook and eat their own rice dish for lunch.

In *Yoko* (Wells, 1998) the various animal children in Yoko's class bring lunch boxes full of all sorts of food from peanut butter sandwiches to egg salad on pumpernickel. But when the children see Yoko's sushi rice rolls stuffed with shrimp, tuna, and seaweed, they begin a hurtful teasing, shouting "Yuck-o-rama!" The teacher tries having an International Food Day the next week with everyone bringing in a food from a different country and everyone trying a bite of everything. Still no one will try Yoko's sushi until hungry Timothy sneaks a piece. He loves it so much he persuades Yoko to bring sushi every day, and they push their desks together and open a restaurant.

Children's dwellings are another area of commonality, yet with many differences. In *Paul and Sebastian* (Escudie & Wensell, 1988), the boys' mothers have trouble accepting each other because one lives in a blue apartment with green curtains, and the other in a green trailer with blue curtains. In *Space Travelers* (Wild, 1992), Zac and his mother Mandy sleep, not in a house, but in a rocketship climber in the city park. In other words, they are homeless. Children can block-build, easel-paint, or role-play scenes from their own or pretend dwellings after hearing these stories.

In *It's Okay to be Different* (Parr, 2001) listeners find out through zany cartoons that it's okay to have a different nose (an elephant's), to be a different color (a zebra), to have wheels (child in wheelchair), to come from a different place (Saturn), to come in last (a turtle), or to have different moms (a yellow and a blue one).

And what about their different hair styles? Everyone has hair, but you won't believe how excitingly different it can be until you read to your children *Hats Off to Hair!* (Kroll, 1995), with thirty-six different children's heads peering from framed pages, showing off their bangs, bobs, buzzes, dreadlocks, ducktails, and on and on, with their names and hairdos in rhyme.

In *I Love My Hair!* (Tarpley, 1998), Keyana sits down between her mother's knees every night while she combs out her hair. Sometimes it hurts, but her mother tells her how lucky she is to have such a wonderful head of hair. Keyana then pictures all the different hairdos she has worn and which one she likes best, even when the kids at school tease her.

Clearly, the adults and older children around them are the ones who most strongly influence young children's attitudes about accepting differences in people, places, food, clothing, skin color, hairstyles, and disabilities. Be sure your own attitude of acceptance comes across strongly to the youngsters by the way you treat all of them and their families as special persons.

Build on Each Child's Strengths

You can begin to help any children who do not seem to feel good about themselves by identifying their strengths and helping them to build on them. For example, a child who speaks Spanish can help the others learn to count in Spanish. The others can help her learn to count in English. Bring in books and tapes to support this language exchange.

A child with a hearing impairment may be able to show the other children how to sign "hello." *The Handmade Alphabet* (Rankin, 1991) displays a different hand on each page, with fingers showing the sign for a particular alphabet letter from *A* to *Z*. White hands, brown hands, gloved hands, and even the X-ray of a hand demonstrate the letters. Your children can learn to sign their own initials or names.

Everyone can do something well. Help each child discover her particular skill and then build on it. The aggressive child may be an expert climber who can help less skillful climbers to master the jungle gym. The shy child may turn out to be the class computer expert who can share her skills with the rest.

Perhaps the child with poor motor coordination can grasp a spoon and stir well. It is up to you, then, to provide activities in which that child can experience similar success: mixing gelatin or powdered drinks or play dough. Add other similar activities to extend the successful experience. Let children put together a fruit salad with that child in charge of the melon baller. Think of other implements that the child might use successfully: a paper punch to count the number of children in class each day or a food mill to grind up cooked apples or pumpkins. Maybe that child can be a drummer in your music-making activities.

Be sure to read *Cleversticks* (Ashley, 1992), a story about Ling Sung, the Chinese boy who enters preschool but is unable to accomplish tasks the other children complete with ease, for example, tying his shoes, printing his name, buttoning his jacket, or fastening his painting apron. Then by accident he discovers what he is good at: picking up the pieces of the cookie he dropped by using inverted paintbrushes as chopsticks. All the children clap for his accomplishment and his dad calls him "Cleversticks."

You may want to list such skills on individual cards for each child, with space for the dates when they accomplish something new. Parents need to know about your goals for their children, and you need to know about their goals, as well. Discuss with them what children are able to do by themselves in your classroom, so that parents can encourage them to accomplish similar things at home.

Have High Expectations for Everyone

Finally, you should have high expectations for everyone in the class. With your support and guidance, each child should be able to participate in most of the activities. A child who must use a wheelchair may not be able to climb the monkey bars but may be able to pull himself *around* them with a rope for physical exercise. A shy child can whisper through a puppet if speaking aloud is too painful. A non-English-speaking child can tape-record her original story of a wordless picture book in her own language for another child to hear.

Whatever the activity, you should expect and encourage (but not force) everyone to join in. If the children are singing, a child with a hearing impairment can join in by playing a rhythm instrument or beating a drum. A child who doesn't speak the language can hum the song on a comb covered with waxed paper. The shy or withdrawn child can have her puppet sing the words.

Invite the children to set up challenges for themselves. Instead of competing with other children, let them compete with themselves. How far did they jump last week? Can they do better today? Use a tape measure and record the results. Alfredo has learned to count to 10 in English. What would he like to learn next? Counting to 20? The children in the block area are timing their pickup with a stopwatch every day. They are recording their times on a chart and trying to set a new record each time they pick up and stack the blocks accurately. Children and parents, too, may want to suggest new challenges.

Cultural Influences on Children's Self-Concept

As you accept children from a variety of ethnic, cultural, and racial backgrounds be aware that the cultural values of the children and their families may very well affect how children from different backgrounds tend to feel about themselves. Marshall (2001) points out that:

> Children who are shy, reticent, and quiet are likely to be considered competent and well behaved by parents and teachers in the People's Republic of China. . . . Mothers from Latino cultures are likely to focus on respectfulness. In contrast the Anglo mothers focused on autonomy and active exploration, reflecting more independent values. (p. 20)

Preschool teachers need to be aware of these cultural differences when assessing the self-concepts of their children. As Marshall continues: "Some cultures such as traditional

Navajo cultures expect children to observe before attempting to try things. For these children standing back and observing should not be taken as an indication of low self-esteem" (p. 20). You need to keep this in mind when assessing such children.

Teachers also need to talk with parents and families about what sort of behavior the parents value and expect from their children, as well as discussing your own program's goals. The children themselves tend to be quite resilient about such differences, mainly behaving both at home and at school as expected. Young children are very observant, noting what is going on around them, what is expected of them in different situations, and trying to fit in as best they can.

HELPS EVERY CHILD TO EXPERIENCE SUCCESS IN THE CLASSROOM

One of the most important factors influencing the development of a healthy self-concept is success. Children of this age need to experience success to feel good about themselves. The activities and materials you provide can boost the children's positive self-concepts if they find that they can accomplish them successfully. Achieving suc-

Make sure that activities and materials are appropriate for children's development levels. Children need to experience success.

cess outside their home environment is very important for young children. They need to experience success repeatedly to feel good about themselves and to feel confident that they are able to accomplish meaningful things.

You should make sure that activities and materials are appropriate for your children's developmental levels. In other words, don't put out the most complicated puzzles, books, and art projects at the beginning of the year. Nor should you stress competition in your classroom. Your children will meet that soon enough in the outside world. Their experience in your classroom should give them breathing space—a time to develop positive feelings about themselves, as worthy persons who can accomplish the interesting and challenging activities in your program. Winning or losing can come later in life when their positive self-concept has grown strong.

Although children should be able to choose from among any of the games and materials you provide, you can steer those who have difficulties to the simpler materials and activities. For those who seldom sit still long enough to complete an activity, consider sitting with them and encouraging them to complete it.

Some children are so fearful of failure that they just won't try. You may need to help them to succeed step by step. Hand the puzzle maker a puzzle piece and let him try to find where it goes. Encourage him to try again. "You can find it, Jeremy, look again." Hand him another piece if he doesn't take one on his own. When the puzzle is completed, ask him if he wants a photo of the puzzle for his personal scrapbook. This may be the first time Jeremy has completed a puzzle. He will be proud of his accomplishment if you show him that you are, too.

Strengthening a Child's Independence

Children's concepts of themselves receive an additional boost when they learn how to do things on their own. Some preschool teachers do not realize this. They think they are helping children by tying their shoes, zipping their jackets, serving their food, and pouring their milk. They think they are making things easier for the children if they put out art materials, start up computer programs, and have puzzles and table blocks ready and waiting. Children do not protest. After all, they have been little and helpless all those years before coming to preschool.

As children grow and change, the adults around them should change, too. They must begin to let go of their children and allow them the freedom to do things independently. Helping young children grow and develop independence should be one of the principal goals for any child development center. In current terms, we call this "empowering children."

> Central to this definition is the idea that young children are active learners who can initiate their own learning activities and function as active learners, rather than mere passive recipients of information from others. Such active learning empowers children to assume a measure of control over their environment and develop the conviction that they have some control over their lives. (Schweinhart & Weikart, 1993, p. 56)

Control over the Classroom Environment

Think about your own classroom. What control do the children have? You might make a list of the things that children can complete by themselves or that they have personal responsibility for. Such a list might include these items:

1. Hang up outer garments in personal cubbies.
2. Choose and carry out daily or weekly chore listed on job chart.
   a. Water plants.
   b. Feed fish.
   c. Feed and water guinea pig.
   d. Set table for snack or lunch.
   e. Help teacher with cots for nap.
   f. Take mail to office.
3. Choose curriculum area to play/work in during free choice.
4. Get out own art materials, puzzles, and table games.
5. Put on own paint or water-play apron, or goggles.
6. Help make play dough.
7. Operate tape recorder.
8. Operate computer.
9. Use hammer and saw.
10. Cut with scissors and knife.
11. Follow recipe chart for cooking activity.
12. Sign up with name scribble when waiting for turn.
13. Help with cleanup and pickup.
14. Use the bathroom independently.
15. Wash hands and brush teeth.
16. Serve own food and pour own milk and juice.
17. Clear own table area.
18. Get out and put away own sheet and blanket.
19. Sign out and return picture books for overnight.
20. Put on outer garments and tie shoes.

This is only a partial list. Can the children in your program do these things? More important, are they allowed to? Some teachers say, "I would never allow a 3-year-old to use a sharp knife. He might cut himself." But many other teachers reply, "All my children learn to handle dangerous implements such as knives and saws so that they won't get hurt. If they should ever slip and cut themselves (but none have), that too is a learning experience, and we have bandages and sympathy always at hand."

It is important for children to use record players and adult-type equipment successfully on their own.

Some teachers worry about children using tape recorders, record players, and computers because they are expensive and may be broken by children. Other teachers report that they purchase only the most durable childproof recorders: those that will best survive children's handling. As for computers, these machines are surprisingly durable as long as they are not dropped and liquid is not spilled on them. A simple chart in the computer area can remind children of these rules:

1. Two children at a time
2. One finger at a time
3. No liquids
4. Wash hands first

Teachers who give young children adult-type responsibilities believe it is of primary importance for children to use record players and computers on their own. They are willing to spend as much time as necessary to instruct young children in their value and proper use and to monitor the children until they are able to use these devices independently. If children are to learn through exploratory manipulation, mastery, and meaning, then they need the freedom to experiment using all the classroom materials and equipment on their own. When children find that they can be success-ful even with adult implements, their concepts of themselves as worthy people im-prove significantly.

Children's Activity Choices

Another important ingredient of children's success in early childhood programs is al-lowing them to choose the learning center of their interest during the free-choice or work/play period. Children need to see what is available and then have the freedom to choose an activity that interests them. If the center they select is full, they can pick another area while waiting for their turn. It is a good idea to have a sign-up sheet for popular centers so that every child who wants one actually gets a turn.

Make each learning center in the classroom as equally attractive as possible. For example, don't expect children to choose the book center if it contains only a few books on a shelf against the wall and if there is no place to read the book but a wooden chair and table. Instead, fill this area with brightly colored pillows and a throw rug, a new selection of books with colorful covers facing out, a beanbag chair, and a selection of stuffed animals, character dolls, and puppets to go with the books available. You'll soon have children signing up for a turn in the center.

Have something interesting and different going on in each center every week. Put up challenging question signs and directions. For example, in the book center have a sign that asks, "What do kids *dream* about in the book *KIDS*? Look in the shoebox and find one thing." Then have a shoebox with photocopied pictures made from the book for the children to choose from. Children will first have to figure out what the sign asks them to do. Then they will have to match the picture they select with one of the "dream page" pictures.

In the manipulative/math center have a tape recorder ready with a blank tape and a large sealed clear plastic jar with felt-tip pens inside. Have a sign that says, "How many pens are in this jar? Tell your name and answer to the tape recorder." When chil-dren find out what the words say, they will be flocking to this center to count the pens and tape-record their answer. In the block-building center, have a box full of little farm animals and a sign that says, "Please build a barn for us."

When every learning center is equally attractive, then children will choose each one eagerly. Be sure it is their choice and not yours. Some teachers assign certain chil-dren to particular centers because they feel that the children need experience in the center. This may serve the teacher's purpose, but not necessarily the child's. Even when children repeatedly choose the same center, we must remember that young children's learning involves manipulation, mastery (repetition), and meaning. Be sure everyone has plenty of time for the necessary repetition. Only the children know how much time they personally need.

Children's Special Skills

Every child usually has at least one special skill she can accomplish with ease. Some children already know what their best skill is. Lily can jump rope out on the play-ground 10 times without missing. Loren knows how to build enormous block towers. Ronnie is a natural at strumming the teacher's autoharp. But some children seem to spend much of their time observing what others can do, without revealing any special skills of their own. Keep track of these children as they work and play in the different learning centers to see if they also may excel at something in particular. Talk with the children at the lunch table about their interests at home. Leaf through a magazine or toy catalogue with a youngster to see if any items seem to attract their interest.

Once you have unearthed a special interest for a child, follow up with books, puzzles, games, and activities that support such an interest. One teacher discovered that Maurice wanted to be an artist like his father but everyone ridiculed his attempts at art. The teacher decided to introduce Maurice to Fred, a storybook boy, who also wanted to be an artist but didn't know how to draw, by reading Maurice the book *The Class Artist* (Karas, 2001). In it Fred's sister shows him a simple way to draw a pilgrim, and Fred is on his way—almost. Several other children joined Maurice in listening to the story, and before long there are a number of new "class artists" practicing their skills in Maurice's class.

Teacher's Role

How can you be sure that children are succeeding? Have file cards on every child and record every day what learning center the child played in and what he or she accomplished. Then at the weekly planning session go over these cards with the team to hear what others have to say and to plan new activities appropriate for this child and the others.

Your primary role in the classroom is to set up stimulating activities that involve every child but to choose activities that have specific benefits for certain children. Then, by observing how individual children interact with materials and other children, you can plan what to do next to help each one succeed.

You are not alone in this role. Whether you are a teacher, a student teacher, an assistant, or a community volunteer, you are part of a team. When one of the team is leading a children's group project, for example, someone else is free to operate on a one-to-one basis with a child who may need special help in improving her self-concept.

SUMMARY

This chapter discusses methods for improving the self-concept of your children through your attitude and behavior. First of all, you must accept yourself by listing your positive qualities and then working to develop other qualities you would like to possess. Next you must accept each of the children unconditionally and show them that you do through nonverbal and verbal cues. Smile at them. Encourage them with words. Let them know how you feel about them. For children you have difficulty accepting, observe and record the positive things they do for three days. Show them that you approve with nonverbal cues, and eventually their attitude should change.

Use the Self-Concept Checklist in Figure 8–1 to assess each child's behavior, which is an indication of how they feel about themselves. Make plans to help individuals feel better about themselves with mirrors, photos, tapes, self-concept name games, self-concept art, and self-concept picture books.

Children begin to accept themselves in the classroom when they find that they can succeed in the activities and tasks they encounter. They begin to accept one another when they see you model unconditional acceptance of all of the other children no matter what their background, appearance, or differences are. By stressing similarities in children and honoring their differences, you can help others develop a similar attitude. Focus on areas such as food or dwellings to demonstrate children's common bonds, but show how interesting different people's dwellings or food can be.

Identify and build on children's strengths to help them feel good about themselves. Everyone can do something well, and you must find out what that is for each child. Then challenge them to use their skills in new ways. Help children to succeed in the learning centers of the classroom by encouraging their independence and allowing them to control their environment and to choose their own activities. Then observe and record their choices and accomplishments to determine your next step in helping them to improve their self-concepts.

LEARNING ACTIVITIES

1. Read Chapter 8, "Building a Positive Self-Concept," and write out answers to Question Sheet 8.

2. Meet with your trainer or instructor and discuss answers to Question Sheet 8.

3. View one of the videotapes listed and make 10 file cards with specific ideas for helping children build a positive self-concept.

4. Read one or more of the references cited or suggested readings. Add 10 cards to your file with specific ideas for helping children develop a positive self-concept. Include the reference source on each card.

5. Assess the self-concept of every child in your classroom using the Self-Concept Checklist in Figure 8–1.

6. Make a list of all the children in your class. After each name write down frankly and honestly what you like about the child and why, what changes you think are needed and why, and your reaction to the child in class.

7. Choose a child you have perhaps not accepted unconditionally and try to change your attitude by listing for three days all the positive things you see that child do. Show your approval with nonverbal cues and record the results.

8. Plan and carry out several activities, based on ideas in this chapter, with a child who seems to have a poor self-concept. Record the results.

9. Make a list of every child in the class and record what he or she can do well. Choose one of the children who may need special help and use her strengths to help her experience success in an activity. Record the results.

10. Complete the Chapter 8 Evaluation Sheet and return it to your trainer or college supervisor.

QUESTION SHEET 8

1. How is a child's self-concept formed?

2. What is the first step you should take to help a child accept himself?

3. Why is acceptance of yourself important in your goal of helping children improve their self-concept? How can you do it?

4. Why are nonverbal cues important to young children? What are some important cues?

5. How can using the Self-Concept Checklist in Figure 8–1 help you and the child?

6. What art activities can help improve a child's self-concept? How?

7. Why is it important for children to experience success? How can they do so in your classroom?

8. How should you go about accepting diversity in the children? How can they accept it in one another?

9. How can children build on their strengths? Give an example.

10. Why should you not emphasize competition in your classroom?

11. How does developing independence help improve a child's self-concept? Give an example.

12. In what ways are children able to control their environment in your classroom?

13. Why should children be allowed to use the computer on their own? What are some rules you could establish to prevent any damage to the computers?

14. What activity choices do your children have?

15. How can you make a learning center especially attractive to the youngsters?

REFERENCES

Eaton, M. (1997). Positive discipline: Fostering the self-esteem of young children. *Young Children, 52*(6), 43–46.

Marshall, H. H. (2001). Cultural influences on the development of self-concept: Updating our thinking. *Young Children, 56*(6), 19–25.

Schweinhart, L. J., & Weikart, D. P. (1993). Success by empowerment: The High/Scope Perry Preschool study through age 27. *Young Children, 49*(1), 54–58.

Warner, L. (1999). Self-Esteem: A byproduct of quality classroom music. *Childhood Education, 76*(1), 19–23.

SUGGESTED READINGS

Beaty, J. J. (1997). *Building bridges with multicultural picture books.* Upper Saddle River, NJ: Merrill/Prentice Hall.

Beaty, J. J., & Pratt, L. (2003). *Early literacy in preschool and kindergarten.* Upper Saddle River, NJ: Merrill/Prentice Hall.

Briggs, D. C. (1970). *Your child's self-esteem.* Garden City, NY: Doubleday.

Bronson, M. B. (2000). Recognizing and supporting the development of self-regulation in young children. *Young Children, 55*(2), 32–37.

Ferber, J. (1996). A look in the mirror: Self-concept in preschool children. In Likoplow (Ed.), *Unsmiling faces: How preschools can heal.* New York: Teachers College.

Hopkins, S., & Winters, J. (Eds.). (1990). *Discover the world. Empowering children to value themselves, others, and the earth.* Philadelphia: New Society Publishers.

Hopson, D. P., & Hopson, D. S. (1993). *Raising the rainbow generation: Teaching your children to be successful in a multicultural society.* New York: Simon & Schuster.

Howell, N. M. (1999). Cooking up a learning community with corn, beans, and rice. *Young Children, 54*(5), 36–38.

Hunt, R. (1999). Making positive multicultural early childhood education happen. *Young Children, 54*(5), 39–43.

Kendall, F. E. (1996). *Diversity in the classroom: New approaches to the education of young children.* New York: Teachers College.

Kostelnik, M. J., Stein, L. C., & Whiren, A. P. (1988). Children's self-esteem: The verbal environment. *Childhood Education, 65*(1), 29–32.

Mallory, B. L., & New, R. S. (Eds.). (1994). *Diversity & developmentally appropriate practices: Challenges for early childhood education.* New York: Teachers College.

Milner, S. (1996). Helping children develop healthy self-concepts. *Children Our Concern, 21*(1), 24–25.

Purkey, W. W., & Novak, J. M. (1984). *Inviting school success: A self-concept approach to teaching and learning.* Belmont, CA: Wadsworth.

Ramsey, P. G. (1998). *Teaching and learning in a diverse world: Multicultural education for young children.* New York: Teachers College Press.

Strasser, J. K. (2000/01). Beautiful me! Celebrating diversity through literature and art. *Childhood Education, 77*(2), 76–80.

CHILDREN'S BOOKS

Anholt, C., & Anholt, L. (1992). *KIDS.* Cambridge, MA: Candlewick.

Ashley, B. (1992). *Cleversticks.* New York: Crown.

Baker, L. (2001). *I love you because you're you.* New York: Scholastic.

Carlson, N. (2001). *How about a hug?* New York: Viking.

Dooley, N. (1991). *Everybody cooks rice.* Minneapolis, MN: Carolrhoda.

Gliori, D. (1999). *No matter what.* San Diego: Harcourt.

Escudie, R., & Wensell, U. (1988). *Paul and Sebastian.* Brooklyn: Kane/Miller.

Karas, G. B. (2001). *The class artist.* New York: Greenwillow.

Krauss, R. (1998). *You're just what I need.* New York: HarperCollins.

Kroll, V. (1995). *Hats off to hair.* Watertown, MA: Charlesbridge.

Lovell, P. (2001). *Stand tall, Molly Lou Melon.* New York: Putnam's.

Minarik, E. H. (1992). *Am I beautiful?* New York: Greenwillow.

Moss, T. (1993). *I want to be.* New York: Dial.

Parr, T. (2001). *It's okay to be different.* Boston: Little Brown.

Rankin, L. (1991). *The handmade alphabet.* New York: Dial.

Tarpley, N. A. (1998). *I love my hair!* Boston: Little, Brown.

Wells, R. (1998). *Yoko.* New York: Hyperion.

Wild, M. (1992). *Space travelers.* New York: Scholastic.

Winter, S. (1993). *I CAN.* New York: Dorling Kindersley.

VIDEOTAPES

Redleaf Press (Producer). *Start seeing diversity: The basic guide to an anti-bias curriculum.* St. Paul, MN: Author.

South Carolina Educational Television (Producer). *Building quality child care: Independence.* Washington, DC: Author.

State of Indiana (Producer). *Welcoming all children.* Washington, DC: National Association for the Education of Young Children.

CHAPTER 8 EVALUATION SHEET
BUILDING A POSITIVE SELF-CONCEPT

1. Student _____

2. Trainer _____

3. Center where training occurred _____

4. Beginning date _____ Ending date _____

5. Describe what student did to accomplish General Objective.

    _____

    _____

6. Describe what student did to accomplish Specific Objectives.

    Objective 1 _____

    _____

    Objective 2 _____

    _____

    Objective 3 _____

    _____

7. Evaluation of student's Learning Activities

    _____

    _____

    Comments:

    _____

    _____

    _____

    _____

    _____

    _____

Permission is granted by the publisher to reproduce this page for evaluation and record keeping.

Promoting Social Skills

GENERAL OBJECTIVE

To help children develop the social skills of interacting in harmony with others

☑ SPECIFIC OBJECTIVES

____ Helps children learn to work and play cooperatively through sharing and turn-taking

____ Helps children learn to enter ongoing play without disruptions

____ Helps children learn to make friends

Learning **social skills** has long been one of the important goals for children in early childhood programs. Early childhood educators understand that young children are highly self-centered beings and that this is a necessary step in the human growth pattern for the individual to survive infancy. But as children grow older, they need to develop into social beings who can get along with others outside their homes.

Children in your center must learn to work and play cooperatively not only because we expect it of them but also because they are in a group situation that demands it. They need to learn to get along with the other children through sharing and turn-taking; enter ongoing play without creating a fuss; and find friends to play with. It may not be easy for some.

HELPS CHILDREN LEARN TO WORK AND PLAY COOPERATIVELY THROUGH SHARING AND TURN-TAKING

Three-year-olds, for instance, may be more attuned to adults than to other children. After all, they are not far removed from the toddler stage, when they were almost completely dependent on adult caregivers. Now they are thrust into a group, where adults do not have time for them exclusively and where they are expected *not* to act as dependent, self-centered beings. Many young children do not realize that this will happen to them when they go to preschool. It is quite an adjustment for some children.

SOCIAL SKILLS CHECKLIST

Child's Name_____Date_____

_____Plays in solitary manner away from group.

_____Plays parallel to other children, but alone.

_____Seeks other children to play with or joins group.

_____Enters ongoing play without a fuss.

_____Takes turns with roles, toys, and equipment.

_____Waits for turn without a fuss.

_____Shares toys, materials, and equipment.

_____Solves interpersonal conflicts on own.

Figure 9–1   Social Skills Checklist

Permission is granted by publisher to reproduce this checklist for evaluation and record keeping.

You and the other staff members should recognize this problem and help ease children into becoming social beings who can work and play happily with other children. This is no chore for some children; they have learned these skills elsewhere. For others, you must work carefully to set up opportunities for them to become part of the group.

To recognize which children already display social skills and which ones may need help in developing these skills, you may want to observe each of your children by using the Social Skills Checklist in Figure 9–1. Be as unobtrusive as possible as you observe each child during group play. This information will give you insights into the social development of individual children so that you can determine which ones are able to share and take turns, gain access to group play, and resolve conflicts on their own.

Children learn these skills by being involved in spontaneous play with other children. These are not skills that are "taught" by a teacher. The teacher's role is to set up situations in which children can play together and to observe each child using a checklist like the one in Figure 9–1 to determine to what extent the child is developing social skills. For those who need special help, the teacher can then help—but not pressure—them to become involved with others. For children who need special help in learning to take turns or to resolve conflicts, for instance, the teacher can set up special situations outside of group play where children can practice the skills they will be learning spontaneously during the play.

Social Play

Play is the primary means through which young children learn: about themselves, about others, and about the world around them. Whereas adults often view play as recreation, play for young children is their work, and they spend a great deal of time, energy and concentration in their play with the materials and people around them. When children play with other children we call it "social play." Edwards (2002) has this to say about it:

> Social play is the "umbrella" of all play experiences, encompassing several different levels of social interactions. Young children engage in all types of social play, such as when they are playing chase, or sitting side-by-side working on puzzles, or involved in spontaneous play such as playing "heroes" while running around the playground. These social interactions provide children opportunities to practice and learn self-related and interpersonal related social skills. (p. 192)

Early childhood specialists have been interested in learning how children use spontaneous social play to develop the skills to get along with one another ever since Mildred Parten published her early study "Social Participation Among Pre-School Children" in 1932. Parten defined six categories of play behavior:

1. *Unoccupied behavior:* The child does not participate in the play around him. He stays in one spot, follows the teacher or wanders around.
2. *Onlooker behavior:* The child spends much time watching what other children are doing and may even talk to them, but he does not join or interact with them physically.
3. *Solitary independent play:* The child engages in play activities, but he plays on his own and not with others or with their toys.
4. *Parallel activity:* The child plays independently but he plays next to other children and often uses their toys or materials.
5. *Associative play:* The child plays with other children using the same materials and even talking with them, but he acts on his own and does not subordinate his interests to those of the group.
6. *Cooperative play:* The child plays in a group that has organized itself to do a particular thing, and whose members have taken on different play roles. (pp. 248–251)

As you observe your children at play throughout the year you may also recognize that many of them progress through this natural sequence of play behaviors from onlooker to solitary play to parallel play to group play. These levels of play seem to be age-related, with the youngest, least mature children starting as onlookers, then progressing spontaneously through the other levels until they finally are able to play with a group. Your role as teacher is to:

1. Set up the physical arrangement of the classroom to accommodate small group activities.
2. Schedule enough free-choice time for children to become deeply involved in their play.
3. Accept children wherever they are in this developmental sequence.
4. Observe and record the social skills being demonstrated by each of the children.

5. Help (but not force) them to progress through this sequence of social skill development (see Beaty, 2002, pp. 135–137).

Sharing and Turn-Taking

When young children first enter a preschool program they are often bewildered by the number of toys, games, materials, and pieces of equipment available. Are all of these wonders for them? Because of their egocentric point of view, some children begin to act as if this is the case. These toys are for them alone. If they want a toy another child is playing with, they may simply take it—by force if necessary.

Children who act like this are not trying to be mean; rather the social skills of sharing, taking turns, and waiting for turns are simply not yet part of their behavior. The ability to control their impulses, to wait, or to negotiate or bargain for a turn needs to be learned through observation of others or trial-and-error interactions on their part. As noted by Katz and McClellan (1997):

> Turn taking involves being able to detect cues in a partner's behavior that indicate that he is about to bring his turn to an end, to discern the moment that would be the most propitious to press for one's own turn, and so forth. Mastery of these skills takes time and lots of experience. (p. 91)

The teacher can help by asking the child to ask for a turn rather than trying to take the desired toy by force. The following are some additional strategies.

Modeling and Demonstrating Turn-Taking Behavior

Children can learn from your example and that of the other adults in the classroom. Make it obvious that you respect their rights and will stand up for them if necessary. Make it a point of thanking children who wait for a turn or who share. Do this again and again, and some of the children will soon imitate your behavior. Thank children for saying thanks. That will help other children to remember. Because children also imitate peer behavior, your modeling will spread throughout the classroom as other children see the original child behaving this way.

Bring in a special toy or activity for sharing and taking turns. For example, to demonstrate taking turns, the teacher can show a small group of children some new toy or stuffed animal that they might all want to play with. How can they decide who will get the first turn, and the next? How long should a child be allowed to play with the toy? These problems can be talked about and decided on at group meeting time. Perhaps the children would like a sign-up list where those who want a turn can sign their own name (even in scribble writing). Or perhaps they would like to regulate turns by drawing tickets out of a hat with numbers on them to determine the order. They can also manage the time with a three-minute egg timer. Then it is up to the children to put these skills to use in the spontaneous group play situations that you promote during free-choice time.

Puppets

For children who still have difficulty sharing toys, you might bring in two puppets, one for you and one for a child who gets involved frequently in sharing conflicts with another child. Ask the child if she would like to play puppets with you. Introduce the puppets. Hers can be "Sadie-Share-the-Toy." Yours can be "Donna-Don't-Give-It-Up." Have your puppet get involved with her puppet over a sharing conflict. For example, you could have your puppet say: "Look what I've got. I found this neat dinosaur over on the toy shelf." (Have a real toy dinosaur to get the child's attention.) Her puppet might respond: "Can I see it? I want to play with it too." Yours can reply: "No, it's mine. I found it first. You can't have it."

At this point you can intervene to speak as yourself. Ask the child what Sadie-Share-the-Toy could say to persuade Donna-Don't-Give-It-Up to share the dinosaur toy with her. Also discuss the strategies that probably won't work: getting angry, yelling, or taking the toy by force. Then continue the role play until Sadie finally gets the toy. Getting the real toy when she exhibits the proper behavior reinforces the behavior and helps the child understand what works and what doesn't work in sharing.

Books with Sharing and Turn-Taking Themes

Reading a book about a sharing conflict works best *after* the child has experienced the conflict rather than before. Children need real and concrete experiences on which to base the more abstract ideas gained from books. However, stories are an effective follow-up to reinforce the learning children gain from conflicts. In *Just Not the Same* (Lacoe, 1992), three little sisters always want the first, the biggest, or the best of everything. When they fight over who gets the biggest piece of apple, their mother takes all the pieces and makes them into applesauce. But it is just not the same. Finally after many trials, they learn to share one puppy among all three.

Ruby to the Rescue (Glen, 1992) is the story of toy bears that some preschool children have sharing fights about and the little talking bear, Ruby, who comes to their rescue. *Me First* (Lester, 1992) tells the story of Pinkerton, a pushy little pig who makes sure he is first to get everything no matter who gets shoved aside. On a picnic to the beach, he learns a powerful lesson about other people and their rights, when the sandwich that he hurries to grab turns out to be a "sand witch." Read books like these to individuals or small groups so that everyone has a chance to see the pictures. Then talk with the children afterward to find out what they would have done.

Computer Turn-Taking

Children learn powerful lessons about cooperating with others when they have direct experience with equipment calling for more than one child to use at a time. The classroom computer, for instance, should be set up for two children to use at a time, as discussed previously. Children can choose to use the computer during free-choice

Children learn powerful lessons about cooperating with one another when they have direct experience with equipment calling for more than one child to use at a time.

time by selecting the two computer area necklaces. Then let the two users work out their own turn-taking scheme for each program.

Observers have noted that computer turn-taking problems are frequently settled through conversation rather than physical struggle, as is often the case with other classroom materials. Because turn-taking has to be worked out for nearly every program, computer partners learn lessons about who gets the first choice of program, who goes first, and how many key presses each person gets. Onlookers learn about waiting for turns, not pushing ahead of someone who was there first, and sharing ideas (through conversation) with someone who already has a turn.

For children who have difficulty interacting with others like this, you may need to help them get started, but with great care and without pressure. If a child doesn't seem to participate in group enterprises at all, you will first want to assess the situation by observing and recording.

HELPS CHILDREN LEARN TO ENTER ONGOING PLAY WITHOUT DISRUPTIONS

Children's free play in a preschool setting often ebbs and flows like waves on a beach. No one is still for long. Youngsters come together for a short time in the block area; someone is painting at the easel; a few children wander into the dramatic play kitchen; someone dresses up in high heels and takes the baby doll for a ride in the carriage; two children operate the computer; others are busy at the arts and crafts tables; several are involved with counting blocks and stringing beads; someone is up on the loft listening to a tape with a headset. In the next instant everything changes, and different children are occupied with or trying to gain access to the same activities.

You may wonder why children don't stay longer in one place. Then you remember about the short attention spans of children 3 to 5 years of age. You also recognize their boundless energy and endless drive for finding out what is going on everywhere. If you watch long enough, you are sure to encounter one of the common access struggles that arises when someone wants to enter an ongoing play situation. "I want to do what they're doing, and they won't let me!" is a complaint sounded over and over in early childhood programs.

If a child has not been invited to join or does not know how to establish contact with the ongoing players, he or she is almost always rejected. As noted by early childhood specialist Ramsey (1991):

> Interactions in preschool classrooms are short, so children are constantly having to gain entry into new groups. This process is made more difficult because children who are already engaged with each other tend to protect their interactive space and reject newcomers. (p. 27)

What is a child to do who sees his favorite toy animals being lined up on the floor by two other children but is rejected when he wants to join them? This typical group-entry conflict can be a frustrating dilemma for the child, and he may end up disrupting the play of the other children or coming to you in tears. Your knowledge of group-access strategies can help such a child convert the conflict into a positive social skill learning situation for all involved.

Group-Access Strategies

What do you need to know? You need to be aware of what works for most children who try to enter ongoing play and what does not work. Observers of young children have noted that one of the best strategies for a child who has been rejected is to hover silently near the group, carefully observing what they are doing. Once the child knows what the group is doing, he can do parallel play with similar materials near them. When the time seems right, he can try again to enter the group.

In this case you could suggest to Lanny, the rejected child, that he get a few more animals from the shelf and line them up on the floor next to the other two children. In a little while they might let him into their play, but if they don't, he can continue playing on his own. Most children who have been rejected don't try to enter the play again. Child observers have noted, however, that youngsters who make a second attempt to gain entry are much more likely to be accepted on the second try.

In the case of ongoing dramatic play, a rejected child should also watch what the others are doing and then begin playing in her own way nearby. For example, if Shelly has been refused entry into the ongoing doctor's-office play of three other children, she can observe what's happening until she notes that two of the girls are taking their baby dolls to the doctor's for a shot. She might then get a doll of her own and enter the play, saying, "My baby needs a shot, too." If a child wants you to intervene, you can suggest, "Why don't you watch what the girls are doing? They may let you play after a while." If the child cannot figure out on her own how to insert herself into the play, you can suggest, "Why don't you get a doll and play too?"

Not all strategies work. Asking the players questions that refer to oneself does not seem to help. For example, "Can I play?" or "Can I have that doll?" almost always results in the answer no. Children who make aggressive claims against the players are also rejected. For example, saying "I was here first!" or "That's mine!" or "I got it first" only irritates the other players rather than allowing the new child entrance. If rejected

Figure 9–2   Entering
Ongoing Play

Strategies that work for young children:

1. Observing silently

2. Mimicking the play

3. Trying again to enter group

Strategies to help children avoid:

1. Asking "I" questions

2. Making aggressive claims

3. Disrupting the play physically

children disrupt ongoing play by taking the materials, shouting, or throwing things, they succeed only in stopping the play altogether. Furthermore, the other children remember such actions and may ostracize the outsiders from their further activities. Some of the strategies for entering ongoing play are listed in Figure 9–2.

Why shouldn't you as the teacher simply tell the players to let the outside child into their activity? You certainly have the authority and power to do this. But should you? A teacher's intervention in an interpersonal conflict that can be resolved by the children themselves misses an important point. Children have come to your classroom to learn how to get along with one another. The only way they can really learn such social skills is by becoming involved in interpersonal conflicts and attempting to resolve them on their own.

Your role should be a supportive one in children's conflicts. If someone is hurt or crying or if physical aggression is taking place, you must of course intervene. But if the situation is a common group-access conflict, then give the children a chance to resolve it on their own.

> Play access struggles with other children are the most critical learning opportunities that young children must deal with. Such conflicts teach profound lessons in getting along with others: how to watch and wait; when to initiate contact; how to learn what is going on in the play; how to blend in with the group; what to say so you won't be rejected; what to do in case you are rejected. These crucial lessons are repeated over and over as children ebb and flow during free play. (Beaty, 1995, p. 108)

Books to Read

When the time is right, read to small groups the book *This Is Our House* (Rosen, 1996), a story about the cardboard carton house that the children take out to the playground but that George quickly climbs into and claims for his own. Every time another child comes to play in the house, George keeps him out, declaring, "This house is mine and no one else is coming in." One after another he forces other children out, until at last he has to leave to go to the bathroom. Everyone quickly squeezes into the house, and when George comes back, there is no room for him, until he finally decides that the house is a house for everyone. Ask your listeners what they would have done to get into George's house.

Hoberman's (1999) action-packed *And to Think That We Thought That We'd Never Be Friends* starts out with a brother and sister having a fight over a croquet game that ends when another sister happens by with soda pop to share if they will make up, so they do. But arguments keep flaring up in this rhyming multicultural story, each one ending with more and more people playing musical instruments until a huge parade ensues, marches around the world, and includes all the animals, as well. Have your listeners help end each conflict by chiming in with the title refrain: "And to think that we thought that we'd never be friends!"

Dramatic Play

One of the most effective opportunities for children to learn and practice social skills of all kinds is through the spontaneous pretend play that takes place in the dramatic play center, sometimes called "sociodramatic play." Edwards (2002) defines it as:

> Play in which children assume roles and act out episodes. Sociodramatic play is also described as play that involves social role-playing with others and refers to children's pretend play when two or more children assume related roles and interact with each other. (pp. 194–195)

Most classrooms have a dramatic play center where children are encouraged to pretend and take on roles. Sometimes called the "housekeeping" or "family area," it contains equipment such as a play stove, refrigerator, sink, and table, as well as kitchen equipment and dress-up clothes. These props encourage children to take on spontaneously the family roles they see at home: mother, father, baby, sister, brother. (See Chapter 3, "Dramatic Play Center.")

In a preschool classroom, this kind of activity gives children an opportunity to be part of a group. If they are shy about interacting, they can become acquainted with others through the roles they take on. They can "hide" behind their roles, so to speak, in the way a shy child hides behind a puppet. Dramatic play is one of the most unique opportunities you can provide for learning social skills. To get along with the other players, children must learn to share, to take turns, to adjust their actions to the group, and to resolve conflicts without an adult's help.

We know how important peer pressure is with older children. Child development research has only recently come to recognize how important peers are to younger children as well. They exchange information about the world around them; they offer suggestions to one another on appropriate ways to behave; and some even try to impose their will on others in the group. Children learn what is expected of them and whether or not to conform to this pressure.

In addition, children observe how other children are treated by their peers, what works and what doesn't work in interpersonal conflicts, and how far a peer can go in trying to get his own way. Aggressive children learn that others will not accept their

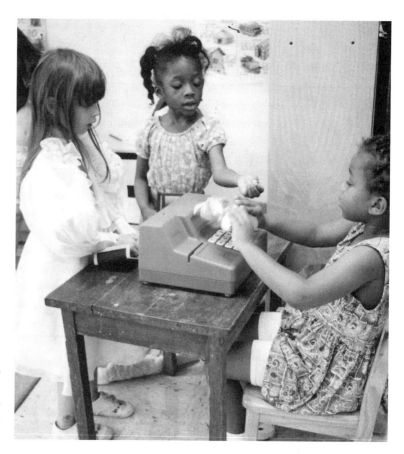

Besides teaching them social skills, dramatic play gives children the opportunity to try out the real-life roles they see enacted around them.

overbearing ways. The group may demonstrate its feelings by stopping the play altogether when things get out of hand or by not allowing their aggressive peer to join them the next time. Not only do aggressive children learn a lesson when such negative peer responses happen again and again, but other child players also learn that similar reactions from the group could happen to them if they behave in a similar aggressive manner.

Besides teaching them social skills, dramatic play also gives children the opportunity to try out the real-life roles they see enacted around them. It helps them understand what it is like to be a mother or a brother. They begin to see things from another perspective, often trying on for size the roles they will eventually play as adults. While they play these roles in the classroom, they are becoming socialized in a much more effective way than any adult could teach them. They learn to follow peer directions, to take leader or follower roles, to compromise their own desires, to resolve interpeer conflict—all through spontaneous play.

Dramatic play also helps children master uncomfortable feelings. Adults are sometimes unaware of the frustrations children feel at being small and helpless in a grown-up world. Pretending to be an adult helps them gain some control over their world and helps them work out fears and frustrations. They can pretend about going to the doctor and getting a shot, about going to a strange school next year, or about staying overnight with a baby-sitter and thus lessen the trauma of the real event.

Furthermore, dramatic play helps children clarify new ideas and concepts about society and the world around them. As they gain information about unfamiliar people and situations, they are able to make it understandable by incorporating it into their imaginative play. The child who has a plumber come to her house plays out this situation in the housekeeping corner and begins to understand it better. Dramatic play, in other words, gives concrete meaning to abstract ideas.

Finally, such play helps young children develop creative skills by forcing them to use their imaginations. They make up the roles, the rules, the situations, and the solutions. The drama can be as elaborate or simple as the players make it. And strange as it seems, it is through imaginative play like this that children come to understand the difference between fantasy and reality. The real world becomes more real to children who have opportunities to pretend.

Dramatic Play Areas

You will want to have a permanent area in your classroom for this kind of dress-up play, as discussed in Chapter 3. In addition to the permanent household area, other dramatic play areas may also be appropriate from time to time. For example, you may want to set up a supermarket, shoe store, or post office, especially after the children have visited one of these sites on a field trip. Children can bring empty cartons, cans, and boxes to fill the shelves of a store.

Dramatic play can also take place with smaller toys in many other areas of the classroom, and it serves the same socialization purpose. You can encourage dramatic play in the block corner by mounting, at child's eye level, pictures of activities involving the field trip sites the children have visited: stores, farm, zoo, pet store, post office, or park. Then you must provide appropriate toys and props to accompany the play: figures of people and animals, little cars and trucks, string, aquarium tubing, or little boxes. Let the children use these props on their own in any way they want. To be effective, pretend play must be spontaneous.

Do the same near the sand or water table and in the manipulative area. A supply of miniature people, animals, cars, trucks, boats, and doll furniture is essential if you are committed to promoting imaginative play.

Teacher's Role

Your initial role may be as an observer. You will want to determine which children take part in dramatic play and which never do. Can they take turns? Can they resolve conflicts? Who are the leaders? The followers? What other roles do they play? How long can they sustain their roles? Do they allow other children to participate in their play?

Children's fear of going to a doctor or dentist may surface in dramatic play. If you observe that children have mistaken ideas about what doctors or dentists do, do not interrupt the play to "set them straight." Instead, take note of their misconceptions. Later you may want to read them a book about visiting the doctor or dentist. Or you may think that the children have been able to work out their fears satisfactorily on their own in their dramatic play.

What happens in the dramatic play area is often determined by the way you set it up, what equipment and furniture are available, and what paraphernalia you put out. If the children have expressed fear of police officers, for example, you may want to put out appropriate props—say a police cap—especially after a classroom visit from an officer.

If you observe that certain children are not participating in dramatic play, are not staying with a role, or are not really interacting with others in their roles, you may want to help them get involved by playing a role yourself. For example, you might say: "C'mon, Shandra, let's visit Jayce's store. You carry the pretend money. What shall we buy?" When the child seems involved and comfortable, you can ease out of your role the same way you entered.

For new groups of children who seem to have no idea how to get started in dramatic play, you may even have to assign roles and start the play by taking a role yourself. When things are going smoothly, you can withdraw. "Let's go to the beach," you might say. "Does anybody want to go to the beach with me? Okay, let's pack our swimming suits. The bags are on the shelf. Rachel, you bring the picnic basket. Rob, you bring the beach ball. I'll bring the towels. Sharon, would you like to drive the bus to the beach?"

All of this is, of course, pretend. If you happen to have beach bags or picnic baskets for props, all the better. If not, the children can pretend they have them. If going to the beach turns out to be a favorite theme, then create a prop box that you fill with necessary props (e.g., beach toys, towels, sunglasses), and store it on a shelf along with other prop boxes in a designated area. Computer paper boxes covered with colored contact paper and labeled with a title or picture make fine prop-storage containers.

Ask the children what other dramatic play themes they would like to try. Some will probably mention places they have visited with their parents or where their parents work: office, restaurant, gas station, convenience store, museum, flower shop, bakery, repair shop, factory, school, hairdresser, or sports shop. Fill the prop boxes with appropriate implements from home, from flea markets, or from the actual sites themselves. Then introduce the boxes one at a time when it seems appropriate.

When dramatic play begins to get wild or seems to disintegrate, you may need to step in and change its direction. When a race with tiny cars in the block-building center has deteriorated into squabbles and shouting, you might say, "What do race car drivers do when the race is finished?" If you have the props on hand, you may be able to redirect the children into "washing and polishing their race cars." Children can use milk cartons open at both ends as car wash buildings to drive through, old cut-off toothbrushes to clean the cars, and paper tissues to polish them. Or you can help them improvise in other ways.

Block-Building

Social skills can also be learned and practiced in the block-building center. Children do role playing in this center just as in the dramatic play center but in a scaled-down manner. Unit blocks are used realistically to construct roads, bridges, and buildings or more abstractly as cars, planes, spaceships, or anything else a child's imagination can conceive. Children play with the constructions they create both realistically and imaginatively, depending on their experience with life, with blocks, and with pretending.

Occasionally a child does not seem to know how to get started in block building. This is an instance where you might want to intervene. How should you go about it? Sometimes simply your presence in the block corner will entice a shy or insecure child into the area. You might then ask the child to get you a long block from the shelf if she doesn't seem to know what to do. Put the block down and ask her to get another block. Ask the child where to place it. Get her involved in selecting and placing other blocks one by one. Once she is involved, you can withdraw, as in dramatic play. Tell her you'll be back in a few minutes to see how many other blocks she has placed on her structure and what it will look like. Your role should be one of support for the shy or unsure child and that of observer for the rest.

You will soon become aware of which children build by themselves (solitary play), who builds next to the others but independently (parallel play), and finally who is able to build cooperatively with other children (group play), the final step in the socialization process. Keep records of the children's progress on individual file cards along with the results of the Social Skills Checklist shown in Figure 9–1.

It is important not to pressure children to socialize. It is not up to you to make Paul play with Mike. You may need to provide the opportunity for both, but the children must make the contact on their own. This will often happen automatically after both feel secure in the block area. That means they will have experimented with blocks on their own. Many children need to do a great deal of solitary and parallel block building before they gain the confidence to cooperate with other children.

Handling Interpersonal Conflicts

Frequently, the first social contacts are ones of conflict. "He took my block!" or "She won't let me play!" Often, as a teacher or student teacher, you will be drawn into the situation because the children want you to settle it. Situations of uncontrolled anger, destruction of materials, or harm to other children demand that you step in. Firmly but calmly, you must enforce previously established limits of not letting children hurt one another or damage materials.

On the other hand, you can let the children handle many of their own interpersonal conflicts once they feel they have your support. Give them masking tape to mark off boundaries for building, if that seems to help. Help them make a sign that asks others not to knock down the building. Help them set the kitchen timer to five minutes so that they can take turns with a favorite truck in the block area. Let children give out tickets to other builders who would like to join in. Ask the children

Many children need to do a great deal of solitary and parallel block building before they gain the confidence to cooperate with another child.

themselves what they want to do to solve the problem. You and the children can come up with dozens of similar ideas to help them resolve conflicts.

You must remember, of course, that adult direction stifles children's own problem solving. You may need to encourage children at the outset to help them get started, but then you should tactfully withdraw. You may need to help redirect their play when it gets out of hand, but then you should step aside. For group play to be truly effective in promoting the development of social skills, children need to manage their social roles by themselves.

Other-Esteem Conflict Conversion

On the other hand, children need to know you will respect each child's rights; then you can help individuals stand up for their own rights. When conflicts arise, it is often impossible for the teacher to determine who was right and who was wrong. Try not to deal with children's conflicts on the basis of right and wrong or blame and shame. Instead, listen to each child in a noncommittal way.

You can best help two children in conflict by listening to each and then asking how each one thinks the other child feels.

For example, Michelle says Anthony took the toy cash register that she was playing with. She starts to cry. Anthony says that he had it first and left it for only a few minutes to find some toy money. When he came back, Michelle had taken it, so he took it away from her.

You can best help both children recognize each other's points of view and empathize with their feelings by listening to each, thanking them for telling you what happened, and then by asking how each one thinks the other child feels about it. This is quite different from the usual blame-and-shame approach, or asking a child how she feels. Children are usually surprised to be asked how the *other* child feels. After they finally reply, then you can ask what each one thinks should be done to make the other child feel better. This approach is known as "other-esteem conflict conversion." It is a new learning approach to handling social conflicts rather than a blame-and-punishment approach.

For example, Michelle tells the teacher that it's Anthony's fault because he took the cash register away from her. Anthony says that it's Michelle's fault because he was playing with it first and left it for just a minute to get some money. She took it away from him. The teacher listens carefully to each point of view and then says to each child, "Thanks for telling me what happened." She does not blame either child or let the two children get into their own who's-to-blame argument. Instead, she next asks: "Michelle,

1. Listen to each child.

2. Thank each child for telling you what happened.

3. Do not blame either one or get into a blaming argument.

4. Ask each child how he thinks the *other* child feels.

5. Ask each child what should be done to make the *other* child feel better.

6. Follow the agreed-on solution.

Figure 9–3   Teacher's Role in Children's Conflicts

how do you think Anthony feels about what happened?" Michelle may be very surprised at this question, and say: "But it's his fault. He took my cash register." The teacher can then reply, "I know, you already told me, but now we're talking about feelings. How do you think Anthony feels? Look at his face."

When Michelle finally is able to answer that Anthony looks mad, then the teacher can ask Anthony how he thinks Michelle feels. He is also surprised at this turn of events and still wants to blame Michelle. But the teacher insists on talking about feelings. Anthony may finally say that he thinks Michelle feels bad because she is crying. This is where the "conflict conversion" happens. Instead of blame and shame, the teacher has converted the situation to feelings: how does the other child feel? Most youngsters can respond honestly to this question. Then the teacher concludes by asking each child what they think will make the other child feel better.

This is generally a big relief for each child because they are not being blamed or punished. Furthermore, the children themselves have control over the resolution. This usually means they will abide by whatever they decide to do and not carry on the conflict later. An adult-imposed solution is never that satisfactory and often results in bad feelings or a continuation of the conflict. On the other hand, children's solutions are often more creative than an adult's might be. Perhaps they decide to takes turns with the cash register using a kitchen timer, or both use the cash register at the same time, or to play a different game altogether; or they might even decide to give each other a big hug! Figure 9–3 outlines the steps the teacher can take in an "other-esteem conflict conversion" situation.

No matter how you finally handle conflict, it is important to be consistent. If you handle interpersonal problems in the same objective manner every time, the children will come to trust you and to understand that you will treat each of them fairly in their dealings with one another. This gives them a good basis for handling problems on their own. Then they can try out different strategies to see which ones work best. Sometimes the only solution is to have the teacher put away the disputed toy until another day.

As these ideas become internalized through the children's experiences in the classroom, their social behavior should also change from self-centeredness to cooperation and other-esteem.

The Shy Child

The shy or unsure child, on the other hand, may need your help to get started, or she may never attempt group entry. One way to help the child is to take a role yourself for a brief period and then extract yourself when the child seems comfortable playing with others. "Shall we visit Rosa's house today, Denise? You knock on the door and see if she is home." If the shy child lacks the social skills to gain entry to play groups, your modeling of the appropriate behavior and dialogue can help.

Classroom materials can sometimes help shy children become involved with others. Materials through which they can project, yet not reveal themselves totally, are best. A toy telephone, for instance, allows them to talk with other children indirectly, until they feel comfortable enough for a more direct encounter. A teacher can initiate such a pretend phone call. Puppets and dolls or toy animals also allow shy children the same protection. A stuffed animal can act as a security blanket and provide a way for an unsure child to approach someone else. In the classic book *Will I Have a Friend?* (Cohen, 1967), Paul makes his initial contact with Jim through a tiny truck he shows Jim.

Sometimes the seemingly shy child has other reasons for not interacting with others. One teacher learned that a boy who usually played by himself in a vacant corner was not shy at all. He came from a family of 10 and had no toys or space of his own at home. He simply needed to get off by himself. In another program, an extremely bright child who was reading at age 4 was simply not challenged by the activities the others engaged in and preferred to play quietly at solitary tasks.

If a child seems happy in self-contained play, invite but don't push him into a group activity. He may in fact do better on his own. We need to respect these differences in children as we do in adults. Don't give up entirely on the so-called loner, however. Some children are simply overwhelmed by large groups. You might begin by inviting them to do something with one other friend: look at a book together, help pick up toys together, set the table together, get out the cots for nap time, or go to the office to get the mail. The friends may eventually participate in group activities on their own.

Making friends with the classroom guinea pig or rabbit can be the first step toward making friends with another child. The teacher can help children become involved with a classroom animal like this to get this process started. Find out what shy youngsters are interested in and use that knowledge to motivate them to become involved with others. You might read the child Dick King-Smith's (1997) *I Love Guinea Pigs,* and then ask the child to be in charge of feeding the classroom guinea pig if she agrees.

 ## HELPS CHILDREN LEARN TO MAKE FRIENDS

Friendship among young children is not necessarily the same as it is among older children or adults. Preschoolers often value friends for their abilities to meet their (the preschooler's) needs rather than for their personalities. Young children need a friend

Figure 9–4   Children's
Friendship-Building Skills

1. Inviting another child to play or work together

2. Sharing toys and materials

3. Carrying on a conversation

4. Offering to help

5. Exchanging play ideas

6. Reading or listening to a friendship book together

7. Following another child's lead, or leading another

8. Walking, eating, playing together

9. Being partners on a field trip

10. Laughing together

11. Having fun together

to help them build a block building, or play firefighter, or push a wagon around. Because young children are so self-centered, early friendships are often one-sided and fluid. A friend is valued if he satisfies certain needs of the other child. Someone who shares a toy or plays with a preschool child is considered a friend, for the moment at least.

For a child who has difficulty finding a friend in the classroom, the teacher can sometimes help by modeling the appropriate behavior. Put on a hand puppet and have the child put on one, if she will. Have your puppet ask the child's puppet to do something. Could they build a tower together? Perhaps this child could also show another child how to do something she is familiar with. Could they saw wood together, make a puppet talk, read a book, or build a Lego building together? These activities can provide the means for a shy child to enter other group activities where she might form a friendship. McCay and Keyes (2001/02) comment:

> Making friends, or relating positively to others, is a major component of social competence and a central concern throughout childhood. All children want to know that their peers like and respect them. While some skills related to friendship-building may be taught through modeling, specifically teaching these skills can be more successful. (p. 75)

Some of the skills related to children's friendship-building include those listed in Figure 9–4.

Finding friends and forming friendships on their own is sometimes beyond the capabilities of preschool children. As Katz and McClellan (1997) report:

> For example, teachers report that some families move so frequently that children's budding relationships are broken too often to allow them to master social skills or form real friendships. (p. 8)

Some children learn to find a friend by "reading" a book together.

Listening Partners

You as teacher may have to help. You might start by reading a book about friendship to two children. You can choose the book, pick pairs of children, and invite them to listen to the story. If the book characters are boys, for instance, you may want two boys to listen.

Yo! Yes? (Raschka, 1993) shows large pictures of two lonely boys, one black and one white, on opposite pages, standing and looking at one another. One says "Yo!" and the other says "Yes?" as they tentatively approach one another with single words in oversize type. Each is looking for a friend, and when they finally come together, they both say "Yow!"

Ask your listeners what they would say if they met someone they wanted for a friend. What else would they say if the person agreed to be their friend? If your listeners ask you to read the book again, be sure you comply. Then ask if they could "read" it to one another themselves. Tell them to make up their own words for this simple story if they forget the words in the book.

Margaret and Margarita (Reiser, 1993) are two little girls taken to a park by their mothers who end up on the same park bench. Margaret, with her toy rabbit Susan, speaks English, but Margarita, with her toy cat Susana, speaks Spanish. What will they do? While the adults sit with their backs turned, the two little girls make tentative advances toward one another, saying "Hello" and "Hola" and finally having their toy pets respond in the opposite language. Soon they are friends, although each speaking her own language. If you cannot read these simple Spanish words, find someone who can. What would your listening partners do if they were Margaret or Margarita?

Often it is toys like this that bring children together. In *Building a Bridge* (Begaye, 1993), an Anglo girl named Anna and a Navajo girl named Juanita are excited but worried about their first day of school on the Navajo reservation because they don't know anyone. Anna is uncomfortable because she looks so different from the Navajo children. The teacher, Mrs. Yazzie, asks Juanita to take a bucket of purple and green blocks over to Anna and see if she would help her build something. She tells them the blocks are magic. They each build their own purple bridge or green bridge with the blocks, but then the magic clicks in. They find that by putting the blocks together they can build a really big bridge, and the colors don't make any difference. If your listening partners like this story, be sure to read it again. Then ask the two of them if they can build their own bridge in your block center. Will it help bring them together as friends?

Children with Special Needs

Often children with special needs may have trouble finding friends in the classroom, sometimes because children outside the classroom have not treated them well. As McCay and Keyes (2001/02) note:

> Children with disabilities in the regular classroom tend to have more difficulty building friendships, because they may have learned that other children can hurt them. Children's behavior is guided by their interpretation of social cues based on prior experience. (p. 75)

You as a teacher can help not by scolding others or pointing out the need for special help regarding such children, but by treating children with special needs in the same loving way you treat all of the children. You can help them participate in all of the classroom activities, as well as taking on simple leadership roles such as being in charge of getting out materials and equipment for art or outdoor play, feeding the aquarium fish, or helping to get out naptime cots. They too can become listening partners when you read appropriate books to two children at a time, or computer partners if they want to take turns on the computer. You can also help them find friends just as you do with other children who need assistance. As Honig and Wittmer (1996) note:

> Children with disabilities need your inventive interventions to learn how to make a friend, use positive and assertive techniques to enter a play group, and sustain friendly play bouts with peers. (p. 65)

However, teachers need to be aware that friendship evolves and cannot be forced. Talking to the children about who is friends with whom does not help the situation. Some children do seem to prefer the company of a particular child, but this is no reason to point out to the others that Sandra and Rachel are such close friends. Such statements may unknowingly put pressure on children who do not have identifiable friends. Finding a personal friend is not the point in preschool. Most children have not yet developed to this level. Having a playmate is more important, but talking about it is not.

Creating a Kindness Class

The class itself can reflect your focus on treating one another with respect and kindness. Friendship grows out of little acts of kindness such as one child helping another to pick up the blocks without being asked, sharing a lunch sandwich with another, or giving up a computer turn to someone else. You can alert the children to these acts of kindness in several ways. For instance, one teacher began by commenting to the children on every kind act she saw and writing it down on a slip of paper that she posted on the bulletin board under the label "Acts of Kindness." Another teacher wrote down such acts on cards and put them into a large glass "Kindness Jar."

But that was just the beginning. Soon the children were contributing their own "sightings of kindness." This time the staff members asked the children themselves to record such acts on cards the best way they could by scribbling, printing, drawing pictures, or asking one another to write their names. Such cards could then be put into a jar or a basket, or pasted in a "kindness scrapbook" for everyone to look at in the book center. Some children also wanted to give their "kindness cards" to the children who performed the kind acts to take home or put in their personal journals. The teacher in this class noted:

> I realized that, for the children, sharing a personal kind act was not really different from showing one's picture or journal to the class. Telling about their kind acts was a way for them to affirm their growth in thoughtfulness. (Whitin, 2001, p. 20)

Before the year was up some children were also reporting their conflict resolutions as acts of kindness. The teacher was especially gratified to hear "we decided that we would be friends" as the solution to a conflict over a toy. What everyone including the teaching staff learned was that when you look for kindness you find it; when you expect children—and teachers—to be kind to one another, it happens. Who else could this class include in their kindness campaign: What about parents? Cooks? Bus drivers? Visitors? Children and teachers from other classes? When will you start your own "kindness class"?

SUMMARY

This chapter discusses ways to promote children's social development by helping them to learn to get along with one another. It is often difficult for children of this age, who are egocentric in nature, to work and play cooperatively in a group setting.

To facilitate such play, the teacher needs to observe and record information about individuals and their social skills development, such as who seeks other children to play with, who can take turns, or who can solve interpersonal conflicts on their own. Teachers help children learn turn-taking by demonstrating with toys and pup-pets, by reading books about sharing and turn-taking, and by setting up turn-taking situations such as partners at the computer.

For children who need assistance in learn-ing to enter ongoing group play, teachers help them to use strategies that have been found to work and to avoid strategies that do not work. Their experiences in the dramatic play and block-building areas can provide opportunities for children to work out relationship problems with their peers. Through dramatic play, children learn to see things from another's point of view. They exchange information with one another, often about appropriate ways to behave. They learn to share, take turns, and wait for a turn.

The teacher's role is to stimulate such play in the first place by helping children become in-volved in pretend play. When play disintegrates, she finds ways to extend it further by posing a question or suggesting a new direction. To help the shy child become involved in such play the teacher may take on a role herself, modeling ap-propriate dialogue and behavior.

A friend for preschool children is often someone who shares a toy or plays with them. Teachers can help children find friends through their modeling behavior, use of puppets, and pairing children to listen to books with friend-ship themes. Toys and play materials can also bring children together as playmates and friends. Children with special needs may need direct help from the teaching staff to find friends. Friendship itself can grow out of little acts of kindness noted by the teaching staff and chil-dren as they record and share these acts.

LEARNING ACTIVITIES

1. Read Chapter 9 and write answers to Question Sheet 9.

2. Meet with your trainer or instructor and discuss answers to Question Sheet 9.

3. View one of the videotapes listed and make 10 file cards with specific ideas for helping children develop social skills.

4. Read one or more of the references cited or sug-gested readings. Add 10 cards to your file, with specific ideas for helping children develop social skills. Include the reference source on each card.

5. Use the Social Skills Checklist in Figure 9–1 to guide your observation of children as they en-gage in dramatic play or block building. Record and interpret the results, noting children who may need help.

6. Choose one or more of the children who may need help developing social skills and use ideas from this chapter to help them improve.

7. Bring in a prop box with items for children to use in dramatic play or block building based on a new theme from a field trip or other classroom activity. Observe and record the children's use of props.

8. Help children who are having difficulty enter-ing ongoing play to use one or more of the strategies described in this chapter. Record the results.

9. Help shy children to become involved in activi-ties or to find a friend using ideas presented in this chapter. Record the results.

10. Help children resolve turn-taking conflicts by demonstrating how to take turns with toys or puppets, learning how the other child in the con-flict feels, and helping the other child feel better. Record the results.

11. Complete the Chapter 9 Evaluation Sheet and re-turn it to your trainer or college supervisor.

QUESTION SHEET 9

1. Why should children have to change their ego-centric natures when they come to your center or classroom?

2. How can you help bring about this change?

3. How can a teacher help the children learn to share and take turns?

4. How can puppets be used to help children with turn-taking problems?

5. How can using the computer teach children about turn-taking?

6. Why do children have trouble entering ongoing play without a fuss?

7. What group-access strategies work best for children?

8. What should a child do who has been denied admission to a group's ongoing play?

9. What social skills can children learn through dramatic play?

10. How can you help a child become involved in dramatic play who doesn't seem to know what to do?

11. How can you help involve a child who does not seem to know how to play with blocks?

12. What is the teacher's role in conflicts that children have difficulty resolving on their own?

13. How can the use of classroom materials help a shy child overcome shyness?

14. How do friendships between preschoolers differ from those between older children?

15. How can you help a child with special needs find a friend?

REFERENCES

Beaty, J. J. (1995). *Converting conflicts in preschool.* Fort Worth, TX: Harcourt Brace.

Beaty, J. J. (2002). *Observing development of the young child.* Upper Saddle River, NJ: Merrill/Prentice Hall.

Edwards, L. C. (2002). *The creative arts: A process approach for teachers and children.* Upper Saddle River, NJ: Merrill/Prentice Hall.

Honig, A. S., & Wittmer, D. S. (1996). Helping children become more prosocial: Ideas for classrooms, families, schools, and communities. *Young Children, 51*(2), 62–70.

Katz, L. G., & McClellan, D. E. (1997). *Fostering children's social competence: The teacher's role.*

Washington, DC: National Association for the Education of Young Children.

McCay, L. O., & Keyes, D. W. (2001/02). Developing social competence in the inclusive primary classroom. *Childhood Education, 78*(2), 70–77.

Parten, M. B. (1932). Social participation among preschool children. *Journal of Abnormal and Social Psychology, 27,* 243–369.

Ramsey, P. G. (1991). *Making friends in school: Promoting peer relationships in early childhood.* New York: Teachers College.

Whitin, P. (2001). Kindness in a jar. *Young Children, 56*(5), 18–22.

SUGGESTED READINGS

Beaty, J. J. (1999). *Prosocial guidance for the preschool child.* Upper Saddle River, NJ: Merrill/Prentice Hall.

Buzelli, C. A., & File, N. (1989). Building trust in friends. *Young Children, 44*(3), 70–75.

Caldwell, B. (1998). Early experiences shape social development. *Child Care Information Exchange, 121,* 53–59.

Cartledge, G., & Milburn, J. F. (1995). *Teaching social skills to children and youth.* Boston: Allyn and Bacon.

Honig, A. S. (1987). The shy child. *Young Children, 42*(4), 54–64.

Kostelnik, M. J., Stein, L. C., Whiren, A. P., & Soderman, A. K. (1993). *Guiding children's social development.* Albany, NY: Delmar.

Myhre, S. M. (1993). Enhancing your dramatic-play area through the use of prop boxes. *Young Children, 48*(5), 6–11.

Niffenegger, J. P., & Willer, L. R. (1998). Friendship behavior during early childhood and beyond. *Early Childhood Education Journal, 26*(2), 95–99.

O'Brien, M., Roy, C., Jacobs, A., Macaluso, M., & Peyton, V. (1999). Conflict in the dyadic play of 3-year-old children. *Early Education & Development, 10*(3), 289–313.

Provenzo, E. F. Jr., & Brett, A. (1983). *The complete block book.* Syracuse, NY: Syracuse University Press.

Rogers, D. L., & Ross, D. D. (1986). Encouraging positive social interaction among young children, *Young Children, 41*(3), 12–17.

Van Hoorn, J., Nourot, P., Scales, B., & Alward, K. (1999). *Play at the center of the curriculum.* Upper Saddle River, NJ: Merrill/Prentice Hall.

Walden, T., Lemeirie, E., & Smith, M. C. (1999). Friendship and popularity in preschool classrooms. *Early Education & Development, 10*(3), 351–371.

CHILDREN'S BOOKS

Begaye, L. S. (1993). *Building a bridge.* Flagstaff, AZ: Northland.

Cohen, M. (1967). *Will I have a friend?* New York: Macmillan.

Glen, M. (1992). *Ruby to the rescue.* New York: G. P. Putnam's.

Hoberman, M. A. (1999). *And to think that we thought that we'd never be friends.* New York: Crown.

King-Smith, D. (1997). *I love guinea pigs.* Cambridge, MA: Candlewick.

Lacoe, A. (1992). *Just not the same.* Boston: Houghton Mifflin.

Lester, H. (1992). *Me first.* Boston: Houghton Mifflin.

Raschka, C. (1993). *Yo! Yes?* New York: Orchard.

Reiser, L. (1993). *Margaret and Margarita.* New York: Greenwillow.

Rosen, M. (1996). *This is our house.* Cambridge, MA: Candlewick.

VIDEOTAPES

High/Scope Press (Producer). *Supporting children in resolving conflicts.* St. Paul, MN: Redleaf Press.

Indiana Steps Ahead. (Producer). *Dramatic play: More than playing house.* Washington, DC: National Association for the Education of Young Children.

National Association for the Education of Young Children. (Producer). *Play—The Seed of Learning.* Washington, DC: Author.

South Carolina Educational Television. (Producer). *Block play: Constructing realities.* Washington, DC: National Association for the Education of Young Children.

CHAPTER 9 EVALUATION SHEET
PROMOTING SOCIAL SKILLS

1.   Student _____

2.   Trainer _____

3.   Center where training occurred _____

4.   Beginning date _____ Ending date _____

5.   Describe what student did to accomplish General Objective.

_____

_____

6.   Describe what student did to accomplish Specific Objectives.

Objective 1 _____

_____

Objective 2 _____

_____

Objective 3 _____

_____

7.   Evaluation of student's Learning Activities

_____

_____

Comments:

_____

_____

_____

_____

_____

_____

Permission is granted by the publisher to reproduce this page for evaluation and record keeping.

Providing Guidance

To promote the development of self-control in young children through positive guidance

✓ SPECIFIC OBJECTIVES

_____ Uses positive prevention measures to help eliminate inappropriate behavior in the classroom

_____ Uses positive intervention measures to help children control their inappropriate behavior

_____ Uses positive reinforcement techniques to help children learn appropriate behavior

Positive guidance that helps children develop control over inappropriate behavior also helps improve their self-esteem. Children who feel good about themselves are less prone to exhibit disruptive, negative behavior. Some children enter your classroom smiling, with good feelings about their self-worth and cooperative behavior that reflects these feelings. Other children come with as many as three or four years of accumulated negative experiences that are reflected in their disruptive behavior. How can you help such children learn appropriate behavior?

Some teachers have long responded with traditional "discipline," some type of punishment for a child's inappropriate behavior. This kind of behavior management may stop a child's actions, but it creates other serious problems. Because the control comes from outside the child, she fails to develop her own self-control and becomes dependent on the adult to manage her behavior. Secondly, most discipline makes a child feel ashamed and often angry, ready to strike out again at the next opportunity. The action has been stopped, but the negative feelings created often go on and on.

If you are aware that much of young children's inappropriate behavior stems from insecurities and a negative self-image, you will eventually conclude that punishment, harsh treatment, loud commands, or scolding on your part do not provide solutions. These responses are themselves inappropriate behavior and only reinforce a child's poor self-image. Such discipline does not help the child feel good about herself or build the inner control needed to get along in the world.

Today many preschool teachers are turning instead to guidance, a positive response that keeps the child's self-image in mind. As defined by Gartrell (1997):

> Teachers who practice guidance believe in the positive potential of children. . . . Teachers who use guidance think beyond conventional classroom discipline—the intent of which is to keep children in line. Rather than simply being a reaction to crises, guidance involves developmentally appropriate, culturally responsive education to reduce the occurrence of classroom problems. Guidance means creating a positive learning environment for each child in the group. (pp. 34–35)

Preschool children come to your classroom to develop manipulative skills, to improve large motor coordination, to learn social skills, to develop language, to develop creativity, to learn cognitive concepts, and to improve their self-image. Learning to control their behavior should also be a learning goal. You should put this goal at the top of your list for certain children and go about teaching it as you would any skill. Young children need objective, not emotional, guidance in the area of learning appropriate behavior.

USES POSITIVE PREVENTION MEASURES TO HELP ELIMINATE INAPPROPRIATE BEHAVIOR IN THE CLASSROOM

Learning Environment

First, you need to anticipate problem behavior and set up your learning environment so that it does not happen. Young children may run around wildly if your classroom arrangement gives them the space to do this. Children may squabble over toys and materials if there are not enough for everyone or if toys are not at the appropriate developmental level of the children. Likewise, children may become bored with books and toys if the "same old ones" are always on the shelves, with nothing new ever added or none of the old ones put away.

Some of the causes for disruptive behavior in a preschool classroom that can be resolved by rearranging the room and providing more materials include those identified in Figure 10–1. By setting up your classroom as described in Chapter 3, you will go a long way toward reducing friction between children, in addition to freeing yourself to work with small groups and individuals who need special help. The way space is used to define learning centers, to allow for pathways between areas, and to prevent overcrowding can help prevent disruptive behavior before it starts. As Ratcliff (2001) notes:

> Research shows that placing young children in relatively small areas may increase aggressive behavior. More accidental physical encounters—head bumping and fingers getting stepped on—occur in crowded areas, and children's play and/or creations can be interrupted or accidentally destroyed. Young children often don't see a difference between accidental and intentional actions and respond with aggression. (p. 84)

1. Learning centers not clearly defined or too crowded
2. Not enough learning centers to engage everyone
3. No pathways between learning centers
4. Too much room to run around
5. Activities and materials not appropriate for developmental level of children
6. Too few activities and materials
7. No duplicates of favorite toys or materials
8. No change in old materials, books, or toys
9. Classroom geared for total group activities rather than individual and small group activities

Figure 10–1 Causes for Disruptive Behavior

New Materials

Teachers can also help by introducing new toys or equipment to the entire class during morning circle time, by passing around the new materials and later storing them on a labeled shelf or location that everyone recognizes. If teachers anticipate conflicts over the new material, they can ask youngsters ahead of time how they would like to set up a turn-taking arrangement for the new object. Another method for preventing possession squabbles is to obtain at least two of the favorite toys.

Books to Read

If conflicts over toys and materials occur regularly in your classroom, read books with this theme to individuals or small groups. Then discuss what your children would have done in the same situation. In *It's Mine!* (Lionni, 1986), three frogs fight all day long over the water in the pond, their island, the air, and the bugs they eat, until a flood and a big toad set them straight. In *The Rainbow Fish* (Pfister, 1992), a gorgeous fish with glittery scales will not give up even one small scale until he learns through loneliness that it is better to have friends than to be beautiful. In *Jamaica and Brianna* (Havill, 1993), the African American girl Jamaica and the Asian American girl Brianna struggle over getting the best boots.

Orderly Sequence of Events

Another positive measure you can take to prevent disruptive behavior among children is to maintain a stable and orderly sequence of events each day. The daily schedule should be maintained in the same order so that children feel secure in knowing what will occur and what comes next. Although the home life of some of your children may be chaotic, their classroom life should be stable enough to have a calming influence on their behavior. Have an illustrated daily schedule chart mounted at the children's eye level. Refer to it daily so that children begin to feel comfortable with the sequence of events.

The sequence should be a balanced one. For example, active play should be followed by quiet activities. Have a quiet or rest period after vigorous outdoor play. But do not force children to rest if they have not been active enough to make this necessary. If you do schedule a mid-morning rest period but the children are not tired, you may spend the whole time trying to force the children to be quiet and rest.

A Minimum of Waiting

Don't keep children waiting. You can anticipate that some youngsters will act disruptively if you make them stand or sit for long periods while waiting to go out or if you make them sit at tables with nothing to do while waiting for lunch. If inappropriate behavior occurs, it is your fault, not the children's. Plan your schedule so that long waits are unnecessary. However, if unanticipated waiting should occur, then be prepared with a transition activity to hold the children's interest and attention. Read or tell them a story, do a fingerplay, sing a song, or play a guessing game or a name game.

A Maximum of Time

Giving children plenty of time is another "trick of the trade" that experienced preschool teachers have found to be valuable in preventing inappropriate behavior. Give them time to choose activities, time to get involved, time to talk with friends, time to complete what they are doing, and time to pick up. Your program should be relaxed and unhurried. Young children take longer to do everything than we often anticipate. They need this time to accomplish things on their own. If they feel pressured because you impose your own time limits on them, they may be disruptive.

Pickup time is often a period of disruptive behavior on the part of some children. If this is the case in your classroom, you can anticipate this behavior and diffuse it. Some teachers inform the class: "It's five minutes to pickup time." This direction is not always effective. Most preschool children have a poor concept of five minutes, or any length of time, for that matter. For certain children, it may be the signal to leave their learning center quickly so that they won't have to pick up!

It may be more effective for you to go to certain areas and tell the children quietly: "You can finish playing now. I'll be around in a few minutes to help you get started picking up." It is important for adults to contribute to pickup. Some children are too overwhelmed with all of the blocks or toys scattered across the floor to know how to get started. Involve them in a pickup game, such as: "Let's use a big block as a bulldozer to push all the little blocks over to the shelf." Once they get started, you can leave and go to another area.

Child Involvement in Rules

Another positive measure for preventing negative behavior is to involve the children in making classroom rules. If children know what is expected of them, they are often

If children are involved in making block pick-up rules, they will be more cooperative in complying with them.

better behaved and more cooperative in complying with the rules. At meeting time, talk to the children about rules. Ask what kind of rule they should have about the toys and materials. Rules such as "the children who got materials out should help pick up" and "use materials carefully" may be among those that evolve from this discussion. Have the children help you make a few simple rules about materials and equipment. You may want to post these rules, illustrated with stick figures, in the appropriate learning centers:

Block Center: "Build Only as High as You Can Reach"

Computer Center: "Wash Hands Before Using Keyboard"

"Two Children at a Time on Computer"

"Sign Up on Clipboard for a Turn"

Children can then help regulate themselves. Even preliterate children will soon be interpreting these signs if they are read aloud and referred to by the teacher and other children. Children can regulate their own turns in learning centers, as well as with favorite toys and activities. (Turn-taking has already been discussed in Chapter 9.) Some of the self-regulating devices children can use include those that are listed in Figure 10–2. The children themselves can help to decide which of these devices

Figure 10–2   Self-Regulating
Devices

1. Learning center necklaces or tags
2. Tickets for popular centers or toys
3. Drawing names out of a hat for a turn
4. Sign-up sheets or clipboards for turn-taking
5. Kitchen timer or egg hourglass for controlling amount of time

they want to use to control access to learning centers, use of the computer, taking . turns with the tricycle, or borrowing a favorite book.

Setting Limits

When children clearly understand the limits to their behavior in the classroom, they are more inclined to accept them. This means that the limits should be simple and few in number. You and your co-workers need to agree ahead of time on the behavior limits that you will enforce firmly, consistently, and without shame or blame on the children. Many programs subscribe to the following behavior limits: *Children will not be allowed to hurt themselves, to hurt each other, or to damage materials.* These are not rules to be posted in the classroom but limits that everyone has agreed on and all will enforce. Without such limits, children may frequently test you to see how far you will let them go. They need to be satisfied that you will not allow destructive things to happen. They need to feel secure in the classroom environment to expend their energies on constructive activities.

Your co-workers also need to keep these limits clearly in mind, since they too will be responsible for enforcing them firmly, consistently, but not sternly. Other rules regarding the number of children in activity areas, taking turns, and sharing materials can be regulated mainly by the children themselves through the physical arrangement of the classroom and turn-taking methods previously set up.

Force Unacceptable

Finally, you should not force young children to participate in group activities. Some are not ready to be involved with large and, to them, overwhelming groups. Others may not feel secure enough in the classroom environment to join a group. You should invite but not pressure such children.

If you anticipate that certain children who do not join in will instead be disruptive, then have an activity or task ready for them. Give them a choice: "If you don't want to join us, Jeffrey, here is a storybook for you to read. When you're finished, you may want to join us. If not, you can watch what we are doing."

1. Set up classroom in well-defined spacious learning centers.
2. Provide enough materials and activities at appropriate developmental levels.
3. Introduce new materials to everyone and set up turn-taking arrangements.
4. Maintain a balanced daily schedule.
5. Minimize length of children's waiting time.
6. Use transitions between activities.
7. Allow children time to choose and become deeply involved in activities.
8. Involve children in making their own rules and choosing their own self-regulating devices.
9. Set a few simple behavior limits and enforce them consistently.

Figure 10–3   Strategies for Preventing Inappropriate Behavior

These, then, are a few of the preventative steps you and your co-workers can take to decrease inappropriate behavior by the children (see Figure 10–3). What other strategies have you used?

USES POSITIVE INTERVENTION MEASURES TO HELP CHILDREN CONTROL THEIR INAPPROPRIATE BEHAVIOR

Accepting Negative Feelings

What will you do when children become angry or upset and begin to act out their feelings? First of all, don't wait for this to happen and then be forced to react inappropriately yourself. You need to anticipate the children's behavior and be prepared for them to be out of sorts, as you yourself are from time to time.

Once you acknowledge that negative feelings are a natural part of a young child's growth and development, you will be able to take the next step more readily, that is, accepting these feelings. It is natural for children to feel angry, frustrated, or upset. Acceptance does not mean approval; it means only that you recognize that children have both negative and positive feelings. Acceptance is the next step in helping children control the inappropriate aspects of their behavior.

In addition, accepting a child's negative feelings helps to diffuse them. You need to display your acceptance by not becoming angry or upset yourself. You need to stay calm and respond to the child in a matter-of-fact tone of voice. Your unruffled behavior is another step in calming the child. Your actions say, "If the teacher doesn't get upset, then it can't be so bad."

Accepting a child's negative feelings helps to diffuse them.

Helping Children Verbalize Negative Feelings

Next, you need to help children express their negative feelings in an acceptable manner. Helping them find a harmless way to express these feelings diffuses them. Otherwise, they may burst out again as soon as you turn your back.

Verbalizing feelings, that is, expressing them in words, is one of the most effective ways to resolve them. Expressing anger, jealousy, or frustration in words helps to relieve these negative emotions. Your calm voice saying, "How do you feel, Jennifer? Tell me how you feel," may be all it takes to calm down the child. If the child will not talk directly to you, she may talk to a hand puppet you hold or through a hand puppet she holds. Be patient. A child caught up in an emotional outburst often needs time to calm down enough to talk.

Books to Read

For the youngest children who do not know enough words to express their feelings, you can read them a book about children expressing their feelings in words, when the time is right. Be sure to have some of the following books on hand:

How Are You Peeling? Foods with Moods (Freymann, 1999)

I Feel Happy and Sad and Angry and Glad (Murphy, 2000)

Kinda Blue (Grifalconi, 1993)

The Owl Who Was Afraid of the Dark (Tomlinson, 2000)

Sometimes I Feel Like a Mouse: A Book About Feelings (Modesitt, 1992)

The Way I Feel . . . Sometimes (deRegniers, 1988) (children's poems)

What Makes Me Happy? (Anholt & Anholt, 1994)

When Emily Woke Up Angry (Duncan, 1989)

When Sophie Gets Angry—Really, Really Angry (Bang, 1999)

You can mount pictures of children laughing, crying, or feeling lonely in your total group area for a talk at meeting time. If you have no pictures, simply make photocopies of the characters in these books to motivate your children to talk about their own feelings. Then when children burst out with actions instead of words during an emotional situation, remind them gently but firmly: "Tell him how you feel, Calvin. Don't hit him," or "Use words, Natalie, not fists." If you are consistent with your reminders, children will eventually learn to speak first, rather than act. When you hear *them reminding each other* to "Tell her. Don't hit her," you will know that verbalizing feelings has finally become a habit with the children.

Redirecting Inappropriate Behavior

On the other hand, a hostile, crying child may not be able to respond verbally. Instead, a classroom activity may help him calm down and regain control of himself. Water play is an especially soothing activity. If you don't have a water table, you can fill the toy sink in the housekeeping corner or a plastic basin on a table for an upset child to play with.

Clay and dough are also excellent for children to use in working out frustrations. Encourage them to knead the material or pound it with their fists or a wooden mallet. Beanbags serve the same purpose. Let children expend their negative energy constructively by throwing beanbags or a foam ball at a target.

Finger painting also helps children release negative energy. Consider setting up a quiet corner with a comfortable rocking chair and space for water play, dough, or finger painting. If children know you will help and support them in releasing negative feelings nondestructively, they will begin to assume more control themselves.

No "Time-Out" Chair

One of the intervention methods frequently used in early childhood classrooms for out-of-control children has been the "time-out" chair. No longer. The time-out chair is "out" in many classrooms today, as far as positive intervention methods are concerned. Most teachers heave a sigh of relief when they hear about its demise. It was always a struggle for teachers to make out-of-control children sit in it in the first place. Their noisy protests and crying tended to disrupt the entire classroom.

The more submissive children allowed themselves to be placed in the chair, but at what cost to their self-concepts? They were not supposed to be isolated, since the chair was within the classroom, but the other children kept away anyway. It was not supposed to be a punishment, just a time-out for disruptive children to calm down. Nevertheless, their peers treated them as being punished and shunned them—a particularly unpleasant punishment. It was not supposed to be a threat, yet there it sat, a definite threatening presence in an otherwise pleasant environment—like a dunce's chair from an old-time schoolroom waiting to be occupied. We are glad to see it go, along with other negative intervention techniques that tend to insult children instead of teaching them appropriate behavior. Gartrell (2001) notes:

> When used as a discipline, the time-out is one of a group of techniques—including name-on-the-board, an assigned yellow or red "light," and the disciplinary referral slip—that still rely on blame and shame to bring a child's behavior "back into line." This is the modern equivalent of the dunce stool. (p. 9)

Still, a question remains. What about out-of-control children who are not calm enough to rejoin the group or respond to any verbal interchange? Many teachers, assistants, and student teachers find that their most effective action is to take such children aside—but not to a designated time-out chair—and remain with them until they are calm enough to return to the group. It may mean holding the crying child on your lap or sitting close by. It may mean waiting quietly until they feel better. Talking to out-of-control children is usually futile and often provokes further outbursts from them. What they need is the time and space to recover their control. Volunteers such as Foster Grandparents from the Foster Grandparents Program are especially effective at holding and calming such upset children.

If the child in question is having a temper tantrum on the floor of the block area, you may need to direct other children away from the area while the tantrum runs its course. At the appropriate time, you can speak calmly and softly to the child, redirecting his attention to some activity you wish him to do to take his mind off the tantrum. For example, you can say, "Rodney, when you feel that you can, would you please bring me the truck over by the block shelf." Once Rodney brings the truck, you can talk to him softly about feelings—telling him that you want him to feel better or asking what might help him to get over feeling so upset. When he has finally regained control, he can choose to rejoin the others.

Intervening in Interpersonal Conflicts

Child development researchers have discovered that more than 90 percent of the interpersonal conflicts that occur in preschool programs involve squabbles over possessions. Young children with their self-centered point of view often start out by thinking that the toys and activities in the classroom are for them alone, as discussed in Chapter 9. "It's mine!" or "I had it first!" are frequently heard complaints in many

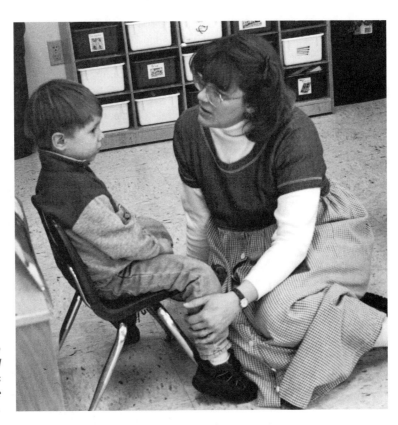

An effective strategy is taking an out-of-control child aside and remaining with him until he is calm enough to return to the group.

preschool programs. It takes young children a great deal of time and much hands-on experience before they can learn to share and take turns with their classmates. As children grow older, however, the number of possession conflicts seems to decrease, although conflicts over materials are still the most frequent cause for dissention in the classroom.

Most of these conflicts are brief interruptions in play, resolved by the children themselves. One or the other gets the toy or gives up a turn. Sometimes they come running to you to resolve their dilemma. Your response should be one that helps the children solve the problem on their own.

Occasionally, however, the conflict becomes so overpowering that you must intervene. When children are hitting, fighting, throwing materials, or crying, it is time for you to take action. What will you do? One of the most effective forms of intervention is known as "conflict conversion" as discussed in Chapter 9. Take the children in conflict aside—usually two youngsters, the instigator and the victim. When they are calm enough to talk, ask each to tell you what happened. Accept whatever they say. Then ask each to tell *how they think the other child feels.* Finally, ask each child to tell what would make the other child feel better. Conflict conversion like this helps each child look at the conflict from the other child's point of view, something quite different for them.

1. Accept children's negative feelings.

2. Remain calm and unruffled.

3. Help children to verbalize their feelings.

4. Read and discuss books about feelings with children.

5. Redirect inappropriate behavior.

6. Use "time-out" technique only when an adult can share the time-out.

7. Use conflict conversion techniques in children's out-of-control interpersonal conflicts.

Figure 10–4   Positive Intervention Methods

Many children are surprised to find that there is another side to the conflict. Most youngsters have never been asked to consider the feelings of the other child. But most children are also able and willing to respond like this when they realize that this is what you want them to do. They are relieved to find that you do not blame them for the conflict and that you are not going to punish them. Instead, you are asking them to think about the other child's feelings and then to help decide what can make the other child feel better.

Considering the feelings of the other person is often a great revelation to them. It is something most preschoolers had not contemplated before. But when asked how they think the other person feels, they can respond with accuracy. Lillard and Curenton (1999) point out that even very young children "show surprising awareness of what other people feel, want, and know. By the time they are seven or eight months old, babies pay special attention to the emotional expressions of adults. By the second year of life, toddlers are beginning to know when others are feeling happy, angry or sad. They may even comfort someone in distress" (p. 52).

When both parties to a classroom conflict finally agree on a solution based on the other's feelings, they can shake hands or give a "high five" if they want to. It is a satisfying way to end a conflict, especially when children have control of the solution. Other children also notice what is happening and may even change their behavior as a result of it. Learning about "the other person's feelings" is indeed an important contribution to the preschool classroom in these turbulent days. Positive intervention methods like this that help children develop self-control include those listed in Figure 10–4.

USES POSITIVE REINFORCEMENT TECHNIQUES TO HELP CHILDREN LEARN APPROPRIATE BEHAVIOR

Positive Reinforcement

Positive reinforcement helps the teacher focus attention on a child's desirable behaviors and ignore the inappropriate behaviors. Teachers frequently focus on inappropriate behavior because it is so attention-getting. The disruptive child is frequently crying out for adult attention, even if it means punishment. When we respond to such misbehavior, even with punishment, we do not change it—even though we may stop it temporarily. Instead, we reinforce it in a negative way. A response of any kind leads the child to believe, "If I do this, they will pay attention to me."

Therefore, we must shift our attention from the undesirable to the desirable behavior. This is no simple task. It will take a concerted effort on your part and that of the other staff members to shift attention to the positive and ignore the disruptive behaviors of the children. This kind of shift requires the changing of a mind-set. You must take a definite action to bring about the change in yourself first, before you can expect a child to change.

You can begin to accomplish this change by making a list of the positive behaviors that a disruptive child exhibits during the day. Share the list with other staff members. Each time the child displays a positive behavior, reinforce her with a smile, a nod, or a word of encouragement. Each time she displays a disruptive behavior, try to ignore it. If you must stop it because it involves harm to another child or damage to a material, simply remove the other child or the material. Do not make eye or verbal contact with the disruptive child at this time. But as soon as the child exhibits desirable behavior, go to her and express your pleasure. Do this as soon as possible so that the child receives the message that you will respond to her positive behavior but not to her undesirable actions.

Be sure the other adults in the classroom respond to the disruptive child in the same way. There is no need to get angry or upset, to speak loudly, or to punish the child. You and your co-workers need to keep in mind that "discipline" for young children is really "guidance," which means "learning appropriate behavior" or "learning self-control." For young children to learn self-control means that you and your staff must provide them with many, many such learning opportunities.

You may have to practice this new way of responding a number of times before you can expect results from the children. Have another staff member watch you do it, then talk about what you did and how it worked. Let that person try it, too, with the same child. Work on this method until you make it work for you. It takes more time to get results this way than forcing a child to stop his misbehavior. In the end, however, it is more worthwhile because the behavior control comes from within the child rather than from the outside. Such efforts take the child one step closer to developing self-control and another step away from depending on the adults around him to control his behavior.

Focus on Victim Not Aggressor

When things get out of hand and one child hurts another, your first concern should be for the victim rather than the aggressor. You must, of course, stop the unacceptable behavior, but you do it by removing the victim. This is contrary to the ordinary actions of most adults in cases of aggressive child conflict. Ordinarily the teacher rushes to the aggressor to stop her and may even punish her. This reaction, however, tends to reinforce the aggressor's misbehavior by giving her the first attention. If you go first to the victim, the surprised aggressor will get the message that she cannot gain your attention with such misbehavior.

Do not forget, however, to respond to the aggressor as soon as he or she displays positive behavior. Tell her how you appreciate the way she is behaving now and ask her if there is a different way she can handle her anger in the future so that no one gets hurt. If the child does not seem to know, you might try using puppet role-plays. As Adams and Wittmer (2001) note:

> Puppets can be used to role-play problems based on common classroom situations (such as name calling, lack of sharing, or difficulty in taking turns), or in response to actual conflicts (such as two children arguing over who gets to use the watering can to water the plants). (p. 12)

When using puppets with one child the teacher can play the role of one conflictee and the child the role of the other. If the child refuses, the teacher can put a puppet on each hand and play both roles, acting out the conflict while the child watches. Afterwards the teacher and child can discuss what happened, what caused it, and how the puppet handled it. Would the child now like to be one of the puppets and try a different resolution? Keep at least two "problem-puppets" in a small box to be used by the children or the teacher with individuals or the whole class at a class meeting when conflicts arise.

Model Appropriate Behavior

How else can a disruptive child learn acceptable, appropriate behavior? You and your co-workers need first to explain and then to model this behavior. Children learn a great deal by example. Say to a child: "When you are angry with another child, you need to tell that child how you feel. What could you say to her? Try it." If the child does not know how to express anger in words, you can demonstrate. Tell him: "Say to Sharon: 'Sharon, you spilled paint on my paper. That makes me angry!'"

You need to model this behavior. You need to express your own feelings to the child: "Rob, I am really upset that you hit Sharon instead of talking to her. You need to tell her in words how you feel, and not hit her." If you model this advice again and again, children will notice. Eventually you will hear the children saying to one another: "Tell her in words. Don't hit her."

You also need to maintain your own self-control. When you become angry with children, you need to calm down first before talking to them. Yelling at children puts you in the same position as the child who is out of control. Anger is not helpful to either of you. Children are in your program to learn how to handle their own strong emotions. They want someone to prevent them from getting out of control. They look to you to model this controlled behavior. As Marion (1997) notes:

> Adults who are most effective in helping children manage anger model responsible anger management by acknowledging, accepting, and taking responsibility for their own angry feelings and by expressing anger in direct and nonaggressive ways. (p. 65)

You can say, "That really made me angry when the paint was spilled this morning. People need to watch what they are doing."

1. Shift your attention from inappropriate to appropriate child behavior.

2. Look for and reinforce the positive actions of children who disrupt.

3. Focus on the victim, not the aggressor at first.

4. Make eye or verbal contact with disruptive children only after their inappropriate behavior has ceased.

5. Model appropriate classroom behavior yourself.

Figure 10–5 Positive Reinforcement Methods

Or together you could make "mean soup." Save the mean-soup activity for a day when everyone is out of sorts. Then read the book *Mean Soup* (Everitt, 1992) to the group, about Horace who has such a bad day at school that he comes home feeling really mean. His mother suggests they make "mean soup" and proceeds to put on a pot of water to heat up. Then each of them takes turns screaming into the pot until they feel better and can stir their troubles away.

You can plug in a hotpot, fill it with water and canned vegetables or vegetable soup, and have every child who wants to participate come up and scream into the pot and stir it for a bit. Afterward serve it for lunch or for a crackers-and-soup snack. Leave the book out for everyone to look at and be prepared to repeat this activity every week or so.

You should also model courteous behavior. Treat children with the same respect as you would treat a friend. Don't yell across the room at a child who is demonstrating inappropriate behavior. Walk over to the child and talk to her quietly, in a courteous but firm manner: "Brenda, you took the paint brush away from Rachel before she was finished. She is really upset about it. You will need to give it back to her now. If you want to paint, you can sign up for a turn."

You may also need to let a child practice or role-play her actions or words: "Rachel let's go over to Brenda, and you tell her how you feel. What are you going to say to her?" In this way you model for the children how they should act. Figure 10–5 summarizes some of these reinforcement methods.

Your efforts to improve the children's self-control will be rewarded as they learn to control their behavior in the classroom. Parents, too, may notice their children's growth in this regard and help support your efforts at home. A child with special behavior problems may require concerted and cooperative effort on the part of both home and school to affect a change. It is surely worth the effort.

The Child as a Spiritual Being

As discussed in Chapter 1, we must remember that, like us, all children are also spiritual beings. But they are not yet adults, and thus often need our help to learn appropriate behavior and self-control. If we keep this in mind when we are dealing with their inappropriate behavior, we will make sure our responses are loving. We will not

When dealing with children's inappropriate behavior, make sure your responses are loving, not scolding.

use anger, scolding, or punishments to "correct" their behavior. Instead, our positive prevention, intervention, and reinforcement strategies will, at the appropriate time, include:

Closeness: hugs, touches, pats, hand-holding
Body language: smiles, nods, eye-contact, twinkling eyes
Verbal expressions: acceptance, delight, appreciation
Reciprocal feelings: other-esteem, empathy, affection, goodwill

Children who are treated as spiritual beings will often respond to the adults around them in the same manner. Your classroom can then become a happy, delightful place to be, where everyone is accepted and treated with respect no matter what their behavior.

SUMMARY

The goal of guidance should be to promote the development of self-control in young children. This is accomplished through positive prevention measures such as arranging the learning environment to prevent disruptive behavior, by offering an orderly sequence of daily activities to promote feelings of security, by minimizing the length of time that children have to wait, by maximizing the length of time allowed for children to accomplish things, and by involving children in making classroom rules and setting their own limits.

Positive intervention techniques that help children control out-of-bounds behavior no longer include the "time-out" chair because of its detrimental effects on children. Instead, teachers intervene first by accepting children's negative feelings, then by helping children verbalize their feelings, and finally by redirecting children's inappropriate behavior into constructive activities such as finger painting and using play dough, water play, and beanbags. Your own modeling of calm yet firm behavior should also help children feel less upset and more in control during times of stress.

For out-of-control children involved in interpersonal conflicts, a new and effective technique called other-esteem conflict conversion is helpful. By taking the two children with the conflict aside and asking each what happened, you allow them to state their position without being blamed. Then they must think about how the other child feels and consider what will make the other child feel better. Children find themselves in control of the solution and therefore begin to develop better self-control over their own actions.

In addition, children learn self-control by being reinforced positively for their appropriate behavior. For example, each time disruptive children display a positive behavior you can give them a smile, a nod, or a word of praise. Their inappropriate behavior can be ignored as much as possible or responded to matter-of-factly without making eye contact. Focusing on the victim rather than the aggressor also helps children realize that inappropriate behavior will not get your attention. Treating children respectfully by realizing they are also spiritual beings like us helps them to develop the positive behaviors we model. Little by little the youngsters begin to develop control over their own behaviors and a concern for the feelings of their peers.

LEARNING ACTIVITIES

1. Read Chapter 10 and answer Question Sheet 10.

2. Meet with your trainer or instructor and discuss answers to Question Sheet 10.

3. View one of the videotapes listed and make 10 file cards with specific ideas for helping children develop self-control.

4. Read one or more of the references cited or suggested readings. Add 10 cards to your file, with specific ideas for helping children develop self-control. Include reference sources on each card.

5. Make an assessment of your classroom based on the seven items listed in Figure 10–1, Causes for Disruptive Behavior. Make necessary changes and record the results.

6. Make a list of the rules, limits, and self-regulating devices used in your classroom. Tell how they were arrived at, how they are used, and what difference they make in children's behavior.

7. Observe a disruptive child for a day and write down all of the positive behaviors he or she displays.

Show that you approve by smiling or giving a word of praise. Record the results.

8. Read one of the books about feelings to children who display negative feelings. Help them to verbalize their feelings. Record the results.

9. Use the conflict conversion method with two children involved in an interpersonal squabble over possession of a toy or piece of equipment. Record the results.

10. Complete the Chapter 10 Evaluation Sheet and return it to your trainer or college supervisor.

QUESTION SHEET 10

1. Why is punishment an inappropriate method for correcting a child's disruptive behavior?

2. How can your arrangement of the learning environment prevent inappropriate behavior?

3. Why is an orderly sequence of daily events important in helping to eliminate inappropriate behavior?

4. Why is it your fault if children's disruptive behavior occurs while they stand in line or wait for lunch?

5. Why should children be involved in making rules and establishing limits? What should these limits be?

6. What is positive reinforcement and how does it work to bring about self-control in children with behavior problems?

7. Why should you focus on the victim rather than the aggressor when one child hits another?

8. How do children learn appropriate behavior in the classroom?

9. How can you introduce a new toy to the children in a way that eliminates the potential for squabbles over playing with it?

10. Why is the time-out chair no longer considered an effective method for controlling children's disruptive behavior?

11. How does the redirecting of inappropriate behavior work?

12. Why should children learn to verbalize their feelings? How can they learn it?

13. What is conflict conversion and how can you use it to help two children resolve an interpersonal conflict? Be specific.

14. How does your modeling of appropriate behavior help a child learn self-control?

15. When should you make eye contact or verbal contact with disruptive children? Why?

REFERENCES

Adams, S. K., & Wittmer, D. S. (2001). "I had it first." Teaching young children to solve problems peacefully. *Childhood Education, 78*(1), 10–16.

Gartrell, D. (1997). Beyond guidance to discipline. *Young Children, 52*(6), 34–42.

Gartrell, D. (2001). Replacing time-out: Using guidance to build and encouraging classroom. *Young Children, 56*(6), 8–16.

Lillard, A., & Curenton, S. (1999). Do young children understand what others feel, want, and know? *Young Children, 54*(5), 52–57.

Marion, M. (1997). Guiding young children's understanding and management of anger. *Young Children, 52*(7), 62–67.

Ratcliff, N. (2001). Use the environment to prevent discipline problems and support learning. *Young Children, 56*(5), 84–88.

SUGGESTED READINGS

Bailey, B. (1996). Understanding temper tantrums. *Children Our Concern, 21*(1), 22–23.

Beaty, J. J. (1999). *Prosocial guidance for the preschool child.* Upper Saddle River, NJ: Merrill/Prentice Hall.

Betz, C. (1994). Beyond time out: Tips from a teacher. *Young Children, 49*(3), 10–14.

Cherry, C. (1983). *Please don't sit on the kids.* Belmont, CA: Pitman.

Clewett, A. S. (1988). Guidance and discipline: Teaching young children appropriate behavior. *Young Children, 43*(4), 26–31.

Duffy, R. (1996). Time out: How it is abused. *Child Care Information Exchange, 111*, 61.

Eaton, M. (1997). Positive discipline: Fostering the self-esteem of young children. *Young Children, 52*(6), 43–46.

Fields, M. V., & Boesser, C. (2002). *Constructive guidance and discipline: Preschool and primary education.* Upper Saddle River, NJ: Merrill/Prentice Hall.

Froschl, M., & Sprung. (1999). On purpose: Addressing teasing and bullying in early childhood. *Young Children, 54*(2), 70–73.

Gartrell, D. (1994). *A guidance approach to discipline.* Albany, NY: Delmar.

Marion, M. (1995). *Guidance of young children.* Upper Saddle River, NJ: Merrill/ Prentice Hall.

McCloskey, C. M. (1996). Taking positive steps toward classroom management in preschool: Loosening up without letting it all fall apart. *Young Children, 51*(3), 14–16.

Miller, D. F. (1996). *Positive child guidance.* Albany, NY: Delmar.

Ramsey, P. G. (1986). Possession disputes in preschool classrooms. *Child Study Journal, 16*(3), 173–181.

Schreiber, M. E. (1999). Time-outs for toddlers: Is our goal punishment or education? *Young Children, 54*(4), 22–25.

Wolfson-Steinberg, L. (2000). "Teacher! He hit me!" "She pushed me!"— Where does it start? How can it stop? *Young Children, 55*(3), 38–42.

CHILDREN'S BOOKS

Anholt, C., & Anholt, L. (1994). *What makes me happy?* Cambridge, MA: Candlewick.

Bang, M. (1999). *When Sophie gets angry—really, really angry.* New York: Blue Sky Press.

deRegniers, B. S. (1988). *The way I feel . . . sometimes.* New York: Clarion.

Duncan, R. (1989). *When Emily woke up angry.* Hauppauge, NY: Barron's.

Everitt, B. (1992). *Mean soup.* San Diego: Harcourt Brace.

Freymann, S. (1999). *How are you peeling? Foods with moods.* Arthur A. Levine Books.

Grifalconi, A. (1993). *Kinda blue.* Boston: Little, Brown.

Havill, J. (1993). *Jamaica and Brianna.* Boston: Houghton Mifflin.

Lionni, L. (1986). *It's mine!* New York: Alfred A. Knopf.

Modesitt, J. (1992). *Sometimes I feel like a mouse: A book about feelings.* New York: Scholastic.

Murphy, M. (2000). *I feel happy.* New York: Dorling Kindersley.

Pfister, M. (1992). *The rainbow fish.* New York: North-South Books.

Tomlinson, J. (2000). *The owl who was afraid of the dark.* Cambridge, MA: Candlewick.

VIDEOTAPES

High/Scope Press (Producer). *Supporting children in resolving conflicts.* St. Paul, MN: Redleaf Press.

Indiana Steps Ahead. (Producer). *Painting a positive picture: Proactive behavior management.* Washington, DC: National Association for the Education of Young Children.

National Association for the Education of Young Children: *Discipline.* Washington, DC: Author.

South Carolina Educational TV. (Producer). *Discipline: Appropriate guidance of young children.* Washington, DC: National Association for the Education of Young Children.

CHAPTER 10 EVALUATION SHEET
PROVIDING GUIDANCE

1. Student _____

2. Trainer _____

3. Center where training occurred _____

4. Beginning date _____ Ending date _____

5. Describe what student did to accomplish General Objective.

    _____

    _____

6. Describe what student did to accomplish Specific Objectives.

    Objective 1 _____

    _____

    Objective 2 _____

    _____

    Objective 3 _____

    _____

7. Evaluation of student's Learning Activities

    _____

    _____

Comments:

Permission is granted by the publisher to reproduce this page for evaluation and record keeping.

Promoting Family Involvement

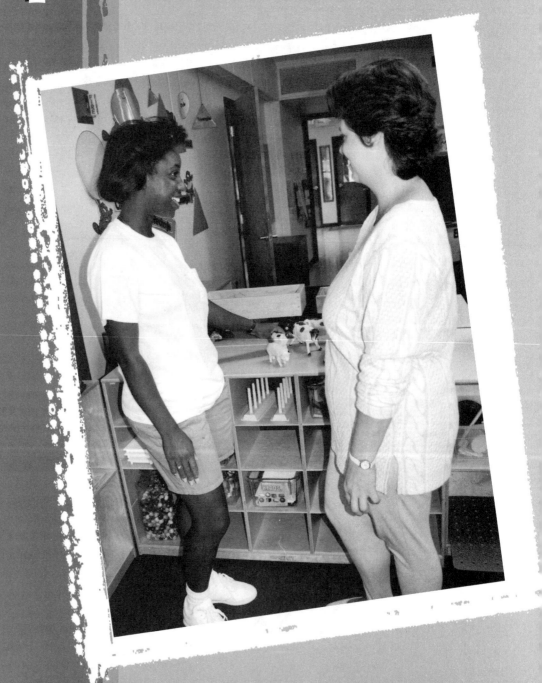

GENERAL OBJECTIVE

To encourage family involvement in center activities to promote their children's positive development

✓ SPECIFIC OBJECTIVES

____ Involves parents in participating in children's program

____ Recognizes and supports families of different makeup

____ Builds teacher-family relationships through family classroom meetings

P arent involvement has long been a part of most preschool programs, but only in recent years have we come to realize just how important this involvement can be. Research shows us that programs in which parents are highly involved have the longest lasting positive effects on children. Not only do children change their behavior and improve their skills because of their preschool experience, but their parents change as well. As Eldridge (2001) reports:

> Parents involved with school in parent-related activities show increased self-confidence in parenting, more knowledge of child development, and an expanded understanding of the home as an environment for student learning. (p. 66)

Parents who are directly involved in their children's preschool programs are much more likely to encourage their children's development at home and to support their learning during the later school years. And parents who are not directly involved but show enthusiasm for their children's preschool programs promote their children's self-esteem and reduce discipline problems both at home and at school.

Most parents will not become involved automatically. Teachers must take the initiative, letting them know they are welcome and helping them find a comfortable way to contribute to their child's welfare while in your program. They may not realize how important their role is to their child's success in the classroom. Parents of preschool children are their child's most important role model. If parents ignore or downplay their child's school experience, the child may not take it seriously either. Furthermore, if parents do not know what kind of learning is going on in the preschool, they can hardly support or extend that learning at home.

Thus, it is vital for teachers to find ways to involve the parents of each child in some aspect of the program. Gaining the support and involvement of parents may not be easy, especially with parents who work during the day or with parents whose own school experience has left them with negative feelings about classrooms and teachers. Nevertheless, if you are committed to parent participation, then you can find ways to bring parents into your program.

INVOLVES PARENTS IN PARTICIPATING IN CHILDREN'S PROGRAMS

Parents can be involved at many different levels in their children's programs. Several of the possibilities are shown in Figure 11–1.

Focus on the Child

The most effective approach to parent involvement is to focus on the child, not the program. What is the child like? What kinds of activities are his or her favorites? Does she like to sing or color? Have books been read to the child? Which ones? Should the program know anything special about the child and his needs? Parents are concerned

---

1. Visiting the program
2. Attending the classroom team meeting to help plan for their children
3. Volunteering as a teacher's assistant
4. Receiving training and working as a paid classroom assistant
5. Helping the classroom staff on a field trip
6. Visiting the program to read a story or sing a song with the children
7. Making equipment, materials, or toys for the program
8. Bringing something of their culture or language to the program (stories, songs, dances, foods, or words)
9. Putting on a fund-raising project for the class
10. Visiting the classroom as a community helper or to demonstrate their occupation
11. Becoming a member of the board or policy council or other decision-making body
12. Carrying out at home with their children an activity they have learned at the center
13. Joining the program's parent club and participating in activities
14. Taking instruction in nutrition, cooking, parenting, or another topic in a workshop sponsored by the program.
15. Taking instruction in how to choose books and read to young children.

Figure 11–1   Parent Involvement in Children's Programs

The most effective approach to parent involvement is to focus on the child, not the program.

about their children's welfare, and if you focus on this from the beginning, you will quickly capture their attention.

At the intake interview or enrollment process at the beginning of the year, you or another program member can invite parents to become involved and offer them several choices. For example, a parent could eat lunch with her or his child once a month, read a story to a small group at "story time" on any Friday, walk to the park with the group any time they go, be the librarian for the parent group in charge of child care magazines and pamphlets, be a "telephone parent" and call other parents when it is time for the monthly parent meeting, be the "transportation parent" and bring to the meetings parents without cars, or gather news from parents for the parent newsletter. On the other hand, parents may have ideas for the monthly workshops, perhaps something he or she would like to learn about topics such as low-fat cooking, shopping on a tight budget, games to make from throwaway items, or positive discipline techniques for the hard-to-manage child.

You may not meet the parents of the children until school actually begins. Some teachers, however, visit the children's homes before school begins and take a picture of the child and family by their front door to include in the child's own personal book he will be making in school. Children not only need to make a transition from home to school but also need to be assured that the teacher and the program accept and respect their home and parents.

Building Trust in Parents and Parental Trust in the Program

Just as the parents of the children need to build confidence in you and the program, you also must come to trust the parents. After all, parents, not teachers, are the children's most influential adult guides. It is important for you to realize that your role is

You should start your relationship with parents by asking them what they want their child to accomplish during the year.

secondary. The parents or guardians of the children are their most important teachers. However, you must be the one to initiate a relationship with these significant people; you must find out what parents expect of the program and then convey to them how the program operates to support their children's growth and development. As Workman and Gage (1997) explain:

> We have come to believe that trust between family members and staff is the single most important factor in promoting individual growth, involvement, and the development of self-sufficiency. Establishing relationships and developing trust involve entering into a dialogue to explore issues together and offer information, resources, and personal assistance. (p. 11)

Not every parent may understand or agree with "what" or "how" you are teaching their child. "I want my child to learn her ABCs," a parent may tell you. "She needs to learn to read. Where are the worksheets she should be doing?" Parents who say this may expect you to stand in front of the whole class and "teach." To argue with parents that "young children learn through play" or "young children learn best as individuals" is unproductive and, in the end, unnecessary.

Instead, you should start your relationship with parents by asking them what they want their children to accomplish during the year. Some may have very specific ideas. Others may not have a clue. You should take seriously whatever parents have to say about their children, because they are expressing what they think and what they want. It is important to write down parents' goals for their children, as well as their ideas and suggestions. Parents need to know that you are concerned about their children, that you will listen to them, and that you will take them seriously.

Some programs ask parents to fill out a list of learning goals for their children. This not only helps you to determine what areas are important to them but also helps parents realize how broad and rich the program is. Furthermore, such a list does not indicate "how" you will help their children to accomplish each goal. Thus, you need not debate with parents about self-learning versus direct teaching or play versus worksheets. A list like this also gives you a basis for talking with the parents about what they want for their children and why certain items are important.

You can use a list, such as the one shown in Figure 11–2, at the beginning of the year, just as you use an intake interview to give you information about families and their goals for their children. Make the list personal for parents. Go over it together with them; don't just mail it to them and ask them to return it. It can be a focus for conversation about their children and your program. Make a second list for yourself at the same time so that both you and the parents have a record of the goals they consider important.

Once parents understand the scope of the program, they may be more willing to contribute by helping their children to accomplish these goals both at home and in the classroom. Ask them if they would also consider volunteering to help other children in the classroom in one of the six areas listed. You can start a sign-up sheet for parent volunteers. Tell parents you will contact them when the children are involved in the area they have signed up for.

Be sure to add to the list the parents' own learning goals for their children. Later, when you communicate with the parents, be sure to refer to the goals that parents consider most important. Discuss with them how their children are doing in these areas.

However, do not use such a goals list later as a "report card" for children's accomplishments. Their children may not, in fact, accomplish all of the goals, nor should they be expected to. Instead, you can talk to parents about their children's positive accomplishments without using the list when you see them from time to time throughout the year. File the list away for your own further reference.

Beginning School

Many programs begin the school year with a staggered entrance process so that all the parents and children do not come on the same day at the same time. Half the children, for instance, may come on the first day and half on the next, or half in the morning and the other half in the afternoon. On those first days, each half of the class stays only part time. Parents or other family caregivers can be invited to bring their children and stay themselves for the brief class session. You and your co-workers can then better divide your time between the parents and their children. The children and parents should be invited to explore the room. You can set up puzzles or a water table for them, as well as show them the permanent learning centers.

In the meantime, one of you can talk with the parents, asking them about some of the things their child likes to do at home and more about what the parents hope to

Child's Name _____ Age _____

Your Name _____ Date _____

(Fill in the number that tells how important this goal is for you and your child.)

Very important . . . . ._1_

Somewhat important. . . . . . . _2_

Not important . . . . ._3_

I WANT MY CHILD TO LEARN THESE SKILLS:

Physical

    1. To climb up and down a climber   _____

    2. To balance on a balance beam   _____

    3. To throw and catch a ball   _____

    4. To put on a jacket and zip it   _____

    5. To tie or fasten shoes   _____

    6. To cut with scissors   _____

    7. To pour without spilling   _____

Cognitive

    8. To identify colors and basic shapes   _____

    9. To sort things that are alike   _____

    10. To count   _____

    11. To understand that numbers represent objects   _____

    12. To care for plants   _____

    13. To care for animals   _____

    14. To care for the environment   _____

Language

    15. To speak clearly   _____

    16. To say words in another language   _____

    17. To enjoy a storybook   _____

    18. To pretend with hand puppets and dress-up clothes   _____

    19. To use words for rhymes and fingerplays   _____

    20. To write his or her name   _____

    21. To use a computer learning game   _____

Figure 11–2 Parent's Learning Goals for Children

Creativity

    22. To make up a story   _____

    23. To sing a song   _____

    24. To play a rhythm instrument   _____

    25. To play a tape on a tape recorder   _____

    26. To paint at an easel   _____

    27. To use play dough and clay   _____

Social Skills

    28. To get along with other children   _____

    29. To take turns   _____

    30. To share toys and materials   _____

    31. To play cooperatively   _____

    32. To make friends   _____

    33. To control inappropriate behavior   _____

    34. To settle conflicts over toys   _____

    35. To talk about feelings   _____

Self-Esteem

    36. To feel not afraid of people or things   _____

    37. To be successful in classroom activities   _____

    38. To be happy in preschool   _____

    39. To like the other children   _____

    40. To feel good about himself or herself   _____

Other

_____

_____

_____

_____

_____

Permission is granted by the publisher to reproduce this list for evaluation and record keeping.

see the child accomplish in the program. Jot down this information on a file card for each child. The parents may have already talked with the program's parent worker about this, but it is still a good idea for the classroom staff to reinforce the notion that the program cares about them and their child and wants their input. This may be the time to go over with each family the Parents' Learning Goals for Children (Figure 11–2) they filled out earlier.

Invite parents to stay until the child feels comfortable without them. This may take several days for some children. If parents work, they may be able to manage to come to work late on the first day of the program. If not, they may be able to send another family member. Family members who have difficulty knowing when to leave after staying with a child for several days can be assisted by the staff. Let parents know from the beginning that they should plan to stay a shorter time every day as their child becomes more involved in the classroom activities. In the meantime, a staff member needs to make sure the child does become busily engaged so that she can signal to the family member when it is a good time to leave.

Two-Way Communication

We often pay mere lip service to the notion that the child's parents are his first and most important teachers; yet it is true. To recognize this fact, we must turn our parent-involvement effort into a reciprocal process in which we are not the only ones speaking and telling our story. Parents also need to communicate to us how their children are doing and what is happening in the family that may affect their children. This does not mean we should pry into family matters. Again, the focus is on the child. It means we should try to come together on common ground regarding what is best for the child. We will support parents in their efforts and will expect them to support us in ours.

If we find that the two sets of goals for children are different, we need to find ways to communicate to parents why we are doing what we are doing and to elicit the same information from them. Parents need to know that their youngster's preschool program will support their efforts to help their child grow and learn. Parents also need to know that the program wants their support, too. The program's child-rearing techniques may, indeed, be different from their own, but they need to understand that both are acceptable.

Child abuse, of course, is not acceptable. However, two-way communication with parents involved in child abuse is just as important to help such families correct the situation and to support them while they are getting help.

Sometimes the differences in expectations focus on behavioral goals. A parent may expect her child to play quietly, to sit still and listen to the teacher, or to keep her clothes clean. The program, on the other hand, may expect the same child to become involved with all activities—both quiet and noisy ones—to become independent of the teacher, to make her own choices, and to be less concerned about keeping clean when it is more important to experience all the activities. According to Workman and Gage (1997):

Teachers who are effective, respectful partners realize that it is their job to support parent's goals for their children whenever possible and appropriate. When it is not, careful negotiation and sharing of available resources with families can help the teachers maintain their position as partners. (p. 12)

Teachers and parents need to talk about these goals face-to-face if at all possible. Set up a time when you can meet with each family. Can one of the parents visit the class, perhaps on a lunch hour if both are working? Can you visit a child's home in the evening? Can parents come to an evening, early morning, or weekend parent group meeting? Can the group meeting take place in an informal location, such as a restaurant, where parents may feel more at ease?

If parents are unaware that young children learn best through exploratory play, you might consider showing a videotape to illustrate such activities. On the other hand, if you learn from a parent how important they feel it is that, for example, their child keep clean because of limited clothing resources at home, you will need to find ways to make sure that the child's clothing will not be damaged. A collection of men's shirts for wearing over good clothes may do the trick.

Home Visits

The beginning of school may be the time to arrange home visits. You can mention to parents that you want to drop by in a few weeks to let them know how their child has adjusted to the center and that you plan to visit all the parents to give them this information. Plan it for a mutually agreeable time. It is important to mention your intention to have this visit at the beginning of the program; otherwise, parents may feel threatened by a home visit later on, fearing that their child has done something wrong. You must, of course, follow up with the visit once you have mentioned it.

Some parents may not be at ease with a teacher visiting their home if they think their home doesn't measure up to the teacher's expectations. Some teachers may not be at ease with home visits because they find themselves out of their own comfortable classroom "territory." Both teachers and parents will feel more at ease with each other if the meeting focuses on the child. The purpose of the home visit is to see the child in the home setting and talk with the parents about how he or she is getting along in preschool.

The teacher should take along a photo of the child taken in the classroom engaging in a favorite activity, for example, a block building he has made, a dress-up role she has taken, an art project she is engaged in, or a puzzle she is making. The teacher may also want to take some of the child's artwork to share or a book the child particularly likes.

The teacher could also talk about the scribbles on the child's paper as being the first step in a child's development of drawing or writing skills. She could leave the favorite book behind for a family member to read to the child. Before leaving, the teacher can invite family members to visit the school at a particular time to watch or participate in some activity.

A home visit like this is important not only for the teacher to gain a feeling for the child's home and family background but also for the family to learn that the program and teacher care enough about their child to take time to visit his home.

*Michael's grandmother read a
story on the day she visited.*

Family Members' Classroom Visits

What should a family member do during a visit to the child's classroom? Sit and
watch? Join in their child's activity? You can greet visitors at the door and let them
know what they can do. They will probably want to sit and watch at first. Later they
can participate in some way if they want. Raymond's father was invited to stir the instant gelatin the children were making for a snack. Michael's grandmother read the
children a story on the day that she came. Jordan's mother went with the class on a
nature walk, when they gathered colored leaves.

Parents need to be aware that some children may act up when their parents are in
the classroom. This is not unusual nor is anything wrong. To distract such children from
the discomfort of having their parents present in school or having to share their parents
with other children, you might give such children a special role to play, an errand to do,
or something to be in charge of to take their minds off their parents. On the other hand,
you might also give such parents a teacher's role, for example, reading a book to a small
group, overseeing the woodworking area, or being in charge of playing a record or tape.

For some children, the best thing to calm them down is actually working with their parents on an activity. Perhaps they can make a puzzle with their parent, do an easel painting, or build with blocks. Or, you might invite the child and parent to look at the classroom book collection and to select a book to sign out and take home.

Books and Materials as Connectors

For some families, materials make the best connector between home and school. Parents can understand the purpose for bringing home a book or for sending to school some empty containers for use in the dramatic play area. Again the focus is on the child. Keep a duplicate collection of children's books in paperback to be loaned on a daily basis and taken home. Children can sign out for one book at a time at the end of the session. They can return it in the morning. If they forget, they will need to wait until they return it before taking out another book. In the same manner, you can have a toy lending library of a duplicate set of the same little toys you use in the classroom, with, for example, cars, trucks, figures of people, animals, and doll furniture. Children can sign out their favorite toy and keep it overnight.

This is a good time for you to exchange notes with a parent. Put a file card in the book the child is borrowing. On it you can write a brief message about the child or the program and ask the parent to reply on the back of the card.

At home, parents can be asked to collect and send to school empty containers to be used for the children's pretend supermarket or shoe boxes for mailboxes. They can also be asked to send dress-up clothes such as hats, shoes, belts, wallets, and purses. Scraps of cloth, scraps of wood, Styrofoam containers, margarine cups, and paper towel tubes are other useful items to be saved for the classroom.

You may not have time to make all of the materials for individuals that you would like. Parents can help. Invite parents to a puzzle-making session and provide them with two enlarged copy-machine photos of their children, along with clear contact paper and cardboard backing. They can make two picture puzzles of each child by gluing the photo to the cardboard, laminating it with clear contact paper, and cutting it into simple puzzle sections to be kept in a manila envelope. One puzzle will be left on the manipulative materials shelf, but the other one can be taken home. Talk about what children learn from such puzzle-making activities (see Figure 11–3).

Figure 11–3   Children's Learning from Puzzle-Making

1. Eye–hand coordination
2. Small motor skills of picking up and inserting
3. Matching shapes and configurations
4. Visual-perceptual skills of identifying whole-to-part relationships
5. Positive self-concept of seeing a completed picture of themselves

Parents as Classroom Volunteers

Parents can be encouraged to volunteer in the classroom regularly if they feel comfortable in this role. Parents who interact successfully with the children when they come for a visit may want to return as volunteers. You will need to talk with such parents about program goals, your goals for individual children, and what the parents themselves would be comfortable doing during their stay in the classroom.

It is important to stress teamwork and how they will be a part of the classroom team. The roles of the other team members also need to be addressed so that parents understand what their own role will be and how they should carry it out. Remember, it takes time and effort on the part of the classroom staff to have a successful volunteer effort.

You can post signs in each activity area to tell volunteers and visitors what the children are doing and what the volunteers' roles can be. For example, in the book area, the sign might say: "Children are free to choose any book to read during free-choice period. Volunteers and visitors may want to read a book to a child if the child is interested." In the art area, the sign might say: "Children are encouraged to try out art materials on their own. Volunteers and visitors may want to observe the children and encourage them, but let them do art activities without adult help."

In the beginning, you may want the parent volunteers to observe both children and teachers, focusing on certain areas of the Teacher Skills Checklist (see this checklist in the Introduction), so that they have a better understanding of how staff members carry out program goals. The area of guidance is one that often needs an explanation. Let each parent spend time observing how staff members "use positive intervention methods to help children control their inappropriate behavior" or how they "use positive reinforcement techniques to help children learn appropriate behavior." At the end of the observation time, you or another staff member will want to sit down with the parent and discuss what she or he observed. You should discuss the methods for guiding children and also explain why certain methods are used. Ask the parent how she handles the same behavior at home.

At first you may want volunteers to work in only one or two learning centers of the classroom, until they get to know the children and the program. You or one of your team members needs to give help and support to the volunteer or to intervene with sensitivity when things do not go well. Have how-to booklets available to lend to volunteers or suggest that they view a videotape about the learning center or guidance method they are working with. Invite volunteers to planning sessions and in-service training programs. When they have acquired enough contact hours in your program, certain volunteers may want to prepare for CDA (Child Development Associate) assessment (see Appendix A).

You will soon recognize which volunteers are most helpful. Make rules governing classroom volunteers so that the program is not overwhelmed with them. Select one day a week for one volunteer at a time if you find there are too many. You may need to regulate the number of times a person can volunteer if this becomes a problem. Remember, volunteers should be a help in the program, not a hindrance.

You may want parent volunteers to work in only one or two learning centers until they get to know the children and the program.

Parent Conferences

You will want to have parent conferences from time to time during the year. Most of them will be called by you to speak positively with parents about how their child is doing. A few conferences may be called by the parent to discuss a particular issue. All parent conferences can be satisfying for everyone concerned if you plan for them ahead of time.

Because both you and the parent are busy people, be sure to schedule the conferences for a certain time period, say 30 minutes, and then try to keep to the schedule. State at the outset that you want to spend as much time as necessary but that for today you need to finish as close to your allotted time as possible. This statement gives both you and the parent the knowledge that the conference will not drag on and on and that you will need to focus clearly on the topic at hand.

Relax and enjoy yourself. Your relaxed manner will also put the parent at ease. Many parent conferences start off a bit strained because both of you may be ill at ease with one another. You need not be. You are going to be talking about a fine child and a good program. Focus enthusiastically on these positive things and the conference will take on an affirmative tone. If the parent sounds intimidating, listen carefully and take notes. You do not need to be defensive. When it is your turn to speak, do so with confidence and with facts, not with an argument.

Parent conferences are most successful when you are able to establish rapport with the parent. To do so you need to plan the conference around the parents' needs and concerns, rather than yours. Duffy (1997, p. 41) suggests structuring the conference in three parts:

1. Listening and sharing stories
2. Discussing child's school performance
3. Preparing for the future

Let the parent talk first and listen carefully to what she or he has to say. If she has trouble getting started, you can prompt her with an anecdote about her child and his involvement with activities and friends. Perhaps she can reply with an anecdote of her own. As Duffy notes:

> When parents and children separate for long periods each day, there is a tremendous need to hear stories about each other. What did you eat today? Did you learn a new song, or were you sad, mad, glad over something? Parent conferences are a formal time for parents and teachers to share stories. (p. 40)

After sharing stories about the child, you can ask the parent to describe any specific concerns about the child. Come prepared with child observation notes, individual plans you have used, photos of the child and his accomplishments, and art or writing products the child has done. Share these with the parent. Talk in specifics, not in vague generalities about the child. Not "Oh, he's doing fine" but "Yesterday Josh joined us in singing for the first time. Did you know how well he could sing?" If problems arise, do not be defensive but listen carefully to what parents have to say. Koch and McDonough (1999) suggest that teachers have "collaborative conversations" with parents in which they examine solutions rather than focusing on problems. As they note:

> Too often conferences are characterized by extensive dialogue about the problem. This frequently leads to blaming others for the problem, designating certain individuals as sole experts on the child, categorizing and labeling individuals as impaired, and making one person responsible for changes. (p. 11)

On the other hand, collaborative conversations focus on multiple solutions to problems and treat parents as partners in arriving at solutions. Both parents and teachers should share with each other their personal experiences and possible solutions. Neither one needs to try to convince the other that they are right, but instead, "to ask questions and understand experiences in ways that illuminate resources and spur people to action" (p. 11).

Often it is good to have a facilitator who understands about problem-solving conversations to facilitate the meeting. She or he will welcome everyone and establish rapport among them with small talk at first. The conversation should begin with trying to define a mutual goal that they all share. Participants can then describe what they have noticed about the child's behavior, both the inappropriate behavior and the acceptable behavior—even the littlest thing. How can this acceptable behavior be encouraged? What can each of the participants do to help?

When the time is up, you or the facilitator can conclude the meeting by summarizing what has been discussed and describing any actions you and the parents plan to take. Be sure to make the meeting positive and reciprocal. Both of you have concern for the child, and both of you need to be specific about the plans. If you need to follow up on the concerns expressed by either of you, now is the time to decide when and what will be done. Finally, thank the parent for coming and invite her to the classroom to see how things are working out.

RECOGNIZES AND SUPPORTS FAMILIES OF DIFFERENT MAKEUP

Lifestyles and family styles of the 2000s are far different from those of the traditional American family of the past. Even as recently as 15 years ago, many families consisted of mother as homemaker, father as breadwinner, and children whose first group experience occurred in public school kindergarten. Today's families, however, may be blended, extended, single-parented, bilingual, culturally diverse, and dependent on child care, often from infancy on.

Single-Parent Families

A tremendous increase in the number of single-parent families occurred between 1980 and 2000. The increased divorce rate along with the increased number of births among single teenage girls was principally responsible. Adoption of children by single parents was also on the rise. Although women head most single-parent families, more men have joined the ranks.

Early childhood programs need to recognize and accept such families. Single parents can maintain strong, functioning families with the proper support. Teachers must be aware, though, that children need special support during the turmoil of family breakup and that parents may need special arrangements to meet with preschool teachers. Some early mornings, evenings, or weekends may need to be set aside for parent-teacher meetings. It is your professional responsibility to make the initial contact and arrange your schedule to meet that of a family member.

Book to Read

Some single children may be upset when they find themselves with only a single mother while other children they know have both a mother and father and other siblings. Be sure to read them *Love Is a Family* (Downey, 2001) about little Lily who complains loudly to her mother that she wants a real family like Melissa who has four brothers and two sisters and whose house is never quiet and never, never neat. Her mother tells her that love is what makes a family, and they've got plenty of that. When Family Fun Night arrives at Lily's school, she finds that plenty of the families don't look a bit like Melissa's. There are stepdads and stepmoms, half sisters and half brothers, and families made up of different colors of skin. Everyone is laughing and showing their love by being together just like Lily and her mother.

Mixed/Blended Families

Many divorced parents eventually remarry. In situations where both parents bring children from a previous marriage, the new family is often referred to as "mixed" or "blended." Blended families can offer their children the same kind of support as their primary families did. Often, however, it takes time for families and children to build secure relationships with one another, especially if the original family breakup was difficult. Young children seem to suffer most immediately from this stress, often taking on feelings of guilt, shame, and rejection.

Preschool teachers need to be aware of the stress factors possible in blended families and show both children and their parents that they are accepted and cherished by the program. Again, it is up to the teacher to make the initial contact and set up parent–teacher meetings at the convenience of the family.

Many programs find that having children's picture books available on the themes discussed here makes a difference with children. You can read the books in class or put them out for children to look at, but especially have them available for families to borrow and read together.

Books to Read

Sam Is My Half Brother (Boyd, 1990) tells the story of a Caucasian girl named Hessie; her daddy and new wife have a baby. Hessie visits them during the summer and finally comes to appreciate her new half brother Sam. Numeroff's (1998) double book *What Mommies Do Best* and when turned upside down becoming *What Daddies Do Best,* shows animal mommies, one on every page, doing things such as teaching their child to ride a bicycle, make a snowman, and bake a birthday cake. Turn the book upside down and see animal daddies on every page doing the same things the mommies do, ending with giving them lots and lots of love.

Some children are living with grandparents rather than their real parents. Buckley's (1994) *Grandmother and I* is a sensitive tale told by a little African American girl sitting on her grandmother's lap being rocked back and forth as she considers other people's laps such as mothers, fathers, brothers, and sisters. But Grandmother's lap is just right.

Culturally Diverse Families

Families from cultures different from that of the majority of classroom parents are referred to as culturally diverse. They may be recent immigrants to the United States from Haiti, Cuba, Puerto Rico, Mexico, Vietnam, Pacific islands, India, Japan, China, Korea, or other areas of the world. The families may be ethnic minorities such as Hispanics, Asian Americans, Native Americans, or African Americans. They may speak only their native language or be bilingual. Their economic background will be as diverse as their nationalities.

Most immigrants come to this country for economic opportunities as well as political refuge. This has always been the case in the United States. These families expect that a program like yours will help their children to become adjusted to their new country, its language, and its customs. They also expect that their own culture and language will be respected, not ignored or ridiculed.

You or a member of your classroom team needs to make the initial contact with these families. If the parents do not speak English, then take with you a native language speaker or arrange for an older sibling who speaks English to be present. It is important that initial meetings be face-to-face at a location convenient to the parents. It is important also that you establish rapport with the parents. As Lee (1997) notes:

> When a parent speaks another language, it is important to establish a relationship which is one of equality and respect from the start, setting the tone for the future. If parents feel embarrassed about their English skills, it is sometimes helpful for (care) providers to share how frustrated they feel at not being able to communicate in the parents' language. (p. 58)

Books to Read

Children coming to preschool need to be welcomed and made to feel a part of the class. One book that everyone may enjoy is *Cleversticks* (Ashley, 1991), mentioned previously, a story about a little Chinese boy named Ling Sung who begins attending a multiethnic child care facility but can't seem to do things like the other children. His use of paintbrushes as chopsticks finally brings him acclaim and the help of all the others.

Another book about cultural diversity is *Will You Come Back for Me?* (Tompert, 1988), in which an Asian American girl named Suki, who is from a multicultural family, is worried that her mother will not come back for her when she starts at a child care program. She finally learns from the sensitive mother and her teddy bear Lulu that her mother will always come back.

Two Mrs. Gibsons (Igus, 1996) is a special story told by an African American girl about the two loving women in her life, both called Mrs. Gibson. One was a laughing, singing African American Mrs. Gibson from Tennessee who helped her play dress-up in fancy hats, sing gospel music in church, and catch fireflies at night. The other was a quiet little Japanese Mrs. Gibson from Gifu, Japan, who helped her play dress-up in a kimono and obi, cooked rice with meat and vegetables for her, and folded paper napkins into cranes for her. The first Mrs. Gibson she called nanny, because she was her grandmother, and the second Mrs. Gibson she called mommy. It is a wonderful true story showing how love can truly overcome major cultural differences.

In other instances families may have adopted children from another country or culture. They and their children also need your help to feel accepted even within their own families. A book that expresses this need is *Families Are Different* (Pelligrini, 1991), narrated by the little adopted Korean girl Nico who becomes uncomfortable because she looks so different from other members of her Anglo American family. Her mother tells Nico that "there are different kinds of families . . . that they are glued together with a special kind of glue called *love*." Nico finds this to be true as she looks around and sees nine familiar families at a family night gathering who seem to be more different than alike within themselves. She decides: "Now I don't think I'm strange at all. I'm just like everyone else . . . I'm different."

Working Parents

No matter what the makeup of the family, it is to be expected that the parents will be working and not at home during the day. This means that they depend heavily on their child's preschool for quality care, concern, and support for their children. Help your children's parents to be assured that this is the case. Take the initiative to contact the parents and arrange for meetings at their convenience. This should be an important part of the job description of every teacher and early childhood caregiver.

As a child caregiver, you need to recognize and support every type of family that your children represent. Families set the stage for their children's successes or failures in life. Thus, early childhood programs must be deeply involved in supporting the families of their children.

Books to Read

Picture books concerning children who worry about their working parents include *Friday Night Is Papa Night* (Sonneborn, 1970), the classic story about a Puerto Rican boy named Pedro who is always worried about his father coming home, because he can come only on the weekend. In *My Mom Travels a Lot* (Bauer, 1981), a little girl lists all of the good and bad things about her mother's traveling. But the best of all is "She always comes back!" *My Dad Takes Care of Me* (Quinlan, 1987) is about a boy whose father is out of work and stays home to take care of him while his mother works. In *Tucking Mommy In* (Loh, 1987), two little girls in an Asian American family help to put their very tired working mother to bed. Isadora's (1991) *At the Crossroads* is a wonderfully illustrated African story about a group of children who wait all night at the crossroads outside their settlement for their fathers to come home from 10 months of working in the mines.

Family Support of Programs

It is just as important that the children's families support your program. This, in fact, seems to be the key to child gains in preschool: If parents show enthusiasm for their children's preschool program, then children profit greatly from them. In cases where parents do not show enthusiasm or may be negative about the program, children do not seem to gain in self-esteem or behavior improvement. Thus, it is up to you to get across to parents and families your program's message: The program can help children to grow and develop emotionally, socially, physically, intellectually, creatively, and in language skills if parents and families support what you are doing.

You, in turn, must recognize and support the families in their role in raising their children. How do you do this? First, you must recognize the families of your children by accepting them, just as you accept their children. You may not understand or even agree with their lifestyles. However, that is their business, not yours. Your particular role in accepting your children's families is to support them in their child rearing. To do this, you must develop a two-way communication with parents and families. You must not only communicate to parents what is happening with their children in your program but also elicit from them what their expectations are and how you can support what they are trying to achieve.

BUILDS TEACHER–FAMILY RELATIONSHIPS THROUGH FAMILY CLASSROOM MEETINGS

Monthly family classroom meetings have proved to be the most successful family involvement activities that many programs have attempted. Parents often find these family meetings less intimidating than other kinds of school meetings. They are different from one-on-one parent conferences where parents only hear about their own child, or all-school meetings where parents may not know anyone else (Diffily, 2001, p. 8). As Diffily has found: "An investment of 2 hours per month—in a family meeting—cultivates relationships among teachers and families, which in turn promotes family involvement in children's daily activities" (p. 5).

Such meetings usually take place in the early evening, and should be set up in a special way that also includes the preschool children. At first the children can become involved in the classroom activities just as they were during the day, while their parents get better acquainted with the staff and each other. Then it is the parents' turn in the classroom while the children go to another room to listen to storytelling, story reading, or for quiet play with little toys. Parents are given name tags, sit in an opening circle to introduce themselves, and then choose a learning center to work in for a brief period. It is helpful to have signs in each center telling what academic and developmental skills that the children learn in that particular center. You and your coworkers can circulate to the various centers, acting as you would with children. At the end of a brief period, the parents can rotate to another center until they have visited as many centers as time allows.

At the end of the meeting, bring the parents back together for a closing circle where they will sing a song, hear a story, and report on what they did in the various centers. Be sure to have a handout for parents to take with them that lists the learning center activities they experienced, tells what children learn from each one, and gives suggestions on how parents can follow up with similar learning activities at home. As you note, the focus here is on how and what their children learn in the various learning centers, rather than on their children's behavior problems.

Each monthly meeting can focus on different issues or topics. Emergent literacy is one. Have the classroom full of signs and labels. Put picture books with character cutouts or dolls in certain learning centers. Have new computer literacy programs available, along with follow up activities in the various centers. For instance, you might have the CD-ROM alphabet program *Chicka Chicka Boom Boom* on the computer; the book *Chicka Chicka Boom Boom* in the book center; a broom "tree" wrapped in burlap with foam letters that can stick to it standing up in the loft; alphabet songs on tapes in the music center along with headsets for listening to them; alphabet matching games with plastic letters in the manipulative center; alphabet beanbags and a target in the large motor center; alphabet dough stampers and play dough in the art center, and so on.

Staff members can help parents get involved in the activities the various centers offer, as well as posing other problems they must solve, just as they would with the children: "Find the magnetic letter your name starts with." "See how many of that same letter you can find in this box of magnetic letters and put them on the magnet board." "Look at the name cards of all the people in the room. Find what names start with the same letter as yours." "Can you paint your name on the easel?" "Can you stamp your name in the play dough?" "Can you climb all the letters up to the top of the alphabet tree? Which ones fall off?" Afterward, when the parents come together to discuss what they have done, you can talk to them about how children teach themselves to recognize certain letters; how children first learn letters that are important to them; how it is not necessary to learn to name all the letters of the alphabet at first; why children may first write letters backwards or upside down; what letter games children might play at home.

At another meeting you may focus on the social skills of turn-taking, waiting for a turn, making friends, entering ongoing play, or getting along with others. Be sure to have picture books with stories featuring these topics available. Afterward, have parents talk about theirs and their children's experiences. How can they help their children at home with follow-up activities? Parents also have a chance to express concerns and get answers to their questions.

Relationships also develop among families. As Diffily (2001) notes: "Simply getting to know other parents who have children of the same age, and being able to talk about their children, is reassuring to many parents" (p. 8). Family classroom meetings soon take on the characteristics of friends getting together. Teachers benefit by finding that parents who attend are often more willing to share books and materials from home and to become directly involved in helping in the program. Even parents who do not enter the discussions gain from such meetings, according to Diffily :

> Family meetings enable adults who prefer to sit back and listen to the discussion to feel comfortable. All of the information discussed at a family meeting is important to them because it is directly related to their child. (p. 8)

It is important to have regular family classroom meetings so that parents get used to the idea. They can select the best evening to meet, and also telephone one another to remind them to come. Parents who speak little English can be encouraged to come with either you or they providing a translator—perhaps even one of their older children. If the activity is enjoyable and useful to them and their children, they will come. Soon the word will get around and most of the other parents may join in. Be sure to ask for and act on parents' ideas for topics to feature and for children's activities they know about. It can be an exciting learning get-together for everyone.

Select an evening for the monthly family meeting and telephone to one another to remind family members to come.

SUMMARY

Families can be involved in program activities in a variety of ways. They can visit the classroom to assist the staff in daily activities, field trips, or making materials. They can share with the children a song, a story, or a cultural practice. They can serve on committees or policy councils. The classroom staff should make the initial contact with families and arrange for them to visit or participate. The focus should be on the child and should be a positive one. Teachers can get parents' input about goals for their children if they fill out a Parents' Learning Goals for Children, as shown in Figure 11–2. Family members also can be encouraged to volunteer their services, but then they need to be assisted and supported by the staff through discussion and being given specific tasks.

The program and staff need to recognize and support nontraditional families such as single-parent families, blended families, and culturally diverse families. When both parents work, teachers need to arrange meetings at times convenient for the family. Two-way, face-to-face communication is important for both the program and the family to understand the goals each has for the child involved. It is just as important for the child's development to have his family support the program with enthusiasm as it is for the program to support the child. One of the most successful family involvement activities is often a monthly family classroom meeting where parents take the roles of their children and learn how children learn in the various classroom centers.

LEARNING ACTIVITIES

1. Read Chapter 11 and write out answers to Question Sheet 11.

2. Meet with your trainer or instructor and discuss answers to Question Sheet 11.

3. View one of the videotapes listed and make 10 file cards with specific ideas for parent involvement.

4. Read one or more of the references cited or suggested readings and add 10 cards to your file, with specific ideas for helping parents become involved in the classroom. Include the reference source on each card.

5. Communicate with a parent using the Parents' Learning Goals for Children (Figure 11–2) or another idea from this chapter that focuses on their child.

6. Get parents involved in the program as classroom volunteers and work with them in a classroom area in which they feel comfortable.

7. It is important to talk face-to-face with family members from culturally diverse, single-parent, or blended families about their children. Find out what the family member's goals are for the child and discuss the program's goals with him or her.

8. Plan a program at the school that parents can attend, get their input into what should be presented, or try to involve them in working on the program in some way.

9. Help to set up the learning centers for a family classroom meeting, printing up signs that tell what and how children learn in each center; participate in the meeting, talking with the parents who come about their children and the program.

10. Complete the Chapter 11 Evaluation Sheet and return it to your trainer or college supervisor.

QUESTION SHEET 11

1. Why do preschool programs with strong parent involvement have the longest positive effects on their children?

2. What are some of the ways a parent can become involved in a preschool classroom?

3. How can the teacher help get parents involved?

4. Why should you have a staggered entrance process at the beginning of the school year?

5. How can you set up home visits without seeming threatening to parents?

6. How can you involve parents in volunteering in the classroom?

7. How can you conduct a parent conference so that both sides get the most out of it?

8. How can you get parent support of your program from a single-parent, blended family, or culturally diverse family?

9. What does two-way communication in the parent-involvement process mean, and how can you get it started?

10. What should you do if you find that the program's goals and the parents' goals for their child are different?

11. How can children's books support children from families of different makeup? Give examples.

12. How can you build trust in the parents and have parents build trust in the program?

13. How can the Parents' Learning Goals for Children (Figure 11–2) help both you, the parent, and the child?

14. How do family meetings in the classroom help parents to understand the program? Give examples.

15. How should you conduct a home visit?

REFERENCES

Diffily, D. (2001). Family meetings: Teachers and families build relationships. *Dimensions of Early Childhood, 29*(3), 5–10.

Duffy, R. (1997). Parents' perspectives on conferencing. *Child Care Information Exchange, 116*, 40–43.

Eldridge, D. (2001). Parent involvement: It's worth the effort. *Young Children, 56*(4), 65–69.

Koch, P. K., & McDonough, M. (1999). Improving parent-teacher conferences through collaborative conversations. *Young Children, 54*(2), 11–15.

Lee, L. (1997). Working with non-English speaking families. *Child Care Information Exchange, 116*, 57–58.

Workman, S. H., & Gage, J. A. (1997). Family-school partnerships: A family strengths approach. *Young Children, 52*(4), 10–14.

SUGGESTED READINGS

Beaty, J. J., & Pratt, L. (2003). *Early literacy for preschool and kindergarten.* Upper Saddle River, NJ: Merrill/Prentice Hall.

Coleman, M. (1997). Families and schools: In search of common ground. *Young Children, 52*(5), 14–21.

Coleman, M., & Churchill, S. (1997). Challenges to family involvement. *Childhood Education, 73*(3), 144–148.

DeSteno, N. (2000). Parent involvement in the classroom: The fine line. *Young Children, 55*(3), 13–17.

Diffy, D., & Morrison, K. (Eds.). (1996). *Family-friendly communication for early childhood programs.* Washington, DC: National Association for the Education of Young Children.

Gonzalez-Mena, J. (1997). Cross cultural conferences. *Child Care Information Exchange, 116*, 55–57.

Gonzalez-Mena, J. (1998). *The child in the family and community.* Upper Saddle River, NJ: Merrill/Prentice Hall.

Kaufman, H. O. (2001). Skills for working with all families. *Young Children, 56*(4), 81–84.

Kendall, F. E. (1996). *Diversity in the classroom: New approaches to the education of young children.* New York: Teachers College.

Kieff, J., & Wellhousen, K. (2000). Planning family involvement in early childhood programs. *Young Children, 55*(3), 18–25.

Lake, J. (1997). Teachers and parents define diversity in an Oregon preschool cooperative. *Young Children, 52*(4), 20–28.

Lynch, E. W., & Hanson, M. J. (1992). *Developing cross-cultural competence: A guide for working with young children and their families.* Baltimore, MD: Brookes Publishing.

Manning, D., & Schindler, P. J. (1997). Communicating with parents when their children have difficulties. *Young Children, 52*(5), 27–33.

Murphy, D. M. (1997). Parent and teacher plan for the child. *Young Children, 52*(4), 32–36.

Sturm, C. (1997). Creating parent-teacher dialogue: Intercultural communication in child care. *Young Children, 52*(5), 34–38.

Walker-Dalhouse, D., & Dalhouse, A. D. (2001). Parent-school relations: Communicating more effectively with African American parents. *Young Children, 56*(4), 75–80.

Webb, N. C. (1997). Working with parents from cradle to preschool: A university collaborates with an urban public school. *Young Children, 52*(4), 15–19.

CHILDREN'S BOOKS

Ashley, B. (1991). *Cleversticks.* New York: Crown.

Bauer, C. F. (1981). *My mom travels a lot.* New York: Frederick Warne.

Boyd, L. (1990). *Sam is my half brother.* New York: Puffin.

Buckley, H. E. (1994). *Grandmother and I.* New York: Lothrop, Lee and Shepard.

Downey, R. (2001). *Love is a family.* New York: ReganBooks.

Igus, T. (1996). *Two Mrs. Gibsons.* San Francisco: Childrens Book Press.

Isadora, R. (1991). *At the crossroads.* New York: Greenwillow.

Loh, M. (1987). *Tucking Mommy in.* New York: Orchard.

Numeroff, L. (1998). *What mommies do best; What daddies do best.* New York: Simon & Schuster.

Pelligrini, N. (1991). *Families are different.* New York: Scholastic.

Quinlan, P. (1987). *My dad takes care of me.* Toronto: Annick.

Sonneborn, R. A. (1970). *Friday night is Papa night.* New York: Puffin.

Tompert, A. (1988). *Will you come back for me?* Morton Grove, IL: Whitman.

VIDEOTAPES

National Association for the Education of Young Children. (Producer). *Cultivating Roots—Home/School Partnerships. (The Early Childhood Program: A Place to Learn and Grow* video series). Washington, DC: Author. #870.

South Carolina Educational TV. (Producer). *Partnerships with Parents.* Washington, DC: National Association for the Education of Young Children. #857.

Staton, J. (Producer). *Building a Family Partnership.* Van Nuys, CA: Child Development Media.

CHAPTER 11 EVALUATION SHEET
PROMOTING FAMILY INVOLVEMENT

1. Student _____

2. Trainer _____

3. Center where training occurred _____

4. Beginning date _____ Ending date _____

5. Describe what student did to accomplish General Objective.

   _____

   _____

6. Describe what student did to accomplish Specific Objectives.

   Objective 1 _____

   _____

   Objective 2 _____

   _____

   Objective 3 _____

   _____

7. Evaluation of student's Learning Activities

   _____

   _____

Comments:

Permission is granted by the publisher to reproduce this page for evaluation and record keeping.

Providing Program Management

GENERAL OBJECTIVE

To develop an effective early childhood classroom program based on the needs and interests of the children

SPECIFIC OBJECTIVES

____ Uses a team approach to plan a flexible curriculum

____ Plans and implements an emergent curriculum to assure a quality program

____ Evaluates curriculum outcomes through child observations and team conferences

Program management for an early childhood classroom requires planning on the part of all those who will carry it out, that is, teachers, assistants, student teachers, and volunteers. Even the children themselves are part of the planning process. As Patricia Berl (1998), an early childhood administration specialist, points out:

> Ask any director, stop any teacher, and he will tell you that planning makes the difference. With time to plan, chaos can become calm, tension can give way to decent relations, seat-of-the-pants classroom management can become quality education. (p. 61)

If you don't plan for something to happen, nothing will happen, say knowledgeable teachers. This is only common sense. Yet for some early childhood teaching teams, very little planning takes place. In many instances the teacher decides what art project to put out, what science activity to pursue, or what material to fill in the sensory table. Other staff members merely go along with whatever the teacher decides. The daily activities may or may not interest the children but seldom have any connection with one another or with whatever activities are available next week.

How can you tell what children have accomplished in your program if you have not planned for them to accomplish anything? How will you know what concerns staff members may be harboring if they have no forum for expressing their concerns? Where is the excitement that new ideas generate if there is no time to brainstorm? Without a specific time for planning, you and your team members will miss the great satisfaction of working together, creating new plans

317

1. All team members have the opportunity to give input and help plan the curriculum.
2. Team members better understand their responsibilities.
3. Team members are more eager to carry out activities with children because they have helped to plan them.
4. Team members are better able to build on what they have done in the past because there is continuity in the planning.
5. Team members feel an ownership in the program and a sense of accomplishment in their work.

Figure 12–1   Advantages for Team Planning

to help children grow and learn. You may also miss the pride and satisfaction of having your own ideas accepted by the others and put into practice with great enthusiasm by the children.

Classroom planning is not just an exercise to satisfy your administration. It is a necessity for everyone involved in a quality early childhood program. Advantages for team planning are listed in Figure 12–1.

 ## USES A TEAM APPROACH TO PLAN A FLEXIBLE CURRICULUM

Team Planning Sessions

For programs to operate smoothly and with continuity, weekly planning sessions for all team members must be held regularly. Some programs choose a portion of Friday afternoons for planning time. They may call in a substitute while the team carries out its planning, schedule a senior volunteer to read to the children, or if permissible, dismiss the children early.

Everyone on the classroom team must be aware of how plans are made, when they are made, and who is involved. If you are the lead teacher, you realize that for plans to be made and carried out, everyone on the team must participate. Carrying out plans is much more effective if the participants take part in planning for them. If you are an assistant, a student teacher, or a volunteer, you realize that the effectiveness of your contribution to the program depends on your own input in planning the activities you are responsible for.

Weekly team sessions should be threefold in nature. Everyone needs to contribute to the discussion of these three questions:

1. Where are we now?
2. Where do we want to go?
3. How can we get there?

A *summary* of what has been happening in the classroom during the week can be led by the teacher who will record the information from others on newsprint or a chalkboard for all to see. Observation records, data about group and individual accomplishments, and how particular activities worked out can be part of the summary.

Plans for the following week will be based on what has been happening, as well as certain individual and group goals everyone has been working on. Brainstorming can help to generate new ideas as well as follow-ups for ongoing activities. Tasks and duties for every team member are then determined.

No single person in an early childhood classroom can or should do everything. But successful management of the program depends as much on staff interpersonal relations and cooperation as on any other single element. Balance is the key here as the entire staff becomes involved in planning.

Team Roles and Responsibilities

The teacher is, of necessity, the leader, and therefore needs to take the lead in encouraging expression of ideas and concerns of other team members. This lead teacher must not dominate nor allow others to dominate. She should ask for suggestions from the others and then either ask them to volunteer or give them the responsibility to carry out classroom activities without interference from her. Other team members should also be willing to offer suggestions and take on responsibility. Classroom duties, for example, can be rotated throughout the team. Assistants, student teachers, and volunteers, as well as the lead teacher, can be responsible for most of the following on a rotating basis:

Classroom Duties

1. Participating daily in setup and cleanup of the classroom
2. Being in charge of a small group
3. Working with individual children
4. Reading books to individuals and small groups
5. Observing and recording children's behavior
6. Attending and participating in weekly classroom planning sessions
7. Attending family classroom meetings

Everyone can observe individual children and record pertinent information. Everyone can be involved in reading to individuals and attending meetings. Each should also have a chance to be in charge of a small group as well as work with individuals. Teachers need to join with other team members in classroom setup and cleanup. This should not be relegated to an assistant while the teacher occupies herself with more "important" activities. All classroom activities are important for everyone involved.

Teamwork means that everyone on the teaching team shares *all* the responsibilities of the classroom. When teamwork operates effectively, a visitor to the classroom will not be able to tell who is the teacher and who are the assistants.

Teachers need to join with other team members in classroom setup and cleanup.

Good interpersonal communication makes teamwork possible. The team recognizes that the leader has overall responsibility but is willing to work together toward a common goal. Each member trusts and respects the others, so when things go wrong, team members are able to communicate problems and resolve them in the friendly atmosphere of team meetings.

Overcoming Team Problems

Problems do occur from time to time. When more than one person is involved in working closely in the same room with the same children and staff members for long periods of time, it is only natural that conflicts arise. It is the team's responsibility to take time to resolve such problems. When problems arise, the team should choose someone from the program to lead an informal dialogue. This could be the program

1. Choose someone from the program but outside the classroom to be the team leader.
2. Have each team member write a brief note to include the following:
   a. A positive action or accomplishment of the team during the past month
   b. An area of concern needing discussion or action
   c. Any questions regarding the team approach
3. Have the team leader collect and read from these notes, and then conduct the meeting as an open discussion, using good listening and communication skills.
4. Have the leader summarize:
   a. What has been said
   b. What has been agreed on
   c. What will be done and by whom

Figure 12–2   Guidelines for Team Problem-Solving Meetings

director, the educational coordinator, the family worker, or anyone else the team agrees on. Guidelines for conducting such a meeting are shown in Figure 12–2.

Programs that schedule monthly team sessions like this are often able to resolve problems successfully. At these sessions, all of the team members are asked to contribute in a positive manner, following the guidelines. The leader reads the notes that have been written and prepares for the session, keeping in mind the necessity for a positive orientation. These sessions are not only follow-ups of concerns that surfaced the month before but also general problem-solving and brainstorming sessions.

To set the tone, the leader begins the session by sharing the positive accomplishments that were stated through writing. Participants add any additional achievements that come to mind. The leader then chooses one area of concern and opens it for discussion. Whatever resolution is finally agreed on can be recorded on the newsprint or chalkboard.

Teams that have used this approach find that writing down "areas of concern" in their initial notes to the leader helps to diffuse emotional issues and can state their case objectively. Having meetings like this every month rather than only when problems arise also helps to prevent interpersonal problems from developing into major communication breakdowns.

Planning a Flexible Daily Schedule

The keynote of curriculum planning in early childhood programs is flexibility. Your plans must accommodate a group of 15 to 20 lively youngsters and at the same time meet the particular needs of individuals. The children themselves need time to let off steam as well as periods of quiet relaxation. They need to develop large motor abilities but also the fine skill of eye-hand coordination. They should be exposed to total group doings but not at the neglect of small-group or individual activities. While the children may be indoors for most of the day, the necessity for some outdoor activity must still be met. And all of these activities should flow smoothly from one to the other so that children will feel the satisfying rhythm of a well-planned day.

How do you do it? If you have arranged your classroom according to the ideas presented in Chapter 3, you have already begun. The physical arrangement of the room already indicates what curriculum activities are available and how many children can participate in each.

You may wonder whether planning, then, is merely a matter of scheduling time. That is, of course, a part of it, but planning is so much more. First, it involves knowing the children in your care, knowing what they are like as a group as well as how they differ as individuals. Planning also involves getting a feeling for how the children feel at different times of the day.

Take the first thing in the morning, for instance. Do your children walk to the child-care center or ride? Do they come bursting in from a bus in a mob or straggling in one by one with mothers in tow? Are they sleepy, cranky, hungry, or happy? What happens during the first half hour in the morning? What would you like to have happen?

Goals

What goals do you have for your entire group of children for a single day? For part of the day? What special goals do you have for individuals? A group goal may be something such as "helping the children learn to work and play together in harmony." A goal for a certain part of the day could be "to improve nap time so that nonsleepers don't disturb sleepers." Individual goals can be many and varied, for example, "to help Shayla come out of her shell and respond to the other children and activities around her." These goals will be recorded during team planning sessions and referred to at the next session to determine if they have been carried out.

Time Blocks

A simple but effective way many programs schedule activities is in the form of time blocks. Time blocks are labeled periods of time of *unspecified length* that occur in approximately the same order every day, but within which there is flexibility for many things to happen. The time blocks used in many programs include the following:

1. arrival
2. opening circle
3. free choice (A.M.)
4. snack time (A.M.)
5. playground
6. story time
7. lunchtime
8. nap time
9. snack (P.M.)

10. free choice (P.M.)

11. closing circle

12. departure

If yours is a half-day program, the children's departure could occur after lunch. If lunch is not included in your half-day schedule, you could add a closing circle, after which the children would depart. The length of each time block and the order in which you schedule it depends on your goals, your children's needs, and daily circumstances.

One advantage of using time blocks is flexibility. The length of time blocks can vary according to circumstances, although their order will remain the same. For example, arrival usually takes about 15 minutes every morning. But occasionally the bus will be late, so arrival time might stretch to 30 minutes or more. You may decide to omit the free-choice period entirely that morning and go immediately out to the playground, because the children have been cooped up on the bus so long that they need to get out in the open, where they can release their pent-up energy. Another day you may find the children are just too restless for circle time. What they really need is a run around the playground.

In other words, time blocks do not tie you to specific times. Rather, they refer to activities and their sequential order. Their flexibility frees you and your staff to plan for a variety of activities within a certain block. It does not lock you into the kind of schedule that dictates, for example, that snack time must occur at 10:00 A.M. All you know about snack time is that it follows the playground time block (however long that should last)—and that snack time and playground time could occur simultaneously if you decide to serve the juice for a snack outside on a hot day.

Another advantage of time blocks is their built-in balance. You can easily alternate contrasting kinds of activities simply by the order in which you schedule the particular time blocks. Just as important is the stability your program acquires through the use of time blocks. The same periods tend to occur in about the same order every day. This promotes a sense of security among the children. To enjoy a variety of activities, young children need this kind of structure that they understand and within which they feel comfortable. Once you have determined your general time block order, make a simple illustrated chart showing each time block so that children, volunteers, and visitors can tell at a glance what is going on and when.

Finally, time blocks provide a simple system of program management for classroom workers. Student teachers, Foster Grandparents, and other volunteers are much more at ease if they too can readily understand a daily schedule and become comfortable with it.

Let us look at each of the time blocks, one by one, as we would use them to plan a daily program according to the goals mentioned.

Arrival

"Helping the children learn to work and play together in harmony" was one program's daily goal. To accomplish it, the staff first looked at each time block to see (a) what elements promote the goal, (b) what elements hinder the goal, and (c) what changes need to be made.

In reviewing their present morning arrival time block, the staff noted that their 17 children came from two separate neighborhoods. About half of them walked to the center or were driven by their parents between 8:30 and 9:00. The others came by bus in a group between 8:50 and 9:00. The teachers were on hand to greet each child individually, although they found this difficult when all the bus children came swarming in at one time.

As the staff reviewed the arrival period, they decided that the most helpful element was greeting children individually and having a brief conversation. The obvious negative element was the crowd of bus children arriving all at once. What began harmoniously with the walkers soon dissolved into bedlam. The staff decided to try having some individual activities on hand that would separate the crowd as they burst into the room.

Their most successful effort along this line turned out to be a two-part activity involving "tickets and crowns." The tickets sorted out the children, and the crowns made the center a fun place to come to every morning. The staff made a cardboard name ticket for each child. Every morning this was placed in some part of the room, usually on one of the tables, for each child to find when he or she entered. Then the child would present his ticket to one of the teachers, who would give him a cutout paper crown to wear, along with a cheery "Hello, Josh! It's nice to see you this morning!" The children so enjoyed this activity that it evolved into the children making various headpieces for morning greeting time, including paper hats, chef hats, and even sports headbands.

Another teacher resolved the morning mass arrival woes by taking a photograph of each child, fastening a tab hook at the top, and hanging it on a pegboard. When a child arrived, he would find his picture and then hang it on the Job for a Day Chart next to the "job" he wanted. Then he would go to the teacher for his greeting and directions on his job. For instance, "Zoo Keeper" might mean "feed the guinea pig" or it could mean "find a picture of a guinea pig in one of our library books." The children loved challenges like this.

Some teachers use books to make the connection between a child's home and the center, as discussed in Chapter 11. Morning arrival time might then become a book check-in time as well as individualized greeting time for each child.

Once you have assessed your arrival time block on the basis of elements that promote your daily goal for children and those that hinder the goal's accomplishment, you should be able to institute changes that will make your center an exciting place to enter every day of the year.

Opening Circle

Once children have arrived and received greetings from a staff member, many programs schedule a brief opening circle as a transition from home to school. Children and each staff member sit in a circle on the floor and participate in a greeting song, a listening activity, and an introduction to learning center activities for the day. Because of children's short attention span and eagerness to get right into the activities, keep this time block short (20 minutes max) and peppy.

A song that names each child in turn helps everyone feel happy about being there. Almost any familiar nursery rhyme song can be converted to a name greeting. For instance, *Here We Go Round the Mulberry Bush* can become "Here we sit in our circle, our circle, our circle; here we sit in our circle, this lovely Monday morning. Say hello to Melissa, to Bobby, to Samantha; say hello to Bartholomew this lovely Monday morning" (and so on).

Some children are bursting to tell about something that happened to them, but attention-spans being what they are for young children, the rest of the group may have the patience to listen to only two or three. This should not be a "show-and-tell" time for everyone, but instead, a "tell-and-listen" time in which perhaps only three children draw numbered cards out of a hat to see in which order they go. If only one child has something to say, then have one card available. You can control the number of speakers by the number of cards available. Keep track of who has something to say each day, so that certain children do not dominate and others remain silent as the days progress.

Finally, it is time to introduce special free-choice activities in certain learning centers. Let the staff member who is in charge of that center briefly describe the activity. Afterward everyone can join in a familiar song, or perhaps learn a new song.

Dismiss the children from circle time with a transition activity to prevent a mad rush for the activities and squabbles over the center necklaces or sign up clipboards. You can call one or two children by name to leave the circle and go to the activity of their choice. Or say "Children with something red on may go to free-choice activities." Or "Children who can whisper the name of the child sitting next to them may go." Then you and the staff members must go around the circle listening for the whispered names and telling the children they can go.

Free Choice (A.M.)

Most programs schedule a free-choice period immediately after arrival or circle time. Each classroom staff member is responsible for a different planned activity. This will mean three such special activities can be available at a time while the other children play in the remaining permanent learning centers. Activities can be as varied as: a table of play dough, rolling pins, and cookie cutters for making cookies; a table of yarn and uncooked macaroni for stringing necklaces; a portable climber and mats for jumping; a table of vegetable scrapers, carrots, celery, mayonnaise, and ketchup for making snacks and dips; a table of torn paper, buttons, paper clips, and glue for collages; cutting out "frog legs" for making a paper-bag frog; or any one of a hundred other special activities the adult staff has planned for the children.

In light of your daily goal of "helping children learn to work and play together in harmony," the staff needs to identify those elements in the free-choice period that promote this goal and those that hinder its accomplishment. You may decide that your free-choice period's most important strength is the number and quality of activities available daily and that its principal hindrance is getting the children involved

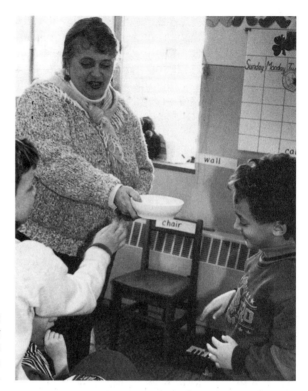

Children can regulate their own movement from one learning center to another by taking a color-coded ticket that they can trade with one another.

in favorite activities without a fuss. When many children insist on participating in favorite activities at the same time, soon a squabble ensues. Thus, you need to either make changes in the way children select an activity or offer more variations of favorite activities.

First, decide which ones are the favorite activities. Those can be identified at staff planning sessions. For example, cooking and water play were identified in one classroom. Many children have trouble waiting for turns when those activities are set up. One solution is to have three tables of the favorite activity going at the same time. For example, set up three tables, instead of one, for cooking. Each table can then feature the same type of cooking activity, or each can be a different variation: for instance, making cherry gelatin with banana slices at the first table; making lemon gelatin with pineapple chunks at the second; and making orange gelatin with mandarin orange sections at the third. Together, the portions made should be just enough of the gelatin fruit dessert for the whole class.

It is no more difficult for a staff to set up three of the same type of activity than three different ones. In fact, such activities provide an excellent way to extend learning experiences. For example, one water activity could be to explore which things float and which sink; another could be to dissolve different food colors and pour the colored water through funnels into plastic bottles; a third activity might be to put detergent into a dishpan full of water and whip it into suds with an eggbeater and pour it into bottles.

Children can regulate their own movement from one activity to another during the free-choice period in a number of ways: (a) when one child leaves his chair, another can take it; (b) for each activity, you can give out color-coded tickets that the children can trade with one another; or (c) four hooks, card pockets, or pegs can be fastened in each area for children to hang name tags on—when a hook is empty, another child may hang her tag on it to join in; (d) or a certain number of learning center necklaces may be hanging up which children can select and wear while they are in that center. You may want to set up these same activities for several days running, until all the children have had their chance at every activity.

How long should the morning free-choice period last? It may vary from day to day, depending on the children's involvement or restlessness. If children are working and playing in harmony, it can last much of the morning. You and your staff can decide daily.

Transitions

If you use transition activities to help children move from one time block to another smoothly, you will not only be helping children understand how the schedule works, but also be preventing squabbles, confusion, and unnecessary running around. Such activities can be brief songs, fingerplays, marching games, follow-the-leader games, puppet fun, or whatever else your creativity can conjure up. Children may first need to pick up the learning centers and put away materials they are finished with. Staff members can help children play pickup games in each center to start the transition. Then at a signal (drum beat, record, musical chimes, etc.), everyone can join in the transition game; perhaps marching around the room with an animal puppet in the lead who tells everyone what motions to make as they march until they finally arrive at the snack tables. If they must wait for the snack to appear, continue with another transition game, perhaps a fingerplay or song led by the puppet. Be sure to keep a record of your and the children's favorite transitions. In other words, don't keep the children waiting with nothing to do. Make waiting fun. Petersen (2000) tells us:

> Using small increments of time—be it lining up at the door, moving from one group time to table work, or just a change of pace during the day—can prove to be challenging if teachers don't have a bag full of ideas to motivate and entice children. (p. 24)

Snack Time (A.M./P.M.)

Snack time in the early childhood classroom may be a group or individual activity, depending on the feelings of teacher, staff, and children. Most programs have snacks as a total group activity in the middle of the morning. Many teachers believe that young children need the nourishment and that it is good to come together as a total group at some point after working individually or in small groups.

Others believe that children themselves should determine when to snack and how much snack they need. Instead of setting up tables for a total group snack, they keep a "snack bar" going on a single table for much of the morning, encouraging children to use it whenever they want. Their rationale is a reluctance to pull children away from activities they are deeply involved in.

The same considerations apply to afternoon snack time. If the children take a long nap, you may want to have a snack ready for them as they awaken. It gives them a chance to become reoriented to their surroundings after a deep sleep. If your snack time has not been all that harmonious, ask the children themselves how they would like snack time to be organized.

Playground

Scheduling this time block depends primarily on the children and their circumstances. Are they city children who seldom get a chance to play outside? Do they come every day from long distances on a bus? If so, you may want to schedule a playground period after arrival. This gives bus children a chance to let off steam and restless children an opportunity to expend their energy constructively. Some teachers like to schedule playground first because the children already have on their outside clothing, making it easier and less time consuming for the dressing-undressing ritual. Otherwise, playground is usually scheduled toward the end of the morning.

One team found that the main hindrance to the playground period was that all three of the center's classes were outside at the same time, creating turn-taking squabbles over equipment. The simple solution was for the three teams to meet together and decide on alternating their playground time blocks.

Children who have been inside all day need to get outside and engage in some kind of vigorous activity on a daily basis. If you have no playground, you may want to take the children on a run around the building, or a hop, skip, and jump down the sidewalk. If your parking lot is safe, you might mark out hopscotch games with sidewalk chalk.

Story Time

Once children come inside after a vigorous workout they need to sit down for a moment and catch their breath before proceeding to lunch. This is the time for a brief total-group listening activity such as story time (not to be confused with individual or small group picture book reading during free-choice). You may want to do oral storytelling without using a book, or invite a special reader (parent, friend, librarian, retired teacher, book-store owner, etc.) to read a book they have brought. Transition to lunch can come after children wash up and use the bathroom.

Lunchtime

Does your lunchtime arrangement fulfill the daily goal of "helping children work and play together in harmony"? What are its strong points? How can it be improved? Most programs consider eating together family style in the classroom to be one of the most beneficial aspects of lunchtime. Teachers, student teachers, volunteers, and visitors sit at the tables with the children, sharing the food and the conversation. It is a time of enjoyment and relaxation.

Most children love to eat, and even reluctant eaters find it hard to resist food when everyone around them is so totally absorbed. The wise classroom staff keeps rules to a minimum, discourages nagging and pressure, and promotes a happy atmosphere at the table. Dessert is a nutritious part of the meal, not a reward or bribe for "cleaning your plate."

Children feel good when adults sit next to them at the table and eat the same food they do. They feel even better when adults converse with them as equals. Fascinating information about children's understandings of themselves and their world comes out of lunchtime conversations.

Public schools sometimes require early childhood programs to use the school cafeteria. However, staff should be aware of the possible difficulties with this arrangement. A noisy cafeteria full of older youngsters presents an intimidating atmosphere for 3- and 4-year-olds, a situation that is not at all conducive to relaxed eating. If the children must go through the regular cafeteria line, they are often given portions much too large for them to handle, and as a result, end up eating very little. Furthermore, the time pressure to finish and move out often achieves the opposite result with preschoolers. Some programs in these circumstances have been able to arrange with the cafeteria staff to have the food sent to their rooms for family-style eating. School officials will usually cooperate once they understand the situation. After lunch be sure to have the children brush their teeth. Then they can help get out their cots for nap time.

Nap Time

Another goal for a particular part of the day might concern "improving nap time so nonsleepers don't disturb sleepers." If yours is an all-day program, you will need to schedule a nap period in the afternoon after lunch. Not all children need a nap. Some, however, can hardly function without their regular afternoon nap. For the nonsleepers, lying quietly for an hour or so in the same room with sleepers is nearly impossible. Some provision needs to be made for them.

If your center has more than one classroom, you may be able to arrange to use one as the sleeping room and another for nonsleepers. The focus, even for nonsleepers, should be on quiet solitary activities, with the rest of the room sectioned off.

If you have only one room, you can reserve a section for nonsleepers, where they can play quietly on mats without disturbing the sleepers. Perhaps the block corner can serve this purpose, if it is well sectioned off. Have a tray, box, or special cart of materials available to the children in this area. If you talk to them in a low voice or whisper, you will soon find the children imitating you. If you have no other means of separating sleepers from nonsleepers, cut apart a large cardboard packing carton and unfold it for a divider.

Free Choice (P.M.)

How much time is available in your program between wake up from nap until departure? A half hour? An hour? Some activities should be available to children during this late afternoon time block. Most programs rely on their regular room equipment, but some insist that children not get out all the blocks or dress-up clothes. These restrictions tend to be more for the adult's convenience than the children's. This is justifiable as long as there are other interesting substitute activities for the children. Activities different from those in the morning are best.

The answer may be a table with a different kind of art from that available in the morning or one with different puzzles or different manipulative games saved for afternoon play. If you have not used your water or sand table in the morning, this can be an excellent time to open it. You can make this time block convenient for you yet enticing for the children if you and your staff use your imaginations during planning sessions.

Closing Circle

Half-day programs often schedule circle time just before lunch or departure. Full-day programs often schedule theirs at the conclusion of the day. The purpose is to pull together the daily happenings and help the children make sense of them. "What did you do this morning, Karen, that you liked best of all?" If teachers listen carefully to children's answers, they can gain valuable insights about the activities that made the greatest or the least impression on the children, and why.

Closing circle may be another good time for conducting music or storytelling for the whole group. Parents or special visitors can be invited to take part. Guitar players or storytellers might put in an appearance, or the teacher might demonstrate a new game or introduce a puppet that wants to talk with the children.

Just as in the morning, this circle time should be shorter than most other time blocks because of preschool children's short attention spans and restlessness in large groups. Student teachers and volunteers can serve as listening models for the children around them to imitate.

Departure

A good ending to the day is as essential as a good beginning. Children need to feel satisfied about the day they have just finished to look forward with pleasure to the next. The staff should be on hand to help the children prepare to go home. Helping children dress or supporting them in their own efforts, conversing about what they have done during the day, checking out a book or a toy to take home overnight, greeting parents who pick up their children, saying a final farewell and a "See you tomorrow!"—these should be pleasurable activities for all involved. If you have planned well, this will signal the end of a happy, satisfying day.

Recording the Daily Schedule

You need to write down your daily plans, not merely as an exercise to please an administrator, but for you and your staff to use for these purposes:

1. To keep you on target

2. To help you remember what you planned to do

3. To help staff members keep track of their own roles

Daily Schedule for Week of _____

Goal _____ Theme _____

Follow-up _____

	Monday	Tuesday	Wednesday	Thursday	Friday
Arrival					
Opening Circle					
Free Choice					
Snack Time					
Playground					
Story Time					
Lunchtime					
Nap Time					
Snack Time					
Free Choice					
Closing Circle					
Departure					

Figure 12–3 Daily Schedule

Permission is granted by the publisher to reproduce this schedule for evaluation and record keeping.

Run off a number of blank daily schedule forms like the one shown in Figure 12–3, Daily Schedule. Fill them in together at your weekly planning session. Then bring them to the next planning session to evaluate how your plans worked out. Write comments directly on the schedules and keep them on file for future reference.

Managing Time

As you make team plans for what will occur daily in the various time blocks, you should take special note of the longest and most important activity periods of the day: the free-choice time blocks. It is here that the children will spend the majority of their

Young children learn best through self-directed playful discovery.

time, working and playing in the learning centers, listening to books being read, and participating in art, crafts, science, cooking, and manipulative activities on the activity tables—see Free Choice (A.M.). How long should these time blocks be? Should they be the same length every day, or will they need to change in length depending on circumstances? How will you know?

What we have discovered about young children's learning through brain research, European preschools, and our own observations of children's behavior in the classroom leads us to these conclusions:

1. Real learning takes time (much longer than we realized).

2. Real learning involves continuity and repetition (much more than we realized).

3. Young children learn best through self-directed playful discovery.

4. Young children have problems learning when they are under pressure to hurry up and finish.

5. Young children can accomplish much more than we ever realized if we raise our own expectations and give children the time, freedom, and opportunity to choose and pursue activities on their own.

American visitors to the Reggio Emilia preschools in Italy were at first astounded at the high level of art and writing accomplishments of very young children. Then they discovered that the children are allowed to work on their self-chosen projects for as long as they want or need to—sometimes for days or even weeks. As Seefeldt (1995) notes:

> Time is used differently in Reggio preschools than in preschools in the United States. Experiences and themes last months, as opposed to the one- or two-week units typical in the United States. And children are never expected to move on to something new until they have exhausted their own ideas fully. Often, in Reggio, children were observed painting at easels for an entire morning or working with clay for hours. (p. 42)

Does this mean that American preschools should abandon the idea of time blocks altogether and open the days to long work/play periods where children pursue a certain project to its conclusion? Not necessarily. As the observers came to realize, it is not the children's products that are important, but the process the child goes through to produce the art or the writing. Because this process is treated so seriously and given so much time in the Reggio preschools, the children's products are extraordinary. Observers also found many Europeans to be more relaxed about time than their American counterparts. Perhaps, instead of lengthening or eliminating time blocks, American preschool teachers should consider keeping the same activities going in the time blocks for more than one or two days, because they realize that children's experiences need to be repeated over and over for them to learn from the process (Beaty, 2002, p. 264). Gandini (2002) has more to say about time in Reggio Emilia schools:

> Time is not set by a clock, and continuity is not interrupted by the calendar. Children's own sense of time and their personal rhythm are considered in the planning and carrying out activities and projects. Teachers get to know the personal time of the children and each child's particular characteristics because children stay with the same teacher and the same peer group for three-year cycles. This process of looping further promotes the concept of *an education based on relationships*. (pp. 17–18)

No matter how you finally decide to schedule time in your classroom, you will need to observe carefully how your children use the time. When programs force children to stop what they are doing and move on to something else, they may be short-circuiting the children's learning process. You will know this is happening when the children show great reluctance to stop or change what they are doing. Does this happen in your program? On the other hand, some time periods may need to be cut shorter than the time allotted because the children are finished with their activities and seem to be milling around looking for something new.

How you schedule time in your program should be based on the children's interests and needs rather than on the convenience of the teacher. Careful observation of the children's behavior can help you determine how long or short the time periods need to be. After all, the free-choice time blocks can be regulated on a daily basis to be different lengths, long or short, as determined by the children's use of them. What goes on within the time blocks themselves can be determined by the curriculum you and the children have planned.

PLANS AND IMPLEMENTS AN EMERGENT CURRICULUM TO ASSURE A QUALITY PROGRAM

Emergent Curriculum Themes

What is an *emergent curriculum* and how does it differ from the traditional curriculum often planned for the preschool classroom? An emergent curriculum grows from the ideas, activities, and interests of both the teachers and the children as they happen, rather than being planned ahead of time by teachers alone as in the traditional sense. As Jones and Nimmo (1994) tell us:

> An emergent curriculum is a continuous revision process, an honest response to what is actually happening. Good teachers plan and let go. If you are paying attention to children, an accurate lesson plan can be written only after the fact. It is important to be accountable for what really happens, as distinguished from one's good intentions. Teachers are often hoodwinked by their good intentions. (p. 12)

The educational plan and how it is carried out is often referred to as the "curriculum" in early childhood programs. But as Jones and Nimmo note, "In early childhood education, curriculum isn't the focus, children are. It's easy for teachers to get hooked on curriculum because it's so much more manageable than children. But curriculum is *what happens* in an educational environment—not what is rationally planned to happen, but what actually takes place" (p. 12).

Programs based on an emergent curriculum often start with general or specific themes the staff and children have brainstormed together and go on from there, responding to children's interest and concerns as they evolve over the course of time. Such curriculum themes are broad topics that give the program an overall learning focus. They are concerned with the child and her world rather than academic subjects such as social studies and language arts. To support each theme, the learning centers of the classroom contribute specific learning activities for individuals and small groups, thus giving the program an integrated approach.

Curriculum themes can emerge from many sources: teachers' or children's expressed interests, science projects, a favorite book, a news item, a holiday, family concerns, or child development topics. A popular overall theme currently used by many programs concerns the environment and our use of it. Translated into children's terms, one such theme might read: "The Earth cares for us; we must care for the Earth." How could you and your team translate that into appropriate ongoing activities for the children?

Jones (1999) has a word of caution:

> Emergent curriculum is scary for some teachers. For those who haven't yet learned how to plan well, it may be too much to undertake. For those with some practice in observing and reflecting on child behavior, it's a well-timed challenge in taking children's interests seriously and becoming co-players with them. (p. 16)

Using Curriculum Webs in Planning

Many programs are currently using a process known as "webbing" to explore broad curriculum ideas and convert them into activities. Team members (and in most instances, children) brainstorm ideas at a planning session. The team leader writes these ideas on easel paper or a chalkboard, connecting each idea with a line to any other ideas deriving from it, eventually creating what looks like a spider web of topics. Jones and Nimmo (1994) discuss such webs:

> A web is a tentative plan. It doesn't tell you exactly what will happen or in what order. That depends in large part on the children's response. So, first you plan and then you start trying your ideas, paying attention to what happens, evaluating, and moving on with further activities. (p. 11)

What is the advantage of doing webbing to help plan your curriculum? Jones and Nimmo believe "it gives a staff of adults a chance to explore the possibilities of any material or idea in order to make decisions about use" (p. 11). This process can also invite children and even parents to brainstorm ideas. The results are known as an "emergent curriculum," one that evolves from the needs and interests of the adult–child classroom community.

For example, to make a web of topics about the curriculum theme "we must care for the Earth," the leader writes "caring for the Earth" in the middle of a sheet of newsprint and asks the group to brainstorm ideas about this theme. As the leader enters on the paper the topics mentioned, she draws lines from the initial topic to subtopics leading from it. This first rather informal web might look like Figure 12–4, Curriculum Web—Caring for the Earth.

Next, the team considers all of the ideas generated to decide where to start with plans for actual classroom activities. Do any of these topics or subtopics strike a chord with the planners? What about the children? Have any of them shown a strong interest in any of these topics? Jones and Nimmo suggest: "In deciding what interests to plan for and actively support, teachers need to assess the potential of any interest for in-depth learning by both the individual child and other members of the adult–child classroom community" (p. 33). In other words, you may not know much about a particular topic yourself, but if it seems important to the children, you can learn about it along with them.

The assistant teacher on one team mentioned that the children had been collecting and bringing in pinecones but had no idea the pinecones contained seeds that would make new pine trees grow. The team then created a web about "trees" to see

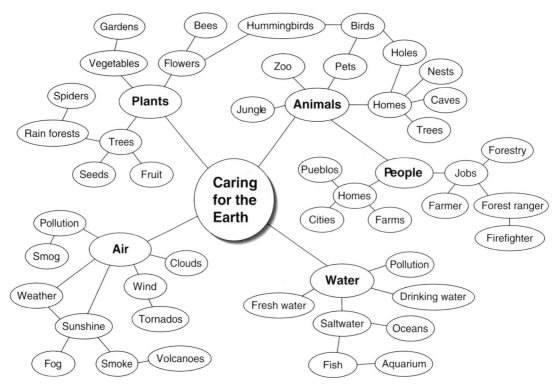

Figure 12–4   Curriculum Web—Caring for the Earth

if this topic would be broad yet interesting enough to build the curriculum around. They asked the children to contribute their ideas to the web. Figure 12–5 shows a curriculum web about trees.

Field Trips

Some teachers introduce new curriculum topics through real experiences outside the classroom, such as field trips. A field trip to look at trees is an exciting introduction that can include making bark rubbings; taking photos; gathering leaves, nuts, and cones; picking apples; or helping to plant a tree. In the Northeast, children can visit a "sugarbush," where maple syrup is tapped from maple trees; in the South, children can visit a pecan grove; in Florida, children can visit an orange grove; in Arizona, they can visit saguaro cactus trees; in Hawaii and Puerto Rico, they can look for coconuts; and in many areas, they can visit a tree nursery or perhaps a national park or national forest.

Walking trips around the center building are just as valuable as long distance traveling. Then, when the children return to the classroom, learning centers can integrate their emergent curriculum topic of trees with specific activities. Following are some examples:

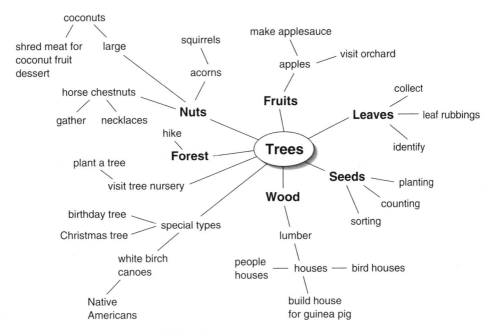

Figure 12–5   Curriculum Web—Trees

Block Center: Build a park; put twigs in a clay base for trees. Build a house for the guinea pig.

Book Center: Have available and read books about trees to individuals and small groups. Following are some suggestions:

> *Baseball Bats for Christmas* (Kusugak, 1990)
>
> *The Bee Tree* (Polacco, 1993)
>
> *Brother Eagle, Sister Sky* (Jeffers, 1991)
>
> *Every Time I Climb a Tree* (poems) (McCord, 1967)
>
> *Gregory Cool* (Binch, 1994)
>
> *The Great Kapok Tree* (Cherry, 1990)
>
> *Jen and the Great One* (Eyvindson, 1990)
>
> *Pablo's Tree* (Mora, 1994)
>
> *The Tree* (Jeunesse & de Bourgoing, 1989)
>
> *We're Going on a Bear Hunt* (Rosen, 1989)

Dramatic Play Center: Have prop boxes to support pretending themes such as "Going on a Bear Hunt," "Being a Forest Ranger or a Tree Nursery Worker," "Living in a Tree House," and "Visiting a Rain Forest."

Manipulative/Math Center: Count nuts gathered or guess how many nuts or maple seeds are in a jar. Make a tree puzzle. String horse chestnuts. Measure how much new tree has grown.

Art Center: Press leaves. Make leaf rubbings or collages.

Large Motor Center: Climb the loft to a "tree house." Place a log on the playground for climbing.

Music Center: Play tapes and do creative movement to storm music (e.g., Groffe's *Grand Canyon Suite*). Make up words to familiar tunes (e.g., "This is the way the maple tree looks, when the wind blows wildly"—to the tune "Here We Go Round the Mulberry Bush").

Science Center: Discover what insects and birds live in nearby trees and how they help trees. Grow trees from seeds and seedlings. Plant a tree.

Woodworking Center: Bring in tree stumps for pounding nails. Bring in different kinds of wood.

Writing Center: Dictate a story about the class tree planting or a field trip to a tree.

Computer Area: Do activities with the CD-ROM *The Treehouse* (Library Video Company, 1-800-843-3620) program to explore a treehouse.

Sand Table: Have children gather twigs to use for trees in the sand table; bring in miniature houses, people, and cars.

Cooking: Make applesauce, nut bread, or cookies; shred coconut and cut up fruits for fruit salad.

How long should you continue with these activities? You must be aware of the responses of the children. As long as they show interest and enthusiasm, keep the activities going. Make changes in the various learning centers when interest lags, using the ideas listed above, but especially using children's own suggestions. One thing should lead to another in an emergent curriculum, just as it did in your planning.

The learning centers themselves are the framework for an integrated curriculum if you stock them with materials and activities to support the theme or topic you have chosen. It is not necessary to change the entire classroom at once. Instead, try adding new tree activities to each of the centers as the need and interest arises. Safety and health, physical, cognitive, communication, creative, social, and emotional skills are accomplished as children work and play together in the learning centers. But you as a staff member must keep your eyes and ears open to children's interests, suggestions, and needs to keep the program evolving.

A Curriculum Theme from a Picture Book

In one program a staff member noticed that the children, especially the boys, became interested in the boy character doll that the teacher had purchased earlier to go along with the book *Carlos and the Squash Plant* (Stevens, 1993), which she was reading to the small groups. Everyone wanted to play with Carlos. At the weekly planning ses-

The boys became interested in the character doll from the book Carlos and the Squash Plant.

sion, the staff member asked whether curriculum plans could come from a doll and book like this. The lead teacher invited everyone, including the children, to try webbing the idea to see if something could come from it.

The team and the children became excited when the web filled up so easily with ideas and subtopics. After the initial meeting with the children, the team decided to make their own refined version of this web, showing learning centers and activities to support the Carlos project (see Figure 12–6). It was quite evident that almost any topic could become the focus for an emergent curriculum, especially a book the children enjoyed.

The Carlos project seemed to be a sound one, especially because of the children's strong interest in the story itself, with its large colorful illustrations. The story is about how Carlos, a Hispanic boy, helps his father harvest vegetables but gets into trouble with his mother because he won't wash his ears. Carlos loves the squash they grow because his mother makes his favorite food, *calabacitas,* from it. But he hates taking baths after working in the field. His mother warns him that if he doesn't wash his ears, a squash plant will grow in them; but Carlos doesn't listen, and that is what happens. The Spanish version of the story fills the lower half of every page, and the recipe for *calabacitas* appears at the end.

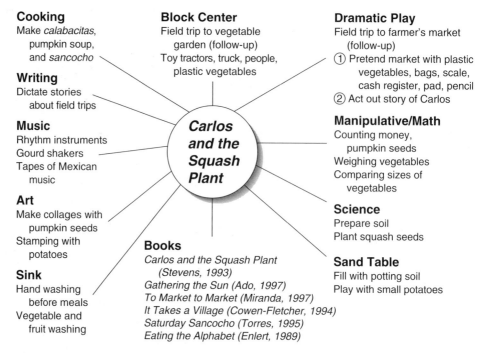

Cooking
Make *calabacitas*,
  pumpkin soup,
  and *sancocho*

Writing
Dictate stories
  about field trips

Music
Rhythm instruments
Gourd shakers
Tapes of Mexican
  music

Art
Make collages with
  pumpkin seeds
Stamping with
  potatoes

Sink
Hand washing
  before meals
Vegetable and
  fruit washing

Block Center
Field trip to vegetable
  garden (follow-up)
Toy tractors, truck, people,
  plastic vegetables

Carlos and the Squash Plant

Books
Carlos and the Squash Plant
  (Stevens, 1993)
Gathering the Sun (Ado, 1997)
To Market to Market (Miranda, 1997)
It Takes a Village (Cowen-Fletcher, 1994)
Saturday Sancocho (Torres, 1995)
Eating the Alphabet (Enlert, 1989)

Dramatic Play
Field trip to farmer's market
  (follow-up)
① Pretend market with plastic
    vegetables, bags, scale,
    cash register, pad, pencil
② Act out story of Carlos

Manipulative/Math
Counting money,
  pumpkin seeds
Weighing vegetables
Comparing sizes of
  vegetables

Science
Prepare soil
Plant squash seeds

Sand Table
Fill with potting soil
Play with small potatoes

Figure 12–6   Learning Center Curriculum Web—Carlos

The children were intrigued with the growing squash plant in Carlos's ear and had great discussions about whether such a thing could really happen. They couldn't wait to act out the story using a big straw *sombrero* to hide their pretend squash plant. They even included the classroom sink in their reenactment, making each Carlos character wash up before he came to supper.

A field trip to a vegetable garden the first week, followed by a trip to a farmer's market to buy squash the next week, were highlights of the time spent on this project. Finally, a Spanish speaking parent visited the class and read the story in Spanish. And, of course, everyone helped prepare *calabacitas* to eat!

After this successful experience, the staff members chose another favorite book and developed a new curriculum web from it. The lead teacher suggested a good follow-up book, one that supported the activities they had been pursuing. *A Kente Dress for Kenya* (Ford, 1996) was their eventual choice. The subtopic of markets (from the curriculum web) led them to read to the children about African markets in *It Takes a Village* (Cowen-Fletcher, 1994). It's illustrations of beautifully colored dresses reminded one of the children about the African dress her grandma made for her out of Kente cloth. When the girl wore her dress to class the next day, the teachers realized they had found a new topic.

They even found other books to support this new topic: *Kente Colors* (Chocolate, 1996), about what each of these colors represents in Africa; *Kofi and His Magic* (Angelou, 1996), about an African boy who weaves Kente cloth; and their best book discovery of all, *Boundless Grace* (Hoffman, 1995), about the African visit of their familiar African American girl, Grace—from their favorite book, *Amazing Grace* (Hoffman, 1991). There was even a Grace character doll that went with the book. One thing truly can lead to another in an early childhood curriculum.

Evaluates Curriculum Outcomes Through Child Observation and Team Conferences

How can you tell if your team plans have been successful? Evaluating curriculum outcomes requires you to collect information about the children and their actions. Which learning centers are they involved in? Which ones do they avoid? What do they have to say about the activities available? Are they able to complete them with ease? Do the activities hold their interest for long? What do they seem most enthusiastic about?

Information about the success of daily and weekly activities can be gathered during weekly team meetings. Team members can report on the activities they were responsible for, how they worked out, and what the children accomplished. The lead teacher usually jots down notes after the daily closing circle, when different children tell what they did and what they liked that day. She can share such information with the team as they plan for the next week. If problems arise about individual children, team members can plan to observe and record the child for brief time periods on several days.

Someone on the staff must step back unobtrusively and observe the child, giving special attention to the identified needs. This observation of the child's interactions with materials and other children can be recorded as a "running record" of the child's actions and words as they occur or as a checking off of behaviors on a checklist. You will be gathering observational data not only to help the child but also to assist the staff in evaluating the curriculum you all have planned.

Some programs make their own checklists to help observers focus on particular behaviors. Others use a prepared checklist such as the Child Involvement Checklist in Figure 12–7, which is arranged according to learning centers. The items are stated in positive terms. The observer should check any item she sees the child perform and place an "N" before any item for which there is *no opportunity to observe.* Thus, the blanks may indicate areas of need.

Team Conferences

As you summarize and interpret the results with members of the classroom team, remember that you are looking at one child's behavior and how she uses the learning centers you have set up. What are this child's strengths? Jot down several. What areas need strengthening? Jot them down, too. Is there a way you can help the child improve in the areas where you have left blanks? Are there other activities that would suit this child better? Team members can give their input as you plan the next week's

Child's Name_____

Time _____ Date _____

Observer _____

(Check items you see the child performing. Use *N* for *no opportunity to observe*.)

1. **Child in classroom**

   _____ Chooses activity area without a fuss

   _____ Stays with one activity long enough to complete it

   _____ Changes from one activity to another without a fuss

   _____ Plays with other children peacefully

   _____ Handles bathroom routine by himself/herself

   _____ Retreats to private area only infrequently

2. **Child in block-building center**

   _____ Carries blocks, fills and dumps, doesn't build

   _____ Builds in flat rows on floor or stacks vertically

   _____ Makes "bridges" (two blocks with space between connected by third block)

   _____ Makes "enclosures" (at least four blocks enclosing a space)

   _____ Makes representations, names buildings, role-plays

   _____ Builds in solitary manner

   _____ Builds parallel to other child(ren)

   _____ Builds cooperatively with other child(ren)

   _____ Follows block-building rules/limits without a fuss

3. **Child in book center**

   _____ Shows interest in the pictures in a book

   _____ Talks about the pictures

   _____ Pretends to read

   _____ Recognizes some words at sight

   _____ Handles books carefully

   _____ Asks adults to read to him or her

   _____ Use books in dramatic play

Figure 12–7 Child Involvement Checklist

Permission is granted by the publisher to reproduce these pages for evaluation and record keeping.

4. **Child in dramatic play center**

_____ Plays a role (pretends to be someone else)

_____ Makes believe in regard to inanimate objects (pretends about a thing)

_____ Makes believe in regard to situations and actions (pretends to do something or go somewhere)

_____ Stays with role for at least 10 minutes

_____ Interacts with others in his or her role

_____ Uses verbal communication during the role play

5. **Child in large motor center**

_____ Balances on a board

_____ Goes up and down steps easily

_____ Runs without falling

_____ Climbs easily

_____ Gets down from high places easily

_____ Jumps with both feet over an object

_____ Rides wheeled equipment with ease

_____ Throws a ball/beanbag

_____ Catches a ball/beanbag

6. **Child in manipulative/math center**

_____ Stacks objects with ease

_____ Fastens and unfastens buttons

_____ Fastens and unfastens zippers

_____ Threads objects on a string

_____ Laces shoes or a lacing frame

_____ Makes puzzles easily

_____ Traces around an object

_____ Crayons inside a space fairly well

_____ Stays with activity until finished

7. **Child in art center**

_____ Handles materials without assistance from teachers or other adults

_____ Paints with brushes

_____ Does finger painting

_____ Plays with dough/clay

(continued)

_____ Cuts well with scissors

_____ Uses paste or glue appropriately

_____ Mixes colors with understanding

_____ Uses materials creatively

8. **Child in music center**

_____ Plays record player without adult help

_____ Sings songs by himself/herself

_____ Sings songs with others

_____ Participates in movement activities

_____ Plays rhythm instrument

_____ Shows enjoyment of musical activities

9. **Child in science center**

_____ Explores materials in area

_____ Asks questions about materials

_____ Brings in new materials for area

_____ Uses senses to examine things

_____ Counts materials accurately up to _____

_____ Sorts materials accurately by size, shape, and color

_____ Shows understanding of likeness and difference

_____ Participates in recording/record-keeping

_____ Takes care of classroom plants, animals

10. **Child in sand/water center**

_____ Becomes absorbed in sand/water play

_____ Respects established rules or limits

_____ Helps regulate number of children playing

_____ Can share or take turns with classroom materials without too much fuss

_____ Uses sand/water in imaginative ways

_____ Talks about what he or she is doing

11. **Child in woodworking center**

_____ Handles tools with confidence

_____ Pounds in nails

_____ Saws wood

_____ Makes things out of wood

Figure 12–7 *(Continued)*

_____ Uses vise without help

_____ Respects rules or limits

12. Child in cooking center

_____ Peels or slices fruit or vegetables with knife

_____ Uses utensils with minimum adult help

_____ Uses names of utensils and foods

_____ Understands recipe chart

_____ Talks with others about what he or she is doing

13. Child in outdoor playground

_____ Uses swings without adult help

_____ Uses slides with confidence

_____ Climbs to top of monkey bars

_____ Gets down from high places without help

_____ Runs without falling

_____ Participates with others in play

14. Child's health condition

_____ Has good attendance

_____ Is seldom ill

_____ Looks generally healthy

_____ Seldom complains about feeling sick

_____ Goes to sleep at nap time

_____ Eats most of lunch

_____ Does not get tired easily

15. Child's visual and auditory skills

_____ Makes comments or notices new pictures or materials

_____ Recognizes his or her written name

_____ Plays lotto or visual matching games easily

_____ Matches things of similar color

_____ Matches things of similar shape

_____ Identifies sounds in sound games

_____ Listens to directions

_____ Listens to stories

(continued)

16. Child's communication skills

_____	Talks with adults
_____	Talks with other children
_____	Talks with animals, dolls, or toys
_____	Adults can understand him/her
_____	Children can understand him/her
_____	Uses whole sentences
_____	Seldom uses "baby talk"
_____	Talks spontaneously when playing
_____	Talks spontaneously at mealtime
_____	Uses language props such as toy telephone
_____	Starts conversations sometimes
_____	Expresses his or her feelings in words

17. Child's self-image

_____	Can identify himself/herself by first and last name
_____	Looks at you without covering face when you speak to him/her
_____	Seeks other children to play with or will join in play when asked by others
_____	Seldom shows fear of new or different things
_____	Is seldom destructive of materials or disruptive of activities
_____	Smiles; seems happy much of the time
_____	Shows pride in his/her accomplishments
_____	Stands up for his/her rights
_____	Moves confidently with good motor control

18. Child with others

_____	Gets along well with other children
_____	Gets along well with adults
_____	Is willing to share
_____	Is willing to take turns
_____	Has special friend or friends
_____	Plays table games with another child
_____	Joins in group games and activities
_____	Is willing to help in cleanup
_____	Seldom shows hostility toward others
_____	Generally follows rules

Figure 12–7 *(Continued)*

activities—not to single out this child but to integrate her special activities into the plans for everyone.

If this process seems too complex and time consuming, remember that you are looking at only one child at a time and that this is the kind of information you need to be able to help in the child's development and in the staff's future planning. Start by observing children who are having problems in the classroom learning centers. Later as you involve them in activities to improve their skills, you can begin to observe the other children, one at a time, as well. Have more than one team member use the same observation form to look at and record their views of the child. They can then present their findings to the rest of the team at the weekly conference.

SUMMARY

All members of the classroom team, including volunteers, should be involved in the planning process. Then they will be more committed and willing to carry out the plans. Regular weekly planning sessions should address where the group is, where it wants to go, and how it can get there. Team members need to share responsibility for managing various tasks and duties. When team members encounter interpersonal problems, a leader can bring them together using verbal and nonverbal communication, as well as writing and listening skills, to resolve the problem.

Flexibility is the keynote for planning a daily schedule. Using time blocks to indicate the order of the various activities is more helpful than schedules that set specific times for activities. Children should not be forced to hurry up and finish. Instead, the time blocks themselves can be lengthened. The curriculum itself can be planned using emergent themes derived from children's or teachers' interests or needs, science projects, popular children's books, or child development topics. Children can offer input

into planning by brainstorming with the adult team and having their ideas added to the curriculum web being created. Learning centers are then stocked with materials to support the curriculum topic and to integrate the activities being planned. New curriculum topics often emerge naturally as follow-ups of activities the children show interest in.

Evaluating curriculum outcomes is accomplished during weekly planning sessions, when team members bring in data they have collected about what children accomplished in the particular learning centers they were in charge of. The lead teacher gathers information from children during the daily closing circle. When problems arise with certain children, team members take turns observing and recording the children's actions in the various learning centers using a Child Involvement Checklist. After interpreting the results, the team can make plans for these individuals to be integrated into the plans for everyone. Curriculum planning is thus an ongoing process that everyone contributes to, giving everyone ownership in the program—even the children.

LEARNING ACTIVITIES

1. Read Chapter 12 and write out answers to Question Sheet 12.

2. Meet with your trainer or instructor and discuss answers to Question Sheet 12.

3. View one of the videos listed and make 10 file cards with specific ideas for daily, weekly, monthly, and yearly plans.

4. Read one or more of the references cited or suggested readings and add 10 cards to your file, with specific ideas for managing your program more effectively. Include reference sources on each card.

5. Participate in a team planning session. Take notes on the topics discussed and resolved. Make a curriculum web for a topic of interest to the children or staff.

6. Write out suggestions for meeting with and helping two team members with interpersonal problems.

7. Choose one of the subtopics from the web and work up a plan for activities in each of the learning centers to support the subtopic.

8. Observe a child using the Child Involvement Checklist in Figure 12–7. Interpret the results and decide on activities to help him become involved in particular learning centers.

9. Make an evaluation of the current curriculum using data gathered from circle time meetings with the children and observations using the Child Involvement Checklist in Figure 12–7. How can the curriculum be changed to respond to any concerns?

10. Complete the Chapter 12 Evaluation Sheet and return it to your trainer or college supervisor.

QUESTION SHEET 12

1. Why is team planning so important?

2. If interpersonal communication between team members breaks down, how can it be restored?

3. What do you need to know about the children in your care to plan for their arrival?

4. What are time blocks and for what purpose are they used?

5. How can you determine the length of the time blocks?

6. How is the management of time different in Reggio Emilia schools from American preschools?

7. What happens to nonsleeping children during nap time?

8. What is the purpose of a total group activity such as circle time?

10. What is the advantage of using curriculum webs for curriculum planning?

11. How can you convert the data from a curriculum web into specific activities for the children?

12. How long should activities go on in the classroom before you set up new activities? How can you tell?

13. What kinds of activities should you choose for a follow-up of your original activities? Why did you choose them?

14. How can you evaluate an emergent curriculum like this?

15. How can you use data from your evaluation to improve the curriculum?

REFERENCES

Beaty, J. J. (2002). *Observing development of the young child.* Upper Saddle River, NJ: Merrill/Prentice Hall.

Berl, P. (1998). Becoming planners: Finding time and insight. *Child Care Information Exchange, 119,* 61–63.

Dizes, D. E., & Dorl, J. (1999). Your mop is my guitar: Emergent curriculum in our classroom. *Young Children, 54*(4), 14–16.

Gandini, L. (2002). The story and foundations of the Reggio Emilia approach. In Fu, R., Stremmel, A. J., & Hill, L. T. (Eds.), *Teaching and learning: Collaborative exploration of the Reggio Emilia approach.* Upper Saddle River, NJ: Merrill/Prentice Hall.

Jones, E. (1999). An emergent curriculum expert offers this afterthought. *Young Children, 54*(4), 16.

Jones, E., & Nimmo, J. (1994). *Emergent curriculum.* Washington, DC: National Association for the Education of Young Children.

Petersen, D. (2000). Using transitions to promote literacy in preschool and primary classrooms. *Young Children, 55*(4), 24–26.

Seefeldt, C. (1995). Art—A serious work. *Young Children, 50*(3), 39–45.

SUGGESTED READINGS

Booth, C. (1997). The fiber project: One teacher's adventure toward emergent curriculum. *Young Children, 52*(5), 79–85.

Carter, M., & Jones, E. (1990). The teacher as observer: The director as role model. *Child Care Information Exchange, 75,* 27–30.

Dighe, J. (1993). Children and the earth. *Young Children, 48*(3), 58–62.

Edwards, C., Gandini, L., & Forman, G. (Eds.). (1993). *The hundred languages of children.* Norwood, NJ: Ablex.

Hendrick, J. (1997). *First steps toward teaching the Reggio way.* Upper Saddle River, NJ: Merrill/Prentice Hall.

Hughes, E. (2002). Planning meaningful curriculum: A mini story of children and teachers learning together. *Childhood Education, 78*(3), 134–139.

Jones, E., & Nimmo, J. (1996). Using circle time as a hub of curriculum. *Child Care Information Exchange, 109,* 44–46.

Nunnelley, J. C. (1990). Beyond turkeys, Santas, snowmen, and hearts: How to plan innovative curriculum themes. *Young Children, 46*(1), 24–29.

Pelo, A. (1997). "Our school's not fair!" A story about emergent curriculum. *Young Children, 52*(7), 57–61.

Satomi, I. T., Morris, V. G., & Cordeau-Young, C. (1997). Field trips in early childhood settings: Expanding the walls of the classroom. *Early Childhood Education Journal, 25*(2), 141–146.

Seefeldt, C. (Ed.). (1999). *The early childhood curriculum: Current findings in theory and practice.* New York: Teachers College.

Spangler, C. B. (1997). The sharing circle: A child-centered curriculum. *Young Children, 52*(5), 74–78.

Taylor, B. J. (2002). *Early childhood program management: People and procedures.* Upper Saddle River, NJ: Merrill/Prentice Hall.

Workman, S., & Anziano, M. C. (1993). Curriculum webs: Weaving connections from children to teachers. *Young Children, 48*(2), 4–9.

Wortham, S. C. (1996). *The integrated classroom: The assessment-curriculum link in early childhood education.* Upper Saddle River, NJ: Merrill/Prentice Hall.

CHILDREN'S BOOKS

Ada, A. F. (1997). *Gathering the sun.* New York: Lothrop, Lee & Shepard.

Angelou, M. (1996). *Kofi and his magic.* New York: Clarkson Potter.

Binch, C. (1994). *Gregory Cool.* New York: Dial.

Cherry, L. (1990). *The great kapok tree.* San Diego, CA: Harcourt.

Chocolate, D. (1996). *Kente colors.* New York: Walker & Co.

Cowen-Fletcher, J. (1994). *It takes a village.* New York: Scholastic.

Ehlert, L. (1989). *Eating the alphabet: Fruits & vegetables from A to Z.* San Diego: Harcourt Brace.

Eyvindson, J. (1990). *Jen and the great one.* Winnipeg, Canada: Pemmican.

Ford, J. G. (1996). *A Kente dress for Kenya.* New York: Scholastic.

Hoffman, M. (1991). *Amazing Grace.* New York: Dial.

Hoffman, M. (1995). *Boundless Grace.* New York: Dial.

Jeffers, S. (1991). *Brother Eagle, Sister Sky.* New York: Dial.

Jeunesse, G., & de Bourgoing, P. (1989). *The tree.* New York: Scholastic.

Kusugak, M. A. (1990). *Baseball bats for Christmas.* Toronto: Annick Press.

McCord, D. (1967). *Every time I climb a tree.* Boston: Little, Brown.

Miranda, A. (1997). *To market to market.* San Diego: Harcourt Brace.

Mora, P. (1994). *Pablo's tree.* New York: Macmillan.

Polacco, P. (1993). *The bee tree.* New York: Philomel.

Rosen, M. (1989). *We're going on a bear hunt.* New York: McElderry.

Stevens, J. R. (1993). *Carlos and the squash plant.* Flagstaff, AZ: Northland.

Torres, L. (1995). *Saturday Sancocho.* New York: Farrar Straus Giroux.

VIDEOTAPES

Carter, M. (Producer). *Children at the center.* St. Paul, MN: Redleaf Press.

Carter, M., Felstiner, S., & Pelo, A. (Producers). *Thinking big: Extending Emergent Curriculum.* St. Paul, MN: Redleaf Press.

Center for Early Education and Development. (Producer). *Looking at young children: Observing in early childhood settings.* New York: Teachers College Press.

Creative Educational Video (Producer). *Children at work.* St. Paul, MN: Redleaf Press.

Curtis, D., & Carter, M. (Producers). *Setting sail.* St. Paul, MN: Redleaf Press.

Dodge, D. T. (Producer). *The creative curriculum for early childhood.* St. Paul, MN: Redleaf Press.

Helm, J. H., Beneke, S., & Steinheimer, K. (Producers). *Windows on learning: A framework for making decisions.* Washington, DC: National Association for the Education of Young Children.

National Association for the Education of Young Children. (Producer). *An idea blossoms: Integrated curriculum.* Washington, DC: Author.

CHAPTER 12 EVALUATION SHEET
PROVIDING PROGRAM MANAGEMENT

1. Student _____

2. Trainer _____

3. Center where training occurred _____

4. Beginning date _____ Ending date _____

5. Describe what student did to accomplish General Objective.

    _____

    _____

6. Describe what student did to accomplish Specific Objectives.

    Objective 1 _____

    _____

    Objective 2 _____

    _____

    Objective 3 _____

    _____

7. Evaluation of student's Learning Activities

    _____

    _____

Comments:

Permission is granted by the publisher to reproduce this page for evaluation and record keeping.

Promoting
Professionalism

SPECIFIC OBJECTIVES

____ Makes a commitment to the early childhood profession

____ Behaves ethically toward children and their families

____ Takes every opportunity to improve professional growth

What is a **professional** in the early childhood field, and what behaviors make a person a professional? Whether you are a college student, a teaching assistant, a parent volunteer, a Child Development Associate (CDA) candidate, or a teacher, this is an important question for you to consider carefully. What qualities do professionals in this particular field possess? What will be expected of you that is different from what you are already doing?

Our professional organization, the National Association for the Education of Young Children (NAEYC) has announced new standards for college and university programs that prepare early childhood professionals. By spring 2003, "all higher education institutions seeking NCATE (National Council for the Accreditation of Teacher Education) accreditation must have responded to these standards or to equivalent standards approved by NAEYC." (Hyson, 2002, p. 78) The standards can be summarized as follows:

1. Promoting child development and learning

2. Building family and community relationships

3. Observing, documenting, and assessing to support young children and families

4. Teaching and learning

    a. Connecting with children and families

    b. Using developmentally effective approaches

    c. Understanding content knowledge in early education

    d. Building meaningful curriculum

5. Becoming a professional

To become a professional, "candidates identify and conduct themselves as members of the early childhood profession. They know and use ethical guidelines and other professional standards related to early childhood practice. They are continuous, collaborative learners who demonstrate knowledgeable, reflective, and critical perspectives on their work, making informed decisions that integrate knowledge from a variety of sources. They are informed advocates for sound educational practices and policies" (p. 78).

Hyson explains that these standards offer "a *shared vision* for the future preparation of *all* who work with young children and their families. The details may differ, but at every level and in every setting the focus is the same. Competent early childhood educators need knowledge, skills, and professional dispositions in the five core areas." (p. 78) The complete document "NAEYC Standards for Early Childhood Professional Preparation: Baccalaureate or Initial Licensure Level" may be downloaded from www.naeyc.org/profdev.

This chapter discusses three important categories of professional development that many early childhood professionals themselves agree on. To be considered a professional in the field of early childhood you must do the following:

1. Make a commitment to the profession.
   a. Gain a knowledge base in the field.
   b. Complete some type of training.
   c. Complete some type of service.
2. Behave ethically toward children, their families, and your co-workers.
   a. Show respect for all.
   b. Demonstrate caring for all children.
   c. Respect privacy.
3. Continue to improve your professional growth.
   a. Become involved in ongoing training.
   b. Join a professional organization, read its publications, and network with colleagues.
   c. Contribute something of value to the field.

The early childhood field is broad, with its principal components including infant care, child care, child teaching, teacher training, health care, children with special needs, family involvement, and administration of programs. The children referred to include infants and toddlers (birth to 3 years old), preschoolers (3 to 5 years), prekindergartners (4 to 5 years), kindergartners (5 to 6 years), and sometimes early elementary children (up to 7 or 8 years).

The programs designed for such children include child care in homes, centers, business and industrial settings, shopping malls, churches, hospitals, senior citizen centers, universities, and military bases. They also include Head Start programs, nursery school and preschool programs, prekindergarten and kindergarten school programs, and before- and after-school programs. These programs are operated by a variety of organizations including private individuals and companies, parent groups, community groups, service organizations, business and industry, public and private schools, religious organizations, the military, colleges and universities, health care facilities, and local, state, and federal government agencies.

The early childhood field is expanding rapidly to meet the needs of the increasing number of working parents, children at risk, and children with special needs, because of the growing realization that early childhood education can benefit all young children. With the increased demand for such services comes a growing concern about the quality of care and education offered to children and the qualifications of the caregivers and teachers involved.

Parents are concerned about the lack of full-day programs, the character and training of those who are caring for their children, the activities offered during the program day, and how they will be able to afford the care. Teachers and caregivers are concerned about their low salaries, how to better themselves in this field, and how they will be able to meet new job qualifications or licensure.

Government regulatory agencies are concerned about how to ensure that all programs meet minimum standards. Professional groups are concerned about how to maintain quality programs when various state licensure regulations for both early childhood facilities and their teaching staffs vary so widely. Colleges and universities are concerned about how to change their course offerings and degree requirements to meet new state regulations and national standards. These are a few of the issues facing this rapidly expanding field that is struggling to become a recognized profession.

The commitment that an early childhood worker makes to this exciting new profession is an important one. Ours is a helping profession, which means that we must put our clients—the children and families we serve—first in our professional lives. Translated into practical terms, our commitment means that we may have to come in early and stay late to make sure that classes are covered and children are served; that we may have to take children home if the bus breaks down or a parent fails to come; that we may miss coffee breaks or even lunch if a classroom emergency demands our attention; that we may have to spend many hours at home preparing activities for the following day.

In other words, our own needs are secondary when it comes to our professional lives. A professional commitment in any of the helping professions requires us to give of ourselves without expecting to be paid for every hour we contribute. Such a commitment means investing time and energy. We may have to work extra hours or even come in when we are not feeling up to par, because a particular situation demands it of us. This behavior is often quite different from that of the paraprofessional or nonprofessional. Often people working part time or paid on an hourly basis look at their work in terms of the hours they put in. They may be reluctant to respond to demands made on them outside of their normal working hours. The professional, on the other hand, must take a broader view of program demands and be willing to sacrifice time and energy if the need arises. *Giving of oneself without expecting a particular reward marks the true professional in fields such as early childhood education.*

A commitment to the early childhood profession means you may have to come in early and stay late to make sure children are served.

 MAKES A COMMITMENT TO THE EARLY
CHILDHOOD PROFESSION

Knowledge Base in the Field of Early Childhood

Professionals in every field must have a familiarity with and understanding of the knowledge on which the field is founded. In early childhood education, this includes familiarity with the foundations of early childhood education and its principal contributors such as Rousseau, Pestalozzi, and Froebel, from the 18th and 19th centuries; Montessori, Pratt, and Mitchell, from the early 20th century; the contributions from the field of psychology by Freud, Gesell, Erikson, Piaget, Vygotsky, and Gardner; the kindergarten and nursery school movements in the United States at the turn of the century; the day-care movement given impetus during World War II; the Head Start and the compensatory education movement born during the War on Poverty of the 1960s; particular curriculum models in vogue today such as those developed by High/Scope, Montessori, or Reggio Emilia; and current research with implications for early childhood development such as the new brain research.

In addition, professionals in the field must have a knowledge of child development, health, psychology, sociology, education, emergent literacy, children's literature, art, music, dance, physical education, special education, and multicultural education because these fields affect young children and their families.

Professionals also need to understand conflicting child development theories such as the maturationist, the behaviorist, and the constructivist points of view. They should be familiar with learning theories such as discovery or exploratory play as they apply to young children to design what is termed *developmentally appropriate practice* for the children in their care.

It is especially important that professionals in the field be aware of the guidelines for developmentally appropriate practice (DAP), as spelled out by our professional organization, the National Association for the Education of Young Children (NAEYC), and being implemented by programs across the country. The revised *Developmentally Appropriate Practice in Early Childhood Programs* (Bredekamp & Copple, 1997) is fast becoming a standard for program practices throughout the country. As noted by Wilt and Monroe (1998): "The guidelines in both instances were developed by a wide variety of leaders in our field. They have helped to crystallize the focus of early childhood educators as to what appropriate educational practice for young children looks like" (p. 18).

The guidelines for developmentally appropriate practice are based on the belief that children's own needs and interests should form the basis for the educational program. Some of the basic guidelines professionals need to be aware of include the following (adapted from Bredekamp & Copple, 1997; Wilt & Monroe, 1998):

1. *Wholeness of the child:* Each area of child development affects every other area.

2. *Active involvement:* Children must actively engage in their own learning.

3. *Interaction with adults and peers:* Learning occurs when children interact with those around them.

4. *Authentic experiences:* Real-life experiences are most effective in children's learning.

5. *Appropriate learning activities:* Hands-on, concrete, and exploratory play activities are most appropriate.

6. *Integrated curriculum:* Activities in each of the learning centers are tied to a central theme.

7. *Intrinsic motivation:* Children become involved in learning activities because of their own interest and excitement.

8. *Authentic assessment:* Evaluation of children's progress comes from ongoing observations and interactions between children and staff members.

In November 1993, the NAEYC first adopted a position statement concerning "A Conceptual Framework for Early Childhood Professional Development." This framework defines what all early childhood professionals must know and be able to do (see Figure 13–1). It is a never-ending task to keep up with developments in this dynamic field. True professionals make the effort to keep abreast of this knowledge by taking college courses and workshops, attending in-service training, reading textbooks and journal articles, inviting knowledgeable guest speakers to their programs, attending conferences where such information is disseminated, and visiting other early childhood programs that feature particular curriculum ideas.

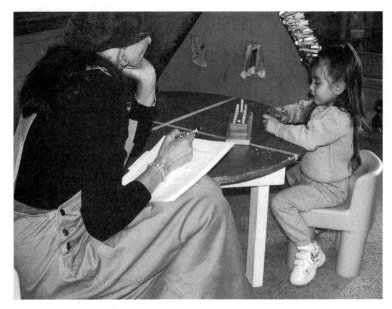

Professional guidelines remind us that evaluation of children's progress comes from ongoing observation of children.

Figure 13–1 Common Knowledge and Abilities of Early Childhood Professionals

Adapted from "NAEYC Position Statement: A Conceptual Framework for Early Childhood Professional Development" by the National Association for the Education of Young Children, 1994, *Young Children, 49,* p. 72. Copyright 1994 by NAEYC. Reprinted by permission.

1. Demonstrates an understanding of child development and applies this knowledge in practice

2. Observes and assesses children's behavior in planning and individualizing teaching practices and curriculum

3. Establishes and maintains a safe and healthy environment for children

4. Plans and implements developmentally appropriate curriculum that advances all areas of children's learning and development, including social, emotional, intellectual, and physical competence

5. Establishes supportive relationships with children and implements developmentally appropriate techniques of guidance and group management

6. Establishes and maintains positive and productive relationships with families

7. Supports the development and learning of individual children and recognizes that children are best understood in the context of their family, culture, and society

8. Demonstrates an understanding of the early childhood profession and makes a commitment to professionalism

New Knowledge

In addition to the commonly recognized knowledge about child development and learning, professionals must always be open to new knowledge as it is discovered by research and technology, developed by professionals in the far corners of the Earth, or even revealed by the children themselves through our observation of them. What a surprise it was for literacy specialists from Argentina to discover that young children could emerge into reading and writing without being formally taught. (Ferreiro & Teberosky, 1982) Children themselves were actually teaching the professionals what they could do by coming into kindergarten programs already knowing how to read. Then it was up to literacy specialists to discover how this had happened and what they could do to support this development. Often it takes many years for professionals to convert such theory into practice.

We must be ever-vigilant to new ideas that may emerge and new ways of doing things that may come forth. The door to understanding child development has not been closed. What we know about young children is perhaps only "the tip of the iceberg." Not so many years ago we believed that infants and young children were "blank slates" waiting to be filled by us with knowledge. Now we realize that children come into this world with the ability to create their own knowledge. Today we talk about six areas of child development that need to be considered: physical, cognitive, language, social, emotional, and creative. Is that all there is? Or might there be undiscovered aspects in the development of the human being that we may not yet have recognized. What about spiritual development? Have we ever thought about this? We tend to see what we look for. That is not enough. We need to keep our antennas up for new insights. (See Beaty, 2002, "The Missing Component of Child Development.")

We need to learn much more about how young children initially operate from the right hemisphere of the brain that controls visual perception, sensory stimulation, emotions, holistic thinking, imagination, humor, art, music, and creativity; and how to help them cross over to adult thinking modes using the left hemisphere of the brain controlling analytic, logical, sequential, and abstract thinking, reading, writing, and math. Or should we first consider the opposite: how adults can regain right hemisphere functions in their own lives? Perhaps the children can teach us. We need to examine the current rise of hyperactivity in children from a positive point of view. How can it help them? Perhaps it is we who are out of sync with the world, not them. How can we change the way we act and react with "hyperactive children" to make a positive difference in their lives?

We need to consider the enormous amount of new knowledge that is surfacing about human development to determine how and whether it can be applied to child development, teaching, and learning. For instance, as Greenspan (1997) notes:

> In recent years, through our research and that of others, we have found unexpected common origins for the mind's highest capacities: intelligence, morality, and sense of self. We have charted critical stages in the mind's early growth, most of which occur even before our first thoughts are registered. At each stage certain critical experiences are necessary. Contrary to traditional notions, these experiences are not cognitive but are types of subtle

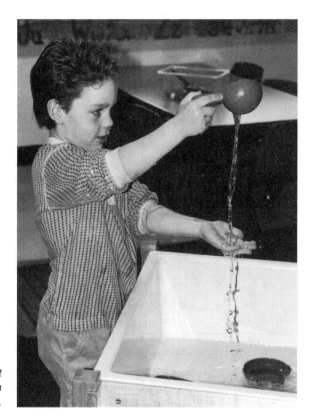

Children learn from teachers but at the same time they teach teachers about children.

emotional exchanges. In fact, emotions, not cognitive stimulation, serve as the mind's primary architect. (p. 1)

How can such new knowledge be used in the early childhood classroom? Professionals in the field will be the ones applying such information now and in the future. Professionals should be persons who do not close their minds to new concepts. They understand that *teaching and learning are reciprocal functions:* teachers teach children, but at the same time they also learn from the children. Children learn from teachers, but at the same time they also teach them things about themselves. All professionals can help to expand this knowledge base in the field of early childhood education by keeping alert for new ideas and sharing their inspirations, observations, and experiences with others in the field.

Training Opportunities in the Field of Early Childhood

Professionals in every field must complete some type of formal training. The field of early childhood requires various types and levels of training or education depending upon the position and state requirements. Child care workers are often required to have 12 to 18 credit hours of courses in early childhood. Teachers may be required to have a two-year or four-year college degree.

Many child-care providers, on the other hand, may have started their early childhood careers informally as baby sitters in their own homes. Then as their own children enter a child care program, those that show interest or promise may be asked to volunteer in a classroom. If the program has an in-service training component, they may be able to receive training and eventual certification from a Head Start Program, a local social services department, or a Military Family Child Care Program. As one director of a Marine Corps Family Care Program reports:

> It has taken quite a while to move providers from seeing themselves as babysitters to looking upon themselves as child care professionals. They are there now. Our next task is to help parents understand the difference. (Nielsen, 2002, p. 13)

Child Development Associate

In addition to the traditional modes of training for early childhood education, there is another increasingly popular method for developing the necessary competence to teach in the field: Child Development Associate (CDA) training, assessment, and credentialing. CDA training is competency-based and performance-based, which means that a certain percentage of the training must occur *in* the early childhood classroom and that the trainee must demonstrate competence with children in such a setting.

The Child Development Associate program emerged in the 1970s as a collaborative effort on the part of early childhood professionals and the federal government, represented by the Administration for Children, Youth, and Families (ACYF), to create a new category of early childhood professional—the Child Development Associate. From the beginning, the program had two separate parts: training that was done by local colleges or early childhood programs themselves and credentialing that was done by the national office (Child Development Associate National Credentialing Program).

Today that program has consolidated both training and credentialing under a new CDA Professional Preparation Program offered by the Council for Early Childhood Professional Recognition, 1341 G. Street, NW, Suite 400, Washington, DC, 20005-3105. Under the program, a candidate may choose to earn his or her CDA credential in one of two ways: through the CDA Professional Preparation Program or by direct assessment. Because many CDA candidates use this text *Skills for Preschool Teachers* for their training, a separate section, Appendix A: "Becoming a CDA: Child Development Associate," has been included. Candidates will find information relating to the two methods of preparation for three types of credentials: center-based, family child care, and home visitor. In addition, more in-depth information is presented on developing the Professional Resource File and how to prepare competency statements.

Why Become a CDA?

Why should you become a CDA? First, it will help you in your work as a classroom teacher or assistant. It will help you improve your skills in working with young children and their families; in setting up an appropriate physical environment; in keeping your children safe and healthy; in providing opportunities for them to improve their physical, cognitive, language, and creative development; and in planning activities and managing individuals and groups.

It will also help you to assess your strengths and areas needing strengthening so that you will be able to make the necessary improvements. You will do this not only through self-evaluation and preparation, but also through the eyes of an early childhood professional, your advisor, whom you will come to know as a friend.

Receiving the CDA credential will elevate your status in your program and enhance the program's status in the community. In some instances, you may receive a promotion or salary raise. This credential may be worth college credit at certain institutions. Since the CDA is a national credential, your talents will also be more marketable in other states if you should move.

Finally, the CDA credential will induct you as a professional into the field of early childhood education. Some professions require a bachelor's degree for entry. The early childhood field is coming more and more to recognize the CDA as the first professional step in an ever-expanding career. Bredekamp (2000) collected a great deal of evidence of the individual impact of the CDA. For example:

> Carolyn Selph from Oklahoma stated, "For me it was a personal thing to think I could take a college class and be successful and continue through the years." Frances Pryor, who is now director of an NAEYC-accredited Head Start program in Florida, had this to say about receiving her CDA: "It was the most exciting day of my life. It helped me in all areas and motivated me to want to do more." (p. 18)

Licensing and Credentialing

Another important mark of professionals in any field is a credential. Professionals need a degree, license, or credential to certify that they are qualified in the field. Credentials of various kinds can be awarded to qualified individuals based on college courses or programs completed, workshops taken, training completed, tests taken, or types and amounts of experience. Licensing or credentialing bodies may be colleges and universities, state departments of education, local programs, or state or national agencies. Types of credentials vary from college degrees to workshop completion certificates. The NAEYC lists six levels of early childhood professional categories (see Figure 13–2).

Service Requirements in the Field of Early Childhood Education

All professions require their members to complete a certain amount of service to be recognized. Taking classroom courses or obtaining general college degrees does not qualify a person as a professional in early childhood. Field experience in an early childhood program or classroom is necessary for all credentials or degrees. The amount of experience varies according to the professional level as indicated in Figure 13–2. Although the levels reflect a conceptual framework rather than standard requirements, many certificates, degrees, or positions do require such service.

Professional Level I

Individuals employed in an early childhood professional role working under supervision and participating in training designed to lead to assessment of competencies or a degree

Professional Level II

Successful completion of CDA Professional Preparation Program or completion of systematic, comprehensive training program leading to CDA Credential through direct assessment

Successful completion of one-year early childhood certificate program

Professional Level III

Successful completion of associate degree from a program conforming to NAEYC guidelines, or

Successful completion of associate degree plus 30 units of professional studies in early childhood development or education including 300 hours of supervised teaching experience in an early childhood program, or

Successful demonstration of the knowledge, performance, and dispositions expected as outcomes of an associate degree program conforming to NAEYC guidelines

Professional Level IV

Successful completion of a baccalaureate degree from a program conforming to NAEYC guidelines, or

State certificate meeting NAEYC/NCATE certification guidelines, or

Successful completion of a baccalaureate degree in another field with more than 30 professional units in early childhood development/ education including 300 hours of supervised teaching experience, including 150 hours each for two of the following three age groups: infants and toddlers, 3- to-5-year-olds, or the primary grades, or

Successful demonstration of the knowledge, performance, and disposition expected as outcomes of a baccalaureate degree program conforming to NAEYC guidelines

Professional Level V

Successful completion of a master's degree in a program that conforms to NAEYC guidelines, or

Successful demonstration of the knowledge, performance, and disposition expected as outcomes of a master's degree program conforming to NAEYC guidelines

Professional Level VI

Successful completion of a Ph.D. or Ed.D. in a program conforming to NAEYC guidelines, or

Successful demonstration of the knowledge, performance, and disposition expected as outcomes of a doctoral degree program conforming to NAEYC guidelines

Figure 13–2 Early Childhood Professional Categories

Adapted from "NAEYC Position Statement: A Conceptual Framework for Early Childhood Professional Development" by the National Association for the Education of Young Children, 1994, *Young Children, 49*, p. 74. Copyright 1994 by NAEYC. Reprinted by permission.

Just to enter CDA training, for instance, a candidate must have completed 480 hours of direct experience working with children in a child-care setting.

Most child-care programs offer opportunities for students or volunteers from the community to gain work experience with children as teacher assistants, one of the first steps up the early childhood career ladder. Colleges and universities require early childhood majors to work a certain number of weeks as student teachers in nursery schools, prekindergartens, preschools, or child-care facilities.

Parents of preschool children often work as volunteers in their child's program to gain necessary experience that can lead to training or job placement in the field. Some training workshops or seminars are held on-site for participants to gain first-hand experience with children. Local child-care agencies can inform you of job opportunities that require specific amounts of training and can often direct you to the training opportunities available in the community.

BEHAVES ETHICALLY TOWARD CHILDREN AND THEIR FAMILIES

Shows Respect for All

A second important area of professionalism in early childhood education is that of ethical behavior, including confidential treatment of information about children and families. In addition to putting children and families first, professionals also demonstrate a positive attitude toward their clients at all times. No matter what the family background, no matter how serious the problems faced by the family, no matter what the past behavior of the child and family, true professionals retain an objective view of the situation and treat the child and family in a positive manner. Parents who abuse their children need your help just as much as or more than parents who treat their children positively. Low-income families deserve the same treatment as affluent families. Children from families of racial, ethnic, or religious backgrounds different from that of the teachers should be treated in the same respectful manner as all others. In other words, children are children—to be accepted, respected, and cherished along with their families by true professionals in the early childhood field.

Demonstrates Caring Toward All Children

Behaving ethically toward children includes relating to them in emotionally positive ways. Figure 13–3 lists positive traits every early child-care professional should exhibit. The original CDA program included these same personal capacities as part of the competencies that early childhood workers need to develop.

Your job is to demonstrate to every one of the children in your class every day that you care about them. Nonverbal cues such as smiling, laughing, talking to them, joking with them, putting a hand on a shoulder, giving them a hug, sitting close to them, or holding them on your lap let children know you care for them personally. You must

Professionals must demonstrate a positive attitude toward families at all times.

Figure 13–3 Personal Capacities of Early Childhood Professionals

1. Is sensitive to children's feelings and the quality of young thinking

2. Is ready to listen to children to understand their feelings

3. Uses nonverbal forms of communication and adapts adult language to maximize communication with children

4. Protects orderliness without sacrificing spontaneity and childlike exuberance

5. Accepts children's individuality and makes positive use of individual differences within the child's group

6. Exercises control without being threatening

7. Is emotionally responsive, takes pleasure in children's successes, and is supportive during times of trouble

8. Brings humor and imagination into the group

9. Is committed to maximizing the child's and family's strengths and potentials

demonstrate this feeling to every child, not to one or two special children. Picking out a favorite child and lavishing attention on her is unethical. Rejecting a child because he is whiny or aggressive or wears dirty clothing is also unethical. Ethical behavior requires you to respond with positive feelings to every child in your class.

Respects Privacy of Children, Families, and Co-Workers

As a preschool teacher, you are probably very much a "people person." You are undoubtedly interested in every aspect of the children and their families. Your position allows you to find out all kinds of information about them. You'll know good things and bad—about health problems, family problems, promotions, firings, new babies, new husbands or wives, and gossip.

As an early childhood professional, you have an ethical duty to treat all such information confidentially. If you hear other staff members gossiping, you should not join in, but remind them as tactfully as possible that this kind of information is confidential. If parents ply you with gossip about other parents or children, let them know in a diplomatic way that this information should not be shared.

Ethical behavior of this type also applies to the children. For example, you should not talk with parents about their children when the children are present. These conversations are confidential and can damage a child's self-concept. If parents start talking to you about their child while the child is standing nearby, tell them you prefer to talk at another time or that perhaps their child can play in another room while you chat. Parents who understand how professionally you treat information about them and others are bound to respect both you and your program.

NAEYC's Code of Ethical Conduct

In 1996 the National Association for the Education for Young Children presented *NAEYC's Code of Ethical Conduct: Guidelines for Responsible Behavior in Early Childhood Education.* The code sets forth important professional responsibilities toward children, families, colleagues, and community and society. As the *Preamble* notes:

> The ideals reflect the aspirations of practitioners. The principles are intended to guide conduct and assist practitioners in resolving ethical dilemmas encountered in the field. (p. 57)

An abbreviated overview of the revised (1997, p. 61) principles affecting the teaching staff as the guidelines apply to children and families is shown in Figure 13–4.

All professions have ethical standards. In a new and expanding profession such as early childhood it is important for practitioners to have such a code as a standard for behavior involving difficult moral actions and decisions. Copies of the complete code found in the brochure *Code of Ethical Conduct and Statement of Commitment* can be obtained from NAEYC, 1509 16th Street NW, Washington, DC, 20036-1426. Applying such standards in the day-to-day life of the classroom can be made easier if your staff explicitly addresses them as part of your preservice and inservice training. As noted by Brophy-Herb, Kostelnik, and Stein (2001):

Ethical Responsibilites to Children

P-1.1 Above all, we shall not harm children in any way. We shall not participate in practices that are disrespectful, degrading, dangerous, exploitative, intimidating, psychologically damaging, or physically harmful to children.

P-1.2 We shall not participate in any practices that discriminate against children by denying benefits, giving special advantages, or excluding them from programs or activities on the basis of their race, religion, gender, national origin, language, ability, or the status, behavior, or beliefs of their parents.

P-1.3 We shall involve all those with relevant knowledge (including staff and parents) in decisions concerning a child.

P-1.5 We shall be familiar with the symptoms of child abuse and neglect, including physical, sexual, verbal, and emotional abuse, and know and follow community and state laws that protect children against abuse and neglect.

P-1.6 When we have evidence of child abuse or neglect, we shall report it to the appropriate agency and follow up to make sure action has been taken.

Ethical Responsibilities to Families

P-2.1 We shall not deny family members access to their child's classroom.

P-2.2 We shall inform families of program philosophy, policies, and personnel qualifications and explain why we teach as we do.

P-2.4 We shall involve families in significant decisions affecting their child.

P-2.5 We shall inform the family of accidents involving their child.

P-2.6 Families shall be fully informed of any proposed research projects involving their children and shall have the opportunity to give or withhold consent without penalty.

P-2.7 We shall not engage in or support exploitation of families. We shall not use our relationship with a family for private advantage or personal gain.

P-2.9 We shall maintain confidentiality and respect the family's right to privacy.

Figure 13–4   Ethical Responsibilities to Children and Families (abbreviated overview)

From *NAEYC's code of ethical conduct and statement of commitment* by the National Association for the Education of Young Children, 1997. Washington, DC: Author. Reprinted with permission.

Ethical concepts and skills are best taught as part of a planned, multilevel approach that includes ample opportunities for facilitated discussions, personal reflections, examinations of professional codes of conduct, and explorations of systematic decision making models for making ethical judgments. (p. 81)

Training About Ethical Conduct

Such training can include: developing an awareness of values, ethics, and the NAEYC's Code of Ethical Conduct, differentiating ethical judgments from other kinds of judgments, analyzing ethical dilemmas, and applying NAEYC's Code of Ethical Conduct in daily practice. For many early childhood practitioners this may be the first time they have dealt with a formal code of ethics. You and your staff should read through the code to become familiar with it. You may be surprised to find that the code does not tell exactly how to handle every case. Instead, the guidelines are general rules of conduct that may be applied to different situations. The idea of the code is to help professionals determine broad categories of ethical and unethical behavior. As Brophy-Herb et al. (2001) note: "Adherence to a code of ethics distinguishes early childhood professionals from lay persons with no commitment to the field" (p. 81).

If you consider each of the guidelines carefully you may find that there is a difference between personal morality and professional ethics. For example, you may need more than a simple knowledge of right and wrong (personal morality) when dealing with a group of people from diverse backgrounds. What makes sense for an individual may not be in accord with agreed-on professional standards. As a professional you must act in accordance with the standards.

From such training you may be surprised to learn that not all dilemmas are ethical. For instance, determining whether to decide a conflict in favor of the child involved or to follow the teacher's previous direction is not an ethical dilemma but one that may reflect educational practices, priorities, convenience, or personal preference. Many ethical dilemmas have no clear-cut solution, but only a choice between two relatively undesirable ethical choices. In other words, there is not necessarily only one correct ethical response. (Brophy-Herb et al., 2001, p. 82) Nevertheless, having the NAEYC guidelines is a valuable starting point.

You may want to discuss any of the real ethical problems that have arisen among your teachers, your colleagues, the children, their families, the sponsoring agency, the school, and even the community. Keep alert for such problems and discuss them at the next staff meeting. Did they really involve ethical problems? How were they resolved? In what way did the NAEYC Code help to make the decisions? How would you handle such problems in the future? What other similar ethical problems can you foresee happening in the future? How will you handle these? Having a professional Code of Ethical Conduct to fall back on helps everyone take an objective view of sensitive situations that may arise. Persons with no commitment to the early childhood field should feel relieved that our profession has come forward with a definite set of guidelines for responsible behavior. You as a new professional in the field should feel more confident that your decisions are in line with those of other professionals in the field.

 ## TAKES EVERY OPPORTUNITY TO IMPROVE PROFESSIONAL GROWTH

Ongoing Training

As you become more professional in your outlook, early childhood training should become an ongoing part of your life. Like Head Start, many programs have in-service training programs built into their schedules. The year begins with a preservice workshop for all teachers and assistants and continues with on-site or regional workshops in the various program component areas such as curriculum, nutrition, health, mental health, career development, and parent involvement.

Ongoing training alerts staff members to current developments in the early childhood field such as the new brain research and its impact on child development. Teaching skills are also sharpened when specialists offer workshops on topics important to the curriculum.

CDA Credential Renewal

Recognizing the necessity for ongoing training, the Child Development Associate (CDA) program requires that CDAs renew their credential three years after its receipt and every five years thereafter. Renewal candidates must meet the following criteria (The Council for Early Childhood Professional Recognition, 1999, p. 15):

1. Have documented proof of a current Red Cross or other agency first-aid certificate
2. Have documented proof of completing at least 4.5 continuing education units (CEUs) or a three-credit-hour course in early childhood education, child development, or family studies within the past five years
3. Have documented proof of recent work experience with young children or families (a minimum of 80 hours within the past year)
4. Have a professional relationship with an early childhood education professional who can complete a letter of recommendation about the renewal candidate's competence with young children or families
5. Have documented proof of recent (within current year) membership in a national or local early childhood professional organization

Join a Professional Organization and Read Its Publications; Network with Colleagues in the Field

The number of professional organizations concerned with young children increases every year. Some of the largest and most important to teachers include the following national organizations:

American Montessori Society (AMS)
150 Fifth Ave.
New York, NY 10011
(*Montessori Life,* quarterly journal)

Association for Childhood Education International (ACEI)
17904 Georgia Avenue, Suite 215
Olney, MD 20832
(*Childhood Education,* journal published six times a year)

National Association for the Education of Young Children (NAEYC)
1509 16th St., NW
Washington, DC 20036-1426
(*Young Children,* bimonthly journal)

Southern Early Childhood Association (SECA)
8500 W. Markham Street, Suite 105
P. O. Box 55930
Little Rock, AR 72215-5930
(*Dimensions of Early Childhood,* quarterly journal)

These national organizations also have state offices and local chapters holding regular meetings. All teachers of young children should join one of these organizations, read its publications, and attend its meetings. Attending local meetings is important for teaching staff to meet and network with other teachers working nearby. Attending state and national meetings can expand participants' points of view, give them the latest information on topics of interest to them, as well as introduce them to leaders in the field.

Every professional field reaches its members through such organizations, publications, and meetings. Early childhood teaching staffs need to become members of such a professional organization to become recognized members of the profession. CDAs are required to join a professional organization to renew their certificates. For others it is imperative that they join an organization to keep up with current issues, trends, and ideas in this ever-expanding field.

In addition to joining a formal organization, some early childhood practitioners get together in a loose network of other professionals with similar concerns. One such group is the Southern Arizona Early Childhood Network, which meets monthly— without an agenda, dues, officers, or bylaws—to talk with kindred spirits about their work, their accomplishments, and their frustrations.

> We have found that building a community of people with similar needs, questions, and concerns can be useful. . . . This professional and personal support helps us continue our journeys. Support is critical. It means the difference between being a productive member of your staff or an absent leader who is continually daydreaming about the next job. (Powers & Butler, 1998, p. 14)

Personal Contribution

In becoming a professional in the early childhood field, you have committed yourself to a career of giving to children, to their families, to your team members, and to your program. In addition, you may be called on to share your knowledge and skills with others in the community and even further afield. As a professional, you should welcome this opportunity. The growing need for qualified early childhood personnel puts special demands on all of us. Spreading the good news about quality programs for young children, helping paraprofessionals in the field to become credentialed, and

Figure 13–5 Personal Contributions of Early Childhood Professionals

1. Serves on board of community child-care program
2. Becomes CDA advisor for another candidate
3. Speaks at a community group about classroom experience
4. Shows slides to parents of how children learn through exploratory play
5. Shares knowledge and skills (plays an instrument; does arts or crafts; speaks a second language) with children in another classroom
6. Submits child-care topic for presentation with a team member at a state, regional, or national conference
7. Advises community librarian about good picture books for the library to purchase
8. Volunteers in a child-care resource center
9. Appears as a guest speaker at a college continuing education class
10. Writes to early childhood book authors about successful new ideas you have tried with children

helping to start new programs are a few of the ways you might contribute. For specific ideas, consider the contributions listed in Figure 13–5.

The list could go on about the many possibilities for sharing your early childhood skills and knowledge with others. The topic of early childhood education is of paramount importance to everyone in the community these days, especially for families with young children. How are these youngsters to grow up in health and happiness, surrounded as many are by broken families, street violence, and environmental destruction?

Simple gifts are just as important to the people you interact with daily as your contributions to the field as listed in Figure 13–5. Jacobs (2001) discusses several simple gifts that early childhood practitioners can give to children and other teachers in their program:

1. Share yourself (give yourself to your children every day)
2. Share your interests (bring in your special talent, hobby, or interest)
3. Help children look at life through the eyes of a photographer (you, if you are one)
4. Help children and others use computer graphics (if you know how)
5. Read a picture book to several children every day
6. Bring in a personal collection of dolls, teapots, pins, magnets, spoons, postcards, whatever (if you have one)
7. Sew something with your children; help them create something with their hands (if you can)

8. Explore science and nature with others (share a pet; do an experiment; take a walk outdoors; make recycled paper, if you can)

9. Bake; write out a recipe and bake something you are familiar with with the children

10. Sing; sing some of your favorite songs with the children, or play an instrument (pp. 77–78)

As Jacobs reminds us:

> Take a few moments from your busy day to think about the gifts you bring each time you walk into the room. Doing this may help you recognize the special strengths in your children as well. When your children and students look back to remember what made an impact in their lives, it may well be the time spent with you as you opened new doors to them; sharing unique talents and interests. It may be the precious moments in which you gave the gift of who you are, and the gift of your time, that made all the difference. (p. 79)

Does this make you a professional? You know it does.

Think about the gifts you bring each time you come to the center. It may be the precious moments in which you give the gift of who you are that makes all the difference.

Early childhood professionals can lead the way with a positive vision of the future for young children. The exuberance of the youngsters, their energy and creativity, and their drive to discover what makes the world tick are topics you are intimately familiar with. You can share this with others. You can help make a difference in the children's world to come when you touch others with your newly acquired knowledge and skills about children and families. For a new professional in the early childhood field, your contribution is no longer an option but a necessity. Children, parents, community members—all of us—we need you!

SUMMARY

To become a professional in the early childhood field, you must first make a commitment to the field by putting children and families first in your professional life. This often means sacrificing time and energy to make sure children and families are served by your program as they should be. It may mean coming to the program early and leaving late. It also means providing services yourself when no one else is available.

To be considered a member of the early childhood profession, you must also gain a knowledge base in the field through workshops, courses, college and university programs, or CDA training. Your training should lead to some sort of credential, certificate, or degree. One of the important methods for acquiring competence as well as being credentialed in the field is by becoming a CDA. This training, assessment, and credentialing program requires trainees to complete a course of study, to perform competently in an early childhood setting, to assemble a Professional Resource File, and to complete a written and oral situational assessment (see Appendix A). In addition, a professional is generally required to complete a period of service in the field as a volunteer, teaching assistant, teacher, or caregiver, using developmentally appropriate practices with children.

A professional also treats information about children and families confidentially. When parents or staff members begin gossiping about children, a professional should not participate and should help others to understand why this behavior is not acceptable. Other ethical behaviors toward children involve being sensitive to their feelings, adapting your language to their understanding, being emotionally responsive, and bringing humor and imagination into the classroom.

To continue your professional growth as a teacher of young children, you should also take every opportunity to gain knowledge and skills in the field by joining a professional organization such as the National Association for the Education of Young Children, reading its journal, *Young Children,* and attending local, state, or national meetings. Some early childhood workers also find networking with other professionals to be especially helpful.

Finally, as a professional, you need to make your own ongoing contribution to the field, perhaps in the form of a presentation to a parent group, a college class, or an early childhood conference; by helping a coworker become a CDA; by giving a librarian information on children's picture books to order; or by sharing one of your skills with the children or another early childhood class. As a new professional in this expanding field, you can truly make a difference.

LEARNING ACTIVITIES

1. Read Chapter 13 and write out answers to Question Sheet 13.

2. Meet with your trainer or instructor and discuss answers to Question Sheet 13.

3. View one of the videos listed and make 10 file cards with specific ideas for professional development.

4. Read one or more of the references cited or suggested readings and add 10 cards to your file, with specific ideas for improving your professional outlook or that of others. Include the reference source on each card.

5. Make a self-assessment using the Teacher Skills Checklist, as discussed in the Introduction. Discuss the results with your trainer or college instructor and together make a training prescription for you to follow.

6. Make a list of organizations or agencies in your community (or county) that are concerned with young children and their families. Attend one of their meetings and write a summary of it.

7. Write to the Council for Early Childhood Professional Recognition for a packet of information on obtaining a CDA. Find out where you can obtain CDA training locally.

8. Join an early childhood organization, obtain a copy of an early childhood professional journal such as *Young Children,* and write a summary of interesting ideas from the articles in one issue.

9. Make a contribution about early childhood education to another group or individuals in your community. Write up the results.

10. Complete the Chapter 13 Evaluation Sheet and return it to your trainer or college supervisor.

QUESTION SHEET 13

1. What does it mean to be a professional in the early childhood field?

2. What is the difference between a professional and a nonprofessional in an early childhood program?

3. What kind of knowledge about the early childhood field must a professional know?

4. What kind of training must a professional have to work in the early childhood field?

5. Which of the NAEYC's professional levels are you on? Which would you like to be on? How do you plan to get there?

6. What kinds of credentials or licenses are available to early childhood professionals?

7. What are two different routes a person could take to obtain the CDA credential? How are they different? (See Appendix A.)

8. How can this textbook be used to help a person become a CDA? (See Appendix A.)

9. Why should a person become a CDA?

10. What kinds of information about children and families must you treat confidentially? Why?

11. What should you do if a parent begins talking to you about her child while the child is present?

12. Why is the Code of Ethics important to an early childhood professional?

13. What is the value of joining a professional organization?

14. How has this reading of *Skills for Preschool Teachers* and your training program changed you as a person and as a teacher or teacher-to-be of young children? Be specific.

15. Why is it important that new professionals like you make a contribution to the field? What will you contribute?

REFERENCES

Beaty, J. J. (2002). *Observing development of the young child.* Upper Saddle River, NJ: Merrill/Prentice Hall.

Bredekamp, S. (2000). CDA at 25: Reflections on the past and projections for the future. *Young Children, 55*(5), 15–19.

Bredekamp, S., & Copple, C. (Eds.). (1997). *Developmentally appropriate practice in early childhood programs* (rev. ed.). Washington, DC: National Association for the Education of Young Children.

Brophy-Herb, H. E., Kostelnik, M. J., & Stein, L. C. (2001). A developmental approach to teaching about ethics using the NAEYC Codes of Ethical Conduct. *Young Children, 56*(1), 80–84.

Council for Early Childhood Professional Recognition. (1999). *Preparing professionals as Child Development Associates.* Washington, DC: Author.

Ferreiro, E., & Teberosky, A. (1982). *Literacy before schooling.* Exeter, NH: Heinemann.

Greenspan, S. I. (1997). *The growth of the mind: And the endangered origins of intelligence.* Reading, MA: Addison-Wesley.

Hyson, M. (2002). Preparing tomorrow's teachers: NAEYC announces new standards. *Young Children, 57*(2), 78–79.

Jacobs, G. M. (2001). Sharing our gifts. *Young Children, 56*(1), 77–79.

National Association for the Education of Young Children. (1994). NAEYC position statement: A conceptual framework for early childhood professional development. *Young Children, 49*(3), 68–77.

National Association for the Education of Young Children. (1996). Code of ethical conduct: Guidelines for responsible behavior in early childhood education. *Young Children, 51*(3), 57–60.

National Association for the Education of Young Children. (1997). *NAEYC's code of ethical conduct and statement of commitment.* Washington, DC: Author.

National Association for the Education of Young Children. (2001). *NAEYC guidelines revision: NAEYC standards for early childhood professional preparation.* http://www.naeyc.org/profdev/prep_review_general.htm. Author.

National Association for the Education of Young Children. (1997). Revisions proposed for NAEYC's code of ethical conduct. *Young Children, 52*(4), 61.

Nielsen, D. M. (2002). The journey from babysitter to child care professional: Military Family Child Care providers. *Young Children, 57*(1), 9–14.

Powers, J., & Butler, M. (1998). Finding kindred spirits. *Child Care Information Exchange, 122,* 13–15.

Wilt, J. L. V., & Monroe, V. (1998). Successfully moving toward developmentally appropriate practice: It takes time and effort! *Young Children, 53*(4), 17–24.

SUGGESTED READINGS

Abbott-Shim, M. S. (1990). In-service training: A means to quality care. *Young Children, 45*(2), 14–18.

Bredekamp, S. (1997). NAEYC issues revised position statement on developmentally appropriate practice in early childhood programs. *Young Children, 52*(2), 34–40.

Bredekamp, S., & Willer, B. (1993). Professionalizing the field of early childhood education: Pros and cons. *Young Children, 48*(3), 82–84.

Cartwright, S. (1999). What makes good early childhood teachers? *Young Children, 54*(4), 4–7.

Caruso, J. J. (2000). Cooperating teacher and student teacher phases of development. *Young Children, 55*(1), 75–81.

Cherry, C. (1989). *Is the left brain always right? A guide to whole child development.* Belmont, CA: Fearon.

Dallman, M. E., & Owens, R. R. (1997). Child Development Associates: Stories from the field. *Young Children, 52*(3), 25–30.

Gordon, A. M., & Williams-Browne, K. W. (1996). *Beginnings and beyond: Foundations in early childhood education.* Albany, NY: Delmar.

Humphryes, J. (1998). The developmental appropriateness of high-quality Montessori programs. *Young Children, 53*(4), 4–16.

Waters, J. V., Frantz, M. T., & Rottmayer, S. (1997). Staff training: Taking the child's perspective. *Young Children, 52*(3), 38–41.

VIDEOTAPES

National Association for the Education of Young Children. (Producer). *Career encounters: Early childhood education.* Washington, DC: Author.

National Association for the Education of Young Children. (Producer). *Seeds of change: Leadership and staff development. (The early childhood program: A place to learn and grow* video series). Washington, DC: Author.

National Association for the Education of Young Children. (Producer). *Tools for teaching developmentally appropriate practice: The leading edge in early childhood education.* Washington, DC: Author.

National Association for the Education of Young Children. (Producer). *The uniqueness of the early childhood profession.* (Milly Almy). Washington, DC: Author.

CHAPTER 13 EVALUATION SHEET
PROMOTING PROFESSIONALISM

1. Student _____

2. Trainer _____

3. Center where training occurred _____

4. Beginning date _____ Ending date _____

5. Describe what student did to accomplish General Objective.

   _____

   _____

6. Describe what student did to accomplish Specific Objectives.

   Objective 1 _____

   _____

   Objective 2 _____

   _____

   Objective 3 _____

   _____

7. Evaluation of student's Learning Activities

   _____

   _____

Comments:

Permission is granted by the publisher to reproduce this page for evaluation or record keeping.

Appendix A

Becoming a CDA: Child Development Associate

In addition to the traditional modes of training for early childhood education, there is another increasingly popular method for developing the necessary competence to teach in the field: Child Development Associate (CDA) training, assessment and credentialing. CDA training is competency-based and performance-based, which means that a certain percentage of the training must occur *in* the early childhood classroom and that the trainee must demonstrate competence with children in such a setting.

The Child Development Associate program emerged in the 1970s as a collaborative effort on the part of early childhood professional and the federal government to create a new category of early childhood professional—the Child Development Associate. From the beginning the program had two parts: training that was done by local colleges or early childhood programs, and credentialing that was done by the national office (Child Development Associate National Credentialing Program).

Today that program has consolidated both training and credentialing under a CDA Professional Preparation Program offered by the Council for Professional Recognition, 2460 16th Street, NW, Washington, DC, 2009-3575. Under the program, a candidate may choose to earn his or her CDA credential in one of two ways: (a) through the CDA Professional Preparation Program, or (b) by local college training and direct assessment.

CDA training programs may enroll candidates for three different types of credentials: center based, family child care, or home visitor. Candidates may also choose a Bilingual Credential if they work in a program that requires them to use a second language as well as English in any of these three settings. (Council for Professional Recognition, 1999, p. 4–5)

CDA Credentials Based on Settings

It is necessary for the training program to decide ahead of time whether to cover all of these options in its training or to concentrate on one setting. Training for *Center-Based CDA* must include a state-approved child development center where the candidate can be observed working as a lead teacher with a specific group of children. Two different endorsements are available: "Preschool" for candidates working with 3-through-5-year old children, and "Infant/Toddler" for candidates working with children from birth to 36 months.

Training for *Family Child Care CDA* must include a family child care home that meets minimum state and local regulations, where candidates can be observed working as primary providers with at least two children, 5 years old or younger and not related to the candidate.

Training for *Home Visitor CDA* must include an established program of home visits to families with children 5 years old or younger to meet the needs of their young children. Candidates can be observed working in the home as an adult educator with the parents. The *Bilingual Specialization* can apply to training in any of these settings. (Council for Professional Recognition, 1999, pp. 4–5)

Training Requirements

If the candidate chooses to be trained under the CDA Professional Preparation Program then she or he must complete the requirements listed in Figure A–1, which include on-site training: that is, working in a child-care setting for at least eight months during which the candidate must complete the readings and exercises in the early childhood curriculum and meet weekly with an advisor. In addition the candidate must complete 120 clock hours of seminar training which includes an introduction to the early childhood profession, observing and recording child growth and development, establishing and maintaining a safe, healthful learning environment, advancing physical and intellectual competence, supporting social and emotional development and guidance, establishing positive relationships with families, ensuring a well-run, purposeful program responsive to participant needs, and maintaining a commitment to professionalism.

If the candidate chooses the second route to CDA credentialing then she or he must complete the requirements listed in Figure A–2 which involves direct assessment by the national program after the candidate has completed the necessary training and data collection. The training can be provided by the early childhood program itself or a local college. This route to CDA credentialing is similar to the program from past years in which the training was provided at the local level and the credentialing at the national level. The LAT (Local Assessment Team) meeting is no longer required, nor is there a requirement for a CDA Portfolio. Instead, the candidate must complete the following Direct Assessment Program (see Figure A–2).

Professional Resource File

In place of the former CDA portfolio, candidates must prepare a Professional Resource File that can be arranged much like the portfolio, either in a bound notebook, inside file folders in a box, or in other creative ways. The candidate must be able to carry the Professional Resource File from a work site, on a home visit, or to a meeting. The file must contain items based on the six CDA competency goals and the 13 functional areas (see p. 384). It must show evidence of what the candidate finds valuable in her or his work. The Resource File has three major sections: (a) Autobiography, (b) Statements of Competence, and (c) Resource Collection.

Eligibility

1. Be 18 years of age or older
2. Hold a high school diploma or GED
3. Identify an advisor to work with during the year of study
4. Have 480 hours working with children within past five years

Application

1. Submit verification of age and high school diploma or GED
2. Submit name and qualifications of advisor
3. Submit required fee

On-Site Training

1. Complete the readings and exercises in the early childhood studies curriculum in about eight months
2. Work in a child care setting either as a staff member, a volunteer, or a student during this time as lead teacher or adult educator
3. Meet weekly with advisor
4. Complete and submit all assignments to advisor for verification

Seminar Training

1. Complete 120 clock hours of classes conducted by seminar instructor under auspices of local postsecondary institution
2. Complete written sections of the Early Childhood Studies Review

Assessment

1. Be formally observed by advisor
2. Complete Professional Resource File
3. Distribute and collect Parent Opinion Questionnaires
4. Complete oral section of situational assessment conducted by council representative
5. Receive notification of decision by council about credential award

Credential Award

1. Receive CDA credential

Figure A–1   CDA Professional Preparation Program

Eligibility

1. Be 18 years of age or older
2. Hold a high school diploma or GED
3. Have 480 hours of experience working with children ages birth through 5 years
4. Have completed 120 clock hours of formal training in early childhood education

Competence

1. Be skilled in the six CDA competency areas
2. Have formal observation by an early childhood professional while working with children in a child care setting
3. Distribute and collect Parent Opinion Questionnaires
4. Complete a Professional Resource File

Application

1. Submit application for direct assessment
2. Submit verification of age, high school diploma, and experience working with children
3. Submit a signed ethical conduct statement
4. Submit a verification of formal training
5. Submit a verification of formal observation
6. Submit required fee

Assessment

1. Be present at designated time and place to complete a situational oral and written Early Childhood Studies Review conducted by a council representative
2. Submit the Parent Opinion Questionnaires and the Professional Resource File for review by the council representative
3. Receive notification of decision by council about credential award

Credential Award

1. Receive CDA credential

Figure A–2   Direct Assessment Program

Autobiography

Candidates must write a 300-word autobiography that tells who they are and the things that influenced their decision to work with young children. Some candidates may feel uncomfortable with writing about themselves. They may first want to discuss what they should say with their trainer. Then they may want to jot down a few reasons why they began their work with children, how they felt about it once they started,

---

Professional Resource File

Candidate's Name: _____

Date: _____

Statement of Competence:
Competency Goal #

Definition:

Functional Area:

Introductory Paragraph:

Goals for Children/Families/Self/Staff:

Statements of Competence: "I" Statements of Competence for each Functional Area that explain *WHAT YOU DO* in the area

Specific example of what you do to achieve each goal: Be sure to give an example of your activities and interaction for each of your goals. This is *HOW* you reach each goal appropriately

Include goals and activities that are age appropriate, culturally appropriate, and individually appropriate.

Figure A–3   Professional Resource File Guide

and what obtaining a CDA credential could mean to them in the future. Although the trainer can lend support in this writing, the ideas and words should be the candidate's own. Such an autobiography should help them sort out their own feelings about working with children and what it has meant in their lives.

Statements of Competence

An in-depth statement of the candidate's competence in each of the 13 CDA Functional Areas under the six CDA Competency Goals should be written out following the Professional Resource File Guide (Figure A–3) which is the required format for this information.

Here is an example of the competency statements for Mary Jones for the Functional Area "Safe" (Figure A–4).

Resource Collection

The bulk of the material in the Professional Resource File is the material the candidate has collected to show competence in each of the 13 Functional Areas: Safe, Healthy, Learning Environment, Physical, Cognitive, Communication, Creative, Self, Social, Guidance, Family, Program Management, Professionalism.

It can contain items such as file cards with children's activities for each of the 13 Functional Areas; pamphlets or brochures from early childhood education association meetings; booklets on how children grow and learn that would be appropriate for parents; observation tools such as checklists for recording information they have gathered about children; lists of agencies in the community that provide help for children with developmental disabilities; emergency telephone numbers; Red Cross certificates; titles of children's books dealing with development of gender identity, separation, family diversity, or multicultural backgrounds; goals of your program; favorite poems and songs for children; file cards from the chapters of this text; or a lists of videos on parenting or other early childhood topics.

Using Skills for Preschool Teachers in CDA Training

This textbook, *Skills for Preschool Teachers,* is designed to be used in CDA training programs either by individuals who prefer the Self-Taught Module Approach (see Introduction) or by colleges or training programs who prefer the classroom or seminar approach. The Teacher Skills Checklist (see Introduction) can be used by any CDA trainee or advisor as an initial assessment tool. Then a training prescription can be developed for the trainee to follow as he or she proceeds through the training. Each chapter of this book represents one of the 13 CDA Functional Areas derived from the six Competency Goals:

1. Establishing and maintaining a safe, healthy learning environment

SAFE	Chapter 1 Maintaining a Safe Classroom
HEALTHY	Chapter 2 Maintaining a Healthy Classroom
LEARNING ENVIRONMENT	Chapter 3 Establishing a Learning Environment

2. Advancing physical and intellectual competence

PHYSICAL	Chapter 4 Advancing Physical Skills
COGNITIVE	Chapter 5 Advancing Cognitive Skills
COMMUNICATION	Chapter 6 Advancing Communication Skills
CREATIVE	Chapter 7 Advancing Creative Skills

3. Supporting social and emotional development and providing positive guidance

SELF	Chapter 8 Building a Positive Self-Concept
SOCIAL	Chapter 9 Promoting Social Skills
GUIDANCE	Chapter 10 Providing Guidance

PROFESSIONAL RESOURCE FILE

CANDIDATE'S NAME   Mary Jones   DATE _____

COMPETENCY GOAL # 1: To establish and maintain a safe, healthy, learning environment

INTRODUCTORY PARAGRAPH: (Write Introductory Paragraph *only at the beginning* of each Competency Goal)

I maintain a safe, healthy learning environment by keeping the indoor and outdoor areas well-organized with enough space for children to move safely from one activity to another. I promote good health and nutrition and provide an environment that encourages play, exploration, and learning.

FUNCTIONAL AREA: SAFE

DEFINITION: Candidate provides a safe environment to prevent and reduce injuries.

GOAL FOR CHILDREN: My goal for children is that they will learn fire safety procedures.

STATEMENT OF COMPETENCE: I plan and practice fire drills monthly.

SPECIFIC EXAMPLES OF WHAT YOU DO TO ACHIEVE YOUR GOAL FOR CHILDREN:

I plan with my classroom team and other building personnel the specific time and procedures for each fire drill. My planning includes a circle time discussion of fire drills and how to leave the classroom safely and quickly when the fire drill alarm sounds. We listen to the sound of the fire alarm so the children will not be afraid. We practice leaving the building following arrows on the floor leading out the door to our classroom's designated location on the lawn. I take the daily attendance sheet with me so I can be certain all children are out of the building. I praise the children for a job well-done to encourage future appropriate fire drill behaviors.

Other fire safety activities I develop are:

Stop/Drop/Roll	A visit from a firefighter
Field trip to fire station	Fire drills on the bus
Home fire safety practices	Books and flannel board stories

I am competent in the Functional Area SAFE because I help the children in my care feel comfortable learning about fire safety through hands-on experiences.

Figure A–4

4. Establishing positive and productive relationships with families

   FAMILIES   Chapter 11 Promoting Family Involvement

5. Ensuring a well-run, purposeful program responsive to participant needs

   PROGRAM MANAGEMENT   Chapter 12 Providing Program Management

6. Maintaining a commitment to professionalism

   PROFESSIONALISM   Chapter 13 Promoting Professionalism

As candidates read the chapters and complete the Learning Activities they will be producing evidence for the 13 sections of their Professional Resource File. Observation checklists, file cards of activities, and lists of children's books are products they can use. Photographs of children using learning centers as suggested in the chapters can be accompanied by descriptions and write-ups of competence.

Other resource materials that candidates can use in their training include those listed under References, Suggested Readings, and Videotapes that follow:

REFERENCES

Council for Professional Recognition. (1999). *Preparing professionals as Child Development Associates.* Washington, DC: Author.

SUGGESTED READINGS

Bredekamp, S. (2000). CDA at 25: Reflections on the past and Projections for the Future. *Young Children, 55*(5), 15–19.

Council for Professional Recognition. (1999). *Essentials for Child Development Associates.* Washington, DC: Author.

Council for Professional Recognition. (1999). *CDA Competency Standards Books* (Preschool, Home Visitor, Infant/Toddler, Family Child Care). Washington, DC: Author.

VIDEOTAPES

Videos to supplement the units in *Essentials for Child Development Associates* (all produced by NAEYC):

Career Encounters: Early Childhood Education
Seeing Infants with New Eyes
Toddler Curriculum: Making Connections
Discipline: Appropriate for Young Children
Sensory Play: Constructing Realities

Developmental Appropriate Practice: Partnership with Parents
Appropriate Curriculum for Young Children: the Role of the Teacher

Council for Professional Recognition, *New Options: The Remodeling of the CDA Program.* Washington, DC: Author.

Index

387